# Social Work during COVID-19

This book focuses on social work in the time of COVID-19. Social workers, their clients, and the organisations they represent have been affected by the pandemic in multiple ways. The pandemic and various efforts to curb the viral outbreak, such as face masks and lockdowns, have forced social workers to adapt to a 'new normal', launch new practices, mobilise social support and networks remotely, and above all, defend the most vulnerable populations. This requires an understanding of how social work and its clients are prepared for, capable to respond to, and further, to recover from a societal crisis and human disasters, like a coronavirus pandemic.

Divided into three parts, it provides a wealth of knowledge related to social work in different local and cultural contexts during the period of the global pandemic. With experienced social work researchers across a diversity of settings, contexts, and research traditions, the book is reflective of the 'glocal' response of social work. Offering new perspectives on challenges social workers have faced in dealing with the pandemic, it makes critical and timely insights into the innovations and adaptations in social work responses, with a strong empirical basis.

It will be of interest to all social work scholars, students, and practitioners.

**Timo Harrikari, PhD,** is a Professor of Social Work at the University of Lapland and Research Professor in Child Welfare at the Finnish Institute for Health and Welfare THL, Finland.

**Joseph Mooney, PhD,** is an Assistant Professor of Social Work at University College Dublin, Ireland, and a former social work practitioner.

**Malathi Adusumalli, PhD,** is a Professor at the faculty of University of Delhi with over two decades of teaching experience and over seven years of working actively with grassroots organisations in the field of social action, disaster management, and development. She has published her work in national and international journals and has three books to her credit. She has successfully guided M.Phil. and PhD research scholars. She is a firm believer in anti-oppressive social work practice.

Paula McFadden, PhD, is a Senior Lecturer in Social Work at Ulster University and teaches at undergraduate, postgraduate, master's, and PhD levels. Paula's main research interests are centred on workforce well-being, resilience, and burnout. Paula has conducted several UK-wide research studies, examining burnout in social workers, workforce ageing in social work, and more recently, well-being and coping during COVID-19, for health and social care professions, including social workers.

Tuomas Leppiaho, B.Soc.Sc., is a research assistant and a master's student in political sciences at the University of Lapland.

# Social Work during COVID-19

## Glocal Perspectives and Implications for the Future of Social Work

Edited by Timo Harrikari,
Joseph Mooney,
Malathi Adusumalli,
Paula McFadden, and
Tuomas Leppiaho

LONDON AND NEW YORK

First published 2023
by Routledge
4 Park Square, Milton Park, Abingdon, Oxon OX14 4RN

and by Routledge
605 Third Avenue, New York, NY 10158

*Routledge is an imprint of the Taylor & Francis Group, an informa business*

*British Library Cataloguing-in-Publication Data*
A catalogue record for this book is available from the British Library

ISBN: 978-1-032-21539-6 (hbk)
ISBN: 978-1-032-44891-6 (pbk)
ISBN: 978-1-003-37437-4 (ebk)

DOI: 10.4324/9781003374374

Typeset in Goudy
by MPS Limited, Dehradun

This edited collection is dedicated to those who lost their lives due to the global COVID-19 pandemic and to those frontline social work practitioners who worked courageously, innovatively, and creatively to support the clients and service users we are privileged to serve.

# Contents

SECTION IV
**Restarting the Dynamics, Relationships, and Connectivity
in Social Work**

SECTION V
**Conclusion**

# Figures

# Tables

# Contributors

**Sareh Abri, PhD,** is an experienced Social Worker with an extensive background in the field and academic domains. Skilled in Lecturing and Research, she has done her Doctor of Philosophy (PhD) in Medical Social Work. After working as a social worker and social work senior expert in Iran for ten years, she did her Post-Doc at Tokyo Metropolitan University from 2018 until 2021. Besides, she received an invitation to serve as a Co-researcher at the Japan College of Social Work.

**Kim Bastaits** is a senior researcher at Social Work Research and a research lecturer at PXL University College of Applied Sciences and Arts, Hasselt, Belgium.

**Anna-Karin Bergman** has a PhD in Sociology of Law and an LLM from Lund University. She currently holds a position as an R&D Director at Helsingborg City Council, Sweden. She has mainly worked in local government coordinating and leading research and development processes and her main scholarly interests are systems innovations, the organization of public sector and change management within the welfare system.

**Priyanka Bhattacharjee** works as an Assistant Professor at the Department of Social Work, Shahjalal University of Science and Technology (SUST), Sylhet, Bangladesh. She completed her undergraduate and graduate (with the first position) degrees in Social Work from Shahjalal University of Science and Technology, Sylhet. **Bhattacharjee** has also received a master's degree in International Project Management in Northumbria University, Newcastle, the UK. Her research interests are government and non-government social services; social development; informal workers and other disadvantaged groups of people; impact of pandemic and gender inequality.

**Marcin Boryczko** is an Associate Professor at the University of Gdańsk/Poland where he teaches Social Work BA and MA. He is a member of the Board of experts of the Polish Federation of Social Workers and Social Service Employees Unions (Polska Federacja Związków Zawodowych Pracowników Socjalnych i Pomocy Społecznej) and Human Rights Commissioner in the European region as a member of International Federation of Social Workers

(IFSW). He is a Board Member of The European Social Work Research Association and a member of The International Advisory Board of the European Social Work Research Journal. His main research interests include social work education, critical thinking in social work, human rights in social work, decolonisation, neoliberal governmentality in social work, and social workers' protests and social engagement.

**Sara Carder** is a PhD Researcher at the University of East Anglia, UK and an independent social work practice consultant and psychotherapist. Her research focuses on the role of teams in child and family social work.

**Declan Coogan, PhD,** is a lecturer in social work and a Research Fellow with the UNESCO Child and Family Research Centre at the University of Galway, a former social work practitioner and current systemic family therapist.

**Laura L. Cook, PhD,** is a Lecturer in Social Work and a member of the Centre for Research and Families (CRCF) at the University of East Anglia, UK. Her research focuses on retention, well-being, and decision-making in child and family social work.

**Tulshi Kumar Das** is a Professor of social work at Shahjalal University of Science and Technology. He has widely published articles with established publishers, such as Sage, Wiley-Blackwell, and Taylor and Francis. He has completed research projects related to such issues as domestic violence, natural disasters, street children, micro-credit, food security, sponsored by e.g. Comic Relief Fund, UK., FAO, Ministry of Social Welfare, European Commission, USAID, GIZ/EPOS (Germany), Japan College of Social Work, Korea International Cooperation Agency (KOICA), and Bangladesh University Grants Commission. He actively works with many welfare organisations in Bangladesh.

**Mie Engen** is PhD in Social Work and associate professor in social work at Department of Sociology and Social Work, Aalborg University, Denmark. Her research focuses on care in social work, social work practices with vulnerable children and families and their connections with broader societal developments. She is head of Master in vulnerable children and young people, professional management at Aalborg University.

**Vera Fiorentino, Ms. Soc. Sc.,** is a Junior Research Fellow and a Doctoral Candidate at the University of Lapland.

**Daniela Gaba** is a Lecturer in social work at the University of Bucharest where she teaches undergraduate and master-level courses and seminars in areas such as international social work, community social work, psychosocial evaluation, and research methods for the social sciences. Her research interests include the internationalisation and professionalisation of social work and mental health social work, with a focus on the application of novel neuropsychological therapeutic methods to social work practice.

**Kristofer Hansson** is a Senior Lecturer at the Department of Social Work, Malmö University, and holds an Associate Professorship in Ethnology. His research focuses on cultural perspectives on immunity, as well as medical praxis in health care and emerging biomedical technologies.

**Timo Harrikari, PhD,** is a Professor of Social work at the University of Lapland and Research Professor in Child Welfare at the Finnish Institute for Health and Welfare THL.

**Andreas Møller Jørgensen** is PhD in Arctic Studies—Culture, Language and Society and Associate Professor at the Department of Sociology and Social Work, Aalborg University, Denmark. His research focuses on changes in social welfare and social work and especially on relations of power, technology, and democracy.

**Tadeja Kodele, PhD,** is a Teaching Assistant at the University of Ljubljana, Faculty of Social Work.

**Kersti Kriisk** (PhD in Social Work and MA in Applied Statistics) is a Lecturer of Social Work at Tallinn University, where she lectures on social policy and research methods, and coordinates internships of social work students. Her fields of research interest are welfare state reforms and local social policy with special focus on social assistance schemes, social care, provision of social services and activation policies from governmental and organisational perspectives.

**Vesna Leskošek, PhD,** is a Professor at the University of Ljubljana, Faculty of Social Work.

**Olive Lyons** is a Professional Social Worker and PhD candidate at the University of Toronto, Canada.

**Melinda Madew, EdD,** is a Professor in international social work at the Protestant University of Applied Sciences Ludwigsburg, Germany. She lectures on postcolonial themes in various European universities where she brings her Global South perspective to social work practice and theory. She is a Research Associate of the University of Johannesburg and member of the board for the European Social Work Research Association. She serves as an external examiner in the graduate program of the University of South Africa, Pretoria. Her commitment to radical social work and postcolonial advocacy began from her years of community work with indigenous women in the Philippines. She currently writes on ecological justice, decolonisation and human rights, and postcolonial feminism.

**Jill Manthorpe (Professor)** is a Director of the National Institute for Health and Care Research (NIHR) Policy Research Unit in Health & Social Care Workforce, Associate Director of NIHR School for Social Care Research and NIHR Applied Research Collaborative (ARC) South London Social Care theme lead at The Policy Institute at King's, King's College London. She has undertaken many studies of social work and social care, including research investigating the impact of COVID-19 on health and social care. In addition, she researches dementia care support, family care, and homelessness services.

**Michiel Massart** is a Senior Researcher at Social Work Research and a Research Lecturer at PXL University College of Applied Sciences and Arts, Hasselt, Belgium.

**Paula McFadden, PhD,** is a Senior Lecturer in Social Work at Ulster University, with research interests centred on workforce well-being, resilience, and burnout. Paula has conducted several UK-wide research studies, examining burnout in social workers, workforce ageing in social work, and more recently, well-being and coping during COVID-19, for health and social care professions, including social workers. In June 2020, Paula was awarded funding by the Health and Social Care Board, Public Health Agency, Northern Ireland to study 'COVID-19: UK Health and Social Care Workforce Wellbeing and Coping' over a 2.5-year period. A website for the study with publications can be found here https://www.hscworkforcestudy.co.uk/

**Caroline McGregor** is a Professor at the School of Political Science and Sociology, University of Galway with lead responsibility for the discipline of social work and a Senior Research Fellow with the UNESCO Child and Family Research Centre.

**Sanna Melling** has a master's degree in Criminology; Crime, Control and Conflict from Middlesex University, UK and a BSc in Sociology and Media Studies from City University, UK. She currently holds a position as a Research and Development Leader, Helsingborg City Council, Sweden. Melling has mainly worked in local government, public health and third-sector organisations driving cross-sector partnership working, developing a whole system approach as well as transformation and change. She has also carried out internal service evaluations and acted as a research assistant. Between 2015 and 2019 Melling acted as an Independent Adoption Panel Member at Haringey Council as a part of the regional North London Adoption and Fostering Consortium.

**Nina Mešl, PhD,** is an Assistant Professor at the University of Ljubljana, Faculty of Social Work.

**Airi Mitendorf, PhD,** is a Head of the Development at The National Institute for Health Development in Estonia as well as a lecturer at the University of Tartu and TTK University of Applied Sciences. She teaches social work theories and social policy. Prior to this, she worked at the Ministry of Social Affairs of Estonia as an adviser on equality policies. Her research interest is concerned with the complex social systems reflected within well-being in general and social work in particular. Mitendorf's previous work has highlighted the implications of a neoliberal culture on contemporary social work practice.

**Joseph Mooney, PhD,** is an Assistant Professor of Social Work at University College Dublin, Ireland and a former social work practitioner.

**Ruth Neill, PhD,** is a Research Assistant working on the Health and Social Care Workforce Study. She completed her BSc Hons in Sports and Exercise Sciences with a Diploma in Professional Practice at Ulster University—School of Sport and her MSc in Sports Management in the Ulster Business School. In 2020, she completed her PhD at Queens University Belfast—School of Social Sciences, Education and Social Work, the project was titled: The development and feasibility of a co-produced mental health and well-being intervention for adolescents in the Northern Ireland post-primary setting. She has published in a number of academic journals and is interested in public health, mental health, education and physical activity-based research.

**Mareks Niklass** is a Senior Researcher at the Faculty of Social Sciences, University of Latvia. His recent articles cover topics such as the burnout of social service employees, in-work poverty and social welfare policy preferences.

**Maria Appel Nissen** is PhD in Sociology and Professor of Social Work at Department of Sociology and Social Work, Aalborg University, Denmark. Her research focuses on changes and challenges in the context of and in social work practice, and how research can contribute to social work theories and professional reflection and change. She is head of Bachelor of social work and of the research group Shaping Concepts, Practices and Advances in Social work (SCOPAS).

**Mie Ohwa, PhD,** is currently Professor at Kwansei Gakuin University. Her introduction to social work came when she was a junior student at Kobe College. She received her MSW and MS in Recreation Administration from the University of North Carolina at Chapel Hill, USA. She received her PhD from Osaka School of International Public Policy (PhD in International Public Policy), Osaka University, Japan. Her interests are social work for older adults, NPO in the field of ageing, and recreation in the later life. She is particularly interested in Long-term Care Insurance Scheme for the elderly and its related issues. Besides her major publication *Towards Retaining Human Resources for Long-Term Care: Exploring the Impact of Job Satisfaction*, she has written many articles and book chapters regarding social work, gerontology, and international social work.

**Inge Pasteels** is head of Social Work Research and research lecturer at PXL University College of Applied Sciences and Arts, Hasselt, Belgium.

**Charlotte C. Petersson** holds a PhD in Social Anthropology and is a Senior Lecturer in Social Work at Malmö University, Sweden. Her research focuses on gender violence, including its global and local manifestations and long-term health implications.

**Maryam Zabihi Poursaadati, PhD,** is a Doctor of Social Work from the University of Social Welfare and Rehabilitation Sciences, Tehran, Iran. She was a member of the social work committee of the Ministry of Health and Medical Education of Iran during 2016–2018, which developed six guidelines for the basic services of hospital social workers. She also has 14 years of experience in the field of psychiatry and has supervised many students with bachelor's and master's degrees in this field and has a chapter and several articles in the field of psychiatry.

**Bart Put** is a Senior Researcher at Social Work Research and a Research Lecturer at PXL University College of Applied Sciences and Arts, Hasselt, Belgium.

**Tamara Rape Žiberna, PhD,** works as a teaching assistant at the University of Ljubljana, Faculty of Social Work.

**Līga Rasnača** is a Senior Researcher at the Faculty of Social Sciences, University of Latvia. Her research interests are changes in social policy and the situation of vulnerable groups. Her recent articles cover topics such as housing vulnerability of seniors and the transformation in service delivery during COVID-19, intergenerational solidarity.

**Endija Rezgale-Straidoma, MA SW, MA Sc.soc.,** is PhD Candidate, Research Assistant at the Faculty of Social Sciences, University of Latvia. Her recent articles were focused on ageing, long-term care, intergenerational relationships, housing needs, and quality of life. She is also a social worker at NGO 'Resilience centre' were working in the youth communication program DARI.

**Marjo Romakkaniemi, PhD,** is a Research Fellow and a University lecturer at the University of Lapland, Faculty of Social Sciences, Social Work.

**Sanna Saraniemi, PhD,** is a Post-Doctoral Research Fellow and a University Lecturer at the University of Lapland, Faculty of Social Sciences, Social Work.

**Reeli Sirotkina** has worked as a lecturer of social work more than 20 years. Her research interests are the role of social work in social policy, the development professional of social work and qualitative social work research. She is experienced in international cooperation in running the projects and lecturing abroad. Currently she works at Tallinn University.

**Lupita Svensson** has a PhD in social work and is working as an assistant professor at School of Social Work, Lund university. Since 2015, her research has been focusing on the digitalization of social services and her main research contribution is in the area of digital automatization and the impact of professional´s discretion, especially social caseworkers. She has also experience of working as a clinical social worker. Besides research, she also teaches law in the bachelor program of social work.

**Junko Wake, PhD,** is currently Professor at Tokyo Metropolitan University. She graduated from Tokyo Women's Christian University, Japan (BA in Sociology), from Washington University in St. Louis, USA (MSW in Social Work), from Toyo University, Japan (PhD in Social Welfare). She is currently Vice President of Japanese Association for Social Work Education (JASWE), and Japanese Representative of International Association of Schools of Social Work (IASSW). She is a Chair of Social Welfare/Social Work Committee of Science Council of Japan, which is the national representing organization of Japanese scientists' community. She also has been elected and served as Vice President of the Japanese Society for the Study of Social Work.

# Preface

This work has been completed as a collaboration of researchers from the global COVID-19 social work forum research network. The network met online for the first time in April 2020 and actively met until the end of 2021. The idea of this book project was launched within the network in the spring of 2021 and the editorial work was started in the summer of 2021. Panda project at the University of Lapland, Finland, has coordinated the network's activities and provided a common platform for the editorial work. We would like to thank all the social work researchers around the world who participated in the network meetings, for the great discussions and mutual support in times of global crisis.

Timo Harrikari, Joseph Mooney, Malathi Adusumalli,
Paula McFadden, and Tuomas Leppiaho

# Acknowledgements

The completion of the book has been supported by several scientific and governmental actors. In Finland, this work was funded by Academy of Finland, The Strategic Research Council, grants 335656/2020, 353971/2022 and 335442/2020, and The Ministry of Social Affairs and Health grant VN/25259/2020. In the UK, this work was funded by the Health and Social Care Research and Development Division of the Public Health Agency, Northern Ireland (COVID Rapid Response Funding Scheme COM/5603/20), the Northern Ireland Social Care Council (NISCC) and the Southern Health and Social Care Trust, with support from England's National Institute for Health and Care Research (NIHR) Policy Research Unit in Health and Social Care Workforce—PR-PRU-1217-21002. Funders were not involved in study design, analysis, and interpretation of results, writing, or reviewing manuscripts.

# 1 Introduction

*Timo Harrikari*

## Introduction

In early 2020, the coronavirus spread across the globe, surprising the entire world and bringing about wide-scale effects on the economy, politics, communities, and people's everyday lives (Dominelli et al. 2020). As of this point of writing the book (26 September 2022), 609 *million* people worldwide have been infected and 6.5 *million* have died from the virus (World Health Organisation n.d.). More recently, the WHO and national governments have conducted continuous risk assessments and issued guidelines for managing the pandemic. The media has presented the primary public concerns as being the availability of healthcare resources and continuous functioning of business and industry.

Since March 2020, continuous speculation has been presented on how COVID-19 first emerged, how it spreads, what types of societal effects it has had, and how the pandemic, as an ecological and social phenomenon, will change our planet. Speculations that the pandemic could be characterised as a 'black swan' (Taleb 2010), a sudden and unexpected series of events with extensive impact, far-reaching effects, and long-term consequences have been presented. However, for scientists, the spread of a worldwide pandemic was not a surprise. Even if social scientists have envisaged an emerging global risk society for nearly 40 years (Beck 1986) and had plenty of experience from previous pandemics, the world today seemed to be rather unprepared and vulnerable to the arising COVID-19 epidemic in the spring of 2020.

In terms of social research and current societies, the COVID-19 pandemic is a new type of phenomenon. It is true that epidemics have occurred throughout world history, but the current complexity of societal phenomena and their mutual interdependence may manifest some kind of new dynamic. Global economic interdependence, air travel and digital, real-time communication have increased drastically over the past three decades (Gomez et al. 2013; Ductor and Leiva-Leon 2016; Kumar et al. 2009). Consequently, in the past three years, we have obtained information about the changes in the pandemic from television, social media, and mobile phone feeds. This may indicate an irreversible compression of the world, where the global interconnectedness of events in the 'global village' becomes intense and their local effects unpredictable (Harrikari and Rauhala 2019).

DOI: 10.4324/9781003374374-1

The pandemic era has demonstrated and brought out many kinds of vulnerabilities to which societies, communities, individuals, and institutions have been exposed in different ways. These vulnerabilities have varied depending on geographical location, population density, and age structure, among other things. There also seem to have been regional and age group–specific differences in the countermeasures aimed at spreading and eradicating the virus. However, the COVID-19 pandemic has proven to be a very complex phenomenon to control. Even if the viral outbreak could be controlled through epidemiological means, the multiplier effects of the pandemic on other sectors of society, such as the economy and politics, may be unpredictable. All of this requires a systemic-oriented view, in which the changes in the socio-ecological fabric of society are analysed and appraised holistically, hence outlining the importance of the emergence, interconnectedness, and interdependence of events (Boyd and Folke 2012).

In the autumn of 2022, it was no way obvious whether—and if so how—various social and ecological entities, such as continents, nation-states, provinces, cities, or local communities, had begun to organise themselves in a new way because of the pandemic, referred to as a 'new normal' by several governments. In a broad sense, the whole pandemic era raises the question of whether—and if so, to what extent—the pandemic and its consequences could be viewed as indicators of a new world age. However, questions arise as to whether we tend to overestimate the effects of crises and count on developments that would have happened anyway or that have only accelerated during crises. In terms of limiting the constitutional and human rights of citizens, the reactions and countermeasures of governments and authorities to curb the viral outbreak have been extraordinary and powerful. All types of countermeasures have received a wide and rather unquestioned legitimacy among citizens because the fear of getting infected has been so overwhelming. Furthermore, if we assume that something like a 'new normal' has really emerged, it follows that there may be definitions of a 'new deviance', leading to new kinds of stigmatisation because of the response to the outbreak. Governmental restrictions affect the entire population, but they have the harshest impact on marginalised individuals who already have difficulties in coping with their daily lives.

### Social work in disasters and humanitarian crises

Social work is a global, practice-based profession, and academic discipline that promotes social change and development, social cohesion, and the empowerment and liberation of people. The principles of social justice, human rights, collective responsibility, and respect for diversity are central to social work. Underpinned by the theories of social work, the social sciences, humanities, and indigenous knowledge, social work engages with people and structures to address life's challenges and enhance well-being (IFSW 2018; see also Adams et al. 2009; Payne 2012).

Together with health care, social welfare, social development, and social work form the core structure of the service system that maintains the well-being of the population. Although social welfare provides systemic-level support to the entire population, the specific role of social work aims to work with, support, and take care of the most vulnerable sections of the population (Jordan 2007; Gehlert and Browne 2019; Metteri et al. 2013). At the heart of social work is the concern for marginalised groups, who experience recurring difficulties in coping with their daily lives and who often come into conflict with their environment and are stigmatised by their communities. Social work bears the ultimate responsibility for the homeless, drug users, abused children, people with mental health problems, and those convicted of a crime, to name just a few.

Much has been written about social work in disasters and times of crisis (e.g. Aghabakhshi and Gregor 2007; Dominelli 2012; Mathbor 2007; Chou 2003). According to Zakour (1996), 'disasters' are crisis situations involving more than one household and that are precipitated by natural agents, technological accidents, environmental, contaminations, transportation accidents, mass violence, and the sudden death of key individuals in an organisation. Social work research on disasters seeks to improve the understanding of the *mitigation, preparedness, response, and recovery* from these situations of traumatic stress and collective suffering. In addition to protecting people, research has placed a great deal of emphasis on how people and various human communities can mobilise a variety of adaptive capacities and organise adaptive governance in crises (Zakour 1996; Yeong-Tsyr Wang et al. 2020). Even if we know quite a lot about crisis preparedness and the best practices of social work in disasters, it is possible that something quite unexpected can come up that society is not prepared for and for which no ready-made professional modes or organisational guidelines are available.

Social work and its basic functions are shaped by societal crises and humanitarian catastrophes. Indeed, social work is predominantly a transformative practice aiming to change the lives of individuals, groups, or communities in a way that increases their well-being, empowerment, and the realisation of their rights (IFSW 2018). The key tasks of social work are reducing harms in clients' lives, providing resources to increase the well-being of vulnerable groups, and opening up opportunities for them through the work of social activism (Dominelli 2012). During societal crises, however, the functions of social work tend to shift from a transformative to a conservative mode. The key duties of social work in disasters are supporting individuals and families, securing their well-being, preventing more serious consequences in their lives, and linking the clients' needs and available resources together, to mention a few (Chou 2003). In times of rapid change, the mandate of social work is to stabilise the everyday life of vulnerable populations, protect them from serious health consequences, safeguard their livelihoods, and make institutions and inter-institutional resources more accessible. Thus, problems tend to become more difficult in times of crisis, but crises may also generate qualitatively new challenges for social work. This all changes the nature of social work, social workers' work tasks and how they position themselves in their multi-professional environments. Shifts in social workers' positions not only indicate, but also set, new types of requirements for professional knowledge, competencies, and know-how in a unique societal context (Romakkaniemi et al. 2021).

### COVID-19: Social work in pandemic settings

Even if there is plenty of experience in social work practice and research on working in human emergencies and natural disasters, the global COVID-19 pandemic has been a novel kind of experience for social work professionals, teams, and organisations. Social workers, their clients, and the organisations they represent have been affected by the pandemic in multiple ways. The pandemic has called for social workers to reflect, adapt, innovate, and change their professional activities. The status of social work as a mandatory emergency profession has varied in countries during the pandemic (Dominelli et al. 2020). The primary public concerns presented in the media have focused on the availability of healthcare resources and functioning of business and industry. However, the voices of frontline social work professionals are rarely heard in the public debate over the pandemic.

Among the efforts to stem the pandemic, various public health and medical interventions have been highlighted. Interventions, such as instituting lockdowns and improving hygiene, have been pivotal in preventing viral outbreaks. However, not only everyday experiences, but also empirical social studies have indicated that the pandemic has been a highly 'social' phenomenon (Aluffi Pentini and Lorenz 2020). The pandemic setting has caused difficulties in people's everyday lives, livelihoods, and financial status, as well as their social relations and safety networks. In recent times, social work has raised concerns regarding the homeless during lockdowns, the loneliness of people with mental health problems in isolation, and hidden problems in child protection, to name a few.

These examples illustrate that frontline social workers and social welfare institutions have had to adapt to these new circumstances and respond to the challenges caused by a powerful biological mechanism that is invisible in everyday activities but has a fundamental impact on the functioning of society. Face-to-face interactions, human touch, and compassion are at the heart of social work, so we have been forced to ask how this pandemic has changed people's daily lives and the functions of social work institutions. Social work is increasingly surrounded by multidirectional and cross-scalar dynamics, in which the social systems are complex, emergent, and stratified. The ethical principles of social work have constantly been tested, and pressures to deviate from them tend to intensify in exceptional situations. Thus, although the well-being of healthcare staff has been a primary concern in many countries during the pandemic, it is worth seriously considering social workers' workload, well-being, and resilience (McFadden et al. 2021; Rapeli et al. 2018).

The pandemic and various efforts to curb the viral outbreak, such as face masks and lockdowns, have forced social workers to adapt to a 'new normal', launch new practices, mobilise social support and networks remotely, and, above all, defend the most vulnerable populations. The events and developments of the past few years have led us to consider how social work and its clients are prepared, and capable of responding to and further recovering from a societal crisis and human disasters such as the COVID-19 pandemic. When assessing the ability to prevent, respond to, and recover from external crises, such as pandemics, the adaptive capacity of social workers and social work organisations to mobilise resources is crucial (Yeong-Tsyr Wang et al. 2020). We believe that this requires an understanding of the irreversible complexity and interconnectedness of the world and its spatially social-ecological fabrics, capabilities to mobilise adaptive capacities to respond to immediate threats and launching new innovations that improve the preparedness of social work for dealing with future pandemics. Resistance to external shocks, the ability to recover from external shocks and the ability to adapt to new circumstances require strengthening the resilience of social work professionals and social welfare institutions (Rapeli et al. 2018). During the pandemic, social work has faced significant challenges, being forced to adopt *a new type of adaptive governance* (Boyd and Folke 2012), that is, new arrangements and innovations in the ways to provide social care for those in need.

### This book

This book will focus on social work during the COVID-19 pandemic. In April 2020, the editors and authors of the proposed book established a global social work researcher network called the COVID-19 Social Work Research Forum. Since then, the network has gathered regularly to reflect on the effects that the pandemic era has had on social work professionals, their clients, and organisations all over the globe. In July 2020, the network published a collection of country reports via the International Association of School of Social Work (IASSW; Dominelli et al. 2020). In mid-April 2021, the editors of the book proposal launched a call for papers for a book called *Social Work during COVID-19: Glocal Reflections and Implications for the Future of Social Work*. As a result, we received 24 abstracts, ranked the proposals, and included 15 chapters organised around four sections. Peer review of the chapters was conducted through a single-blind, cross-review practice.

The objective of this book is to offer a wealth of knowledge related to social work in different local and cultural contexts during the global pandemic. With experienced social work researchers across a diversity of settings, contexts, and research traditions, the book aims to be reflective of the 'glocal' responses of social work, where the phenomenon causing the need for social work is global and shared but in which the solutions being developed are often regional and local (think globally, act locally). Offering new perspectives on the challenges social workers have faced in dealing with the pandemic, the book aims to provide critical and timely insights into the innovations and adaptations in social work responses with a strong empirical basis. In our call, we have welcomed articles from a broad spectrum of empirical research on social work during the time of the COVID-19 pandemic. In particular, the book focuses on the specific challenges that social workers, their organisations, and their clients have faced during the pandemic and the solutions they have developed to prepare, adapt, respond to, and recover from the pandemic in their everyday settings. In this context, we have sought papers that present and reflect upon the various values, methodologies (research or practice), and practices that have been influenced by or emerged from the pandemic. We have encouraged papers from diverse settings and contexts, in terms of both global regions and practice settings, to contribute to a broad mix of international and comparative perspectives. The principle of context-boundness becomes evident in the concepts and terms describing social work, local operating systems, and pandemic, which seem to vary around the world.

This book strongly aims to bring forth knowledge that is deep and wide, here with a range of new concepts, theoretical perspectives, and research innovations that have emerged in the glocal pandemic settings. The goal is to capture the strengths of social work professionals in responding to personal and professional challenges during the pandemic and their readiness and preparedness to respond to the new, altered reality. One of the focuses is on the technological innovations that have replaced and modified 'personal and face-to-face engagement', which has presented its own challenges, with implications for personal and institutional capacities. The book offers some evidence-based practices for advancing social work knowledge, both in practice and in research, specifically in dealing with the pandemic, thus laying the grounds for preparing for social work practice and providing it with an empirical understanding of a 'new normal'.

## Structure of the book

The book consists of an introduction, 15 chapters based on empirical studies and a conclusion. The book is divided into four parts, with each providing slightly different perspectives on our overall theme. In principle, all four sections of the book examine the various challenges social workers have faced in various cultural and spatial contexts, their responses to these challenges and adaptations to the new circumstances in the glocal pandemic settings. The first section, *Policies and Governance Framing Social Work*, contains the analyses, the special feature of which is that social workers' operational possibilities and their structural conditions during a pandemic are made visible. The second section, *Voices from the Field: Facing Challenges and Creating Solutions*, demonstrates what types of challenges social work professionals and teams have faced and what kinds of creative solutions they have developed to adapt and reorganise in pandemic settings. The third section, *Vulnerabilities and Adaptive Capacities at the Client Interface*, continues with this parallel thematic, but the social work analyses focus slightly more on the client interface. The final section, called *Restating the Dynamics, Relationships, and Connectivity in Social Work*, explores the new dynamics in social work launched by the pandemic era and explores whether we could speak about anything such as a 'new normal' in social work. In these articles, the specific focus will be on taking digital leaps, working remotely, and providing digitised services for clients.

The first section of the book, *Policies and Governance Framing Social Work Practice*, contains three empirical analyses. The section begins with a chapter called *Social Workers' Response to COVID-19 in Slovenia: The Interconnectedness of Macro, Mezzo, and Micro Levels of Practice*, written by *Tadeja Kodele, Vesna Leskošek, Tamara Rape Žiberna*, and *Nina Mešl*. In their analysis, the authors explore the multilevel effects of the two waves of the pandemic on social work in Slovenia. The goal is to examine how governmental measures to curb the COVID-19 pandemic in Slovenia have affected the operations of social services and shaped the daily practices of social workers. Through their survey data, which were collected during two waves of the pandemic, the authors demonstrate how the structural and institutional changes made in Slovenia during the past few decades have weakened social work performance at the micro systemic level, resulting in the exclusion of social workers from decision- and policy-making bodies at the macro systemic level. These developments have become particularly visible during the pandemic years.

The impact of neoliberal policies on the operational readiness and adaptive capacity of social work during a pandemic is a subject of interest in the chapter *COVID-19: Social Work in the Expanding Neoliberal Welfare States*, written by *Melinda Madew, Marcin Boryczko, and Daniela Gaba*. In their chapter, the authors examine the results of a cross-national qualitative study undertaken in Poland, Romania, and Germany from December 2020 to April 2021, examining how neoliberal policies affected the daily functioning of frontline social workers during the pandemic. The results suggest that although public organisations were locked in a bureaucratic quagmire, frontline social workers were obliged to make responsible autonomous decisions to avoid the paralysis of inaction in situations of dilemma. The authors state that it is creative resilience that maintains the functionality of social service organisations, especially at the early stages of the pandemic. The employees reported working undeterred by the unpredictable trajectory of the COVID-19 pandemic and the opaqueness of organisational guidelines.

The final chapter of the first section, *Development of Digital Social Work in the Early Phase of COVID-19 Pandemic in Slovenia and Finland*, written by *Vera Fiorentino, Vesna Leskošek, Sanna Saraniemi, Marjo Romakkaniemi*, and *Timo Harrikari*, compares the practices and structures of digital social work in Finland and Slovenia after the outbreak of the COVID-19 pandemic in the spring of 2020. The chapter first focuses on the impact of the pandemic on the uptake of digital devices in Slovenia and Finland before exploring the possibilities and obstacles that social workers viewed in using digital tools while encountering service users. The results suggest that the preconceptions for and against the digital-based implementations of social work services emerged in both national contexts. The digital leap took place in both countries soon after the viral outbreak, but it happened faster in the Finnish context. The authors suggest that this may be because of the well-developed Finnish IT infrastructure, which allowed for expanding the use of digital devices in social work.

The second section of the book, called *Voices from the Field: Facing Challenges and Creating Solutions*, consists of four chapters that demonstrate what types of challenges social work professionals and teams have faced and what kinds of creative solutions they have developed to adapt and reorganise during rapid changes, both at home and at work. In their survey analyses in the chapter titled *UK Social Worker Burnout and Coping during the First Years of the COVID-19 Pandemic, Paula McFadden, Ruth Neill*, and *Jill Manthorpe* explore the impact on social worker well-being and coping across different periods of the pandemic, here starting in 2020. The surveys reveal that, despite increased pressures and changes in practice, social workers mostly continued to work creatively, using online platforms and adaptive risk management approaches to ensure those most at risk of harm were 'seen' or 'heard'. However, these efforts took a toll on their well-being, with burnout reported to be high in relation to personal and work life. The chapter discusses the findings from the research, focusing on the impact of working during the pandemic on well-being when burnout coexists while simultaneously exploring 'how' social workers cope with crises, which may be useful learning in the future.

One of the key innovations of governance during the pandemic was the different practices of controlling the virus by isolating people from each other—in other words, *lockdown*. In their chapter *Social Work during Triple Lockdown: A Restatement of Discourses in Social Workers' Stories in Estonia? Reeli Sirotkina, Airi Mitendorf*, and *Kersti Kriisk* explore how social workers responded to the emergent COVID-19 pandemic in the context of a lockdown on a small island, Saaremaa, in Estonia. The chapter introduces the emergent discourse about social work in circumstances of total isolation, analysing semi-structured focus group interviews with social workers, child protection workers and homecare workers. The analysis suggests four main discourses, revealing that working within complexity and uncertainty calls for social resilience that can be capable of adaptive and transformative capacities from professionals, but also from the community in alignment with emergent situations.

During the pandemic, social work communities were forced to organise themselves in a new way because of physical restrictions. In their chapter *Teams Interrupted: Social Work Teams as Communities of Practice and Coping during COVID-19, Laura L. Cook* and *Sara Carder* examine the impact of the COVID-19 pandemic on child and family social work teams in the UK. During the pandemic, mandatory working from home, coupled with increasingly hybrid working practices, presented both challenges and opportunities for social workers to connect with colleagues. A key concern during the pandemic was how to facilitate effective virtual and hybrid teamwork. The concepts of communities of practice (CoP) and communities of coping (ComC) are introduced as a theoretical framework for conceptualising the functioning of social work teams. The authors consider the legacy of COVID-19 for social work teams, offering recommendations for supporting effective teamwork in this increasingly hybrid, post-pandemic world.

Throughout the pandemic, the challenges caused by the pandemic have been significant in social work, but the challenges also vary over time. The beginning of the pandemic in the spring of 2020 has appeared to be a very special period because the entire phenomenon was new, the activities of societies were stopped, and the fear of the lethality of the virus was at its highest. In Belgium, a national lockdown was declared in March 2020, and companies and organisations had to take appropriate measures and adapt quickly to minimise the impact of COVID-19. In their chapter *Social Work During Crises: Good Practices and Bottlenecks According to Social Workers in Flanders, Belgium*, Michiel Massart, Inge Pasteels, Kim Bastaits, and Bart Put explore the dynamics or adaptations that social workers experienced during the first wave of the pandemic in the spring of 2020. An extensive survey demonstrates how social work organisations and social workers were not prepared for a crisis like the pandemic, but they adapted to this new situation quickly. The chapter sheds light on several good practices and bottlenecks, raising several questions that should be thoughtfully taken into account to establish those systems that benefit the client, social worker, and organisation.

The third section, called Vulnerabilities and Adaptive Capacities at the Client Interface, continues with the same theme as the previous section, but the empirical analyses focus slightly more on the client interface. The section starts with a chapter called *Medical Social Workers' Context of Practice during COVID-19 in Iran*, written by Sareh Abri and Maryam Zabihi Poursaadati. The chapter reminds us how social work acts in close, sometimes even inseparable, connection with health care. Likewise, healthcare social workers are placed in healthcare organisations, and their basic task is to support persons and families suffering from health problems and diseases. Using the data from 16 qualitative interviews, the authors analyse the challenges faced by social workers working in health care during the COVID-19 pandemic and the solutions they developed. The interviews demonstrate how working in health care was completely disorganised and chaotic for social workers at the early stage of the pandemic. The rapidly increasing infection and mortality rates, as well as working unprotected from the virus at the interface of client work, caused particular concern that the virus would be carried from the workplace to home. Social workers were also forced to adapt to many types of new tasks and roles in health care.

One of the most important age-specific groups that caused global concern during the first months of the pandemic were older adults, who, because of their age and diseases, were in a remarkably vulnerable situation regarding viral infection. Likewise, the virus entering nursing homes and its spread among elderly residents has received extensive media attention. In their article *Social Vulnerability of Older Adults and COVID-19: Findings of Surveys of Professionals Providing Care in Japan*, Junko Wake and Mie Ohwa discuss the challenges related to these issues in Japan, whose population is exceptionally old, even by international comparison. The analyses suggest that the COVID-19 pandemic has had many negative impacts on older adults' living in the community, as well as in residential institutions. Because of strict infection prevention measures, it became difficult to provide a place for elderly residents to gather. As a result of the lack of contact with others in the community, a decline in physical function in older adults because of confinement and the psychosocial effects of high anxiety were observed. The authors note that it is paradoxical that the protective measures resulted in the exacerbation of social vulnerability among older adults.

During the pandemic, there has been a global concern about the increase in violence, hidden intimate partner violence, and the ability of services to offer support to victims in acute situations. In their chapter *Experiences of Social Service Officers Working at Safe Home during COVID-19 in Bangladesh*, Priyanka Bhattacharjee and *Tulshi Kumar Das* describe the Bangladeshian social service officers' daunting challenges both at the workplace and at family during COVID-19. Through six in-depth interviews, the study investigates how social service officers met the urgent needs of the inmates, how they ensured their personal and others' safety, and the challenges the officers confronted. The findings show how the officers initiated some noble measures to deal with the situation. The shared responsibilities of the officers and staff were instrumental in ensuring the safety of all concerned. Communicating with the inmates and taking them for testing, convincing them to follow the health guidelines, connecting with the higher authorities, and looking after the family members were the major challenges for the officers. The officers recommended that increasing interdepartmental collaboration to deal with such a situation could be helpful.

The third section ends with a view regarding how, in many respects, social workers and their clients have been 'in the same boat', so to speak, as deaths and viral restrictions have touched the lives of all groups of people and may have caused shared traumatic experiences. The chapter called *Social Work and Lost Contacts with Clients during the COVID-19-Pandemic: Experiences of Shared Trauma from Three Different Civil Society Organisations*, written by *Kristofer Hansson* and *Charlotte Petersson*, focuses on how the COVID-19 pandemic illuminates a dialectical relationship between social workers and their clients and how it affects the vulnerable positions of both. Through telephone interviews with 25 social workers at battered women's shelters, night shelters, and church deacons in Sweden, the authors suggest that the clients' problems were detected at slightly different phases in the institutions. In addition, the outbreak increased the risk of negative psychological impacts on those working as care workers, which elaborates on the concept of shared trauma.

The fourth section, called *Restating the Dynamics, Relationships, and Connectivity in Social Work*, explores the new dynamics in social work launched by the pandemic era. One of the core tasks of social work is organising social relationships in a way that promotes the values of social work. Thus, the chapters included in the final section focus on, with varying perspectives, the changing modes of social interaction with social work clients and teams from an immediate face-to-face setting towards remote, digitalised, and hybrid settings. The section starts with a chapter called *'And I Say, "Yes" Because I Want to Help'—Social Worker's Reflections on Practice in Ireland during COVID 19*, written by *Joseph Mooney, Declan Coogan, Caroline McGregor*, and *Olive Lyons*. Through the constructivist grounded theory approach and interviews and diaries of ten frontline social workers working in child protection and welfare services, the authors explore how the social connections between social workers, their clients, co-workers, and collaborative parties faced ruptures in the early stages of the pandemic, how the parties were disconnected and then, again, reconnected. The findings demonstrate the practice of person-centredness in social work. Moreover, all the participants seemed to value connection with the team, particularly during the pandemic, whether through realising its absence or through its provision of resilience.

The section continues with a chapter called *Transformative Disruption?— Reflections on Care in Social Work under a COVID-19 Pandemic Lockdown*, written by *Andreas Jorgensen, Mie Engen*, and *Maria Appel Nissen*. This chapter focuses on the possibilities for sustaining care in social work with vulnerable families during a pandemic lockdown in the Danish context, discussing whether the disruption of normal practices could be a source of learning and transformation, referring to Hartmut Rosa's concept of '*resonance*'. An analysis of online focus group interviews with child welfare social workers shows how prioritising scarce resources to enable care became paramount in the pandemic context. The authors note that although the social workers experience moments of enabling and (re)discovering the 'essence of social work' and a sense of community with families, they also felt 'worn out', wondering what the future possibilities for care in the aftermath of COVID-19 will be and whether the conditions during the lockdown will become 'the new normal'. Based on these findings, the authors discuss the possibilities for transformative disruption in terms of recognising the caring purpose of social work.

After this, the book focuses more on the changes in interactions and how they have been applied in social work. This topic is addressed in a chapter called *A Shift in Social Interaction in Social Work During the COVID-19 Pandemic*, written by *Līga Rasnača, Mareks Niklass*, and *Endija Rezgale-Straidoma*. This chapter focuses on the shift in social workers' interaction patterns and heuristic decision-making through ecological rationality during the COVID-19 pandemic. Specific attention is paid to social interactions between social workers, their co-workers, service users, and administration in the Latvian context. Through a qualitative study setting, the authors suggest that information and communication technology (ICT) allowed social workers to work remotely, frequently replacing face-to-face contact with service users with virtual meetings. ICT also changed communication and its applications with colleagues and administration during the COVID-19 pandemic.

The final chapter of the fourth section, *COVID-19 as a Game Changer for the Digitalisation of Social Work*, written by *Anna-Karin Bergman, Lupita Svensson*, and *Sanna Melling*, follows the themes of social interaction and digitalisation in social work. In recent years, digitalisation has permeated many fields of society, but in social work, the digital transition has been slow—that is, until the COVID-19 pandemic hit in 2020. Using the theory of reciprocal change management and three perspectives on work, Bergman, Svensson, and Melling examine in the Swedish context how a sudden shift towards digitalisation could be understood and what kind of role COVID-19 may have played in this change. The chapter first explores the COVID-19 pandemic as a driver for the digital leap, then the connections between organisational systems and its social work community of practice, and, finally, the importance of involving a community of practice in the reformatting of social work community standards.

The book ends with a concluding chapter written by Timo Harrikari, in which he summarises the empirical research results included in the chapters. Based on the conceptual frames presented in the introduction, the findings of the empirical analyses and social work studies published elsewhere, social work research insights into the glocal challenges that arose during the pandemic are discussed. The goal is to update our view with the state of social work and the lessons learned during the pandemic, as well as future perspectives, as a way to respond to humanitarian disasters such as the COVID-19 pandemic. Moreover, he aims to discuss new elements in social work practice and research by reflecting on social theory and the methodologies applied in empirical studies. Finally, reminders regarding the limitations of the book are presented and discussed.

## References

Adams, Robert, Lena Dominelli, and Malcolm Payne, eds. 2009. *Social Work: Themes, Issues and Critical Debates*. 3rd ed. Basingstoke: Palgrave Macmillan.

Aghabakhshi, Habib, and Claire Gregor. 2007. "Learning the Lessons of Bam: The Role of Social Capital." *International Social Work* 50 (3): 347–356. 10.1177/0020872807076048.

Aluffi Pentini, Anna, and Walter Lorenz. 2020. "The Corona Crisis and the Erosion of 'the Social' – Giving a Decisive Voice to the Social Professions." *European Journal of Social Work* 23 (4): 543–553. 10.1080/13691457.2020.1783215

Beck, Ulrich. 1986. *Risikogesellschaft. Auf dem Weg in eine andere Moderne*. Frankfurt am Main: Suhrkamp.

Boyd, Emily, and Carl Folke, eds. 2012. *Adapting Institutions: Governance, Complexity and Social- Ecological Resilience*. Cambridge: Cambridge University Press.

Chou, Yueh-Ching. 2003. "Social Workers Involvement in Taiwan's 1999 Earthquake Disaster Aid: Implications for Social Work Education." *Online Journal of Social Work and Society* 1 (1): 14–36. https://ejournals.bib.uni-wuppertal.de/index.php/sws/article/view/251.

Dominelli, Lena 2012. *Green Social Work. From Environmental Crises to Environmental Justice*. Cambridge: Polity Press.

Dominelli, Lena, Timo Harrikari, Jospeh Mooney, Vesna Leskošek, and Erin Kennedy Tsunoda, eds. 2020. *COVID-19 and Social Work: A Collection of Country Reports*. N.p. https://www.iassw-aiets.org/wp-content/uploads/2020/07/IASSW-COVID-19-and-Social-Work-Country-Reports-Final-1.pdf.

Ductor, Lorenzo, and Danilo Leiva-Leon. 2016. "Dynamics of Global Business Cycle Interdependence." *Journal of International Economics* 102: 110–127. 10.1016/j.jinteco.2016.07.003

Gehlert, Sarah, and Tory Browne. 2019. *Handbook of Health Social Work*. 3rd ed. San Francisco: Wiley.

Gomez, David M., Benno Torgler, and Guillermo J. Ortega. 2013. "Measuring Global Economic Interdependence: A Hierarchical Network Approach." *The World Economy* 36 (12): 1632–1648. 10.1111/twec.12080

Harrikari, Timo, and Pirkko-Liisa Rauhala. 2019. *Towards Glocal Social Work in the Era of Compressed Modernity*. London: Routledge.

IFSW (International Federation of Social Workers). 2018. "Global Social Work Statement of Ethical Principles." *International Federation of Social Workers*. Accessed 11 September 2022. https://www.ifsw.org/global-social-work-statement-of-ethical-principles/

Jordan, Bill. 2007. "The Political, Societal and Economic Context of Practice." In *Social Work: A Companion to Learning*, edited by Mark Lymberry, and Karen Postle, 11–19. Los Angeles: Sage.

Kumar, Kuldeep, Paul C. van Fenema, Mary A. von Glinow. 2009. "Offshoring and the Global Distribution of Work: Implications for Task Interdependence Theory and Practice." *Journal of International Business Studies* 40 (4): 642–667. 10.1057/jibs.2008.77

Mathbor, Golan M. 2007. "Enhancement of Community Preparedness for Natural Disasters: The Role of Social Work in Building Social Capital for Sustainable Disaster Relief and Management." *International Social Work* 50 (3): 357–369. 10.1177/0020872807076049

McFadden, Paula, Jana Ross, John Moriarty, John Mallett, Heike Schröder, Jermaine Ravalier, Jill Manthorpe, Denise Currie, Jacklyn Harron, and Patricia Gillen. 2021. "The Role of Coping in the Wellbeing and Work-Related Quality of Life UK Health and Social Care Workers during Covid-19." *International Journal of Environmental Research and Public Health* 18 (2): 815. 10.3390/ijerph18020815

Metteri, Anna, Teppo Kröger, Anneli Pohjola, and Pirkko-Liisa Rauhala, eds. 2013. *Social Work Approaches in Health and Mental Health From Around the Globe*. Binghamton. The Haworth Social Work Practice Press.

Payne, Malcolm. 2012. *Modern Social Work Theory*. 4th ed. Oxford: Oxford University Press.

Rapeli, Merja, Carin Cuadra, Rasmus Dahlberg, Guðný B. Eydal, Björn Hvinden, Ingibjörg L. Omarsdottir, and Tapio Salonen. 2018. "Local Social Services in Disaster Management: Is There a Nordic Model?" *International Journal of Disaster Risk Reduction* 27: 618–624. 10.1016/j.ijdrr.2017.07.018-

Romakkaniemi, Marjo, Timo Harrikari, Sanna Saraniemi, Laura Tiitinen, and Vera Fiorentino. 2021. "Bonding, Bridging and Linking the Last Resort Tailboard': Shifts in Social Workers' Professional Positions and Mobilizing Adaptive Capital during the Coronavirus Pandemic." *Nordic Social Work Research*. Published ahead of print, 25 October, 2021. 10.1080/2156857X.2021.1992489

Taleb, Nassim N. 2010 *The Black Swan: The Impact of Highly Improbable*. 2nd printing. London: Penguin.

World Health Organization. n.d. "WHO Coronavirus (COVID-19) Dashboard." Accessed 26 September 2022. https://covid19.who.int.

Yeong-Tsyr Wang, Kate, Tsai Wen-Hui, Tze-Yin Chuang, and Hsi-Jing Lee. 2020. "Rethinking Four Social Issues of the COVID-19 Pandemic from Social Work Perspectives." *Asia Pacific Journal of Social Work Development* 31 (1–2): 45–51. 10.1080/02185385.2020.1819396

Zakour, Michael J. 1996. "Disaster Research in Social Work." *Journal of Social Service Research* 22 (1–2): 7–25. 10.1300/J079v22n01_02

# Section I

# Policies and Governance Framing Social Work Practice

# 2 Social Workers' Response to COVID-19 in Slovenia: The Interconnectedness of Macro, Mezzo, and Micro Levels of Practice

*Tadeja Kodele, Vesna Leskošek,*
*Tamara Rape Žiberna, and Nina Mešl*

## The complexity of social work in crisis situations

The COVID-19 pandemic of 2020 changed everyday life around the globe but also affected the work of social workers, who faced challenges they could not have foreseen. The pandemic affected people's health and socio-economic circumstances, and exacerbated their psychosocial problems, requiring an active role for social workers on multiple levels—not only in direct contact with service users (Amadasun 2020; Walter-McCabe 2020) but also in addressing social inequalities at the structural level (Huston and Mullan-Jensen 2011, 267). Social work should address the personal and the political as it deals with the daily lives of service users, but also with social inequalities at the structural, macro-level (Hare 2004, 412; Mattocks 2018, 7; Hyslop 2016).

Especially in crisis situations, social workers play an important role in advocating for policies that are responsive, rights-based, and transformative; as these situations are often used to curtail rights, resources, and services (Dominelli et al. 2020, 2). Social work has developed the knowledge and the skills to work in emergencies (Lavalette and Ioakimidis 2011), but comparative research on social work during the pandemic (Dominelli et al. 2020; Harrikari et al. 2021) shows that the sudden impact of the virus affected social work practice and context and challenged the engagement of social workers at all levels. At the forefront were health measures to prevent the spread of the virus, to keep the economy going, and to prevent a rise in unemployment (Harrikari et al. 2021, 3).

To understand how social workers in Slovenia responded to the increased need for services in this unique situation, we conducted a study 'Social Work during COVID-19 in Slovenia'. The analysis was built on the framework of micro, mezzo, and macro practices while being aware of the overlaps between the levels (Hare 2004), as professional conduct is situated in a certain structural framework that influences what social workers do and how they do it (Harrikari and Rauhala 2019). For the purposes of this research, the macro level was

DOI: 10.4324/9781003374374-3

defined as the structural and institutional framework in which the measures against the pandemic were adopted, which determined the functioning of social service. The mezzo level encompasses institutional settings where governmental measures were translated into practice. The micro level refers to the activities of the social workers, who translated measures and institutional practices into their daily work.

There were two main research questions: (1) How did the governmental measures to curb the pandemic affect the operation of the Social Work Centres and shape the daily practice of social workers? and (2) What were the responses and adjustments that best responded to people's needs?

## Structural context of social work

In Slovenia public social services are called Social Work Centres (hereafter SWCs) and are the main organisations in the field of social protection. Their aim is to prevent and resolve various social problems, hardships, and challenges for individuals, families, and various groups of people (Kuzmanič Korva et al. 2004, 20). The state is responsible for the establishment of SWCs, provides funding, and determines the normative framework and social policy. SWCs are organised territorially into 16 regional centres with units, 63 in total. The number of employed professionals (excluding administration) in 2021 was 1198 for a population of 2,100,000 people (Association of Social Work Centres, e-mail to author, 8 June 2022). Staff consists of social workers (counting for approximately 60 percent of all employees), lawyers, psychologists, pedagogues, gerontologists, theologists, sociologists, and other professions.

In 2018 the Ministry of Labour, Family, Social Affairs, and Equal Opportunities (hereafter the Ministry) reformed SWCs by introducing New Public Management (hereafter NPM), which is being implemented to different degrees in most countries in the EU countries (Hammerschmid et al. 2019). Different research reports show that NPM increases governmentality and reduces contacts with service users to brief, centrally directed, and micromanaged meetings (Harlow et al. 2013, 540–43; Healy 2009, 402–6; Heffernan 2006, 142), that applies also to Slovenia. After introducing NPM, the opportunities for social workers for active and close engagement with service users were reduced because of the heavy workload, serious staff shortages, with an intense process of bureaucratisation and specialisation (Rihter 2016, 185–8). The Ministry introduced a pyramidal decision-making structure for SWCs, a performance measurement control system and the rationalisation of administrative processes. This was followed by strong criticism from social workers that emphasised the negative consequences, such as restrictions on professional autonomy, increased control, even greater workload, and reduced opportunities for direct work with people (Rape Žiberna et al. 2020).

The reform was conducted just two years before the pandemic struck and did not yet finish, meaning that SWCs still have to deal with their own structural weaknesses that influenced their capabilities for fast and flexible adaptation to new reality, including measures against the spread of the pandemic. Governmental measures included restrictions in contact with service users, which were allowed just in emergency situations (such as domestic violence, child abuse, or other life-threatening situations), ban on field visits and strict use of personal protective equipment as a condition for contacts in emergencies. Broader measures that also influenced the work of social workers included a ban on public transport, restrictions on mobility between the cities, and restricted movements of older people. This is the context in which we conducted our research, which is presented below.

## Research on social work during COVID-19 in Slovenia

The data used in this chapter are from the research 'Social Work during COVID-19 in Slovenia', which was conducted in December 2021 and covered the periods of the first wave (from 12 March to the end of May 2020) and the second wave of the pandemic (from mid-October 2020 to the end of February 2021). Mixed methods of data collection were used, consisting of interviews, diaries, and online survey. This chapter presents the results of the online survey that asked SWCs staff about how they worked during the first and second waves of the pandemic. Because there is no list of employees in the SWCs, a non-probability sample was used. Invitations for participation in the survey were sent to 796 addresses obtained from the SWCs' websites and to the main institutional email addresses. The questionnaire consisted of 18 questions, of which 13 were mandatory and five were optional. Four questions were open-ended. We asked about the organisation of work in both waves, the choices of direct work with service users and distant work, how much social workers were able to influence these choices, how they have established contacts with service users and about the use of digital tools in these contacts (the latter data are presented in the chapter by Fiorentino et al. in this book). In the open-ended questions participants were asked to comment on the organisation of work, contacts with service users, use of ICT, and overall satisfaction with the organisation.

The survey was available online from 7 to 21 December 2020. In total, 294 persons validly completed the questionnaire, of which 242 were social workers. The data were analysed using the computer program 1ka, which allows partial data processing, complemented by Microsoft Excel and IBM SPSS 28. Univariate descriptive statistics was used, and percentages, averages, and standard deviations were calculated because the conditions for statistical inference are not met, due to nonprobability sample. The open-ended answers were analysed using the MAXQDA qualitative data analysis software and were analysed thematically according to the macro, mezzo, and micro levels.

## The impact of government measures against the pandemic on the daily practice of social workers

The model presented in Table 2.1 is designed as a result of the analysis and it is structured by the themes at micro, mezzo, and macro levels.

*Table 2.1* Model of macro-, mezzo-, and micro-level social work responses to COVID-19

| Level | | |
| --- | --- | --- |
| *Macro* | *Mezzo* | *Micro* |
| Measures and instructions | Management and organisation of work | Contacts with service users |
| Restricted access to essential public services | Trust and participation | Dealing with restriction—defining emergency |
| Invisibility of social work in society—the role of media | Security and safety | Ethical dilemmas |
| The impact of the reform and NPM | | Balancing between fear, care responsibilities, and work |
| Accessibility of social work | | |

Data from closed and open-ended questions were analysed. When using quotations from the open-ended questions the abbreviation Q followed by the number (Q 213 stands for questionnaire number 213) were used.

## The structural barriers to efficient social work

The macro level (see Table 2.1) includes measures and instructions (social distancing, closure of public services, bans on public transport and most of the economy, etc.) set by the Slovenian government based on the recommendations of the National Institute of Public Health and of the Expert Group on the containment and control of the pandemic. This group consisted of medical experts and the Ministry did not adapt the measures to the specifics of the social welfare and care sector. The instructions involved the use of protective measures (washing hands, social distancing) and protective equipment (use of masks and disinfectants) and a prohibition of personal contacts among the staff and service users. Personal contacts were allowed only in cases of emergency. It was not clear what defined an emergency, which led to various and contradictory practices not only among SWCs but also within a particular SWC. Some SWCs defined emergencies in a very broad way and accepted as many service users as possible, while others allowed contacts only exceptionally. Consequently, social workers had relatively continuous personal contacts in some places, while in others did not have them at all.

> We haven't received detailed instructions on what are the emergencies in which contacts are allowed, we were left to our own creativity and each SWC unit found their own way how to handle the situation. [...] The work depended on how individual social workers interpreted instructions—some of them did nothing, because the contacts were prohibited and some of them did everything, pushing themselves to the limits (Q 100).

They [the government, authors note] should think about the alternative ways of having a contact with service users. [...] There are too many regulations on how to prevent it and not enough support for how to make it. [...] It should be considered that the economic crisis [years 2009–2015, authors note] changed the population that uses our services, they are not the same as years back, their problems are much more complex and difficult to solve. It is not possible to help them with one call (Q 26).

In the second wave of the pandemic, there were fewer instructions given by the Ministry and the licences for video conferencing were assured as well as some technical equipment what raised the overall satisfaction with working conditions (see Figure 2.1).

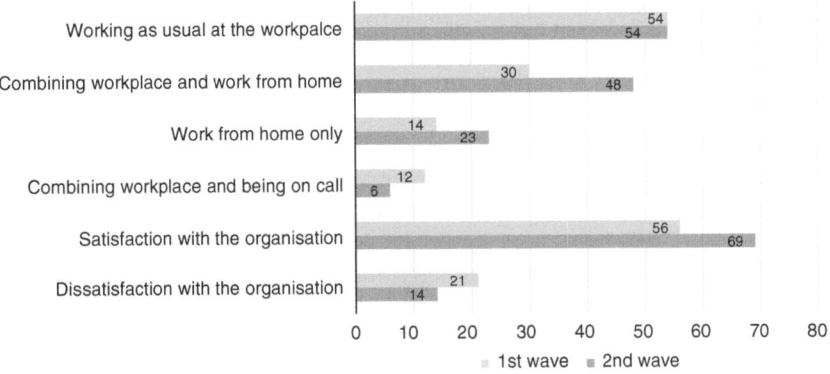

*Figure 2.1* Organisation of work and satisfaction with the organisation (% of replies, n = 247).

One of the important structural barriers was the closure of essential institutions such as schools, courts, administrative units and social services for homeless persons, people with mental health problems, and in-home care services. Admissions to old people's homes were also not possible. The measures banning inter-municipal movement and restricting it to the local community, and the closure of public transport, caused many problems. As a result, in some of the SWCs social workers took the work of other services (e.g., administering medicines, transport to the doctor's, supporting schooling of children from homes).

Everything is fine, but it is very tiring, plight of people is much greater and a lot of supporting services are closed, it is down to us to help. There is a great support from the local community, but one can feel the absence of other services (Q 201).

We had too hard workload, for example, the applications for the acknowledgement of paternity before the child's birth are responsibility of the administrative units, but because they were closed, we did it (this is not the problem for us, but we have taken over the work of other institutions—they didn't do their job). [...] It was similar with schools, parents asked us for support because they couldn't reach the teachers, or they didn't help them. Parents didn't manage Zoom connections, didn't understand the computer programmes, or didn't have internet connection at all (Q 176).

Most social workers feel that social work was more or less invisible and un-recognised by the society. They consider it wrong that the Ministry didn't require the presence of social workers in the bodies where the measures were decided. They also feel that this leaves good practices and their hard work overlooked by the public, while the media only focus on affairs that show them in a bad light. Described exclusion of social workers reduces the impact the profession might have on policies against the pandemic.

[...] The same was with the court, they didn't do divorce cases as this was not considered an emergency, but couples stayed in the same flat that caused extreme problems for them and for the children, and sometimes resulted in the violence. In reality our role is essential, but unrecognised, ignored and by the media often blamed and shamed (Q 176).

The last question in the survey was about the assessment of the overall role of SWCs in the pandemic. Data in Table 2.2 shows that majority of respondents believe that the role of SWCs was important and that they succeeded to adopt to new circumstances.

Participants were additionally asked to explain their opinion on what their role should be and about the dilemmas they had. One hundred and ten respondents decided to share their views. Most often they have mentioned the negative impact of the reform of SWCs and staff shortage. They wrote about the increased bureaucracy, about the computer programs for measuring performance, and about the time shortage because of being overloaded with cases which is also a consequence of staff shortage.

*Table 2.2* Adaptation to new circumstances and addressing the social effects of the epidemic (% of respondents, n = 221)

In both waves of the epidemic, SWCs have adapted their operations accordingly and play an important role in addressing the social effects of the epidemic.

|  | Do not agree | Partly agree | Neither agree nor disagree | Agree | Strongly agree | Total |
|---|---|---|---|---|---|---|
| **First Wave** | 12.0 | 6.9 | 25.0 | 30.6 | 25.5 | 100.0 |
| **Second Wave** | 9.3 | 5.1 | 21.3 | 33.3 | 31.0 | 100.0 |

SWC should play a greater role, it should be involved in certain activities (meetings with civil protection, the Ministry) regarding assistance and alleviation of people's distress. It should be present in the public and media, it should alert decision-makers to the plight of people who have been left alone, without receiving support. Warning decision-makers about the unsustainable situation and inefficiency of the SWCs due to the poor system. All the problems that were there before are now only bigger. I fear the future when the consequences of the epidemic will be fully revealed (Q 55).

## Adapting governmental measures to institutional practices

The mezzo level consists of the following themes (see Table 2.1): management and organisation of work, contacts with service users, relations between the staff, safety issues, trust, and participation. At this level, the differences between the first and the second waves were greater than at the macro level. Differences within SWCs also emerged, with particular importance given to the way in which the SWC management translated the measures into organisational practice. The SWC units depended on the guidance of the regional SWC, which depended on the guidance of the Ministry. In this pyramid structure, differences were generated down the hierarchy as information was lost or re-interpreted, and each unit also depended on a leadership style.

In both waves, approximately half of respondents worked as usual, others combined distant work with being at workplace. The rest had very different working arrangements, most frequently combining distant work with being at workplace and on call. Minor percentage was on sick leave or took annual leave which is partially the response to not being allowed to work from home in some of the SWCs. The data presented in Figure 2.1 show that the possibility of flexible work arrangement and combining different forms of work increased over time. In the first wave 30 percent of staff combined work in the office and work from home, which increased to 48 percent in the second wave. Thirteen percent of staff worked only from home in the first wave, figures increased to 23 percent in the second wave.

The choice of flexible working arrangements increased satisfaction with the organisation from 3.46 to 3.65 (on 5-point scale, both standard deviations are 1.1). Reasons for greater satisfaction in the second wave were manifold. In the open-ended answers respondent mentioned the time they have got to catch up on administration, completing electronic databases, editing files, and writing reports. It was also important that the choices for flexible working arrangement increased, especially the choice of working from home. Some of the respondents pointed to the importance of having the opportunity to propose to the management what they want.

There was a great difference between the waves as I have switched the job from one to another SWC in the second wave. A lot depends on a leadership, here it is about cooperation and participation while before it was top-down. It is much easier now (Q 7).

Several open answers pointed to the importance of having possibilities to make arrangements between co-workers that proved to be efficient and uncomplicated way of organising. Where this was possible the overall satisfaction was higher.

> With respecting the instructions from the leadership, we [the staff, authors note] had agreed between ourselves, how we will organise, and everything went smoothly (Q 24).

Few open answers pointed to the issue of trust. The management should trust the staff that they will do their best for service users and to protect themselves and co-workers in this terrible situation.

> So far, we have no problems with the organisation of work, we can express opinions, wishes, most of us adapt to the situation (Q 56).

At the mezzo level, another relevant issue is security. In the first wave, protective equipment for home visits was severely lacking. Quite a few SWCs had their doors locked and hired security guards which decided who could enter, that caused many complications and unpleasant situations when the service users remained in front of the closed doors. They came to SWCs hoping to be understood but were not allowed into the premises, which increased mistrust.

> [...] (I)n the second wave, we were again unprepared, all the while, even to the most desperate service users, the security guard at the door tells them to make an appointment and points to three phone numbers at the door and sends them away. Hardly anyone comes into the premises. Desperate situation! (Q 97)

Paradoxically, security guards did not supervise only the service users but also the social workers as they were only allowed to accept service users that succeeded to enter the premises.

## Professional autonomy, ethical dilemmas, and innovative ways of work

Compared to the macro and mezzo levels, the micro level is highly complex because here the personal and the professional issues intertwined with the organisational level and with overall measures set by the government. The micro level consists of the following themes (see Table 2.1): contacts with people, defining emergency, ethical dilemmas, and work-family balance.

The needs of people for support and assistance from social workers increased, mostly connected to financial hardship due to sudden loss of the job or reduced salaries. Isolation and restriction in movements, schooling from

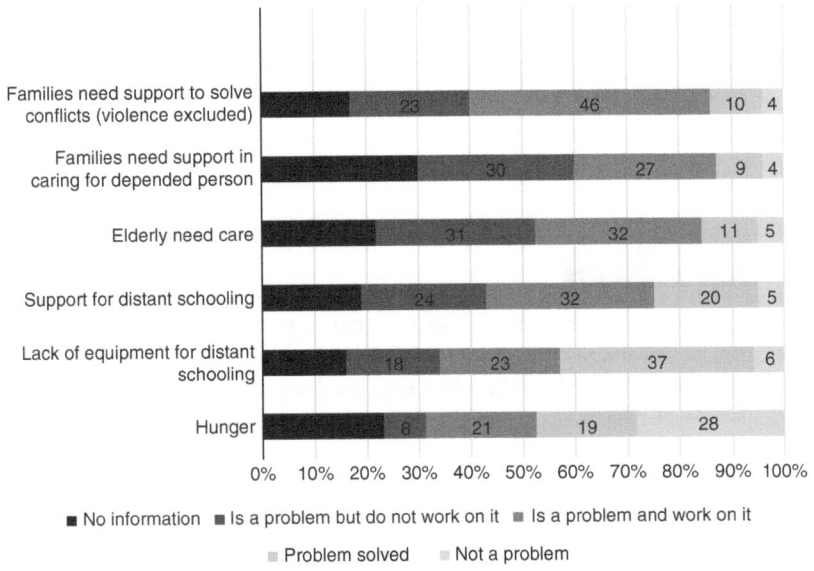

Figure 2.2 Assessment of the needs and response to them (% of responses, n = 226).

home and other measures caused many problems in family dynamics and for people living alone. Data presented in Figure 2.2 shows that family conflicts were in the forefront of the work as 46 percent of respondent are working on it and additional 10 percent already solved it. The second issue are care needs of elderly what is also connected to the fact that for a short time in-home care services were closed and admission to residential care was not possible. And the third issue was distant schooling of children where families needed quite a lot of support.

In the first wave, most SWCs restricted access and contacts but not all of them. Some stopped working altogether for a short time, not allowing staff onto the premises; some allowed staff to work in offices but restricted access of service users; and some organised themselves on an on-call basis and partially allowed service users to enter or allowed work outside the SWC premises (i.e., in the field). Data presented in Figure 2.3 shows that the major difference between the waves was in the work without restrictions. In the first wave, only 8.2 percent were working as usual with no restrictions; this percentage increased to 23.2 percent in the second wave. Consequently, there was a decrease in contact only in emergency from approximately. Seventy-five percent in the first wave to 67 percent in the second wave.

A strong opinion prevailed that people's circumstances became very complex during the pandemic and that they need immediate support. If people experience distress that they cannot resolve on their own, every situation is an emergency for them. Data in Figure 2.3 shows that 19.3 percent of respondents

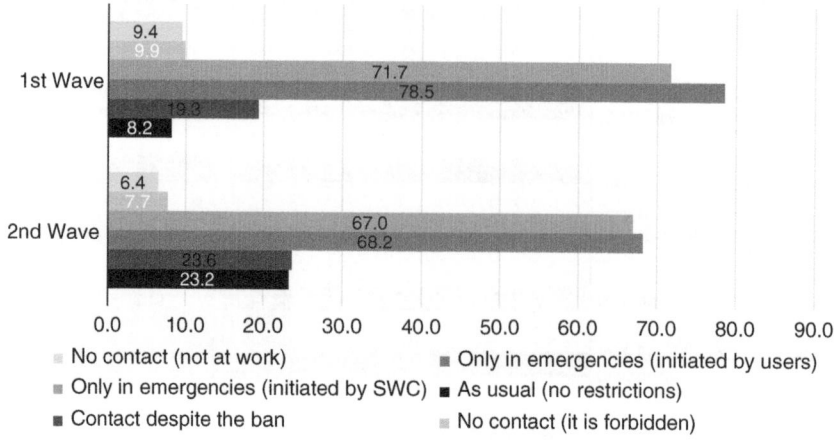

1st Wave
9.4
9.9
71.7
78.5
19.3
8.2

2nd Wave
6.4
7.7
67.0
68.2
23.6
23.2

0.0  10.0  20.0  30.0  40.0  50.0  60.0  70.0  80.0  90.0

▪ No contact (not at work)　　　　　　▪ Only in emergencies (initiated by users)
▪ Only in emergencies (initiated by SWC)　▪ As usual (no restrictions)
▪ Contact despite the ban　　　　　　　▪ No contact (it is forbidden)

*Figure 2.3* Contact with service users (% of selected replies, n = 233).

had contact with service users despite the ban in the first wave and the percentage was even higher in the second wave, explained very well through the open-ended question on professional autonomy in taking decisions and with the ethical conduct.

> Considering wearing masks, we conducted our services smoothly, people were able to come unannounced, as in a time when there is no epidemic. If I were banned from contact, I would still meet people outdoors with a mask, as I find it unprofessional and unethical not to do so (Q 83).

> In some cases, personal contact is very important. I believe that the management protects employees and cannot allow contacts on average, but at the same time the professional decision for an individual case must be left to us (Q 281).

Regarding restrictions in contacts the dilemma of respecting the rules and having contacts with service users was not easy to solve. Social workers had to adopt and find prompt and new ways in responding to the needs, what proved to be quite challenging.

> Here's the ethical dilemma: Should I ignore the Ministry's instructions and go into the field to meet people? Should I admit a service user who comes to my office because they do not know how to fill in the application, despite the fact that all SWCs are closed? (Q 197)

> We should warn decision-makers about the very problematic situation and inefficiency of the SWCs due to the poor system. [...] All the problems that were there before are now only bigger! (Q 57)

Additional dimension of the problem was fear and insecurity about the infection with the new virus. Respondents differed in the extent to which this fear inhibited their functioning, causing some to isolate themselves, refusing to have contact with other staff and service users. This was not a simple situation and cannot be seen as a breach of professional ethics. Some social workers had comorbidities that would normally allow them to work without any difficulty, but the infection could exacerbate their condition, while others had contact at home with parents, grandparents, or dependent family members who could be further endangered by infection. The circumstances were demanding; consequently, it was not easy to make choices and decisions.

## Lessons to be learned for the future

The results of the research point to several important issues that should be considered in future developments in relation to pandemics and beyond. The research showed that in the first wave of the pandemic, operations of SWCs were reduced not only to the micro level but to the minimum of services, although people's needs were greater. Many of these needs resulted from the state's measures and required an immediate response (e.g., Dominelli et al. 2020; Harrikari et al. 2021). The top-down effect of the measures is clearly recorded in Slovenia, but there is no evidence of the bottom-up actions of social workers having influence over measures and policies to prevent the negative effects of the pandemic. Some reasons for this are objective (e.g., office closures, bans on services and public transport, poor ICT, and the lack of medical protective equipment). However, there are also structural and normative reasons for the weak influence of social workers on the macro-level policies what some authors conceptualised as the politics of pandemic (Santiago and Smith 2020; Itzhaki-Braun 2021; Aaltola 2022).

Anna Maria Santiago and Richard Smith (2020, 90) emphasise that the response to the pandemic must be contextualised in the 'neoliberal global order and in rising populism either of which undergird the politicking shaping these responses', which was ignored by medical and political policymakers when deciding on the measures against the pandemic. This is also true in Slovenia, where SWCs were reformed just a few years before the pandemic and resulting in, among other things, increased workloads, less time to work directly with service users, and performance monitoring through electronic databases. This was exacerbated in times of the pandemic and further fuelled by lack of protective equipment, increased control, instructions from the government, and feelings of helplessness and fear.

The Slovenian case shows that the emphasis on safety was complemented by increased control over professional conduct. Here, we refer mainly to the institutional barriers established to contact with service users, such as locking SWCs, banning personal contacts, non-defining emergency, introducing security guards, and assessing eligibility for services, which was declared by some social workers to be the end of professional work, but accepted by others as necessary. It cannot be denied that it is necessity to trade a certain amount of freedom or professional autonomy for safety in times of disaster, but this trade-off can pose a serious threat to human dignity and human rights. As John Chandler et al. (2017) claim, that NPM which was in Great Britain introduced already in the eighties, reduced and reframed professional autonomy and social workers became much more controlled and inspected. In Slovenia NPM was introduced recently and the pandemic was situated in this unstable and vague structural framework resulting in a variety of different institutional and organisational settings that impacted professional autonomy.

It is also necessary to recognise the differences between the first and second waves of the pandemic. As the pandemic progressed into the second wave, SWCs became more flexible and innovative in their responses to staff and service users' needs. The normative framework determined the organisation of SWCs, but it mattered how the management of SWCs responded to the defined framework and how each social worker acted in day-to-day practice. Thus, at the mezzo and micro levels, there were significant differences between the operation of SWC units and their responses to people's needs, not to mention the importance of management's trust and respect of the professional autonomy of employees.

At the micro level, the research results show that some respondents were happy to gain the time to sort out administration, fill-in electronic databases and to write reports but they struggled with ethical dilemmas about what to do for service users, as they were aware of their increased needs for support. Some faced the opposite dilemma of whether to break the law, ignore the measures and instructions and meet with service users. Respondents also had their own fears and wanted to protect themselves and their families from infection. In the context of pandemic politics, Mika Aaltola (2022) coined a term of 'politico-somatics' to capture these feelings and dilemmas. He claims that the lived life of individual somatic level anxieties coupled with the hierarchical interconnectedness of the global polity. The concept can be applied at the national level where the political order is reflected in the behaviours and feelings of an individual person. What matters is how governments frame the politics of the pandemic and how it is implemented and used at the operational levels.

The everyday work of social workers and their relationships with service users thus can't be exempted from the contexts in which it is practised, what is already broadly discussed in social work theory (Healy 2009; Lavalette and Ioakimidis 2011; Hyslop 2016). In the disaster framework this fact becomes not just more visible but has also stronger impact because a collective and orchestrated response is needed at all interconnected levels. Major differences between countries are generated exactly at this point of how well the system works; how it embraces and encourages participation; enables a space for flexible and autonomous adaptation and innovative approaches in unique times. More authoritarian, patriarchal regime intertwined with the neoliberal paradigm is certainly less successful as it does not have respect and trust in professionalism, especially when located in public sector (Gray et al. 2015; Garrett, 2018), which minimises chances for the successful response in times of emergency as it limits the agency. This is the case of Slovenia that needed more than one wave of pandemic to adopt, and consequences are yet to be seen.

## References

Aaltola, Mika. 2022. *Understanding the Policies of Pandemic Emergencies in the time of COVID-19: An Introduction to Global Politosomatics.* Abingdon: Routledge.

Amadasun, Solomon. 2020. "COVID-19 Pandemic in Africa: What Lessons for Social Work Education and Practice?" *International Social Work* 64 (2): 1–5. 10.1177/0020872 820949620

Chandler, John, Elisabeth Berg, Marion Ellison, and Jim Barry. 2017. "Reconfiguring Professional Autonomy? The Case of Social Work in the UK." In *Social and Caring professions in European Welfare State*, edited by Björn Blom, Lars Evertsson, and Marek Parlinski, 69–82. Bristol: Polity Press.

Dominelli, Lena, Timo Harrikari, Joseph Mooney, Vesna Leskošek, and Erin Kennedy Tsunoda, eds. 2020. *COVID-19 and Social Work: A Collection of Country Reports.* N.p. https://www.drugsandalcohol.ie/32880/1/IASW-COVID-19-and-Social-Work-Country-Reports.pdf

Garrett, Paul M. 2018. *Welfare Words: Critical Social Work & Social Policy.* London: Sage. https://www.worldcat.org/title/1016984483

Gray, Mel, Dean Mitchell, Kylie Agllias, Amanda Howard, and Leanne Schubert. 2015. "Perspectives on Neoliberalism for Human Service Professionals." *Social Service Review* 89 (2): 368–392. 10.1086/681644

Hammerschmid, Gerhard, Steven Van de Walle, Rhys Andrew, and Ahmed M.S. Mostafa. 2019. "New Public Management Reforms in Europe and Their Effects: Findings from a 20-Country Top Executive Survey." *International Review of Administrative Sciences* 85 (3): 399–418. 10.1177/0020852317751632

Hare, Isadora. 2004. "Defining Social Work for the 21st Century: The International Federation of Social Workers' Revised Definition of Social Work." *International Social Work* 47 (3): 407–424. 10.1177/0020872804043973

Harlow, Elizabeth, Elisabeth Berg, Jim Barry, and John Chandler. 2013. "Neoliberalism, Managerialism and the Reconfiguring of Social Work in Sweden and the United Kingdom." *Organization* 20 (4): 534–550. 10.1177/1350508412448222

Harrikari, Timo, and Pirkko-Liisa Rauhala. 2019. *Towards Glocal Social Work in the Era of Modernity.* Abingdon: Routledge.

Harrikari, Timo, Marjo Romakkaniemi, Laura Tiitinen, and Sanna Ovaskainen. 2021. "Pandemic and Social Work: Exploring Finnish Social Workers' Experiences through a SWOT Analysis." *The British Journal of Social Work* 51 (5): 1644–1662. 10.1093/bjsw/ bcab052

Healy, Karen. 2009. "A Case of Mistaken Identity: The Social Welfare Professions and New Public Management." *Journal of Sociology* 45 (4): 401–418. 10.1177/1440783309346476

Heffernan, Kristin. 2006. "Social Work, New Public Management and the Language of 'Service' User." *British Journal of Social Work* 36 (1): 139–147. 10.1093/bjsw/bch328

Huston, Stan, and Christine Mullan-Jensen. 2011. "Towards Depth and Width in Qualitative Social Work: Aligning Interpretative Phenomenological Analysis with the Theory of Social Domains." *Qualitative Social Work* 11 (3): 266–281. 10.11 77/1473325011400484

Hyslop, Ian. 2016. "Neoliberalism and Social Work Identity." *European Journal of Social Work* 21 (1): 20–31. 10.1080/13691457.2016.1255927

Itzhaki-Braun, Yael. 2021. "Community Social Workers' Perspectives on the Challenges and Opportunities Presented by the COVID-19 Pandemic." *American Journal of Orthopsychiatry* 91 (6): 714–723. 10.1037/ort0000573

Kuzmanič Korva, Darja, Marija Perkovič, Jure Kovač, Pavla Rapoša-Tanjšek, and Vito Flaker. 2004. *Preoblikovanje organiziranosti centrov za socialno delo v Republiki Sloveniji* [Transforming the Organisation of Social Work Centres in Slovenia]. Ljubljana: Skupnost centrov za socialno delo Slovenije.

Lavalette, Michael, and Vassilis Ioakimidis, eds. 2011. *Social Work in Extremis. Lessons for Social Work Internationally.* Bristol: Policy Press.

Mattocks, Nicole O. 2018. "Social Action among Social Work Practitioners: Examining the Micro–Macro Divide." *Social Work* 63 (1): 7–16. 10.1093/sw/swx057

Rape Žiberna, Tamara, Janko I. Cafuta, Aleš Žnidar and Vito Flaker. 2020. "Začetna analiza stanja po izvedeni reorganizaciji: skupščina kot oblika akcijskega raziskovanja centrov za socialno delo" [Initial Analysis on the Implementation of Reorganisation: Assembly as the Form of Action Research of the Social Work Centres]. *Socialno delo* 59 (1): 5–27. http://www.dlib.si/?URN=URN:NBN:SI:DOC-FPJ57C3G

Rihter, Liljana. 2016. "Zaposlitev in delovne razmere na področju socialnega varstva" [Employment and Working Conditions in the Field of Social Protection]. *Socialno delo* 55 (4): 181–190. http://www.dlib.si/?URN=URN:NBN:SI:DOC-9RPWTJOQ

Santiago, Anna M., and Richard J. Smith. 2020. "Community Practice, Social Action, and the Politics of Pandemics." *Journal of Community Practice* 28 (2): 89–99. 10.1080/10705422.2020.1763744

Walter-McCabe, Heather A. 2020. "Coronavirus Pandemic Calls for an Immediate Social Work Response." *Social Work in Public Health* 35 (3): 69–72. 10.1080/19371918.2020.1751533

# 3 COVID-19 Social Work in the Expanding Neoliberal Welfare States

*Melinda Madew, Marcin Boryczko, and Daniela Gaba*

Social work is shaped by policies, value systems, situated knowledge, and contemporary local development. It is a profession forced into collective introspection by a pandemic affecting societies at various stages of global economic development. Social workers worldwide must learn more about global forces affecting societies at various stages of economic development (Hare 2004, 417). Such contemporary knowledge flow is crucial in understanding the nature and specificity of social work, especially when the context of practice changes under the impact of the COVID-19 pandemic.

Respected experts argue that marketisation, managerialism, and neoliberalism have not only profoundly challenged social work values but greatly impacted social work practice as well (Ferguson 2008; Lorenz 2005; Rogowski 2010). Studies have shown that the impact of neoliberalism on social work is worldwide. However, local variation can be recognised when it comes to public policies, institutional management, and governance (Albuquerque 2018; Garrett 2019; Spolander et al. 2014).

Two main dimensions characterise the neoliberal framework as formulated by David Harvey (2005). First, is the marketisation of the welfare state, and its consequential restructuring to operate for profitable capital accumulation, leading to a 'dramatic shift in government commitments from securing the welfare of citizens to facilitating the flow of global capital' (Baker 2009, 70). Second, is the engagement of a disciplinary regime for governing subordinated populations by incorporating multi-layered mechanisms of oppression. In this chapter, we refer to neoliberalism not just as a concept or a system of ideas, but more on its pragmatics and consequences for social actors beyond simple rhetoric. Neoliberalism as a political and economic ideology compels governments to impose policies of privatisation and marketisation of social services giving rein to the state to abnegate its responsibility to guard citizen welfare and promote community cohesion (Cahill and Konings 2017). By using the concept of neoliberalism, we examine the nature of policies that shape social work practice, an idea that refers to intersections between people's actions, practices, and underlying principles influencing those actions such as normative structures, ideologies, culture, beliefs, or policies. Paul Willis and Mats Trondman (2002)

DOI: 10.4324/9781003374374-4

define these as 'procedural policy work' that is a way in which social actors use their symbolic resources to understand their place and consequences of actions through assimilation of theories, narrations, and ideologies about their particular practice. In this case, we focus on practices determined by neoliberal policies present in the research field.

The expansion of neoliberalism occurred by adapting market policies that significantly restructured welfare states throughout the world, primarily in the European region (Cahill and Konings 2017). Integration in the EU strengthened the neoliberalisation of welfare states in Europe where strategies such as the European Employment Strategy, Single Market Strategy, European Competition Policy, and Economic and Monetary Integration all became European variations of 'neoliberalism in practice' despite the declared European Social Model (Hermann 2007). At the European level, an example of the restructuring of welfare states was the shift from welfare to workfare-oriented social policy that included budgetary austerity, labour market flexibilisation, and privatisation of the public sector all leading to unprecedented inequalities.

Neoliberalisation influenced global social work including the Central and Eastern European (CEE) countries. The main ideological force of welfare reform was neoliberalism as it exerted transitionary pressure on European countries where 'the neoliberal premises of the Washington consensus with their respective advisors, shaped policies that systematically and radically transformed them from non-capitalist regimes to capitalist ones' (Drahokoupil 2007, 408). The specificity of CEE (including Eastern Germany) often described as post-socialist systems had to adjust to new economic conditions and reality labelled as neoliberalism.

The CEE countries spend much less on welfare programs than most countries in the OECD or the EU (Abrahamson 2010; Chelcea and Druță 2016; Inglot 2009) coined the term 'emergency welfare state' to describe CEE countries. The emergency welfare state was designed as a temporary system in the form of shock therapy, but it continued as a permanent structure. However, the CEE region including Romania and Poland stands out in EU statistics as having a low ratio in terms of total general government expenditure on social protection (Eurostat 2022).

## Neoliberal welfare states—Three county experience

### Poland—Victim of non-interventional state

At the beginning of the 1990s, the leitmotiv of public debates in Poland was the welfare state's focus on the pension and family allowance system which was perceived by the general population as a social security base. From that time to the present, the perception of the social security system is limited to financial transfers. This was a reason for criticism against the welfare state by neoliberals who often pictured democracy with a neoliberal face, contrasting this with the 'old and bad' communism. Neoliberal discourse in the context of social policy appeared after 1989 when there was a need to justify the austerity policy. As David Ost (2005) points out, the logic standing after the idea of the non-interventional state was that capitalism was not yet established so the government cannot restrain or fight its social consequences.

The 1990 neoliberal paradigm was the implementation in Poland of the 'shock therapy' locally called 'Balcerowicz plan'. Polish social policies since that time were conceived by policymakers and presented in public media as an unnecessary burden instead of an investment that stimulated socio-economic growth. Therefore, the dominant conviction was that the shift from 'welfare' to 'workfare' was the panacea for all social problems. The post-communist period was oriented toward the so-called active social policy that is based mainly on *employability*. Because of the so-called Europeanisation process, social workers became more engaged in the process of managing social problems rather than solving them (Granosik 2016).

### Romania—Fragile political stability within an inconsistent neoliberal transition

Welfare state reforms in the post-communist period were gradual and non-uniform in CEE countries (Lazăr et al. 2019). While in some states in the region such as Poland and Hungary, reforms took the form of 'shock therapy' through trade liberalisation, price stabilisation, and heavy privatisation. In others, such as Romania, these were slower due to inconsistencies in local-level governance and overall economic instability (Miszczyński 2019, 20). Communism ended violently in Romania, through the execution of the country's communist ruler, Nicolae Ceaușescu, whose economic policy throughout the 1970s and 1980s contrasted with those of other socialist economies as it attempted to isolate Romania from both USSR and Western influences, leaving the country with 'rigid economic and political arrangements' (Pop 2013, 164). The first part of the 1990s was especially turbulent in Romania amid social protests and fragmented and unstable political views from governmental actors struggling for legitimacy. Neoliberal patterns of governance materialised in the mid-1990s, under the auspices and involvement of foreign international actors such as the World Bank, the IMF, and the European Commission all providing technical and financial support for social reforms.

In Romania, social work flourished during the inter-war period only to be dismantled as an occupation and educational field by the communist regime (Lazăr et al. 2019). The reinstatement of social work as a profession during the early transition period faced the difficult challenges of a fragile social protection system and a lack of institutional and legislative coherence (Pop 2013). Amid an increase in the social costs of structural reforms with rising social inequality and poverty, neoliberal influences manifested strongly with an increased focus on individual responsibility employing managerial approaches to reduce social assistance costs (Lazăr et al. 2019).

## Germany and the precariat class

When set against the framework of European politics, there are perplexing contraindications over the much-touted German welfare state. References are often made over Germany's rigorous efficiency since emerging as the European economic miracle or the Wirtschaftswunder of the 20th century. After the Nazi defeat, the country took an outward-facing position, marching unstoppably into the wide-open world market as an industrial powerhouse in the 1950s despite its decimated post-war status. Such status was preserved by Germany standing unscathed in the turbulence of global recession as other countries in the European Union submitted to fiscal restructuring by adapting neoliberal austerity measures (Germann 2021). In his time John Maynard Keynes rightfully predicted how the German machine, like a top to maintain its equilibrium, must spin faster and faster (Slobodian 2021). Its global primacy is secured by a protectionist technological prowess in producing machines that produce other machines.

The export Weltmeister (global champion) spawned a rung in society often referred as the precariat class. They are those who either slide into unemployment, struggle in precarious mini-jobs, or occupy the lowest level of paid work with no long-term job perspective. The government went about setting social reforms with standardised guidelines for welfare payments following a neoliberal justification that only the deserving poor will receive state subsidies. The increasing rank of zero-hour gig workers or flexi-workers within the precariat class is often unrepresented in workers' unions. National data in Germany or perhaps the world over when collected and analysed will yet reveal how COVID-19 morbidity and mortality rates would be highest in the rich world's precariat class (Sablowski 2020).

## Research methodology

Presented here are the results of a cross-national qualitative study undertaken in Poland, Romania, and Germany from December 2020 to April 2021. The general objective was to examine how neoliberal policies affected the daily functioning of frontline social workers in pandemic times. Two specific objectives were formulated. The first objective identified challenges that social workers similarly faced in each country and the strategies they employed to cope with difficulties caused by the pandemic. The second objective examined the perceptions of social workers over the capacity of state institutions to respond with policy and procedural measures to promote and protect the efficacy of frontline work. From the comparative collation of critical insights given by experienced frontline social workers, the study has the potential of encouraging social workers to decisively engage in the reshaping of institutional structures to safeguard the interest of vulnerable groups, while correspondingly calling on the social work profession to expose and oppose state neglect.

A total of 30 frontline social workers, 10 from each participant country were purposively sampled to collect critical perspectives over professional activities and the level of state and organisational support for their work during the pandemic that subsequently affected their private lives. Given the exploratory nature of the research conducted at the backdrop of the unprecedented scenario of the COVID-19 pandemic, a heterogenous sample was sought, with a diversity of experiences and perceptions located in each national pandemic context. At the time of the data collection, the participants in the study were employed either in public institutions or in NGOs or private practices, performing in various areas of practice: child and family protection, work with refugees and asylum seekers, social protection for the elderly, community development, or social economy programs. Only social workers with at least a year of experience in the field were selected to ensure fully formed professional perspectives. The data were collected through semi-structured interviews conducted online or in-person conversations that were recorded and transcribed verbatim. In Germany, the interviews were conducted in English, while in Poland and Romania they were performed in the national official languages, namely Polish and Romanian, respectively. The interview guide was originally developed in English and translated into Polish and Romanian with assistance from foreign language experts.

The interview covered specific areas such as the difficulties they confronted; their perceptions of the capability of state institutions to provide appropriate measures; and the work-life balance mechanisms they initiated. The instrument was pre-tested involving at least one respondent from each country and subsequent improvements were adapted. Interview transcriptions in non-English languages were translated into English. There were occasions for repeated interview sessions to validate the information given. All respondents signed an informed consent document. The research project adhered to the ethical standards of the academic institutions of the authors. No incentives were given to respondents.

This study made references to critical social work theory as the analytical framework used in dissecting the interrelatedness of social problems and relating these to their systemic and historical rootedness in economic and political structures. The complexities confounding social workers in crisis situations are better understood when traced to the history of neoliberalism and the corrosion of the welfare state.

Following a critical reflective approach, participants in the study narrated events to describe interactive critical incidents with client groups. Their critical and reflective analyses of situated experiences were evidential bases of our thematic analysis of the collected qualitative data. Employing participatory methods, follow-up sessions were conducted to validate the interpretation of information and clarification of insights offered by participants.

## Presentation of interview results

The pandemic exposed the vulnerable underbelly of researched countries as social service workers compensated for government failures in securing the basic individual right to state protection in matters of health, physical integrity, and personal security. Social workers have done this not because of institutional compulsion, but more as an expression of professional accountability to groups and individuals, who at the early stages of the chaotic COVID-19 reorganisation were left stranded in bureaucratic limbo. It is often the precariat class that needed social workers in pandemic times. The ones who knocked on office doors during lockdowns to keep appointments with social workers. The precariousness of their economic situation exposes them to greater health hazards. Among the precariat class are migrants, refugees, sex workers, restaurant workers, cleaning women, and others in flexible work conditions. Research findings showed how misdirected social policy measures exacerbated the impact of the crises.

## Social workers and social organisations: Resilience in crises

Most respondents from the three countries described situations where organisations were inadequately prepared at the onset of the pandemic. Internal procedural confusion resulted from the inconsistencies between governmental policy directives on public health measures and social work organisations' capacity to implement these. Rules imposed by authorities encroached on professional self-determination and client autonomy as in the following example:

> Some of the measures taken have been contradictory. There was [the] measure to keep a strict distance of 3 meters from clients, something that was in contradiction with the fact that I needed to take their temperature each time they came in [...] Also, I had to explain all the time to them that, no, no, this is not a medical act, the fact that I'm taking your temperature (Romania, F, one-year work experience, private sector).

Insufficient public health resources in the face of increasing needs stressed social workers. There was a real, yet unspoken expectation that social workers compensate for gaps left open by inadequate organisational and state support. Frontline social workers became immediate responders to calls for help. In the absence of financial or material assistance, social workers compensated with professional skills by providing emotional support, family counselling, child supervision and care.

The research exposed multiple binds in balancing legitimate personal interests with professional duties. Increased professional stress resulted from increasing workload, health risks, and job insecurities taking the form of shortened working hours and salary cuts. Modalities in client-social worker relationships were constantly reconfigured. Many social workers were bound to professional practice while dealing with private fears. As the following testimony would indicate, the social worker feared losing income while forced to use her private equipment to maintain the flow of office work from home.

> In March also, well, for example, they took away the field allowance because, because we didn't go to the clients, so they took that away from us too. [...] Yeah, well they put us on remote work, with our equipment, with our computers, with our phones and yet they took that allowance away from us (Poland, F, two years work experience, public sector).

## Work dilemmas: Professional duty or client autonomy?

In times of crisis, social workers did a balancing act of upholding their professional mandate to serve clients and protect their interests while maintaining professional loyalty to the organisation and the state that employs them. In such cases, duty and personal values became determining factors in decision-making. As in the case cited here, a social worker's value system guides her in respecting client autonomy while pushing the borders of ethical practice and organisational policy.

> My clients are street prostitutes. During pandemic times they are prohibited from working in the streets [n.b.: Sex work in Germany is legal]. There was an undocumented migrant, she had no social security or unemployment insurance. My organisation cannot pay her rent or buy her food. She has to work the streets to survive. Should I call the police? No, I issued her condoms instead! (Germany, F, three years work experience, public sector)

In times of extreme insecurity, there is a tendency to rely on established rules. Conformity to rules provides stabilising assurance in situational decision-making. At the onset of the pandemic, organisations began establishing rules and procedures that were often implemented regardless of the consequences on social workers. The more stringent the rules, the greater the demand for conformity. Yet, the nature of the crisis demanded decisional flexibility and on-the-job adaptation by social workers. Social workers reported fearing the threat of sanctions when engaged in situational decision-making that pushed the limits of rules and regulations. When following directives from the top, the initiative and creativity to search for better alternatives in resolving client needs are curtailed as these testimonies indicate:

> I was afraid to act on my own. Better than I obeyed, then I know I can defend and protect myself by just following orders (Germany, F, 10 years work experience).

> We were never asked for an opinion [in the decision-making process]. We simply executed [the orders] (Romania, F, one-year work experience, public sector).

Budgetary cuts affected social service organisations in the European region resulting in a multi-burdened social worker delivering cheap and efficient labour. The pandemic created a situation where social workers had to compensate for the failings of the state to allocate more personnel resources by assuming multiple roles and responsibilities. Ever bound to a high sense of duty, there were social workers who almost without question fulfilled unrealistic expectations, as this experience suggests:

Generally, we strongly applied as unions to keep that rotational work and then the executive disagreed [...] Everyone knew that it wasn't a joke anymore, because everyone already had a family member somewhere, someone, who, who died of COVID, and here I'm saying, well, the City Hall could work every second day and they were somehow treated like that, and we were just like like it's always just like on the first line of fire (Poland, F, 11 years work experience, public sector).

## Authoritative Control

The issue of control is a dominant factor affecting social worker relationships with employers, and concomitantly the social worker and client interaction. A post-pandemic situation could still offer the social work profession new spaces where established and respected paradigms of practice can be seriously interrogated in public discourse. For now, questions are raised over managerial control in its nuanced and overt manifestations. Revealed to us are patterns of authoritative control which even when subtle, are still at times insidious in their ability to curtail problem-solving creativity and confidence in democratic decision-making processes within organisations.

An overreliance on authority is created in situations of ambiguity and ambivalence in terms of social workers' perceptions. That obedience accorded to authority became possible when individuals seem not to have any other recourse but conformity to rules. In a vacuum of uncertainties, the controlling authority can occupy every space of decision-making and thereby exercise unquestioned control as this testimony shows:

What are we supposed to be doing on this remote work if we don't have that access to the database? [...] Each team had to figure out for themselves what they were going to do on this remote work so that the directors knew that we were really working. We also had to write daily reports of what we did at home and send that in, right? Also, they kind of sent us to work remotely, they didn't tell us what to do, they expected us to know what to do ourselves and yet such a lack of trust, no? That you, that you work from home, no? We had to report it all (Poland, F, two years work experience, public sector).

Managerial neoliberalism installed bureaucracy as a mechanism of social control. Because of its punitive or sanctioning capability, it can enforce rote unquestioning productivity. Some participants in this research submitted to this behavioural tendency:

You simply ask them such questions and sometimes they simply get caught in a lie. In one of my cases, when I had doubts about some people and I asked them to provide some proof. Of course, I have said: I would like to inform you that the statements I write down with you have criminal liability, so please be honest, because sooner or later it will come out anyway (Poland, F, five years work experience, public sector).

The lack of preparedness and procedural confusion within organisations compounded by bureaucratic state control generated two types of coping strategies among social workers. The subsequent examples showed a tendency to over-rely on authority while exhibiting resignation and resentment.

> There were no channels for asking questions. We were too afraid to raise questions. We were waiting for directives from the top. We acted according to what they told us (Germany, F, eight years work experience, private sector).

> Big chaos, nobody knows anything. We did not know how to inform our clients. We didn't know what to tell them and how to proceed at all (Poland, M, age 45, 15 years of experience, public sector).

Others responded with initiative and creativity to rise above the chaos and install calm in a desperate situation when the virus was hardly understood:

> We organised weekly meetings for them [...] where they learned, for example, how to make their T-shirts with prints or something like that so that they could then do it with their families (Poland, F, age 28, two years work experience, public sector).

> I organised seamstresses who sewed face coverings when there was a general lack of supplies. I also organised a team of young people who did shopping errands for the elderly (Germany, F, age 67, 35 years work experience, public sector).

This public health crisis exposed the paradox of attempting to control the uncontrollable and manage the unmanageable. A virus succeeded in exposing the vulnerabilities of neoliberal governmentality which for long was self-assured and convinced about its ability to control critical eventualities.

## Concluding thoughts derived from respondents' testimonies

### Historical differences and the cross-cutting similarities in welfare regimes

Despite differences in history and economic priorities existing in all three countries, social workers recounted how the politics of austerity within a European neoliberal order spawned similar social welfare policies and managerial procedures that required their organisations to submit to state control (Börner 2020). This study exposed similarities in neoliberal welfare regimes in all three countries. These are empirical evidence of staggering unpreparedness in dealing with humanitarian crises and the decades of neglect in social care investment (Hemerijck and Huguenot-Noël 2021). This proves the contention that in Europe, the social vulnerabilities of client groups cut across all countries in similar ways. Respondents in this study gave testimonies of day-to-day struggle with meagre material resources while dealing with authoritative managerialist control.

### Beyond obedience—Confronting authoritative managerialist control

There is empirical evidence that implies the emerging profile of resistance to authoritative control among frontline social workers. When called to duty in a crisis of unprecedented nature, social workers resorted to a range of responses from passive conformity to outright confrontative resistance. Empirical evidence given by social workers in this study showed their professional grit and hardiness when facing government neglect, leadership failure and misappropriated state resources.

When at the crux of difficult decisions that impinge on professional ethics, personal integrity, or administrative sanction, they acted with discretion in taking risks to protect client interest. Respondents gave testimonies over how they reported for work each day despite confusion and ambivalence in administrative guidelines. Based on their responses, this study further gathered evidence of self-assured professional agency and courage to go beyond pre-ordained regulations to uphold client interest. The ability to question authority while upholding the rights of vulnerable individuals is uncompromising professionalism. When their organisations buckled under the weight of bureaucracy, social workers persevered in resilience and creativity. In the fluidity of situations, they cut red tape by creating workable procedures within their locus of responsibility and control to avoid the tedious process of seeking ineffectual guidelines from people in authority. In this pandemic crisis, it is proved that it is the assertive autonomy of service providers that guards them against the demoralising dysfunctionality of a neoliberal welfare regime (Roethig and Durtschi 2021).

### The pandemic paradox—Resilience, dilemmas, and autonomy

While public organisations were locked in a bureaucratic quagmire, frontline social workers made responsible autonomous decisions to avoid the paralysis of inaction in situations of dilemma. It is this creative resiliency that maintained the functionality of social service organisations, especially at the early stages of the pandemic. They reported working undeterred by the unpredictable trajectory of the COVID-19 epidemic and the opaqueness of organisational guidelines. On one hand, there was the pragmatism of keeping a job to protect their own families from further financial precariousness, and on the other, there emerged a compulsion to professional duty. Despite the economic precariousness of social workers' family situation, they made sure service remained uninterrupted. The pandemic exposed the precarity of those who delivered care and service (Pulignano 2021). The pandemic revealed the inseparability of civic duty and private choices that frontline social workers had to navigate. From here we glean lessons in the intersectionality of private issues, civic duty, and professional ethics (Roethig and Durtschi 2021).

In high-risk situations, social workers expected institutional protection from employers (Lynch 2021). When this was not forthcoming, our study revealed how social workers relied on a strategy of collective resiliency to guard against demoralisation and despair.

COVID-19 crisis exposed how the poor will continue to increase in number even when the rate of infections would have subsided because cuts in social welfare spending will further erode the system of care (Isaković 2020). There is this urgent need to systematically collect qualified data on how social workers are relegated as the functional ever-reliant cogs in the welfare apparatus manned by authority figures insulated from frontline social reality. Expressed in this study are patterns of authoritative control which even when nuanced, are still insidious in curtailing effective problem-solving and democratic decision-making processes within organisations. Efforts at unionised activity to address this require qualified data.

Insights from participants in this study can yet reveal lessons in good practice as social service institutions move away from being complacent receivers of diminishing state subsidies to asserting active participation in the appropriation of financial resources (Murphy and McGann 2021). As the pandemic revealed, reliance on political elites to formulate policy decisions has had its dangers. The widespread evidence-based managerialist practice degenerated to a polarising choice between human needs over a rule-based framework on who qualifies for assistance.

The reliance on authoritative rule-based control to guarantee productivity is a long-hidden organisational fault line in managerialist social work, where the unquestioning conformity to rules became the measure of job efficiency. Paradoxical lessons may yet come from frontline social workers whose transgressions to authoritarian rule and disavowal of oppressive structures will challenge and transform our service organisations. The paradox remains that they are actually the change agents in the very system they want to be changed.

### Could there be ways forward?

This study is in debt to social workers who revealed new patterns of discourse from their everyday struggle at the frontline. It is for them that a long-term reshaping of social services is taking place (Truell and Martinez 2020). From insights gathered, we can identify transformative paths worth pursuing forward.

The long-term impact of COVID-19 will require countervailing responses meant not only to mitigate those institutional deficiencies described by respondents in this study, but also the transformation of political and social relationships beyond specific national borders. The profession might have to be called upon to intervene in situations of humanitarian crises across national borders. In hindsight, we could reflect upon the lack of organised intervention by European or international associations to protect social workers in precarious work situations. This research activity made us aware of how social workers were unprotected in situations of reduced family income; the unpredictability of punishing working hours; the imposition of untenable work conditions; and institutional failures by management to lead in crisis situations.

Beyond resiliency and professional commitment, frontline social workers have resorted to their collective creativity in negotiating with authority. Critical experiences under COVID-19 lockdown encouraged flexibility, autonomy, and confidence in responsible decision-making. These experiences could give new impetus among professionals to engage in unionised work. Solidarity among social workers would be the basis for effective work in collective bargaining to create new protocols, safeguards, and guidelines that promote and secure adherence to ethical employment standards.

This study has also become a critic of the global neoliberal world order. COVID-19 pandemic is but one global crisis which resulted in millions of deaths which could have been prevented by effective and proactive social policy measures. Humanitarian crisis such as a pandemic has no respect for national borders so transnational solidarity movements among social workers could only strengthen our preparedness for humanitarian crises. Global inequalities that COVID-19 pandemic exacerbated are systemic and global in character. This pandemic blatantly directs social work to a way forward that can only be a global one.

COVID-19 intensified the urgency for social work education to emphasise the systemic interrelatedness of social problems. 'National walls' do not insulate people from deadly viruses, much in the same way that social work education cannot be an insular project of Europe and the West. While this study addresses the situation of frontline social workers in three European countries, there is a dearth of social work literature focusing on COVID-19 pandemic as experienced by Global South colleagues. The way forward requires education and research that is respectful and inclusive of contributions from Global South partners in our battle to save more lives.

COVID-19 pandemic ushers that historical period in social work when ethical principles are reviewed and reinterpreted. Findings in this study reveal the need to systematically institutionalise the adaption of values in community belonging and collegiality. This has immeasurable power to provide security, comfort, and affirmation among social workers operating in situations of high risk. The social work community needs to function as a safe non-judgemental space where anxiety, doubt, and frustrations are articulated and reflected upon. It is here where knowledge-based mentorship could effectively happen. By dint of necessity, social workers participating in this study, used a crises situation such as COVID-19 pandemic, to create their own communities of learning. Human connection is the very source of strength and its cultivation in our institutions is essential (Navarro 2020). While operating within neoliberal constraints, social workers need to advocate better working conditions for themselves. If self-care is an individual professional responsibility, COVID-19 has elevated the critical question over a mandatory framework from which employing institutions will observe standards protecting the collective well-being of social workers (Lavalette et al. 2021).

COVID-19 inspired the social work profession to raise questions that are critical of itself. This study revealed structural vulnerabilities in the management of our organisations. The profession could be at that historical cusp where an examination of our professional competencies in the advocacy of systemic change is necessary. The pandemic has imposed new demands on social work practice. Post-pandemic reality will compel us to prepare for critical eventualities such as climate catastrophes, wars and conflict, community dislocation, and other forms of collective human suffering (Dominelli 2012).

## References

Abrahamson, Peter. 2010. "European Welfare States Beyond Neoliberalism: Toward the Social Investment State." *Development and Society* 39 (1): 61–95. https://www.jstor.org/stable/deveandsoci.39.1.61

Albuquerque, Cristina P. 2018. "Social Work's 'Black Hole' or 'Phoenix Moment'? Impacts of the Neoliberal Path in Social Work Profession in Portugal." *European Journal of Social Work* 22 (2): 314–325. 10.1080/13691457.2018.1530641

Baker, Joanne. 2009. "Young Mothers in Late Modernity: Sacrifice, Respectability and the Transformation of the Neoliberal Subject." *Journal of Youth Studies* 12 (3): 275–288. 10.1080/13676260902773809

Börner, Stephanie. 2020. "Is the Corona Virus Going to Reshape the European Welfare State?" In *Corona Crisis and the Welfare State: A Social Europe Dossier*, n.e., 20–26. Berlin: Social Europe Publishing. https://www.socialeurope.eu/wp-content/uploads/2021/01/Dossier_Coronavirus-and_the_welfare-state.pdf

Cahill, Damien, and Martijn Konings. 2017. *Neoliberalism*. Cambridge: Polity Press.

Chelcea, Liviu, and Oana Druță. 2016. "Zombie Socialism and the Rise of Neoliberalism in Post-Socialist Central and Eastern Europe." *Eurasian Geography and Economics* 57 (4–5): 521–544. 10.1080/15387216.2016.1266273

Dominelli, Lena. 2012. *Green Social Work: From Environmental Crises to Environmental Justice*. Cambridge: Polity Press.

Drahokoupil, Jan. 2007. "Analysing the Capitalist State in Post-Socialism: Towards the Porterian Workfare Postnational Regime." *International Journal of Urban and Regional Research* 31 (2): 401–424. 10.1111/j.1468-2427.2007.00727.x

Eurostat. 2022. "Government expenditure on social protection." Accessed 30 May 2022. https://ec.europa.eu/eurostat/statistics-explained/index.php?title=Government_expenditure_on_social_protection

Ferguson, Ian. 2008. *Reclaiming Social Work: Challenging Neoliberalism and Promoting Social Justice*. Los Angeles: Sage Publications.

Garrett, Michael P. 2019. "What Are We Talking about When We Talk about 'Neoliberalism'?" *European Journal of Social Work* 22 (2): 188–200. 10.1080/13691457.2018.1530643

Germann, Julian. 2021. *Unwitting Architect: German Primacy and the Origins of Neoliberalism*. Stanford: Stanford University Press.

Granosik, Mariusz. 2016. "Od profesjonalnej nadziei do procedur: dyskursywna instytucjonalizacja polskiej pracy socjalnej." [From professional hope to procedures: discursive institutionalization of Polish social work]. *Problemy Polityki Społecznej. Studia i Dyskusje* 35 (4): 43–58. http://www.problemypolitykispolecznej.pl/pdf-122847-51028?filename= Od%20profesjonalnej%20nadziei.pdf

Hare, Isadora. 2004. "Defining Social Work for the 21st Century." *International Social Work* 47 (3): 407–424. 10.1177/0020872804043973

Harvey, David. 2005. *A Brief History of Neoliberalism.* Oxford: Oxford University Press.

Hemerijck, Anton, and Robin Huguenot-Noël. 2021. "The Covid-19 Wake-Up Call to Buttress Social Investment." *Social Europe.* Accessed 30 May 2022. https:// socialeurope.eu/the-covid-19-wake-up-call-to-buttress-social-investment

Hermann, Christoph. 2007. "Neoliberalism in the European Union." *Studies in Political Economy – A Socialist Review* 79 (1): 61–90. 10.1080/19187033.2007.11675092

Inglot, Tomasz. 2009. "Czech Republic, Hungary, Poland and Slovakia: Adaptation and Reform of the Post-Communist 'Emergency Welfare States'." In *Post-communist Welfare Pathways. Theorizing Social Policy Transformations in Central and Eastern Europe*, edited by Alfio Cerami and Pieter Vanhuysse, 73–95. New York: Palgrave Macmillan.

Isaković, Nela P. 2020. "What has COVID-19 Taught Us about Neoliberalism." *Women's International League for Peace & Freedom (WILPF).* Accessed 10 June 2022. https://www.wilpf.org/covid-19-what-has-covid-19-taught-us-about-neoliberalism

Lavalette, Michael, Vasilos Ioakimidis, and Ian Ferguson, eds. 2021. *Social Work and the COVID-19 Pandemic: International Insights.* Bristol: Bristol University Press and Policy Press.

Lazăr, Florin, Anca Michai, Daniela Gaba, Alexandra Ciocănel, Georgiana Rentea, and Shari Munch. 2019. "Romanian Social Workers Facing the Challenges of Neo-Liberalism." *European Journal of Social Work* 22 (2): 326–337. 10.1080/13691457.2018. 1540405

Lorenz, Walter. 2005. "Social Work and a New Social Order – Challenging Neoliberalism's Erosion of Solidarity." *Social Work & Society* 3 (1): 93–101. https://ejournals. bib.uni-wuppertal.de/index.php/sws/article/view/205

Lynch, Esther. 2021. "Making Work Fit for Workers after Covid-19." In *The Corona Crisis and the Welfare State – Social Europe Dossier*, n.e., 61–67. Berlin: Social Europe Publishing. https://socialeurope.eu/making-work-fit-for-workers-after-covid-19

Miszczyński, Miłosz. 2019. *The Dialectical Meaning of Offshored Work: Neoliberal Desires and Labour Arbitrage in Post-Socialist Romania.* Leiden: Brill.

Murphy, Mary, McGann, Michael. 2021. "Renewing Welfare through Universal Entitlement: Lessons from Covid 19." In *Corona Crisis and the Welfare State – Social Europe Dossier*, n.e., 70–75. Berlin: Social Europe Publsihing. https://www.socialeurope. eu/wp-content/uploads/2021/01/Dossier_Coronavirus-and_the_welfare-state.pdf

Navarro, Vicente. 2020. "The Consequences of Neoliberalism in the Current Pandemic." *International Journal of Health Services* 50 (3): 271–275. 10.1177/0020731420925449

Ost, David. 2005. *The Defeat of Solidarity: Anger and Politics in Postcommunist Europe.* Ithaca: Cornell University Press.

Pop, Luana. 2013. "The Decoupling of Social Policy Reforms in Romania." *Social Policy & Administration* 47 (2): 161–181. 10.1111/spol.12013

Pulignano, Valeria. 2021. "Including the Precariat." In *The Corona Crisis and the Welfare State – Social Europe Dossier*, n.e., 76–81. Berlin: Social Europe Publishing. https:// www.socialeurope.eu/wp-content/uploads/2021/01/Dossier_Coronavirus-and_the_ welfare-state.pdf

Rogowski, Steve. 2010. *Social Work: The Rise and Fall of a Profession*. Bristol: The Policy Press.

Roethig, Oliver and Adrian Durtschi. 2021. "Fixing Care: Refocusing on Those Who Need It and Those Who Deliver It." In *The Corona Crisis and the Welfare State – Social Europe Dossier*, n.e., 27–33. Berlin: Social Europe Publishing. https://www.socialeurope.eu/wp-content/uploads/2021/01/Dossier_Coronavirus-and_the_welfare-state.pdf

Sablowski, Thomas. 2020. "The Deadly Consequences of Neoliberalism: The Covid-19 Pandemic." *Socialist Project – The Bullet*. Accessed 24 August 2022. https://socialistproject.ca/2020/05/deadly-consequences-of-neoliberalism-covid19-pandemic-germany/

Slobodian, Quinn. 2021. "The Three Ways of Looking at the Novel Coronavirus SARS-CoV-2." *Transnational Institute*. Accessed 24 August 2022. https://www.tni.org/en/article/the-three-ways-of-looking-at-the-novel-coronavirus-sars-cov-2

Spolander, Gary, Lambert Engelbrecht, Linda Martin, Marianne Strydom, Irina Pervova, Päivi Marjanen, Petri Tani, Alessandro Sicora, and Francis Adaikalam. 2014. "The Implications of Neoliberalism for Social Work: Reflections from a Six-Country International Research Collaboration." *International Social Work* 57 (4): 301–312. 10.1177/0020872814524964

Truell, Rory, and Silvana Martinez. 2020. *End of Year Report, Promoting Importance of Human Relationships*. Reinfelden: The International Federation of Social Workers. https://www.ifsw.org/wp-content/uploads/2021/01/2020-IFSW-End-of-Year-Report.pdf

Willis, Paul, and Mats Trondman 2002. "Manifesto for Ethnography." *Cultural Studies ↔ Critical Methodologies* 2 (3): 394–402. 10.1177/153270860200200309

# 4 Development of Digital Social Work in the Early Phase of COVID-19 Pandemic in Slovenia and Finland

*Vera Fiorentino, Vesna Leskošek,
Sanna Saraniemi, Marjo Romakkaniemi, and
Timo Harrikari*

## Social impacts of technological changes

In the turn of 2020, the COVID-19 pandemic spread across the globe causing an international crisis. The restrictions set to prevent the pandemic from spreading caused an unprecedented situation in social work and social welfare across European countries and beyond (Banks et al. 2020; Dominelli et al. 2020). Restrictive measures such as social distancing and closing services or weakening access to them affected people's lives. The exceptional challenges caused by the pandemic were addressed largely by digital services.

The pandemic expedited discussions on the digitalisation of social services which had not received sufficient attention in the past decades (Pink et al. 2021), accelerated the digitalisation and 'forced' everyone, also the sceptical, towards it. The main concerns of social workers have been that digital environments raise questions of ethics and make personal presence and face-to-face contacts more difficult to facilitate (Reamer 2013). Technological changes indeed have social impacts and technologies are meaningful on how work is done as they reconfigure relationships between people and the contexts (Wajcman 2006). According to Wajcman (2006, 776) 'technological change is a thoroughly contingent and heterogenous process' and 'technologies must be culturally appropriated to become functional'. Negotiations about implementing technological possibilities in practice are inevitable (Wajcman 2006) to take digital assets into use in social work practice and to overcome the obstacles of client work in digital environments. The main framework in developing relationships with clients in digital surroundings is the concept of digital intimacy (see Pink et al. 2021). It means sharing personal and sensitive experiences in virtual spaces and creating confidential relationships between clients and social workers.

In this chapter, we focus on what kind of perceptions and experiences have been gained from, the advantages and disadvantages of, and how tools can be used to further develop digital social work. Digital surroundings refer to applications such as Zoom, Teams, Skype, WhatsApp, and others. In this context, we also include telephone in digital devices, for it was the most common means of

DOI: 10.4324/9781003374374-5

communication when face-to-face encounters needed to be reorganised in remote mode in the beginning of the pandemic. In general, debates, both in Finland and Slovenia, have taken place on how digital social work promotes the key ethical principles or professional discretion of social work (see Reamer 2013; Hitchcock et al. 2019). The pandemic made visible the basis of digital social work: the possibilities and obstacles that had influenced its utilisation.

Both in Finland and Slovenia attitudes towards digitalisation have been two-fold. Some social workers regard telecommunication as unsuitable for situations that required deepened personal relationships with service users (Leskošek and Mešl 2020; Harrikari et al. 2021). Face-to-face contact is regarded as essential for establishing trust, respect, and an environment in which service users can disclose their intimate experiences (Banks 2012). However, some social workers see multiple possibilities in digital social work. Especially interacting, communicating, and collaborating between social work professionals has increasingly been conducted with digital connections and social work information systems have been a vital part of such daily routines (Lagsten and Andersson 2018).

The aim of the chapter is to compare the similarities and differences of digital social work between Finland and Slovenia after the outbreak of COVID-19 pandemic in spring of 2020. Our research questions are (1) how the pandemic has affected the uptake of digital devices in Slovenia and Finland, and (2) what kind of possibilities and obstacles social workers perceived in using digital tools while encountering service users. We examine the use of digital tools during the first and second waves of the COVID-19 pandemic using survey data gathered in Slovenia and Finland.

## Slovenian context

Slovenia had a strong tradition of a socialist welfare system (Rus 1990), similar to the social-democratic type defined by Esping-Andersen (1990) but it has gone through a significant transformation towards the liberal model during the last few decades (Filipovič Hrast and Rakar 2019). In Slovenia, the public social services, named as Social Work Centres (SWC), are organised by the state. The municipalities have a minor responsibility in organising home care services and local social programs. Social policy and legislation are also in the domain of the state. Social Chamber is a central organisation in the field of social protection. It is responsible for preparing regulations and standards for the services and licensing the programmes of non-governmental and private organisations but there is no agency to monitor their performance (Social Assistance Act 2007). The Social Protection Institute is a research organisation that evaluates programs and collects data from public social services.

Social welfare includes social assistance, social services, and other measures to enhance or maintain the functionality, well-being and inclusion of families and individuals. In the present monograph Kodele et al. (see Chapter 2) note that state welfare provision consists of SWC and the network of residential institutions. The State also funds services provided by non-governmental organisations, private firms, and religious institutions (Resolution on the National Social Assistance Program 2013–2020).

In Slovenia, the first wave of pandemic occurred from 12th March until the end of May 2020. First, all visits to hospitals were prohibited and gatherings at public events were banned. These preventive measures were followed by closing kindergartens, schools, and universities, and moving to remote teaching. Public transportation was banned. Most of the shops, apart from groceries and pharmacies, were also closed. Care homes for the elderly were closed from visitors and social services were open just for emergency cases, otherwise remote contact was recommended. Recommendations regarding social distancing and large restrictions of traffic and mobility were made. The strict measures were gradually softened in May 2020 and at the end of the month mostly all of them were removed. However, masks, testing, and social distancing were still recommended. Large gatherings were prohibited, but all services were reopened. People returned to work, although remote work was still strongly encouraged.

## Finnish context

Finland is one of the Nordic welfare states, based on the principle of universality that ensures the welfare, social security, and equality of its citizens (Esping-Andersen et al. 2002). The guidance of the implementation, preparation of legislation, direction, development, and policy comes from the Ministry of Social Affairs, but the municipalities have responsibility to arrange social services with government support. Regional State Administrative Agencies evaluate, monitor, and guide the quality and availability of the services at local level. (Ministry of Social Affairs and Health 2021).

The provision of social welfare is implemented by the municipalities and they have a broad discretion in providing services by organising services themselves, providing them jointly with other municipalities, and purchasing them from other municipalities, private providers, or other organisations (Ministry of Social Affairs and Health 2021). Social welfare includes social services, related support services and other measures to enhance or maintain the functionality, well-being, inclusion and safety of communities, families, and individuals (Ministry of Social Affairs and Health 2021). The principles of providing social services are promoting well-being, equality and safety, and offering necessary, adequate and high-quality services (Social Welfare Act 2014).

In Finland, the first wave of the pandemic occurred at the same time as in Slovenia and the restrictive measures were similar as well. Schools and universities moved to remote teaching, restaurants were closed, public services like care homes for the elderly and hospitals prohibited visiting, and people aged 70 or above were suggested to stay at home in quarantine. Physical distancing and working remotely when possible were recommended. Many public services were closed, social services were kept open in critical areas and otherwise in remote mode. (Harrikari et al. 2021) The so-called hybrid strategy was enforced at the end of May 2020 including testing, tracing infection chains, and quarantine. The pandemic situation has been reconsidered and the restrictions have been relieved and restricted locally in areas with different pandemic statuses since the first wave of the pandemic.

Slovenian and Finnish socio-ecological situations have specific features as a result of their historical development. Both countries developed strong welfare States, but Slovenia was based on conditioning the access to social rights and Finnish followed a Scandinavian principle of universalism. Both countries have approximately the same at-risk-of-poverty rate, Finland's 12.2 and Slovenia's 12.4 percent in 2020 (Eurostat 2021). Both countries show trends of applying the neoliberal paradigm to the welfare state, but it seems that in Slovenia this development took place later than in Finland. However, the changes in Slovenia are eroding public sector much faster than in Finland. The public sector in Slovenia is critically understaffed, and lagging behind Finland in terms of equipment and technology. The state of the public sector in both countries influenced the capabilities of social workers to respond to the epidemic, especially in adapting to new realities as fast as possible with the institutional support. It is here that we notice major differences between countries that we will illustrate more precisely in this chapter.

## Data and analysis

The data applied in this chapter are based on online surveys conducted separately in Finland and Slovenia. Both surveys consider taking digital devices into practice, the pros and cons social workers observe in digitalisation and experiences on using digital devices in the context of social work. Moreover, both questionnaires also contained open questions.

The Finnish survey data was gathered using Webropol survey platform in June 2021 in cooperation with Talentia Union of Professional Social Workers. A total of 436 respondents participated in the survey, of which 139 have a masters' degree in social work, which allows them to work as legalised social workers in Finland. The survey was focused on the change of working practices during the pandemic. The questions concerned the effects of the pandemic on social welfare professionals' work and well-being, social services, and the life situations of service users. Questions about management, instructions or guidelines, and adequate infrastructure were asked. Also, questions concerning the status of social work in society and how it was utilised in this exceptional situation were asked. In this chapter, we will concentrate on the questions on the utilisation of digital devices.

The Slovenian survey data was gathered in December 2020 using an online programme, 1KA. The invitation to participate in the survey was sent to 796 email addresses of employees at SWC and was also posted on the Facebook group of social workers and Slovene Association of Social Workers was asked to send the invitation to the members. A total of 294 respondents validly completed the survey of which 242 were social workers. The survey consisted of questions about the organisation of work, the choices of direct work with service users and distant work, the ability of social workers to influence these choices, how contact with service users was established, and the use of digital tools. Open questions were included for commenting on the organisation of work, the contacts with service users, the use of ICT, and the overall satisfaction with the mode of operation during both waves of the pandemic. For this chapter, only data on digital devices is used from the Slovene survey.

The Slovenian and Finnish data differ from each other, but they address the same phenomena, and similar kind of questions were asked. Both data were analysed separately and compared to receive a coherent image of the differences and similarities between the two countries. The Finnish data was analysed with quantitative methods, using IBM SPSS Statistics Viewer. The results have been accomplished by examining the frequencies of different answers and cross-tabulating them. The Slovenian analysis has been conducted using a Slovene online programme 1KA that enables production of frequency tables, calculation of descriptive statistics, and graphical presentation of data. Excel and SPSS were used for a more detailed analysis. The open answers from both countries were analysed using qualitative content analysis.

## The change of social work in Slovenia and Finland during the first and second waves of COVID-19

In the findings the quantitative data from both countries are presented separately. Figures 4.1 and 4.3 present Slovenian data and Figures 4.2 and 4.4 concern Finnish data. We examine the changes in contacting clients during the pandemic and move forward to comparing different forms and platforms of communication.

In both countries social workers were committed to relationship-based social work (Leskošek and Mešl 2020; Harrikari et al. 2021). Face-to-face meetings with clients and home visits were daily routines in social work practice, that

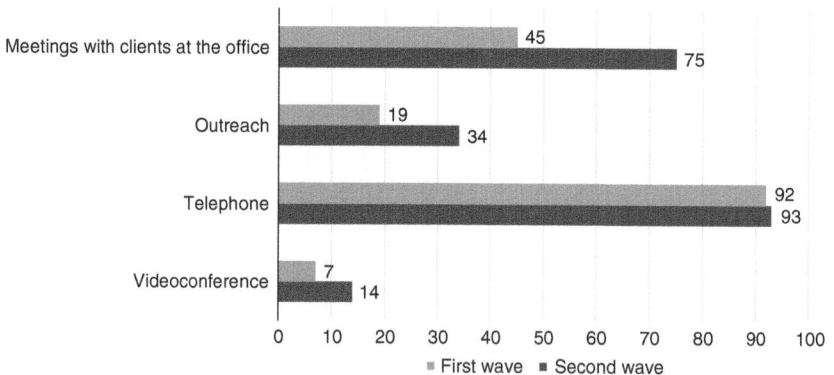

*Figure 4.1* The change of the form of contact with service users during the first and second wave of pandemic in Slovenia (%, n=233).

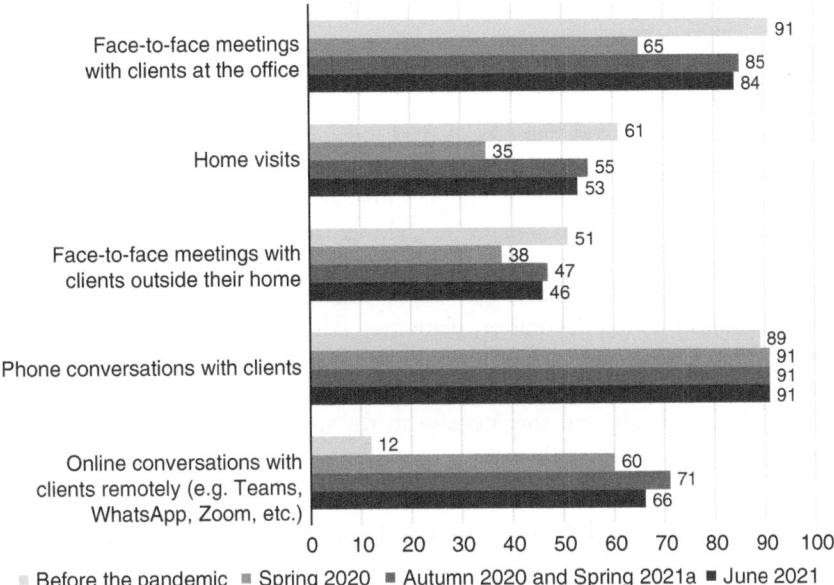

*Figure 4.2* The change of the form of contact with service users during the pandemic in Finland (%, n=139).

were interrupted in the beginning of the pandemic. In Slovenia, the number of face-to-face meetings decreased, and were replaced by phone calls during the first wave of the COVID-19 pandemic. Social workers were asked about the way of contacting service users during the pandemic (Figure 4.1). The most common way of contact was by telephone, percent of which stayed quite the same during the first and second waves. There was a slight increase in the usage of video-conference possibilities during the second wave.

Finnish social workers were asked, what forms of contacting clients were used in different stages of the pandemic (Figure 4.2). Right from the start both phone calls and online conversations were more common than different forms of face-to-face meetings when working with clients. Online meetings increased drastically, from 16 to 60 percent, as digital devices were quickly brought into use. The number of remotely implemented online conversations has remained significantly higher throughout the pandemic than before the outbreak.

Consequently, social workers were obliged to find new ways to implement services in both countries from the very start of the pandemic. Social workers relied on phone calls nearly to the same extent. A significant difference between Slovenia and Finland is in the use of digital platforms, such as Skype, Teams, Zoom, WhatsApp, different client portals, etc., in implementing services digitally. While there was 14 percent of social workers in Slovenia using videoconferences, the percentage in Finland was 60 percent. We may conclude that the introduction of digital and video-based services was much faster and extensive in Finland.

## Implementing social work remotely in Slovenia and Finland

Implementing social work remotely forced social workers to learn using various kinds of software. In Slovenia, Zoom was utilised most frequently, followed by Viber, but the very low use of digital platforms, on average approximately 10–15 percent, must be recognised as being much lower than in Finland (see Figure 4.3).

In Finland, all different forms of remote contacts have increased from the time before the pandemic and the biggest change can be seen in the use of communication and collaboration platforms. Also, in Slovenia social workers report to have used applications for online meetings such as Skype and Zoom. The data (see Figure 4.4) displays, that in Finland, a digital leap was taken at the start of the pandemic and the increase in the use of digital services has continued throughout the pandemic.

## Challenges and possibilities of using digital devices in working with service users

To get a more multifaced picture of digital social work and to explain differences in the extent of the use of digital tools between the countries, open answers were

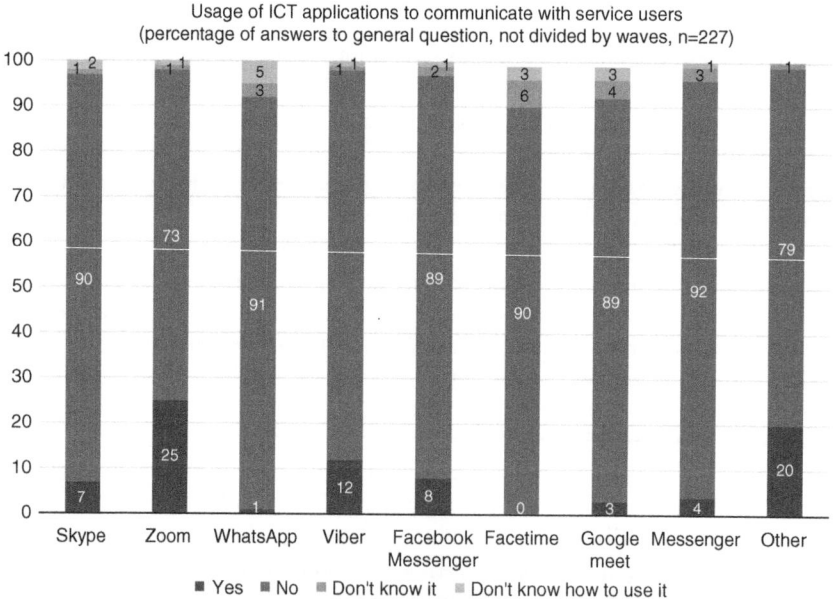

*Figure 4.3* Social workers' digital-based communication channels with clients during the pandemic in Slovenia (%, not divided by waves, n=227).

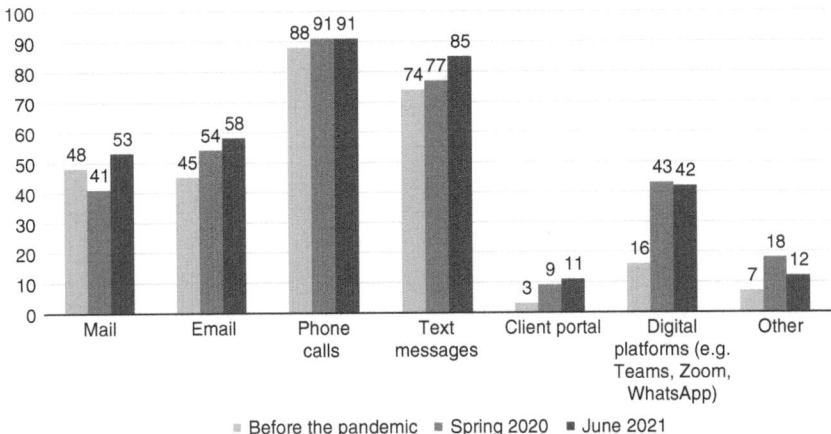

*Figure 4.4* Social workers' digital-based communication channels with clients during the pandemic in Finland (the percentages of answers 'yes', n=139).

also analysed. We analyse the challenges that the social workers faced when taking the digital leap and end with viewing different possibilities of digital implementations that the social workers described. The samples are identified with marking 'Fsw' for Finnish social workers and 'Ssw' for Slovenian social workers.

## Challenges in transition to digital social work in Slovenia

The Slovene social workers perceived many challenges in using ICT, relating to poor ICT provision at workplaces and to their own thoughts about relationships with service users and professional conduct, including ethical dilemmas. As already demonstrated, social workers gradually changed their minds about using ICT as the pandemic progressed and it became necessary to adapt to new circumstances. Still their scepticism towards technology was stronger than in Finland.

Differences between Finland and Slovenia can be explained with the provision of technical equipment. In the Slovene survey the obstacles in using ICT were examined. Results show that 19.4 percent of the respondents were without work phones, 10.1 percent could not access a work computer, and 20.1 percent had a computer without a microphone or a camera. Open answers further explain that in a majority of cases a mobile phone was not provided by the employer and social workers used a stationary phone for work purposes.

> Phones at work are not modern and do not have capability for applications for video calls (Ssw).

> We just have stationary phones at work, and I don't want to use a personal one (Ssw).

The same applies to computers most of which were desktops, not portables. In addition, access to the workplace was restricted. When the offices closed, some social workers could not access the digital equipment and in most cases, they had to rely on personal mobile phones. There were efforts made by the agencies to provide the ICT, but financial resources from the respective ministry were scarce.

> Technological equipment in the second wave is partially better and adapted to the needs of users and the time in which we live (Ssw).

> In the second wave we got just two cameras and one smartphone for the whole SWC! (Ssw)

As a result of the shortage in modern technology, even before the pandemic, there was a problem with IP addresses and licences for applications such as Zoom or Teams.

> In the first wave of epidemic, due to the absence of many employees, only regular tasks were performed. Videocall programmes and equipment have not been yet established. Now we've got some equipment, but it's too little, we also combine it with personal profiles in social media because one IP address (e.g., for Zoom) isn't enough for the whole social work community (Ssw).

Due to flexibility of arranging work during the pandemic (remote work, annual leave, hybrid work), respondents redirected calls from work to their personal phones. They described to hide their phone numbers to keep their privacy and to prevent frequent calls from clients. At the same time, they were critical about such practice and aware that ethical tensions may emerge:

> This is not a relationship based on respect, confidentiality, reciprocity. They give us a mobile phone number, and we call them back from unknown numbers! If an unknown number calls me, I don't pick it up […] (Ssw).

Similar to Finland, the issue of data protection and safety of digital tools was raised also in Slovenia. Especially in using emails and digital applications.

> There is an issue of personal data protection, secure connection, this is not the case at our premises (Ssw).

Others, on the contrary, did not have limitations regarding privacy. They happily shared their personal number but were cautious for other reasons, namely they wanted to avoid additional costs as they were not compensated. As they knew there were financial resources available for supportive measures against the pandemic, they were resisting to personally fund public services.

It is still strange to me, given the fact that the ministry has already planned and allocated money this year, I think it is two billion, that they don't think about the fact that the SWCs should be equipped with mobile phones […] (Ssw).

Another issue was the necessity of teamwork and communication among staff. Weak ICT infrastructure was an obstacle for close collaboration that was needed in the exceptional time in the first wave of the pandemic, but major improvements were made as the pandemic progressed. Technical support for installing programmes or maintaining computers not being available at home was also pointed out to challenge working with remote connections.

The second set of obstacles is related to the capability of establishing or maintaining relationships with service users. This specific issue received most comments in the open answers from both countries. In Slovenia ICT, including mobile phone, was a serious obstacle for service users. In addition, respondents were convinced that social work should be performed face-to-face.

It's a lot different because the phone isn't enough. There is no personal contact, no eye contact. You cannot see if a person is in need, and you cannot comfort the person, saying you will figure something out and all will be fine. It's not personal over the phone. You try to give a feeling that you heard what the person said, that together we can plan the right steps, but this is still not enough (Ssw).

The contact exclusively by telephone and e-mail is not our way of working. I cannot wait for it all to end and we establish a normal relationship with the clients (Ssw).

I think CSWs should remain open to all users during the epidemic. It is already difficult enough for people to come, but if we direct them not to do so, we cause additional damage. We should establish customised modes of operation (conducting outdoor interviews or inside with windows open, etc.), not responding to the needs and closing for users is the least appropriate way (Ssw).

Finally, the respondents noted that digital tools can be used on a short run, but eventually service users would be anxious to meet in person as they felt they cannot go deeper in explaining their life situations and feelings and also, they experienced computer fatigue themselves.

## Challenges in Finnish social work

The beginning of the pandemic was confusing in Finland. The need to shift to remote work brought to light the deficiency of infrastructure. There was a shortage of sufficient equipment and connections, lack or variability of instructions and uncertainty regarding IT security. Social workers used their discretion when deciding the most purposeful way to proceed. Also, the skills in using digital means varied among social workers and service users.

> The use of WhatsApp and text messages in client work is forbidden. The prohibition is silently broken, for their use is crucial when working with the young (Fsw).

> From time-to-time inoperative equipment. At the beginning employee had difficulties choosing what applications can be used for IT security reasons (Fsw).

Furthermore, the Finnish social workers' crucial questions in digital social work related to building relationships with clients, changes in communication, lack of non-verbal communication, and the difficulty of making holistic assessments of the clients' situations continue to exist. The situation was experienced as burdensome. The digitalised work created a new kind of space that demanded learning a different way of listening and focus among other things. There was not, however, enough time to adapt.

> Misunderstanding is easier when one cannot see the facial expressions and other non-verbal communication. [...] The touch and focus are easily lost, and one gets tired when only the sense of hearing can be used (Fsw).

> Supervision cannot be done in child protective services in digital forms, clients cannot be met remotely if enough information on communication and living circumstances etc. needs to be gained (Fsw).

Digitally implemented social work was seen to accelerate the daily pace of working. Without physical transitions the pace of client work became more intense and development work diminished.

> The pace of work accelerates, the meeting start at the same time as the previous end and no physical transitions are needed. The management of work causes major problems for some of the staff (Fsw).

Social workers had worries regarding the closures of services, clients reaching digital services and the adequacy of help.

> Clients have not received the mental help services they need at the beginning of the pandemic. The clients have not had the possibility to meet a worker face-to-face (Fsw).

> All have not wanted or received help from digitally implemented services (Fsw).

## Possibilities in Slovenian social work

Despite scepticism towards using digital tools while working with service users, the Slovenian social workers saw an immense value in it. They searched for practical solutions for situations caused by closures and physical distancing. Digital tools proved to be one of the scarce options of maintaining contact and working in emergency situations.

> Social work is difficult without personal contact, and in general in establishing a working relationship. It is necessary to adapt and explore all possibilities to establish and maintain contact and relationship (Ssw).

Social workers were prepared to learn communication via digital tools. Some of the SWCs were able to find financial resources for Zoom and Teams licences, and organised brief seminars on how to use them. As the pandemic progressed, social workers found effective digital ways for teamwork, supervision and staying in touch with others, which decreased isolation. They also gained better overview and understanding of their clients' situations.

> Cameras and a microphone are particularly important. We also notice exceptional advantages for teamwork, for example, a paediatrician who never comes to the meeting, was present as he did not waste the time for driving (Ssw).

Social workers have emphasised that using digital tools improves availability of services for clients. They felt that making appointments takes less effort and no time or money for transfers is needed. At the same time, greater organisation was needed to balance work and personal life. But with digital implementations they were more responsive to the need for immediate contacts.

## Possibilities in Finnish social work

Finnish social workers described the enabling nature of digital services in their answers. They regarded digital devices as possibilities to enhance practice fluency, focus on tasks, add flexibility in managing time and forthright information flow. These were seen as factors that supported effectiveness, well-being at work, and accessibility of services. Digital services were appraised for making physical distances insignificant as people are more easily reached and services faster received.

> The problems have been diminished once the routines of working have developed. Everything works digitally implemented, in some cases even better (Fsw).

> Enables a wider network, when possible, to attend to meetings from a longer distance, when there is no time to travel on site (Fsw).

> The acute needs for support of the clients are possible to be responded to without delays (Fsw).

Digital services were claimed to enhance the fluency of practice. Routine tasks were easy to handle in digital forms and would not take time off from client work. Social workers further noted that travel time diminished and meetings were easier to arrange. While digital services were seen as good addition to services, social workers saw they would require professional discretion in deciding where digital applications would be suitable.

> Clients are not met face-to-face automatically. If suitable for both parties, the contact can be digitally done. This is an option that could stay [after the pandemic] (Fsw).

## Discussion

In this chapter, we examined the uptake of digital devices in Slovenia and Finland during the first two waves of the COVID-19 pandemic. The analyses of both the Slovenian and Finnish data show prominent increases on the use of remote connections and digital platforms in social work with clients. This exceptional time highlighted the need to develop digital modes of working and social workers' readiness of using digital equipment. The social workers' experiences on the digital leap culminated in the debate whether digital-based implementations are suitable for promoting the ethical principles of social work and professional discretion (see also Reamer 2013).

Digitalisation has been presented as an inevitable trend in social work, being already embedded in everyday life and work practices (Pink et al. 2021). The findings of our comparative analysis also highlight that using digital service tools widely and effectively requires paying attention to digital infrastructure and improving it. Infrastructure forms a basis for the progression of digitalised social work as without adequate equipment digital social work cannot be performed (Fiorentino et al. 2022). The comparison of the data demonstrated that the digital infrastructure enabled a more determined digital leap in Finland than in Slovenia. Moreover, the Finnish social workers also described future options in digital implementations more frequently. However, as Wajcman (2006) claims, technological change is a process, and the changes must be accepted to become functional. Our data demonstrates that the possibilities of digital implementations in social work still need to be reflected both among social work and in cooperation with different specialists responsible for the development of applicable technical solutions.

The issue of relationships is central in the pro-contra debate on the use of digital tools. Debates on digital devices lead to the core of social work; how to enhance well-being and empowerment without face-to-face contact with service users (e.g. Reamer 2013). The question comes to whether social workers see virtual spaces as possible arenas for encountering clients and building personal relationships with them even in complex and sensitive situations. Communication is a crucial part of a relationship and forms from body language, gestures, and the intensity of voices and we must learn how to communicate in digital spaces without losing this complexity.

Building relationships has been discussed from the beginning of professional social work, although its' meaning has changed throughout times. Ward et al. (2018, 13) inquired into the meaning of relationship in contemporary practice 'with its complex bureaucratic and interdisciplinary requirements and its frequent realignments in terms of ideology and professional identity'. However, despite all the changes and turbulent times social work has always had encounters with people and virtual space can be explored as a suitable option for such encounters, but we must be aware of social inequalities in access to digital devices and knowledge and skill in using them (Reamer 2013; Hitchcock et al. 2019; Banks et al. 2020).

Digital intimacy is a concept that answers to the issues of building meaningful relationships in digital surroundings. Pink et al. (2021, 6) propose that proximity and emotional engagement can be created via video, with its claims of realising, 'new modes of closeness, ways of sensing, understanding, care, responsiveness and support'. Daily communication between people exists in virtual spaces such as social media. People are already accustomed to conveying important matters in digital forms in their personal lives. Social workers saw possibilities and enabling features in digital implementations of client work in our analysis too. Modifying interactive digital communication platforms available for professional use appears to be one of the cornerstones of the discussion on hand.

The pandemic forced social work to take a digital leap and made it obvious that digital service forms are an enabling and adequate way to perform social work practice. It can create applicable forms of working in changing environments, enhance social workers' capability to adapt to new situations, increase flexibility when working with clients, and extend possibilities to promote client well-being and the core tasks of social work (Pink et al. 2021). Successful performance in digital implementations requires specific competencies and skills (Zhu and Andersen 2021) and it should be a matter embedded to basic education as well as organisational development instead of being the responsibility of individual social workers or work teams (Fiorentino et al. 2022).

The question of 'new normal' was frequently mentioned in public discussions, when studying the digital leap that happened in the beginning of the pandemic. The changes in societies have been described to mean a 'new normal' and the other side of the conversation has been a constant demand to return to how things were before the pandemic. It may take time for the society to bounce back from the crisis, but over time the 'new normal' can be anticipated to mean something like the normal before the pandemic, but with some restrictions or changes, including health checks when travelling, working from home, shutdowns, social distancing, distant meetings, and so on (Sardar 2021). From the point of social work this could signify changes in work practices and a more permanent nature of the need for digital services.

## References

Banks, Sarah. 2012. *Ethics and Values in Social Work*. 4th edition. Basingstoke: Palgrave Macmillan.

Banks, Sarah, Tian Cai, Ed de Jonge, Jane Shears, Michelle Shum, Ana M. Sobočan, Kim Strom, Rory Truell, María J. Úriz, and Merlinda Weinberg. 2020. "Practising Ethically during COVID-19: Social Work Challenges and Responses." *International Social Work* 63 (5): 569–583. 10.1177%2F0020872820949614

Dominelli, Lena, Timo Harrikari, Joseph Mooney, Vesna Leskošek, and Erin Kennedy Tsunoda, eds. 2020. *COVID-19 and Social Work: A Collection of Country Reports.* https://www.iassw-aiets.org/wp-content/uploads/2020/07/IASSW-COVID-19-and-Social-Work-Country-Reports-Final-1.pdf.

Esping-Andersen, Gøsta, Duncan Gallie, Anton Hemerijck, and John Myles. 2002. *Why We Need a New Welfare State*. Oxford: Oxford University Press.

Eurostat. 2021. "At-risk-of-poverty Rate by Poverty Threshold." Accessed April 25, 2022. https://appsso.eurostat.ec.europa.eu/nui/submitViewTableAction.do.

Filipovič Hrast, Maša, and Tatjana Rakar. 2019. *Socialna politika danes in jutri* [Social policy today and tomorrow]. Ljubljana: Založba FDV.

Finland. The Parliament of Finland. *Social Welfare Act*. 1301/2014. Adopted 1 April 2015. https://finlex.fi/fi/laki/ajantasa/2014/20141301.

Fiorentino, Vera, Marjo Romakkaniemi, Timo Harrikari, Sanna Saraniemi, and Laura Tiitinen. 2022. "Towards Digitally Mediated Social Work – The Impact of the COVID-19 Pandemic on Encountering Clients in Social Work." *Qualitative Social Work*. Published ahead of print, 11 April 2022. 10.1177/14733250221075603

General assembly of Slovenia. 2007. *Social Assistance Act*. Official Gazette, Republic of Slovenia, 3/07.

General assembly of Slovenia. 2014. *Resolution on the National Social Assistance Program 2013–2020*. Official Gazette, Republic of Slovenia, 39/13. http://pisrs.si/Pis.web/pregledPredpisa?id=NACP68#.

Harrikari, Timo, Marjo Romakkaniemi, Laura Tiitinen, and Sanna Ovaskainen. 2021. "Pandemic and Social Work: Exploring Finnish Social Workers' Experiences through a SWOT Analysis." *The British Journal of Social Work* 51 (5): 1644–1662. 10.1093/bjsw/bcab052

Hitchcock, Laurel I., Melanie Sage, and Nancy J. Smyth. 2019. *Teaching Social Work with Digital Technology*. Alexandria: CSWE Press.

Lagsten, Jenny, and Annika Andersson. 2018. "Use of Information Systems in Social Work – Challenges and an Agenda for Future Research." *European Journal of Social Work* 21 (6): 850–862. 10.1080/13691457.2018.1423554

Leskošek, Vesna, and Nina Mešl. 2020. "Slovenia." In *COVID-19 and Social Work: A Collection of Country Reports*, edited by Lena Dominelli, Timo Harrikari, Joseph Mooney, Vesna Leskošek, and Erin Kennedy Tsunoda, 100–110. N.p. https://www.iassw-aiets.org/wp-content/uploads/2020/07/IASSW-COVID-19-and-Social-Work-Country-Reports-Final-1.pdf.

The Ministry of Social Affairs of Finland. 2021. "Social and Health Services." Accessed 14 February 2022. https://stm.fi/en/social-and-health-services.

Pink, Sarah, Harry Ferguson, and Laura Kelly. 2021. "Digital Social Work: Conceptualising a Hybrid Anticipatory Practice." *Qualitative Social Work* 21 (2): 413–430. 10.1177%2F14733250211003647

Reamer, Frederic G. 2013. "Social Work in a Digital Age: Ethical and Risk Management Challenges." *Social Work* 58 (2): 163–172. 10.1093/sw/swt003

Rus, Veljko. 1990. Socialna Država in Družba Blaginje [Social state and the welfare society]. Ljubljana: DOMUS.

Sardar, Ziauddin. 2021. "Afterthoughts: Transnormal, the "New Normal" and Other Varieties of "Normal" in Postnormal Times." *World Futures Review* 13 (2): 54–70. 10.1177/19467567211025755

Wajcman, Judy. 2006. "New Connections: Social Studies of Science and Technology and Studies of Work." *Work, Employment and Society* 20 (4): 773–786. 10.1177/0950017006069814

Ward, Adrian, Gillian Ruch, and Turney Danielle. 2018. "Introduction." In *Relationship-based Social Work: Getting to the Heart of the Practice*, 2nd edition, edited by Gillian Ruch, Danielle Turney, and Adrian Ward, 13–16. London: Jessica Kingsley Publishers.

Zhu, Hong and Synnøve T. Andersen. 2021. "Digital Competence in Social Work Practice and Education: Experiences from Norway." *Nordic Social Work Research*. Published ahead of print, 15 March 2021. 10.1080/2156857X.2021.1899967

Section II

# Voices from the Field: Facing Challenges and Creating Solutions

# 5 UK Social Worker Burnout and Coping during the First Years of the COVID-19 Pandemic

*Paula McFadden, Ruth Neill, and Jill Manthorpe*

## Introduction

Social workers are employed to work with people at risk of harm or ill-being across the life course, from child protection to end-of-life care, and the work is risky, complex, and politically and culturally diverse. The need for social workers to intervene in people's lives often arises at a point of crisis, within a national legal and policy context. The job for social workers is often challenging and stressful since they need to ensure that their practice is based on social justice, human rights, and advocacy for service users. Research on social worker well-being and resilience has assisted understanding of the risk and protective factors associated with stress and burnout (McFadden et al. 2019; Travis et al. 2016). Employment conditions, such as insufficient support with high stress and increasing caseloads, lack of funding and resources, alongside poor work-life balance, contribute to poorer well-being and higher burnout (Geisler et al. 2019; Ravalier et al. 2019; Ravalier 2021). Researchers have been seeking to understand social workers' resilience, both individual resilience and the influence of employer and job characteristics (McFadden et al. 2019). Attention has been given to improving training and curriculum by including, for example, emotional intelligence teaching for students (Grant et al. 2014), preparation for practice (Tham and Lynch 2016), and self-care (Cuartero and Campos-Vidal 2019).

UK research has also learned from international comparisons of selection (admissions) to social work training, practice placement duration, and knowledge and skills for social work students (Tham et al. 2021). Importantly, cross-cultural research has helped to understand how the infrastructures and systems of social work practice enable social workers to withstand some of the exogenous shock of the COVID-19 pandemic through shifts to online contact with service users, online teaching of students and online interviews for admissions to training programmes during widespread social restrictions internationally (see, e.g. Baginsky and Manthorpe 2020; Harrikari et al. 2021; McFadden et al. 2020a).

## Theoretical frame

Resilience factors surrounding social work practice can be understood in the context of systems theory. Adapting Bronfenbrenner's (1992) systems theory,

DOI: 10.4324/9781003374374-7

the levels of systems which surround, interact, and impact on individuals can be considered at different levels. In brief, these include micro (individual), messo (interaction with others, family, social worker, community), exo-system level (political and societal context), and macro systems (global higher-level systems that impact everyone). Social worker well-being and coping are central to being able to work effectively, but this is not just a micro or individual matter. Messo-level support to this workforce has an impact. For example, enabling peer, team, and supervisory supports is critical for sustaining social workers in their jobs (McFadden 2018). It is important to acknowledge the critical responsibilities of employers in providing these messo direct support systems for social workers. Social worker well-being is important, as the quality of social work interventions is connected to service user outcomes, evidenced particularly in children's services. For example, delays in permanency planning for children are impacted by worker turnover (Flower et al. 2005; Schweitzer et al. 2013), and social worker turnover impacts on care experience (Gaskell 2010; Lotty 2021; Strolin-Goltzman et al. 2010). Exo-system level is of course fundamentally important since political and social decisions frame public services, including social work. In the UK these were under considerable strain prior to the Coronavirus pandemic. Policies introduced by the Conservative Coalition government (2010–2015) and continued by Conservative governments since then reduced central government funding for local authorities by a half in real terms between 2010/2011 and 2017/2018. These produced rising demand for social work services which was even harder to meet. As many have argued, the pandemic amplified pre-existing problems in social services (Think Local Act Personal 2020).

Stress and coping theory provide further important context for this chapter since individuals process and appraise challenges and problems at a psychological level. Lazarus (1991) observed that how individuals cope is a process rather than an outcome. The 'process of coping' conceptualises coping methods as changing, adapting and having differing sequencing, over time, with potential for positive or negative trajectories, dependent on risk and protective factors available to individuals. Supportive collegiate relationships and good quality supervision may act as buffers to burnout and workforce turnover (McFadden et al. 2018; Olaniyan et al. 2020).

Burnout theory is central to this chapter. Seminal work on measuring burnout was developed by Christina Maslach, Susan Jackson, and Michael Leiter (Maslach and Jackson 1986; Maslach et al. 1997; Maslach et al. 2016). Maslach and Jackson (1986) defined burnout across three domains, emotional exhaustion coupled with depersonalisation, with reduced feelings of personal accomplishment. Research on the factorial validity of the Maslach Burnout Inventory has evidenced the validity and reliability of the scale, particularly in its application to measure social worker burnout (Doherty et al. 2021; McFadden et al. 2019). However, the Copenhagen Burnout Inventory (CBI) (Kristensen et al. 2005) model of burnout considers personal burnout, work-related burnout, and client-related burnout as separate areas. As there were rapid changes to all areas of life simultaneously under COVID-19, this 'shared traumatic reality', as described by

Rachel Dekel and Nehami Baum (2010) was relevant. Furthermore, evidence of construct validity for use of the CBI for measuring social worker burnout has been presented by Jayme Walters et al. (2018). This ability to discern burnout in relation to separate areas of 'life' and 'work' enabled our analysis of factors that were associated with burnout during the first years of the COVID-19 pandemic.

## Methods

### Demographic characteristics

We set up an anonymous online survey that asked UK health and social care frontline staff (including social workers) about the effects of the COVID-19 pandemic on their work. We also asked for social demographics and characteristics, such as sex, age, ethnicity, country of work, disability status, and years of experience. Details of the methods are available in the full study reports (Gillen et al. 2022; McFadden et al. 2020b, 2021a, 2021b). A further study compared social workers' well-being prior to the pandemic with findings from the COVID-19 survey (McFadden et al. 2021c). The surveys were developed by a team that included researchers with interests in professional well-being in social work, nursing, and midwifery and was funded by a range of government-funded bodies and Ulster University. We refer to the different surveys in this chapter as Phases 2 (November 2020–February 2021) and 3 (May–July 2021). At the time of writing further phases are planned. Common to Phase 2 was some sense that the pandemic might be receding, but that preventive and protective measures remained necessary, while in Phase 3 a resurgence of the virus was occurring albeit with indications that vaccinations were providing hope of risk reduction.

### Outcomes examined

We chose a series of measures to capture frontline professionals' experiences that were easy to complete online and were not burdensome. We chose the seven-item Short Warwick-Edinburg Mental Wellbeing scale (SWEMWBS) to assess how often in the last two weeks respondents had been feeling what was described in the scales' statements (Stewart-Brown et al. 2009). To address the possibility of burnout, we chose the 19-item CBI that consists of three different areas of burnout personal burnout, work-related burnout, and client-related burnout rated on a five-point Likert scale scored from 0 to 100 (Kristensen et al. 2005).

Coping was assessed by two scales in the overall survey, but only one is discussed in this chapter. A total of 20 items from the Brief COPE scale (Carver 1997) were used to assess ten different coping strategies (active coping, planning, positive reframing, acceptance, use of emotional support, use of instrumental support, venting, substance use, behavioural disengagement, self-blame).

## Analysis

Analyses were conducted in SPSS 26 © and all missing data were addressed prior to analyses. Descriptive statistics, independent t-tests, and multiple regression analysis were conducted.

# Results

The sample comprised 1,568 social work respondents; 938 from Phase 2; 630 from Phase 3 (2020–2021); predominately female (85.9 %), and of White ethnicity (94.4 %). Most were aged 50–59, working in the community, mainly in child protection services. Over half said they had been overwhelmed by job pressures during the pandemic (Table 5.1). Descriptive statistics for both Phases are presented in Table 5.2. Results from a correlation analysis indicated a moderate negative relationship between personal burnout and well-being scores; work-related burnout also indicated a moderate negative relationship with well-being across both phases. There were also weak, but statistically significant, negative correlations between client-related burnout and well-being scores. This indicates that as burnout in any area increased, respondents' well-being decreased.

*Table 5.1* Demographics and work-related characteristics of sample

| Variable | Phase 2 (17th Nov 2020–1st Feb 2021) | Phase 3 (10th May 2021–5th July 2021) |
|---|---|---|
| **Sex** | | |
| Female | 809 (86.2%) | 538 (85.4%) |
| Male | 129 (13.8%) | 92 (14.6%) |
| **Age** | | |
| 16–29 | 98 (10.4%) | 37 (5.9%) |
| 30–39 | 240 (25.6%) | 132 (21.0%) |
| 40–49 | 259 (27.6%) | 173 (27.5%) |
| 50–59 | 262 (27.9%) | 232 (36.9%) |
| 60–65 | 79 (8.4%) | 55 (8.7%) |
| **Ethnic background** | | |
| White | 881 (94.0%) | 597 (95.1%) |
| Black | 23 (2.5%) | 12 (1.9%) |
| Asian | 14 (1.5%) | 8 (1.3%) |
| Mixed | 19 (2.0%) | 11 (1.8%) |
| **Country of work** | | |
| England | 352 (37.5%) | 205 (32.5%) |
| Scotland | 56 (6.0%) | 82 (13.0%) |
| Wales | 271 (28.9%) | 77 (12.2%) |
| Northern Ireland | 259 (27.6%) | 266 (42.2%) |
| **Place of work** | | |
| Hospital | 37 (4.0%) | 29 (4.5%) |
| Community | 477 (51.3%) | 354 (56.5%) |
| GP practice based | 10 (1.1%) | 7 (1.1%) |

*(Continued)*

*Table 5.1* (Continued)

| Variable | Phase 2 (17th Nov 2020–1st Feb 2021) | Phase 3 (10th May 2021–5th July 2021) |
|---|---|---|
| Care Home | 28 (3.0%) | 17 (2.7%) |
| Day care | 18 (1.9%) | 6 (1.0%) |
| Other | 360 (38.7%) | 214 (34.1%) |
| **Number of years of work experience** | | |
| Less than 2 years | 60 (6.4%) | 30 (4.8%) |
| 2–5 years | 133 (14.2%) | 83 (13.2%) |
| 6–10 years | 169 (18.0%) | 83 (13.2%) |
| 11–20 years | 290 (30.9%) | 180 (28.6%) |
| 21–30 years | 190 (20.3%) | 161 (25.6%) |
| More than 30 years | 96 (10.2%) | 92 (14.6%) |
| **Area of Practice** | | |
| Children | 432 (46.1%) | 248 (39.4%) |
| Adults | 167 (17.8%) | 133 (21.1%) |
| Physical Disability | 11 (1.2%) | 10 (1.6%) |
| Learning Disability | 68 (7.2%) | 47 (7.5%) |
| Older People | 81 (8.6%) | 61 (9.7%) |
| Mental Health | 104 (11.1%) | 81 (12.9%) |
| Other | 75 (8.0%) | 50 (7.9%) |
| **Disability status** | | |
| Yes | 113 (12.0%) | 109 (17.3%) |
| No | 803 (85.6%) | 509 (80.8%) |
| Unsure | 22 (2.3%) | 12 (1.9%) |
| **Impact of COVID on services** | | |
| Not impacted | 12 (1.3%) | 5 (0.8%) |
| Impacted but not significantly | 390 (41.7%) | 221 (35.1%) |
| Overwhelmed by increased pressures | 534 (57.1%) | 403 (64.0%) |

The use of negative strategies (venting, substance use, behavioural disengagement, self-blame) increased in Phase 3 (May–July 2021), while most positive strategies decreased (recreation and relaxation, working to improve skills/efficiency, positive reframing, use of emotional support, and use of instrumental support). This increase in negative coping strategies may be associated with the increased caseloads and constantly changing working conditions faced by social workers during the pandemic. As shown in Table 5.2, client burnout, work-related burnout, and personal burnout all increased from Phase 2 to Phase 3. UK-wide in Phase 3 for personal burnout, three-quarters (75.7%) of respondents reported moderate to high burnout which was higher than Phase 2 (63.0%). For work-related burnout, almost three-quarters (72.1%) of respondents reported moderate to high burnout which was higher than Phase 2 (69.9%) while for client-related burnout, the same percentage (72.1%) of respondents reported moderate to high burnout which was higher than Phase 2

*Table 5.2* Descriptive statistics for social work respondents

| Variable | Phase 2 (N = 586) M (SD) | Phase 3 (N = 824) | Phase 2 vs. Phase 3 comparison p-value |
|---|---|---|---|
| Well-being | 20.34 (3.21) | 20.35 (3.50) | .995 |
| **Burnout** | | | |
| Personal | 60.91 (19.41) | 63.39 (20.06) | .015 |
| Work-related | 58.48 (20.20) | 62.11 (20.84) | .001* |
| Client-related | 30.07 (20.89) | 31.08 (21.63) | .357 |
| **Coping strategies** | | | |
| Active coping | 5.43 (1.66) | 5.43 (1.71) | .961 |
| Planning | 5.45 (1.82) | 5.51 (1.76) | .569 |
| Positive reframing | 5.67 (1.66) | 5.51 (1.69) | .063 |
| Acceptance | 6.18 (1.48) | 6.01 (1.57) | .028* |
| Use of emotional support | 5.22 (1.67) | 5.08 (1.63) | .104 |
| Use of instrumental support | 4.71 (1.70) | 4.56 (1.63) | .073 |
| Venting | 4.39 (1.63) | 4.45 (1.72) | .507 |
| Substance use | 3.01 (1.55) | 3.05 (1.69) | .596 |
| Behavioural disengagement | 2.86 (1.28) | 3.01 (1.43) | .025* |
| Self-blame | 3.95 (1.79) | 4.28 (1.92) | .000** |

Notes
* p < 0.005,
** p < 0.001.

(69.9%). Respondents whose practice was with older people in Phase 2 had higher personal and work-related burnout, perhaps related to their clients' severe COVID-19 risks, while those working with people with physical disability had higher client-related burnout, perhaps related to the impact of social restrictions on their lives. In Phase 3, all areas of burnout were highest in those working with people with learning disability (intellectual impairment) and this may reflect the pandemic's long-term impact on their social contacts and activities. Overall, with regards to workplace those working in a community setting had lower well-being and quality of life scores but higher levels of burnout (personal, work, and client-related) than those working in hospitals, GP-based, Care homes, daycare, or other settings.

## Discussion

### Main messages

There are several messages from our surveys, one of which is the need to set in context the time of data collection of any research on the impact of the pandemic. Accounts of pandemic 'experiences' need to be considered in relation to which part of the pandemic is being discussed. The deterioration in well-being noted in Phase 3 suggests that the early period of the pandemic had certain novelty and social workers saw themselves as responding to a crisis in which there was a need for immediate problem-solving and substantial resources were newly available, as discussed in Phase 1's results of the wider study (McFadden et al. 2020b). In the UK, home working for social workers initially presented immediate advantages in terms of being able to provide family care and support, and in avoiding travel and personal contacts through use of online communications. By Phase 3 however there were signs of greater stress which others have noted, related to suppressed demand surfacing and families being less able to support their relatives whose jobs reopened, and a certain acknowledgement of the value of face-to-face encounters to explore possible risks of harm or ill-being (Manthorpe et al. 2021). Staff shortages, increasing workloads, and less positive communications from employers all seemed to play their part in the increases in burnout as noted elsewhere (Franza et al. 2020; Kim and Lee 2009; Peinado and Anderson 2020), indicating that these pressures were worsening as the pandemic continued.

In terms of methods, surveys of professionals such as UK social workers who are familiar with online working are clearly easy ways of gaining data in real-time and perhaps enabling personal disclosure of feelings or behaviours which might be hard to articulate to managers and supervisors. However, the benefits of getting such insightful data on this scale needed to be balanced in the context of risk of survey burden and time required from busy social workers to answer open-ended questions. Such responses enabled participants to provide in-depth narrative, providing insights into the realities facing social workers in practice at that time. In the full reports of our surveys, we report some of the open-text responses which help illuminate some of the statistical findings reported in this chapter. The general literature on burnout and coping provided a useful background to the surveys discussed in this chapter, since social work research had previously investigated the difficulties experienced in terms of early exit from the profession because of work-related pressures (see McFadden et al. 2021c). Using measures related to both work and personal well-being in a pandemic context was new, but our surveys suggest that these were effective measures with the additional benefit of facilitating comparisons with others working in human services (McFadden et al. 2021a–c).

Our findings suggest elements of remedial measures to help ensure that professionals are supported in times of crisis. At micro-level individual resilience can be fostered by helping professionals use effective coping mechanisms and enabling them to reap the benefits of peer support and effective supervision. At messo-level there is the influence of employer and job characteristics which may reflect public service values and so encourage morale and feelings of making a positive difference to society. However, in the UK pre-existing problems in social work may have been amplified by the pandemic, suggested by the ways in which many of our respondents were not able to sustain their well-being and resilience when demands increased and pressures continued. What were helpful supports at the start of the pandemic from employers, such as permissions for home working, were perhaps less sustainable when these added to other work and life-related pressures.

The survey findings reported here suggest that it is rarely client-related burnout that leads to an increase in overall burnout amongst social workers, but more the sustained efforts of struggling with the continuing impact of COVID-19 due to increased demand, coupled with reduced staffing. Changed working patterns shifted rapidly, and such changes needed more communication with line managers, colleagues, as well as with service users and their families. The data presented heightened levels of anxieties, perhaps resulting from continual work disruptions, changing work practices, staffing pressures, and sustained demand. Depending on individual circumstances at work and at home, these changes seem to have affected mental well-being and work-related quality of life.

### Implications and limitations

The main strength of our surveys is the rigour of our comparison of well-being, burnout, and coping over the different early periods of the COVID-19 pandemic in the UK (2020–2021). We demonstrate the importance of coping strategies and burnout for mental well-being and work-related quality of life. Significant negative relationships were revealed between negative coping strategies, burnout and mental well-being. Linked to systems theory, resilience, and the stress and coping theory, the evidence suggests that while social workers changed and adapted different strategies during the COVID-19 pandemic, their use of negative coping strategies and burnout increased, suggesting a negative trajectory by mid-2021 in relation to well-being, which links to the different levels of systems available to this workforce. Therefore, within the macro context of social work practices, efforts should be taken to develop and plan interventions to improve well-being and communication in the workplace at both individual and organisational levels. These interventions may reduce burnout and allow for more efficient coping strategies to be developed while showing employees that the leadership in these organisations is willing to take care of and support their personnel. A limitation of the research is that our sample was predominately female and while this gender composition reflects the social work profession in the UK, generalisations to male social workers must be considered tentatively. The large majority were also of White ethnicity. Additionally, as each phase of the research involved cross-sectional data collection, we cannot determine causal inferences.

## Conclusions

Despite increased pressures and changes in the way they operated, many UK social workers reported that they continued to work in creative ways during the pandemic, trying to use online platforms and adaptive risk management approaches to ensure those most at risk of harm or neglect were 'seen' or 'heard' (as outlined in Baginsky and Manthorpe 2020). However, our surveys show that the early years of the pandemic took a disproportionate toll on social worker well-being. Burnout was reported high in relation to personal and work life, but less around client-related burnout, suggesting levels of compassion and empathy for service users were largely sustained. Recovery after the initial COVID-19 shock will need to address the inherent stressors of the job as well as COVID-19-related pressures. This means action at all levels, including political and social support for those working in jobs such as social work. Strategic interventions designed to address burnout risk in social workers may assist in providing evidence of the effectiveness of remedial measures at all levels, to sustain a workforce that was already under extreme pressure prior to this pandemic crisis.

## Disclaimer and acknowledgements

We are most grateful to all participants and to those who facilitated contact with them. The wider study team includes Patricia Gillen, John Mallett, John Moriarty, Heike Schroder, Jermaine Ravalier, Denise Currie, Patricia Nicholl, and Susan McGrory. This research was funded by the Public Health Agency R&D Division in Northern Ireland and supported by the National Institute for Health and Care Research (NIHR) Policy Research Programme, through the NIHR Policy Research Unit in Health and Social Care Workforce, PR-PRU-1217–21002. The views expressed are those of the authors and not necessarily those of the funders, or the NIHR or Department of Health and Social Care.

## References

Baginsky, Mary, and Jill Manthorpe. 2020. *Managing through COVID-19: The Experiences of Children's Social Care in 15 English Local Authorities*. London: NIHR Policy Research Unit in Health and Social Care Workforce, The Policy Institute, King's College London. https://kclpure.kcl.ac.uk/portal/en/publications/managing-through-covid19-the-experiences-of-childrens-social-care-in-15-english-local-authorities(93814072-18ea-4d76-af2d-ec124c6a8494).html

Bronfenbrenner, Urie. 1992. "Ecological Systems Theory." In *Six Theories of Child Development: Revised Formulations and Current Issues*, edited by Ross Vasta, 187–249. London: Jessica Kingsley Publishing.

Carver, Charles S. 1997. "You Want to Measure Coping but Your Protocol's Too Long: Consider the Brief COPE." *International Journal of Behavioral Medicine* 4 (1): 92–100. 10.1207/s15327558ijbm0401_6

Cuartero, M. Elena, and José F. Campos-Vidal. 2019. "Self-Care Behaviours and Their Relationship with Satisfaction and Compassion Fatigue Levels Among Social Workers." *Social Work in Health Care* 58 (3): 274–290. 10.1080/00981389.2018.1558164

Dekel, Rachel, and Nehami Baum. 2010. "Intervention in a Shared Traumatic Reality: A New Challenge for Social Workers." *British Journal of Social Work* 40 (6): 1927–1944. 10.1093/bjsw/bcp137

Doherty, Ann S., John Mallett, Michael P. Leiter, and Paula McFadden. 2021. "Measuring Burnout in Social Work: Factorial Validity of the Maslach Burnout Inventory—Human Services Survey." *European Journal of Psychological Assessment* 37 (1): 6–14. https://doi.org/10.1027/1015-5759/a000568

Flower, Connie, Jess McDonald, and Michael Sumski. 2005. "Review of Turnover in Milwaukee County Private Agency Child Welfare Ongoing Case Management Staff." https://uh.edu/socialwork/_docs/cwep/national-iv-e/turnoverstudy.pdf.

Franza, Francesco, Roberto Basta, Ferdinando Pellegrino, Barbara Solomita, and Vincenzo Fasano. 2020. "The Role of Fatigue of Compassion, Burnout and Hopelessness in Healthcare: Experience in the Time of COVID-19 Outbreak." *Psychiatria Danubina* 32 (S1): 10–14. PubMed.

Gaskell, Carolyn. 2010. "'If the Social Worker Had Called at Least It Would Show They Cared'. Young Care Leaver's Perspectives on the Importance of Care" *Children & Society* 24 (2): 136–147. 10.1111/j.1099-0860.2009.00214.x

Geisler, Martin, Hanne Berthelsen, and Tuija Muhonen. 2019. "Retaining Social Workers: The Role of Quality of Work and Psychosocial Safety Climate for Work Engagement, Job Satisfaction, and Organizational Commitment." *Human Service Organizations: Management, Leadership & Governance* 43 (1): 1–15. 10.1080/23303131. 2019.1569574

Gillen, Patricia, Ruth D. Neill, Jill Manthorpe, John Mallett, Heike Schroder, Patricia Nicholl, Denise Currie, John Moriarty, Jermaine Ravalier, Susan McGory, and Paula McFadden. 2022. "Decreasing Wellbeing and Increasing Use of Negative Coping Strategies: The Effect of the COVID-19 Pandemic on UK Health and Social Care Workforce." *Epidemologia* 3 (1): 26–39. 10.3390/epidemiologia3010003

Grant, Louise, Gail Kinman, and Kelly Alexander. 2014. "What's All This Talk About Emotion? Developing Emotional Intelligence in Social Work Students." *Social Work Education* 33 (7): 874–889. 10.1080/02615479.2014.891012

Harrikari, Timo, Marjo Romakkaniemi, Laura Tiitinen, and Sanna Ovaskainen. 2021. "Pandemic and Social Work: Exploring Finnish Social Workers' Experiences through a SWOT Analysis." *The British Journal of Social Work* 51 (5): 1644–1662. 10.1093/bjsw/bcab052

Kim, Hansung, and Sun Y. Lee. 2009. "Supervisory Communication, Burnout, and Turnover Intention Among Social Workers in Health Care Settings." *Social Work in Health Care* 48 (4): 364–385. 10.1080/00981380802598499

Kristensen, Tage S., Marianne Borritz, Ebbe Villadsen, and Karl B. Christensen. 2005. "The Copenhagen Burnout Inventory: A New Tool for the Assessment of Burnout." *Work & Stress* 19 (3): 192–207. 10.1080/02678370500297720

Lazarus, Richard. 1991. *Emotion and Adaptation.* New York: Oxford University Press.

Lotty, Maria. 2021. "Exploring Trauma-Informed Foster Care as a Framework to Support Collaborative Social Worker – Foster Carer Relationships." *Irish Journal of Applied Social Studies* 21 (1): 4. 10.21427/g1g5-6x52

Manthorpe, Jill, Jess Harris, Stan Burridge, James Fuller, Stephen Martineau, Bruno Ornelas, Michela Tinelli, and Michelle Cornes. 2021. "Social Work Practice with Adults under the Rising Second Wave of Covid-19 in England: Frontline Experiences and the Use of Professional Judgement." *The British Journal of Social Work* 51 (5): 1879–1896. 10.1093/bjsw/bcab080

Maslach, Christina, and Susan E. Jackson. 1986. *Maslach Burnout Inventory Manual* (2nd ed.). Mountain View: Consulting Psychology Press.

Maslach, Christina, Susan E. Jackson, and Michael P. Leiter. 1997. *Maslach Burnout Inventory.* 3rd ed. Palo Alto: Consulting Psychologists Press.

Maslach, Christina, Susan E. Jackson, Michael P. Leiter, Wilmar B. Schaufeli, and Richard L. Schwab. 2016. *Maslach Burnout Inventory Manual [Fourth Edition Manual].* Menlo Park: Mind Garden.

McFadden, Paula. 2018. "Two Sides of One Coin? Relationships Build Resilience or Contribute to Burnout in Child Protection Social Work: Shared Perspectives from

Leavers and Stayers in Northern Ireland." *International Social Work* 63 (2): 164–176. 10.1177/0020872818788393

McFadden, Paula, Gillian Manthorpe, and John Mallett. 2018. "Commonalities and Differences in Social Work with Learning Disability and Child Protection: Findings from a UK 'Burnout' National Survey." *The British Journal of Social Work* 48 (5): 1199–1219. 10.1093/bjsw/bcx070

McFadden, Paula, John Mallett, and Michael Leiter. 2019. "Extending the Two-Process Model of Burnout in Child Protection Workers: The Role of Resilience in Mediating Burnout via Organizational Factors of Control, Values, Fairness, Reward, Workload, and Community Relationships." *Stress and Health* 34 (1): 72–83. 10.1002/smi.2763

McFadden, Paula, John Mallett, Anne Campbell, and Brian Taylor. 2019. "Explaining Self-Rreported Resilience in Child-Protection Social Work: The Role of Organisational Factors, Demographic Information and Job Characteristics." *The British Journal of Social Work* 49 (1): 198–216. 10.1093/bjsw/bcy015

McFadden, Paula, Erica Russ, Paul Blakeman, Gloria Kirwin, Janet Anand, Sanna Lähteinen, Gunn Astrid Baugerud, and Pia Tham. 2020a. "COVID-19 Impact on Social Work Admissions and Education in Seven International Universities." *Social Work Education*, 39 (8): 1154–1163. 10.1080/02615479.2020.1829582

McFadden, Paula, Patricia Gillen, John Moriarty, John Mallett, Heike Schroder, Jermaine Ravalier, Jill Manthorpe, Jaclyn Harron, and Denise Currie. 2020b. *Health and Social Care Workers' Quality of Working Life and Coping While Working during the COVID-19 Pandemic 7th May–3rd July 2020: Findings from a UK Survey.* Belfast: University of Ulster Press. https://577ccd37-5004-401d-b378-2a2af66e499d.filesusr.com/ugd/2749ea_62b10d98a3e84bb79f7d6ee71d226766.pdf.

McFadden, Paula, Patricia Gillen, John Moriarty, John Mallett, Heike Schroder, Jermaine Ravalier, Jill Manthorpe et al. 2021a. *Health and Social Care Workers' Quality of Working Life and Coping While Working during the COVID-19 Pandemic: Findings from a UK Survey Phase 2: 17th November 2020–1st February 2021.* Belfast: University of Ulster Press.

McFadden, Paula, Patricia Gillen, John Moriarty, John Mallett, Heike Schroder, Jermaine Ravalier, Jill Manthorpe et al. 2021b. *Health and Social Care Workers' Quality of Working Life and Coping while Working During the COVID-19 Pandemic: Phase 3: 10th May-2nd July 2021: Finding from a UK Survey.* Belfast: University of Ulster Press. https://kclpure.kcl.ac.uk/portal/files/160297523/2749ea_3a0bc75435ab4657b57e1f66d529b9f3.pdf

McFadden, Paula, Ruth D. Neill, John Mallett, Jill Manthorpe, Patricia Gillen, John Moriarty, Denise Currie, et al. 2021c. "Mental Well-Being and Quality of Working Life in UK Social Workers Before and during the COVID-19 Pandemic: A Propensity Score Matching Study." *The British Journal of Social Work* 52 (5): 2814–2833. 10.1093/bjsw/bcab198

Olaniyan, Oyeniyi Samuel, Hilde Hetland, Sigurd W. Hystad, Anette C. Iversen, and Gaby Ortiz-Barreda. 2020. "Lean on Me: A Scoping Review of the Essence of Workplace Support Among Child Welfare Workers." *Frontiers in Psychology* 11: 287. 10.3389/fpsyg.2020.00287

Peinado, Micaela, and Kelly N. Anderson. 2020. "Reducing Social Worker Burnout during COVID-19." *International Social Work* 63 (6): 757–760. 10.1177/0020872820962196

Ravalier, Jermaine, Rheanna Morton, Lauren Russell, and Antonio R. Fidalgo. 2019. "Zero-Hour Contracts and Stress in UK Domiciliary Care Workers." *Health and Social Care in the Community* 27 (2): 348–355. 10.1111/hsc.12652

Ravalier, Jermaine M., Paula McFadden, Charlotte Boichat, Oliver Clabburn, and John Moriarty. 2021. "Social Worker Well-Being: A Large Mixed-Methods Study." *The British Journal of Social Work* 51 (1): 297–317. 10.1093/bjsw/bcaa078

Schweitzer, Don, Terry Chianello, and Brianne Kothari. 2013. "Compensation in Social Work: Critical for Satisfaction and a Sustainable Profession." *Administration in Social Work* 37 (2): 147–157. 10.1080/03643107.2012.669335

Stewart-Brown, Sarah, Alan Tennant, Ruth Tennant, Stephen Platt, Jane Parkinson, and Scott Weich. 2009. "Internal Construct Validity of the Warwick-Edinburgh Mental Well-Being Scale (WEMWBS): A Rasch Analysis Using Data from The Scottish Health Education Population Survey." *Health and Quality of Life Outcomes* 7: 15. 10.1186/1477-7525-7-15

Strolin-Goltzman, Jessica, Sharon Kollar, and Joanne Trinkle. 2010. "Listening to the Voices of Children in Foster Care: Youths Speak Out about Child Welfare Workforce Turnover and Selection." *Social Work* 55 (1): 47–53. 10.1093/sw/55.1.47

Tham, Pia, and Deborah Lynch. 2016. "Prepared for Practice? Graduating Social Work Students' Reflections on Their Education, Competence and Skills." *Social Work Education* 33 (6): 704–717. 10.1080/02615479.2014.881468

Tham, Pia, Paula McFadden, Erica Russ, Andreas Baldschun, Paul Blakeman, and Austin Griffiths. 2021. "How Do We Prepare Students for the Challenges of Social Work? Examples from Six Countries Around the World." *Social Work Education*. Published ahead of print, 16 September 2021. 10.1080/02615479.2021.1976135

Think Local Act Personal (TLAP). 2020. *A Telling Experience: Understanding the Impact of Covid-19 On People Who Access Care and Support – A Rapid Evidence Review with Recommendations.* London: Think Local Act Personal. https://www.thinklocalactpersonal.org.uk/_assets/TLAP-TIG-report-on-Covid-19.pdf.

Travis, Dinka J., Erica L. Lizano, and Michàlle E. Mor Barak. 2016. "'I'm So Stressed!': A Longitudinal Model of Stress, Burnout and Engagement among Social Workers in Child Welfare Settings." *The British Journal of Social Work* 46 (4): 1076–1095. 10.1093/bjsw/bct205

Walters, Jayme E., Aaron R. Brown, and Aubrey E. Jones. 2018. "Use of the Copenhagen Burnout Inventory with Social Workers: A Confirmatory Factor Analysis." *Human Service Organizations: Management, Leadership & Governance* 42 (5): 437–456. 10.1080/23303131.2018.1532371

# 6 Social Work during Triple Lockdown: A Restatement of Discourses in Estonia?

*Reeli Sirotkina, Airi Mitendorf, and Kersti Kriisk*

## Introduction

This chapter explores how social workers responded to the emergent COVID-19 pandemic in the context of lockdown on a small island in Estonia, where there was a general lack of knowledge on how to deal with protective practices. This chapter introduces the emergent discourse about social work in circumstances of total isolation, analysing interviews with social workers, child protection workers and homecare workers.

In March 2020, the island municipality of Saaremaa became the epicentre of Estonia's COVID-19 outbreak, having more cases per capita than anywhere else in Estonia or Europe more broadly. Although social work has not been considered as an essential component of disaster management (Hay and Pascoe 2021), it played a crucial role in the Saaremaa case as the healthcare and social welfare services encountered wide-ranging emergency regulations and stringent social distancing measures.

Saaremaa Island has about 31,000 inhabitants and a local government that includes a child protection division and a social welfare division with 30 social workers. Local municipalities have an obligation to provide most social care services except labour market services and special care services for persons with mental disabilities which are delegated to the regional level, i.e., they were to be provided by the state institutions on Saaremaa Island.

Saaremaa is a sparsely populated area, with social services needing to cover the whole territory. The COVID-19 isolation period highlighted how intertwined and interdependent are the social work networks and collaborations with the mainland, as the area was faced with a new set of unfamiliar challenges for governance and social workers. Saaremaa experienced a so-called triple lockdown: a national lockdown, special restrictions for the municipality due to its exceptionally high rate of virus transmission, and geographical isolation from the mainland. Initially, Saaremaa was left to deal by itself with the spread of the virus.

During the crisis, public services, on the one hand, had a duty to uphold welfare services but, on the other hand, faced the test of what 'being prepared' for the crisis meant (Nilssen 2020) creating new type of benefits and services (Hidalgo Lavié et al. 2021). Social workers were expected to be experts in

DOI: 10.4324/9781003374374-8

working in challenging environments: new tasks, changing positions, daily updated guidelines from the state, and a constantly changing understanding of the virus and the restrictions. Social workers significantly altered their working patterns to be able to accommodate multiple demands creatively (Hidalgo Lavié et al. 2021), sometimes being regarded as frontline heroes (Miller and Lee 2020; Nilssen 2020) but sometimes being stigmatised because of the fear and misconception of unknown situations. Stigmatisation can happen on a personal, community, or spatial level, especially in unknown situations that develop quickly.

Given these considerations, it is important to understand how social work responded to lockdown and how resilient (Keck and Sakdapolrak 2013) and adaptive (Boyd and Folke 2012) were both, social workers and local governance. This led us to ask the question: how did social workers discursively construct professional social work practice within the context of uncertainty in lockdown, and what underlying components might challenge workers' resilience at individual and local government levels?

While we recognise that working in a complex and unknown context is not unique to social work, it is apparent that the context of a new pandemic and triple lockdown exacerbated the ambiguity and uncertainty. In November 2020, we contacted Saaremaa municipality and asked social workers to recall the spring triple lockdown experience to better understand the profession within this specific context. We conducted three focus group interviews with social workers in the island municipality of Saaremaa. Using discourse analysis, this chapter presents a discourse of the social work profession in Estonia, taking the case of Saaremaa. Discourse analysis reveals the complex situations in small communities facing the stigmatisation of professionals, highlighting the new working methods and new networks that helped to overcome acute crises and communicate the 'hero' discourse (Miller and Lee 2020).

## The COVID-19 pandemic in Saaremaa

The island of Saaremaa became the epicentre of Estonia's outbreak, with as many as 40% of residents in the island's capital believed to have been infected with coronavirus, meaning that, in April 2020, Saaremaa had one of the highest rates of COVID-19 per 100,000 people in Estonia and worldwide. Saaremaa County had, as of the end of June, 16,716 positive results per 100,000 people, at a time when the number of positive results across Estonia was 150 per 100,000 people (Rüütel et al. 2020).

The Estonian Baltic Sea islands, including Saaremaa, were in a triple lockdown from 14th March until 4th of May 2020. As a result, it was possible to go to the island but not to leave it. During the crisis, the island's only hospital was filled within days and the Estonian army was brought in to deploy a field hospital, doubling the number of available beds. A quarter of the medical staff became infected, so the hospital had to depend on support from the local community.

The Estonian government formed a crisis committee that swiftly decided to cut the island off from the rest of the country. Everyone was asked to stay at home and to keep away from the Estonian mainland. Due to the emergency, a prohibition on visiting applied to all social welfare institutions and hospitals. Saaremaa experienced a triple lockdown. The last time that the island was closed to the movement of people in and out was in the Soviet period.

## Adaptive governance

The COVID-19 lockdown, as a unique situation, required greater levels of adaptability and creativity from public policy—including social welfare institutions. Local governments, social welfare institutions, and (frontline) social workers were required to extend and reorganise service provision rapidly; adopting new working methods in the context of social distancing and the isolation of vulnerable groups, network partners, and social workers themselves (Walter-McCabe 2020). These rapid transitions in contemporary complex societies emphasise the increasing need for resilience of all individuals, professionals, and communities, but also highlight changes in the governance of social welfare institutions and local governance (Duit et al. 2010). This raises questions about the flexibility of individuals, professionals, communities, and public actors in adapting norms, rules, working methods, and new networks in the short term, and how to address long-term challenges to deep legacies and belief systems in a changed environment and society (Boyd and Folke 2012).

Hence, new adapted methods and solutions are required at each level—individual, organisational, and societal levels (Bright 2020), taking into account the multiplicity of the component elements with direct and indirect impacts (Alston and Chow 2021). Social resilience requires coping, adaptive, and transformative capacities from all institutions (Keck and Sakdapolrak 2013). In contemporary society, social resilience in institutions and adaptive governance are related to readiness and ICT skills (Young 2019; Wang et al. 2018). For social work, this means being adaptive to actual needs and assets, having in-depth and up-to-date knowledge of the capacities and resources of local organisations; having strong and community-oriented local leadership; flexibility and creativity in service provision with adequate crisis communication (Maglajlic 2019) and capacity for ICT skills. To conclude, adaptive governance and social resilience can be associated in the context of social work with eco-social disasters or long-term crises such as the COVID-19 pandemic, particularly during the first lockdown in the spring 2020.

## Building resilience and overcoming stigmatisation in unknown situations

Outbreaks of unknown, new viruses are related to lack of adequate knowledge of the viruses, leading on the one hand to fear, stigmatisation (Barrett and Brown 2008) and isolation of individuals and even regions, but on the other hand to the development of resilience. Resilience can be an effective way to overcome unknown situations and provide an explanation for the reaction to uncertainty and the unknown on both a personal and an organisational level. The 'professional endurance and resilience' of social workers have garnered attention in pandemic research (Harrikari et al. 2021), highlighting the position of social workers caught between professional and private tensions. Misconception and fear lead to stigmatisation of professionals, clients, and individuals living in certain areas, and to isolation and the lockdown of countries. At the person level, the theory of stigma is well described by Erving Goffman such that the person who carries stigma is:

> an individual who might have been received easily in ordinary social intercourse possesses a trait that can obtrude itself upon attention and turn those of us whom he meets away from him, breaking the claim that his other attributes have on us (Goffman 1963, 5).

Those attributes mentioned by Goffman can be opposites to the *normal*. This leads to a feeling of shame on the part of this person who does not possess normal attributes. During the COVID-19 pandemic, the theory of stigma was connected to stress, discrimination, and fear (Taylor et al. 2020; Ramaci et al. 2020)—mainly associated with being in contact with healthcare workers and becoming infected, though care workers' burnout and stress also prompted stigmatisation.

The first wave of the COVID-19 pandemic was associated with mental health issues, including the burnout of professionals (Choi 2021), increased emotional and mental disorders among schoolchildren after school closures (Lee 2020) and loneliness among the elderly due to prolonged social isolation (Plagg et al. 2020). Furthermore, the situation was associated with stigmatisation in terms of 'we versus they' or 'insider versus outsider'. This was not only notable within the community, in terms of 'healthy people versus people with coronavirus' but also, between the regions, as 'most affected double-lockdown areas versus the rest of the country'. Stigma can usually be experienced at an individual level but universal drivers of stigma, such as misconception and fear, can be felt at community and spatial levels as well (Bologna et al. 2021).

This kind of stigmatisation, in turn, increases the vulnerability of those geographical areas already most affected (Harvey 2019), complicating coping with the situation and challenging the development of resilience at individual, professional, and organisational levels. The geographically disadvantaged areas have to struggle with limited access to social services provided only in larger municipalities, with a limited number of local professionals, organisations, and NGOs—a lack of professional capacities (Pugh 2003; Turbett 2009). However, the stronger role of community members (Walsh and O'Shea 2008) and innovative public solutions, including social service provision (Brown and Keast 2005), have been the everyday practice of isolated and remote areas, increasing social resilience and the capabilities to adapt to changed environments at individual, organisational, and societal levels.

## Exploring the case of Saaremaa

The design of this study is exploratory, as we prioritised an open-minded approach to investigate the experiences and challenges of social workers working within a complex social reality, with multiple demands caused by the novel COVID-19 disease. The empirical material of the study is qualitative, involving semi-structured focus group interviews with five social workers, five child protection workers, and five homecare workers, and an individual interview with the deputy mayor of social welfare in the island municipality of Saaremaa in November 2020. In addition, the heads of departments also participated in all three focus group interviews. All participants in the study were purposefully chosen, all being employed in the first wave of the COVID-19 pandemic. The six- to eight-month gap between the lockdown and the interviews was a suitable period to allow retrospective discussion of experiences that had already been reflected upon by the professionals.

We prepared a series of questions to help us understand the challenges facing professionals due to the pandemic—for example, how field practice changed in general and what the role of social work was and what were the main lessons learned. We decided to create focus groups as these group dynamics bring out aspects of the topic that we, as researchers, might not have anticipated and that might not have emerged in individual interviews (Rubin and Babbie 2014). Using discourse analysis, we looked at the following research questions: how did social workers discursively construct professional social work practice within the context of uncertainty in lockdown, and what underlying components might challenge workers' resilience at both the individual and local governmental levels?

Discourse refers to 'a particular picture that is painted of an event, person or class of persons, a particular way of representing it in a certain light' (Burr 2003, 64) and 'socially specific ways of knowing social practices, they can be, and are used as resources for representing social practices in text' (van Leeuwen 2008, 6). Discourse analysis in our research context means a broader analysis on the representation of social practices, so-called Foucauldian discourse where the object can have many discourses depending on the way people see the event (Burr 2003). Acknowledging that social workers in the context of the COVID-19 pandemic were faced with new complexities, we focused on discourse as a method in which social workers made meaning regarding professional practice in the contexts of the pandemic and triple lockdown. In the first round of analysis, we focused on the content of the detailed transcripts and language being used by participants. For example, the word '*fear*' represented as a generalised phenomenon rather than as an action by specific social actors and was attributed to different discourses— discourse of stigma and discourse of new ways of social work. At the same time, it is also represented as affecting the Saaremaa community. Therefore, the context for the discourse was different. The analysis continued with careful listening to the recordings in order to begin initial construction of discourses based on questions of interest. Faced with transcripts, we searched for the phrases, manifestations and concepts that signified patterns and presented a picture of social work in the middle of a crisis. For this chapter, we selected four discourses in which research participants presented their professional work in the context of the pandemic.

## Emerging discourses during triple lockdown

The overall picture of social work that emerged from the study was a practice that experienced challenges at all levels of professional work—widespread teleworking, leadership, networking, cooperation, and professional positions. Four discourses are presented in the results—working from distance as a new normality in social work, fear and stigma as professional challenges, the guinea pigs for the new social work and adapting to the situation.

Being in triple lockdown, the Saaremaa case was unique because there were no regulations for the crisis established yet at a state level. Moreover, Saaremaa was the first case of lockdown on a regional level as well. Crisis on an island meant constantly finding new working methods and alternative ways to overcome unique situations. Recent administrative reform, from which Saaremaa emerged as one municipality, created the possibility of centralising the decision-making process, which made crisis management easier but also left the leader isolated.

> [...] one thing I've been thinking about is whether one Saaremaa is good or bad compared to the former administrative division. Honestly, I can't imagine what it would have been like if there had been 12 municipalities. How to manage this situation then? Certainly, at that moment it was our victory that there was one municipality. [Name of the municipality] was always with us at the crisis table, but these key decisions were made centrally by Saaremaa, essentially only one person, one institution, but if there had been more of them? (The deputy mayor of social welfare, Admin 1)

The isolation on professional and personal levels as well as challenges emerging every minute required fast thinking in governing. Deputy mayor was responsible for organising the work of health and social welfare and the department was responsible to organise services and help in a new situation.

## Remote working as a new normality in social work

Reflecting on their experiences working within the coronavirus pandemic, participants talked about the widespread teleworking in the field of care work. Even though social care working conditions became rather difficult, a common thread amongst participants was that online methods were essential for secure and effective communication during the pandemic. The communication between each other, teamwork, and belonging to the team became even stronger during the pandemic. The following quotation exemplifies a common attitude: 'Yes, we "met" every morning virtually with our boss sharing everything [...] it kept us informed but also supported' (Care worker, CW 2). In Saaremaa, care workers already had tablets for communication with each other and their head of department before the crisis. Tablets with special programmes that recorded all activity allowed the timely sharing of personal and professional information.

One aspect that participants in the study pointed out is that the core task of social work was changed because networks were broken and cooperation between the mainland and island was cut. As noted, online methods in professional practice were not new in Estonia, but workers considered that teleworking had become a primary method to establish supportive and secure relationships, not only with relatives of clients but also with team members.

> Providing a sense of security to customers and [...] their relatives. We received more calls from relatives and passed on information on how we can cope, how their relatives are doing and how their mother or father is doing (CW 2).

Although the findings show that the increased means of teleworking were greatly appreciated, this created a new challenge: while working remotely, participants experienced teleworking-related loneliness.

## The 'plague stigma' and personal challenges

This discourse shows that isolation had many effects on workers' personal feelings and professional work. The discourse of personal isolation was mixed with feelings of fear, panic, and stigmatisation. We found that workers' own social exclusion was a concern in the interviews with care workers and social workers, as they were frequently confronted with more visible and hidden repellence. This empirical understanding is especially important in the context of a small community, where workers are part of the neighbourhood yet find themselves in conflict stating that: 'We heard from everywhere—avoid shopping, avoid shopping [...] but we went to the store all the time because we had to bring food to the people [...] we were told that we should not come to the store' (CW 1). Evoking multiple discourses, participants highlighted a fundamental fear: 'everybody was afraid of everything and everybody'.

The study participants reflected the feeling of fear within different situations—fear of infecting vulnerable people and colleagues, fear of harming relationships within the community as follows: 'The constant loneliness caused fear for people. Clients feared for themselves and were afraid also of care workers catching the virus' (CW 2). In addition, participants reflected the feeling of fear of catching the virus itself and how to overcome it.

Discourse on stigma about being 'infected in the community' was the most salient discourse amongst study participants as follows: 'It was still a terrible feeling when you're sick [...] The pressure was awful [...] I got a label like that (being sick), *and it stayed*' (Child protection worker, ChPW 2). Beyond that, all of Saaremaa was stigmatised as being the heart of the COVID-19 pandemic. During the first wave, knowledge about the virus was lacking and ideas on how to approach the crisis were being discovered 'from scratch'. The situation itself made everybody vulnerable to 'us' and 'them' labelling.

Panic, fear, and feelings of stigma, made people feel powerless and their professional goals were relegated to a secondary position. This raised the issue of the mental health of professionals, which was very explicitly brought out during the interviews as follows: '*If a person is in trouble, then time is not a criterion for him. And you yourself lose track and in what sense, I turn off the phone at five o'clock. The line between work and private life had completely disappeared*' (Social worker, SW 2). Changes in family life, and the complexity that surrounded professionals in their personal and professional lives, made social workers and care workers often think about their own mental capacity to overcome everyday stressful situations that continued for several months.

The role of the helper exceeded any borders in terms of how family life and professional life were intertwined or how working life took over personal life as a social worker is quoting: '*I really felt that "clients were sitting on my couch" at home. They did not feel it but I felt them at home. […] I haven't still worked out how to maintain my mental health*' (SW 3). The private and public spheres were mixed and professionals were struggling with mental health issues.

Personal isolation mainly manifests in feelings of fear and challenges to tackling mental health issues, which are intertwined with mixed feelings due to the misconceptions and fear of the unknown situation and the rapid spread of the virus.

## Professional fear—we were the guinea pigs for the new social work

The quotations in this section illustrate workers' experiences in upholding public services and child protection tasks, albeit tailored to fit the new context. The uncertainty exemplified a common pattern from study participants, showing how isolation from the mainland restricted the capacity to respond to the vulnerabilities of people in need as follows: '*Lockdown in Saaremaa (and isolating it from the mainland) caused additional fear […] If you can't go and see your parents at all […] and how long will it take*' (CW 4). The frontline workers felt left alone or even as the guinea pigs during the new and complex situation illustrating it as follows: '*We were not ready for the virus to cut us off from everyday life […] We worked on the front line, but it felt like we were working on the back line—no protective equipment was distributed*' (CW 3).

Evoking discourses on professional fear, participants spoke of how uncertainty made people overwhelmed with many questions that nobody could answer. For example, child protection workers brought up the negative effects of the isolation of the island on responding to the needs of the children of victims of domestic violence. According to the Estonian Child Protection Act, the child protection worker is an official of a local authority who provides activities to ensure the rights and well-being of children. The study findings show that isolation from the mainland created significant organisational constraints upon working for the best interest of children. Child protection workers argued that even in a situation where the child was in danger and one parent's ability to take care of the child was limited, there was absolute prohibition on arranging for children to live on the mainland together with their other parent, no matter the character of the risk. The research finding made visible the fear of the relatives supporting children at risk.

> However, at that moment, it became clear to me with that family that this mother could not really handle her children, and in the end she said 'Take them away, I do not want to be with them'. And then we had to organise these children with their fathers on the mainland. And the situation was that the fathers were completely willing to take the children with them, but we could not get them to the mainland. With permission and all this was written out, it was possible, but in the social department, for example [...] that if one father was in Finland and had to come and it was a matter of a few days, these children should not be brought to the mainland, to grandparents or relatives to keep and put them in the family home and let them wait there for their father and then at some point you can take them away (ChPW 2).

These findings reflect the fear that had entered the professional world. Challenges to coping with bureaucracy, and the limited professional cooperation over care of children experiencing neglect and abuse, brought up reflections of disappointment with how they were pushed out from the mainland.

> This situation was extremely difficult that you could not either way or [...] the bureaucratic side was so amplified by the mainland just that the kind of thing that you can't send these children here, you stay there, no one from the island is not coming (here). This statement, too, was that whether or not children could be sent to the mainland with a support person, it was very difficult (ChPW 3).

It was evident in our research that child protection workers felt alone in professional networks facing very urgent situations: the networks were broken due to the isolation from the mainland.

### Adapting to the new situation—new heroes emerging

A common thread amongst study participants was their need for new services because old networks did not work. On the other hand, new networks inside the municipality helped maintain older functions and establish new ones. New networks based on internal resources emerged, e.g. other departments took over certain tasks such as broadening the service of meals on wheels as quoted: '*People from the financial department helped us to deal with the complicated distribution matrix for food delivery for children who attended schools but now stayed at home*' (ChPW 3).

Saaremaa Island had very limited opportunities and help from the mainland was not possible. After a few weeks of crisis there was a demand for a crisis centre using local resources. The crisis centre, which was built up by two enthusiasts, was for people who had moved from hospital to home, who were tested as COVID-19-positive at nursing homes, and people who were signed out from hospital needing a place to be isolated before going home.

> Then later the crisis centre was created, i.e. the people who were not infected, but we did not dare to take them to the care home. And I had to be able to find staff that wasn't available anyway at the time, because many were infected. Many had this phantom disease as well … I had to instruct people by phone, who would then set it up with the accessories and finally all the instructions on how the staff would work in the house [...] where the clean zone is and where the infected zone. I'm not with that education, but I couldn't take people to that house without those instructions (Admin 1).

The work itself was done by one person who took responsibility in very difficult circumstances. Managing the situation alone was challenging and there was a lack of knowledge about crisis management at that time.

> [...] I wrote them (said proudly because she has no preparation for that). And at one point when the Rescue Board came to the rescue and the infectionists came to Saaremaa [...] they examined them and it must be admitted that I succeeded. That it was a complete mystique (Admin 1).

It was evident that crisis management was carried out very differently by the various leaders we interviewed.

## Rephrasing four discourses

The fear of uncertain circumstances, new situations in private life and new professional approaches presented challenges for community reactions to the COVID-19 crisis, for the means to adapt to the new working conditions and how to exchange information. The resilience to cope with new situations was partly seen as an old habit of working as a team but was partly addressed by teleworking and professional isolation.

Four discourses were discovered during analysis. The first opened new ways of working and networking, making remote work a new normality in social work. Importantly, the discourses revealed that working within complexity and uncertainty calls for social resilience as being capable of adaptive and transformative capacities from professionals but also from the community (Walsh and O'Shea 2008), in alignment with emergent situations. For example, the use of organisations' internal resources and competencies, such as accountants, created the logistics to distribute school meals. Although the frontline work of the care workers intensified, they broadened and care responsibilities were taken over from family members who could not access the island to take care of their loved ones. Teleworking has become a normal way to work and it means not only team meetings but meetings with clients are taking place in web-based environments. With regard to teleworking practices, the Spanish case merits mention, where social workers' having previous reluctance to work remotely, after the COVID-19 outbreak assumed that teleworking will become the primary working method for social work in the post-COVID times (Hidalgo Lavié et al. 2021).

Second is the so-called plague stigma, the fear of the *not normal* (Goffman 1963) and using the division of *they* and *us* not only on a personal but also professional level. Last but not the least, the spatial level stigma of being an 'infected island' forced island professionals to find new ways of working. From the point of view of crisis management, it was a collective response to the crisis, but the reactions of the local community and the mainland were obviously stigmatising toward the professional community and the island (Bologna et al. 2021). It is noteworthy that, although the professionals in the social work field worked to keep people's lives and health at the forefront, the reactions of the community weakened rather than reinforced this. Thus, the fear of a new and unknown situation can jeopardise the identity of a community that was previously perceived as strong, something that is connected to the widespread but sometimes contradictory media coverage.

The third discourse concerns fear in the professional field. This was felt as a shock and is akin to a bridge between stigma discourse and discourse about adaptation. This was a period when resilient behaviour was emerging, and new roles and tasks were taken as a new normal. All resources and creativity were used to overcome difficult situations that emerged (Maglajlic 2019). The resources on the island were used and the reality of the triple lockdown was acknowledged. In other words, new methods were found (Harvey 2019) to overcome the new reality, in which the island was isolated and resilience was developed in working with its own resources as a laboratory for a renewed social work.

Fourthly, the isolation on the island brought out a 'hero' discourse regarding those who were alone in deciding on rules and establishing new services. In Saaremaa, external assistance was not possible and resources had to be found and created in the local community—the formation of new institutions, the transformation of the tasks of local government employees (Walter-McCabe 2020). The precondition to the previously mentioned adaptation to the new situation was the existence of rapid and well-equipped teleworking conditions, in terms of equipment and software. Research (Brown and Keast 2005) shows that isolation and remoteness create different ways of working. Homecare workers felt a strong team feeling, social workers and child protection workers were isolated at home, and administrative staff took over many managerial tasks which were new and complicated. We can distinguish strong teamwork on the frontline level and strong individualistic ways of working at the managerial level.

# References

Alston, Margaret, and Amy Y.M. Chow. 2021. "Introduction—When Social Work Meets Disaster: Challenges and Opportunities." *The British Journal of Social Work* 51 (1): 1525–1530. 10.1093/bjsw/bcab154

Barrett, Ron, and Peter J. Brown. 2008. "Stigma in the Time of Influenza: Social and Institutional Responses to Pandemic Emergencies." *The Journal of Infectious Diseases* 197 (S1): S34–S37. 10.1086/524986

Bologna, Lydia, Kathrine V. Stamidis, Sarah Paige, Roma Solomon, Filimona Bisrat, Anthony Kisanga, Samuel Usman, and Ahmed Arale. 2021. "Why Communities Should Be the Focus to Reduce Stigma Attached to COVID-19." *American Journal of Tropical Medicine and Hygiene* 104 (1): 39–44. 10.4269/ajtmh.20-1329

Boyd, Emily, and Carl Folke. 2012. *Adapting Institutions: Governance, Complexity, and Social-Ecological Resilience.* Cambridge: Cambridge University Press.

Bright, Charlotte L. 2020. "Social Work in the Age of a Global Pandemic." *Social Work Research* 44 (2): 83–86. 10.1093/swr/svaa006

Brown, Kerry and Robyn Keast. 2005. "Social Services Policy and Delivery in Australia: Centre-Periphery Mixes." *Policy & Politics* 33 (3): 505–518. 10.1332/0305573054325774

Burr, Vivien. 2003. *Social Constructionism.* London: Routledge.

Choi, Shinwoo. 2021. "'People Look at Me like I AM the Virus': Fear, Stigma, and Discrimination during the COVID-19 Pandemic." *Qualitative Social Work* 20 (1–2): 233–239. 10.1177/1473325020973333

Duit, Andreas, Victor Galaz, Katarina Eckerberg, and Jonas Ebbesson. 2010. "Governance, Complexity, and Resilience." *Global Environmental Change* 20 (3): 363–368. 10.1016/j.gloenvcha.2010.04.006

Goffman, Erving. 1963. *Stigma: Notes on the Management of Spoiled Identity.* New York: Simon and Schuster.

Harrikari, Timo, Marjo Romakkaniemi, Laura Tiitinen, and Sanna Ovaskainen. 2021. "Pandemic and Social Work: Exploring Finnish Social Workers' Experiences through a SWOT Analysis." *The British Journal of Social Work* 51 (5): 1644–1662. 10.1093/bjsw/bcab052

Harvey, David. 2019. *Spaces of Global Capitalism: A Theory of Uneven Geographical Development.* London: Verso.

Hay, Kathryne and Katheryn M. Pascoe. 2021. "Social Workers and Disaster Management: An Aotearoa New Zealand Perspective." *The British Journal of Social Work* 51 (5): 1531–1550. 10.1093/bjsw/bcab127

Hidalgo Lavié, Alfredo, Ana M. González Ramos, and Ana I. Lima Fernández. 2021. "Social Work Practice During the COVID-19 State of Emergency in Spain." *Social Work and Social Sciences Review* 22 (2): 88–102. 10.1921/swssr.v22i2.1585

Keck, Markus, and Patrick Sakdapolrak. 2013. "What Is Social Resilience? Lessons Learned and Ways Forward." *Erdkunde* 67 (1): 5–19. 10.3112/erdkunde.2013.01.02

Lee, Joyce. 2020. "Mental Health Effects of School Closures during COVID-19." *The Lancet Child & Adolescent Health* 4 (6): 421. 10.1016/S2352-4642(20)30109-7

Maglajlic, Reima A. 2019. "Organisation and Delivery of Social Services in Extreme Events: Lessons from Social Work Research on Natural Disasters." *International Social Work* 62 (3): 1146–1158. 10.1177/0020872818768387

Miller, Vivian J., and HeeSoon Lee. 2020. "Social Work Values in Action during COVID-19." *Journal of Gerontological Social Work* 63 (6–7): 565–569. 10.1080/01634372.2020.1769792

Nilssen, Laura. 2020. "Social Work and the Future in a Post-Covid 19 World: A Foresight Lens and a Call to Action for the Profession." *Journal of Technology in Human Services* 38 (4): 309–330. 10.1080/15228835.2020.1796892

Plagg, Barbara, Adolf Engl, Giuliano Piccoliori, and Klaus Eisendle. 2020. "Prolonged Social Isolation of the Elderly during COVID-19: Between Benefit and Damage." *Archives of Gerontology and Geriatrics* 89: 104086. 10.1016/j.archger.2020.104086

Pugh, Richard. 2003. "Considering the Countryside: Is There a Case for Rural Social Work?" *British Journal of Social Work* 33 (1): 67–85. 10.1093/bjsw/33.1.67

Ramaci, Tiziana, Massimiliano Barattucci, Caterina Ledda, and Venerando Rapisarda. 2020. "Social Stigma during COVID-19 and Its Impact on HCWs Outcomes." *Sustainability* 12 (9): 3834. 10.3390/su12093834

Rubin, Allen, and Earl R. Babbie. 2014. *Research Methods for Social Work*. 8th edition. Brooks/Cole Cengage Learning.

Rüütel, Kristi, Liisi Panov, Olga Sadikova, Jevgenia Epštein, Hanna Sepp, Mari-Anne Härma. 2020. *COVID-19 Situation in Estonia. The First Half of 2020*. Tallinn: Health Board, National Institute for Health Development.

Taylor, Steven, Caleigh A. Landry, Geoffrey S. Rachor, Michelle M. Paluszek, and Gordon J.G. Asmundsen. 2020. "Fear and Avoidance of Healthcare Workers: An Important, Under-Recognized Form of Stigmatization during the COVID-19 Pandemic." *Journal of Anxiety Disorders* 75: 102289. 10.1016/j.janxdis.2020.102289

Turbett, Colin. 2009. "Tensions in the Delivery of Social Work Services in Rural and Remote Scotland." *British Journal of Social Work* 39 (3): 506–521. https://www.jstor.org/stable/23724386.

van Leeuwen, Theo. 2008. *Discourse and Practice: New Tools for Critical D iscourse Analysis*. Oxford: Oxford University Press.

Walsh, Kieran, and Eamon O'Shea. 2008. "Responding to Rural Social Care Needs: Older People Empowering Themselves, Others and their Community." *Health & Place* 14 (4): 795–805. 10.1016/j.healthplace.2007.12.006

Walter-McCabe, Heather A. 2020. "Coronavirus Pandemic Calls for an Immediate Social Work Response." *Social Work in Public Health* 35 (3): 69–72. 10.1080/19371918.2020.1751533

Wang, Cancan, Rony Medaglia, and Lei Zheng. 2018. "Towards a Typology of Adaptive Governance in the Digital Government Context: The Role of Decision-making and Accountability." *Government Information Quarterly* 35 (2): 306–322. 10.1016/j.giq.2017.08.003

Young, Jason C. 2019. "Rural Digital Geographies and New Landscapes of Social Resilience." *Journal of Rural Studies* 70: 66–74. 10.1016/j.jrurstud.2019.07.001

# 7 Teams Interrupted: Social Work Teams as Communities of Practice and Coping during COVID-19

*Laura L. Cook and Sara Carder*

## The social work team as a community of practice

Etienne Wenger's (1998) concept of Communities of Practice (CoP) emphasises the role of social interaction in the construction and transmission of knowledge. For Wenger (1998, 73) a CoP consists of three defining characteristics: domain, community, and practice. Practice development occurs in a social context as group members are drawn together by a joint enterprise or activity known as a 'domain', and through mutual engagement over time form a 'community' in which a shared repertoire or 'practice' is created (Wenger 1998, 73). Wenger observed one such CoP forming among nurses, where lunchtime discussions in the cafeteria served as 'one of their main sources of knowledge' about how to care for patients. These informal discussions conveyed the tacit, shared repertoire of their highly specialist practice. Hearing and watching experienced workers share anecdotes and ways around recurrent problems enabled less experienced members to master the skills of the trade from core members.

There are distinct parallels between CoP and the functioning of social work teams, which have been recognised as a key space for decision-making and practice expertise in child welfare social work (Helm and Roesch-Marsh 2017; Helm 2016; Saltiel 2016). Like Wenger's nurses, practice within social work teams consists of highly specialised, often localised expertise with 'privileged knowledge' of the needs of families in the neighbourhoods and communities they serve (Jeyasingham 2018, 87). Conversations and 'backstage case talk' in the office help workers to 'frame' complex information (Helm 2016, 26), assess risk (Saltiel 2016), and make sense of complex or 'borderline' cases in child welfare (Cook and Gregory 2020; Doherty 2017). For this reason, the team has been identified as an essential part of the 'ecology of judgement' in social work (Helm and Roesch-Marsh 2017). Crucially, research has also shown that like Wenger's nurses at lunch, social work teams develop specific artefacts, such as practice-based stories to codify and transmit 'practice wisdom' among social workers, such as how to recognise subtle signs that a child may be at risk, or how to raise a sensitive topic with a family (Cook 2020).

Central to the concept of CoP is a model of social learning (Lave and Wenger 1991). Through social interaction with members of the CoP, learners master the

DOI: 10.4324/9781003374374-9

skills of the trade from core members—a process which Jean Lave and Etienne Wenger (1991, 29) terms 'legitimate peripheral participation'. Similarly, the social work team provides key learning opportunities for less experienced members, such as social work students, newly qualified social workers (NQSWs) and new team members. Vicarious learning has been identified as a core component of social work education, where 'learning on the job' and exposure to the 'practice wisdom' of experienced team colleagues is key to professional development (Scourfield and Pithouse 2006, 331). Shadowing experienced workers, co-working cases, or simply listening to experienced workers talk about their work provides opportunities for legitimate peripheral participation (Lave and Wenger 1991). In this way, social work teams can provide a CoP for social workers, supporting professional socialisation and the development of practice.

## The social work team as a community of coping

Alongside knowledge and practice, social work involves an additional component—emotional labour (Winter et al. 2019). We therefore introduce a second, related concept to our framework for understanding social work teams; Korczynski's (2003) Communities of Coping.

In his ethnographic study of call centres in Australia and America, Korczynski (2003, 58) observed that support from team colleagues allowed workers to 'survive the systematic tensions of their working days'. He noted that responding to customers, particularly those who were hostile, involved emotional labour, a concept originating from Hochschild's (1983) seminal study of airline attendants. Hochschild observed that airline attendants managed their display of emotions to fit with the 'feeling rules' of the workplace, such as feigning a smile when dealing with a difficult customer. Similarly, Korczynski's call centre workers engaged in emotional labour as they made the adjustment needed to respond with polite enthusiasm to irate customers. Although Hochschild's work briefly touched on what she termed 'collective emotional labour' the focus was largely on individual workers. Korczynski therefore extended Hochschild's concept to emphasise the collective aspect of the emotional labour of front-line service work.

For Korczynski's call centre workers, emotions engendered by customers could 'rebound round the whole team' (Korczynski 2003, 66). In response to this, workers both received and provided support to each other, forming Communities of Coping (ComC). These ComCs were informal, spontaneous, and outside of management control, where workers drew on humour, camaraderie, venting, and reassurance to manage the emotional demands of their work. In her study of Danish family law case workers, Stroebaek (2013, 381) noted that ComC were 'created through coffee break encounters', in the 'backstage' areas of the workplace including kitchens and smoking areas, away from the gaze of clients and managers. Whilst Korczynski (2003, 68) argued that ComC plays a vital role in managing the emotional demands of the work, he also identified ComC could become 'communities of antipathy' where cynicism and derogatory language could be used to cope with emotionally painful encounters with customers.

There are distinct parallels between ComC and the functioning of social work teams. Emotional labour has increasingly been recognised as part of social work practice. The intrusive nature of their work with families means that social workers often experience hostility and anger in their day-to-day work, requiring a professional, tempered response. As Winter et al. (2019, 230) observe, social work teams are: '[...] essentially spaces in which social workers can share with peers aspects of emotional labour and its impact'.

Existing research suggests that the team provides a 'secure base' for social workers (Biggart et al. 2017; Winter et al. 2019), helping them to process and manage these emotional demands. The shared office and backstage areas such as kitchens and cigarette breaks can provide the conditions for empathic ComC for social workers. However, like Korzsynski's call centre workers, social work teams can also adopt collective cynicism and antipathy. For instance, teams may use gallows humour (Sullivan 2000) or cynical talk about families (Cook 2020) as a way of coping. We now outline our research on social work teams, using the concepts of CoPs and ComC to consider how teams functioned during the COVID-19 pandemic.

## The research

On Monday 23 March 2020, the English government announced a period of lockdown in response to COVID-19. Excepting essential statutory child protection duties, social workers in England were directed to work from home. While the use of digital technology and agile working is not entirely new to social work teams, the pandemic rapidly accelerated the hybrid model of virtual and face-to-face practice. Below we outline two research studies undertaken in England, which taken together provide a detailed qualitative picture of social work teams during the first year of the pandemic.

Study 1 was undertaken between March and June 2020 and was part of a wider study on the retention of experienced social workers in child protection social work. The research was granted ethical approval from the University of East Anglia (UEA) Research Ethics Committee, the Association of Directors of Children's Services and, where required, from research governance panels of participating local authorities. At the start of the pandemic, the author was carrying out interviews with social workers from several local authorities in England focusing on their career histories. However, as the pandemic hit, social workers experienced rapid changes to their working conditions and found themselves isolated from their team colleagues. They naturally began to talk about these experiences with the researchers. An amendment was approved by the Ethics Committee to gather additional data on social workers' experiences during the first wave of the pandemic. Social workers were therefore interviewed about their experiences of practice in the context of COVID-19 and the findings from this data are reported in this chapter. Semi-structured telephone interviews were conducted with 31 child and family social workers from nine local authorities across England. To capture a range of experiences, the sample included social workers across a range of roles and levels of seniority. The sample included two service managers, team managers, ten senior social workers, and nine social workers. The interviews were recorded, transcribed, and analysed using Virginia Braun and Victoria Clarke's (2006) six-stage model of thematic analysis. A recurrent theme was the impact of remote, virtual working on their access to team support. Social workers' perspectives on practice with vulnerable children and families are considered elsewhere (Cook and Zschomler 2020). The findings reported here focus on their views of team support.

Study 2 was undertaken between September 2020 and March 2021, when hybrid working was more established. This study was granted ethical approval by the UEA research committee and from the two participating local authorities. This ethnographic study was focused on how teams support social workers to manage the emotional demands of practice. It used hybrid ethnographic methods to capture the experiences of two child protection teams. At the start of the pandemic, the research was already underway in the two local authority sites. This meant that the researcher was well-positioned to observe how the two teams adapted as the pandemic unfolded. The findings reported here draw on 30 hours of observations which included the social work office and formal and informal virtual spaces created by the team using Microsoft Teams. In addition, 21 semi-structured individual interviews were undertaken with team members, from manager to student social worker followed by a group team interview. The combination of ethnographic observation and interviews enabled the researcher to identify how teamwork changed during the pandemic as well as how individual team members experienced these changes. Observations and interviews were recorded, transcribed, and analysed using Lyn Brown and Carol Gilligan's (1992) analytical framework the 'Listening Guide'.

A thematic synthesis of data was undertaken from each of the studies, focusing on social workers' perspectives on team support during COVID-19. These themes fell into two categories—firstly, themes around knowledge, decision-making, and practice, and secondly, emotional well-being, support, and belonging. This fitted with the concepts of Communities of Practice and Communities of Coping respectively which we subsequently used as a framework to conceptualise the findings. These concepts were chosen based on 'best fit' with the data from the two studies. While relevance of Communities of Practice for social work has received some prior attention (Cook-Craig and Sabah, 2009; Moore, 2008) the application of Communities of Coping to social work teams is novel.

## Findings

### *The team as a community of practice (CoP) during COVID-19*

Pre-pandemic, the social work team could provide a CoP for social workers, where interactions between team members facilitated learning, decision-making, and the development of practice. However, as COVID-19 unfolded, new working arrangements limited the availability of team members. Pre-pandemic, the office was an important space for reflection, *ad hoc* discussions and the exchange of practice wisdom. As one social worker stated:

> Before you could quite easily just turn around and ... there's someone the other side ... you can have that conversation with (Social Worker, Study 2).

However, during the pandemic some social workers began to work from home exclusively, while others accessed the office with new social distancing restrictions. This affected interactions with colleagues, which in turn impacted practice. As one worker stated:

> If you don't have that face-to-face contact with people, you lose those relationships [...] you lose that confidence [...] picking up the phone to a worker and explaining the situation is very different to going back to the office and seeing a social worker [so] you can talk about something [...] it comes naturally, whereas having to pick up the phone [...] you think twice about who you're going to phone ... you lose the momentum of what's going on (Social Worker, Study 1).

Loss of professional confidence was a common theme among social workers, whose spontaneous interactions with colleagues were limited by the pandemic. Previously, the team was an important part of the 'ecology of judgement' (Helm and Roesch-Marsh 2017) providing a space to resolve and unpick 'borderline' or complex cases (Doherty 2017). However, as these ad hoc discussions were now limited, social workers reported an impact on their capacity to make effective decisions, particularly regarding risk. For instance, one social worker noted that all her assessments were 'coming out positive' which was highly unusual. With fewer opportunities to revise their judgement with colleagues, some social workers were concerned that decisions they had made during COVID-19 were less robust.

In response to these challenges, social work teams began to construct new, online spaces for ad hoc discussion. These spaces functioned as virtual CoP. Team members could 'drop in' with no fixed agenda to exchange practice knowledge or reflect on their work which partially mitigated the need to 'second-guess' the decision to seek advice. However, whilst useful, increased virtual working represented an additional cognitive burden for some workers, who experienced Zoom fatigue and information overload as a result.

An unexpected and positive outcome of increased virtual working was that it prompted an extension of the CoP beyond the confines of the team. Team boundaries became more porous with greater inclusion of other professionals:

> The social work has been much more interactive ... I think there's been a lot more communication amongst professionals [...] I don't know whether they find [...] attending meetings easier via having video [...] rather than directly [...] (Social Worker, Study 1).

This was a point made by many social workers—the increased uptake of online communication meant that professionals from other disciplines (e.g. health, criminal justice, education) were more likely to attend virtual meetings. This in turn increased opportunities for interprofessional learning. However, where social interaction was limited, practice development could be stymied. Since social-distancing limited interactions between team members, social workers experienced a sense of professional inertia:

> I definitely feel quite isolated [...] there is a loss of shared knowledge and information [...] it feels like a real loss of knowledge [...] because there are some really interesting conversations that we have with each other and other cases that you get to hear about that you learn from. I've probably felt a bit stagnant in that sense (Practice Manager, Study 2).

While the issue of professional inertia was an issue for experienced professionals, it was felt most acutely by NQSWs. Prior to the pandemic, simply being in the office could provide important vicarious learning opportunities for NQSWs, such as shadowing a colleague on a home visit, or hearing an experienced worker make a difficult phone call. However, as the pandemic unfolded, increasingly hybrid working led to fewer opportunities for 'legitimate peripheral participation' (Lave and Wenger 1991):

> [...] it is difficult ... you've got to maintain the distance [...] normally [...] you would be close to each other, it's a lot easier to learn whereas now, everything is done distantly [...] it makes it a lot harder, and it takes longer to get on those levels [...] it does affect how you can work (Social Work Student, Study 2).

Social workers expressed concern that opportunities for 'learning on the job' (Scourfield and Pithouse 2006) could not be replicated when working remotely. This affected the process of professional socialisation among newer workers, many of whom reported reduced confidence in their practice. Some NQSWs even began to question their 'fit' as social worker:

> I find it really hard not knowing what I'm doing [...] because of how we're learning at the moment. For example, someone will say 'can you put a referral into this thing'. I don't know how to do that [...] then they have to try and explain that whilst not being near you or doing it online [...] it makes things so difficult [...] It just makes me feel a bit like, oh, maybe I'm not doing the right job [...] (Student Social Worker, Study 2).

This point was also echoed by more experienced social workers, who expressed concern that in the context of remote working, struggling NQSWs could become invisible:

The only thing you've got to be careful of [...] certainly for younger social workers [...] it only takes two or three cases to go over a cliff [...] without the right support people just become isolated and the work drops off [...] I have seen that, some people don't talk about it, and it's only by observing people perhaps in an office situation that you can realise that they're getting into difficulties [...] (Social Worker, Study 1).

COVID-19 brought unexpected challenges as well as benefits to the functioning of the team as a CoP, this was also evident when considering the team as a source of emotional support, explored next.

### The team as a community of coping during the pandemic

Prior to the pandemic, the social work team could function as a ComC for social workers (Korczynski 2003). The 'backstage' areas of the team environment served as important spaces for collective emotional labour where camaraderie, venting, and humour could be spontaneously shared. However, the pandemic created an initial sense of isolation from colleagues:

I think it's very intense working from home, I think what you find is, you are the only one in front of that screen; you are not part of a team (Social worker, Study 1).

Paradoxically, the loss of connection from colleagues through home working also brought with it an increased sense of boundary invasion which added to the emotional burden social workers experienced. Child and family social workers often need to consider emotive and distressing issues, such as child abuse and neglect. Working online at home meant that these issues invaded social worker's private space. For instance, one social worker spoke vividly of:

[...] the darkness that social work can bring in to your own home (Social Worker, Study 1).

Typically, increased homeworking was coupled with fewer opportunities to access the office. There were also restrictions on seating, desks, access to kitchens and informal meeting spaces. These new physical boundaries created a different 'feel' to the workplace, as this ethnographic observation highlights:

Large perspex screens were positioned at the end of each set of desks [...] Some chairs were wrapped in red and white tape [...] 'Not to be used' makeshift laminated signs were hung from a nearby coat rack [...] The Team Manager tells me that only 8 members of the team are allowed into the building at any one time, the reason being 'COVID stuff' (Observation one, Study 2).

These physical barriers created psychological barriers, leading to a sense of disconnection from colleagues:

> I feel like I'm in a movie [...] the atmosphere in the office is definitely different. Before COVID the office used to have a real buzz [...] it is definitely affecting everyone's mental health [...] I was never an extrovert, but I definitely think I have become more of an introvert [...] it's difficult to interact when you come into the office [...] having to adapt [...] it's weird [...] these screens definitely don't help [...] I feel cut off (Social Worker, Study 2).

However, this sense of isolation spurred an immediate flurry of activity among teams to recreate their ComC online. While some teams did have informal online spaces pre-pandemic, during COVID-19 these became more significant. WhatsApp groups for informal chat, online breakfasts, quizzes, and virtual 'water cooler' (social worker, study 1) meetings facilitated the sort of backstage talk that previously occurred in kitchens or smoking areas:

> [...] Every day in the office we would go into the kitchen and get water, so when you're in the kitchen you would meet with other people from the other rooms and have that chat. We've created that in this [Microsoft] Teams thing [...] so the staff can just dial into this meeting and chat about anything they want, really (Social worker, Study 1).

These informal online spaces enabled social workers to vent, share experiences, provide emotional support, and share a sense of solidarity both in relation to the work and the challenges of the pandemic. Post-work drinks at the pub were replaced by online events to de-stress after a difficult day:

> So, we have a lot of pub nights, obviously, before COVID [...] if you've had a bad day or if someone else has had a bad day, it's just quite nice to talk about it with people that [...] know what you're going through and what the job is like [...] when COVID hit, we were doing house parties and things like that, so staying in contact virtually [...] (Social Worker, Study 2).

Korczynski (2003) suggested that ComC were typically outside management control, informally created between workers and sometimes subversive. In this research, however, it was evident that team managers played an active and conscious role in creating and supporting new backstage areas for mutual support, as well as online opportunities to promote team relationships:

> We're [...] doing a Tik Tok talk about bonding, we're going to do our TikTok and then the manager is going to put it together with a little video (Social Worker, Study 1).

The increase in virtual spaces for informal discussion and emotional support enabled teams to function as ComC for social workers during the pandemic. However, this also came with challenges. Pre-pandemic, team interactions were largely limited to the physical space of the office. However, as the ComC moved online, contact with colleagues was possible from home, outside of working hours:

> After office hours they would all be on the WhatsApp group [...] it gave me anxiety [...] in normal life, pre-COVID [...] my office mobile wouldn't be switched on after working hours [...] They say [...] 'make sure you keep in touch with your work colleagues' [...] I've found that a little bit too heavy [...] (Social Worker, Study 1).

For some, the initial shift to virtual team contact meant that rather than acting as a ComC, the team became a source of emotional stress. The worker above was relieved that after the initial flurry of online interaction post-lockdown, the contact began to 'peter out' and become less of a psychological burden. A key aspect of ComC is that they occur spontaneously and in response to the ebb and flow of the emotional demands of the work. This was more difficult online. For instance, one worker observed how:

> [...] you don't know that you need to talk about things, but somebody just picks it up and goes, 'Are you alright, do you want a coffee?' and it might just be enough to set you off [...] (Senior Practitioner, Study 2).

There was also a risk that workers who were struggling could succumb to the temptation to withdraw from online spaces in a way that would be more difficult in person. For team managers, this created a need to be proactive in instigating a 'cameras on' culture for remote working:

> You can hide a lot behind a screen [...] there are times when I go into a call with [team manager] [...] and if I haven't got my camera up, we're not starting that conversation until the camera is up. I think that's quite good because if you are having a bad day it's very easy just to think, oh, I can't be bothered, let's just make it quick, but no, she doesn't allow that (Social Worker, Study 2).

Despite these challenges, in some cases, the physical disconnection from team members created a desire for greater relational connection. Within some teams, the frequency of interaction increased:

> [...] I'm seeing my staff more than I would if I was in the office, because they're in their house and I can just phone them up and we can wave at each other [...] it's improved [...] because I see more of them [...] But, yes, I supervise staff that I just never would have seen as much as I have now, because we check in every day [...] (Social Worker, Study 1).

As well as increased frequency, the adoption of video-calling meant the nature of these interactions changed. Social workers' homes and families, which had been part of their private life, were now visible to the team:

> It's hard to remember what it was like before [COVID-19] [...] some of the people in the team I don't see outside of work, so getting to see them in their homes [...] even just little things, their doorbell might ring [...] and then that leads to a different conversation [...] you get to know people's families as well, which was something maybe with members of the team I didn't know before [...] so I think that's really allowed us to get to know each other more on a personal level (Social Worker, Study 2).

Getting to know colleagues on a more personal level strengthened the team as a ComC. On the other hand, the boundary between work and home became blurred. Prior to COVID, the social worker's home was 'backstage'—a place where to which they could retreat, providing respite from the need to perform their professional identity. However, as this virtual observation highlights, workers now had to consider how to stage their home in professional encounters:

> [The social worker] is sitting in a home space [...] the door behind her is open, with a drying rack hanging from it with what looks like a red dressing gown. She appears to notice this by looking at her own space reflected in the computer screen and quickly gets up, pulls the item of clothing off the door and throws it out of sight. 'I just noticed my dress was hanging up, gotta move that' she says, as she sits back down (Observation 3, Study Two).

These staging decisions were not always straightforward—for instance, one worker described how a colleague joined a meeting sipping water from a glass bottle. As it resembled an alcohol bottle, this had attracted criticism from other professionals. Despite these challenges, for some workers the team began to play a new role during the pandemic. Previously the team had functioned as a ComC in relation to the work, however, it also came to function as a ComC in relation to the anxieties and stresses associated with the pandemic. The team therefore began to serve a compensatory function, acting as a substitute family and source of support for workers separated from family and friends. Communal team lunches, often involving cake and other 'treats', now had a sense of emotional significance and occasion:

> [...] People had got into really bad habits of not having lunch, you know, you're away from your desk a lot of the time [...] It's just, sort of, developed much more over COVID, this ordering food in together [...] And, I suppose, where people aren't seeing friends and family outside of work [...] this time that we spend together in the office has actually become really much more important for people, and lunch is a time to do that (Team Manager, Study 2).

As our research has shown, the social work team as both a CoP and a ComC was impacted upon by the pandemic. The capacity of the team to provide both learning and emotional support to its members created both challenges and unexpected benefits which have left a legacy that has in some ways, shaped the future of social work practice.

## The future: Social work teams as Communities of Practice and Coping post-pandemic

As with any research, there are some limitations. Firstly, the research was carried out during the early stages of the pandemic and may not therefore reflect current practice. However, there are some distinct benefits to capturing this period of rapid 'forced' innovation. The practices of virtual working adopted at the start of the pandemic are now routine, but as we shall explain below, these would benefit from some critical evaluation. Secondly, the two studies employed different methodologies, which makes comparisons between teams difficult. The disparity in methods reflects the opportunistic nature of the studies—both researchers were already engaged in data collection with social work teams during the start of the pandemic, which provided a unique opportunity to capture the impact of COVID-19 on social work as it unfolded. While our claims to generalisability to all teams must remain modest, the research provides a unique, in-depth qualitative picture of social workers' perspectives during a period of historic change.

The concepts of CoP (Wenger 1998) and ComC (Korczynski 2003) provide a useful framework for considering the functions of social work teams. This is supported by existing research, which suggests that interactions within social work teams play a vital role in professional practice, learning, and coping (Biggart et al. 2017; Helm 2016; Saltiel 2016). Consistent with this, our findings suggested that as *ad hoc* interactions between team members were limited by the pandemic, professionals reported their confidence, well-being and practice to be adversely affected. However, we also found that social work teams are adaptable and can function as Communities of Practice and Coping in a hybrid climate if adjustments are made.

The findings suggest that the creation of unscheduled, virtual spaces for reflection can afford new opportunities for learning, peer-aided decision-making, and practice development. They can also allow workers to connect with colleagues in a different way, mitigating the isolation of remote working. However, it was clear that such online spaces could only *partially* replicate being with peers in the office. In order to capitalise on the benefits of remote working, while also avoiding the drawbacks (such as Zoom fatigue and blurring of home/work boundaries) local authorities must offer flexibility. There was particular concern among social workers about the speed and permanence of changes to their working conditions. Some social workers reported that their local authorities were seeking to dramatically reduce, or even remove office space given the perceived success of remote working. However, the message was clear: although social work teams can *survive* as communities of practice and coping when working remotely, *thriving* involves a combination of in-person and remote working.

Lave and Wenger's (1991) concept of legitimate peripheral participation suggests that learning takes place through doing, observing, and participation in a CoP at all levels of experience. Our findings suggest that in an increasingly hybrid working climate, special consideration needs to be given to the professional socialisation and development of all social workers, particularly for newly qualified workers. This could include opportunities for virtual shadowing of experienced workers and ensuring that office time is built into the planning for NQSWs. More broadly, professional development plans for all social workers need to consider the increasingly hybrid context of post-pandemic practice with opportunities for vicarious and in-person learning clearly specified and delineated.

The team became increasingly important as a ComC (Korczynski 2003) during the pandemic as workers turned to colleagues to manage not only the demands of practice (Biggart et al. 2017) but also the personal impact of the pandemic. The extent to which the team could provide support was dependent on the team culture around virtual communication. These unspoken rules were established during the first few weeks of the pandemic and tended to persist. For instance, some teams had a 'cameras on' culture for video calls, while others adopted an audio-only approach. Not 'seeing' colleagues greatly impacted social workers' ability to pick up on their emotional support needs. Similarly, the patterns and rhythms of online team interactions tended to be established early on. While some social workers described this changing over time, for many these patterns of interaction simply became the new normal. It is therefore important for teams and organisations to conduct a thorough review of hybrid practices adopted at the start of the pandemic. For individual teams, the concepts of Communities of Practice and Coping may provide a framework for reviewing, evaluating, and adjusting their teamworking practices in the increasingly hybrid working climate of COVID-19.

# References

Biggart, Laura, Emma Ward, Laura Cook, and Gillian Schofield. 2017. "The Team as a Secure Base: Promoting Resilience and Competence in Child and Family Social Work." *Children and Youth Services Review* 83: 119–130. 10.1016/j.childyouth.2017.10.031

Braun, Virginia, and Victoria Clarke. 2006. "Using Thematic Analysis in Psychology." *Qualitative Research in Psychology* 3 (2): 77–101. 10.1191/1478088706qp063oa

Brown, Lyn M., and Carol Gilligan. 1992. *Meeting at the Crossroads: Women's Psychology and Girls' Development*. Cambridge: Harvard University Press.

Cook, Laura L. 2020. "Storytelling among Child Welfare Social Workers: Constructing Professional Role and Resilience through Team Talk." *Qualitative Social Work* 19 (5–6): 968–986. 10.1177/1473325019865014

Cook, Laura, and Mark Gregory. 2020. "Making Sense of Sensemaking: Conceptualising How Child and Family Social Workers Process Assessment Information." *Childcare in Practice* 26 (2): 182–195. 10.1080/13575279.2019.1685458

Cook, Laura, and Danny Zschomler. 2020. "Virtual Home Visits during the COVID-19 Pandemic: Social Workers' Perspectives." *Practice* 32 (5): 401–408. 10.1080/09503153. 2020.1836142

Cook-Craig, Patricia G., and Yekoutiel Sabah. 2009. "The Role of Virtual Communities of Practice in Supporting Collaborative Learning among Social Workers." *The British Journal of Social Work* 39 (4): 725–739. 10.1093/bjsw/bcp048

Doherty, Paula. 2017. "Child Protection Threshold Talk and Ambivalent Case Formulations in 'Borderline' Care Proceedings Cases." *Qualitative Social Work* 16 (5): 698–716. 10. 1177/1473325016640062

Helm, Duncan. 2016. "Sense-making in a Social Work Office: An Ethnographic Study of Safeguarding Judgements." *Child and Family Social work* 21 (1): 26–35. 10.1111/cfs.12101

Helm, Duncan, and Autumn Roesch-Marsh. 2017. "The Ecology of Judgement: A Model for Understanding and Improving Social Work Judgments." *The British Journal of Social Work* 47 (5): 1361–1376. 10.1093/bjsw/bcw091

Hochschild, Arlie R. 1983. *The Managed Heart: Commercialization of Human Feeling.* Berkeley: University of California Press.

Jeyasingham, Dharman. 2018. "Place and the Uncanny in Child Protection Social Work: Exploring Findings from an Ethnographic Study." *Qualitative Social Work* 17 (1): 81–95. 10.1177/1473325016657867

Korczynski, Marek. 2003. "Communities of Coping: Collective Emotional Labour in Service Work." *Organization* 10 (1): 55–79. 10.1177/1350508403010001479

Lave, Jean, and Etienne Wenger. 1991. *Situated Learning: Legitimate Peripheral Participation.* Cambridge: Cambridge University Press.

Moore, Brenda. 2008. "Using Technology to Promote Communities of Practice (CoP) in Social Work Education." *Social Work Education* 27 (6): 592–600. 10.1080/026154 70802201580

Saltiel, David. 2016. "Observing Frontline Decision-making in Child Protection." *The British Journal of Social Work* 46 (7): 2104–2119. 10.1093/bjsw/bcv112

Scourfield, Jonathan, and Andrew Pithouse. 2006. "Lay and Professional Knowledge in Social Work: Reflections from Ethnographic Work on Child Protection." *European Journal of Social Work* 9 (3): 323–337.

Stroebaek, Pernille S. 2013. "Let's Have a Cup of Coffee! Coffee and Coping Communities at Work." *Symbolic Interaction* 36 (4): 381–397. 10.1002/symb.76

Sullivan, Elizabeth. 2000. "Gallows Humour in Social Work Practice: An Issue for Supervision and Reflexivity." *Practice: Social Work in Action* 12 (2): 45–54. 10.1080/ 09503150008415183.

Wenger, Etienne. 1998. *Communities of Practice: Learning, Meaning and Identity.* New York: Cambridge University Press.

Winter, Karen, Fiona Morrison, Viviene Cree, Gillian Ruch, Mark Hadfield, and Sophie Hallett. 2019. "Emotional Labour in Social Workers' Encounters with Children and Their Families." *The British Journal of Social Work* 49 (1): 217–233. 10.1093/bjsw/bcy016

# 8 Social Work during Crises: Good Practices and Bottlenecks According to Social Workers in Flanders, Belgium

*Michiel Massart, Inge Pasteels, Kim Bastaits, and Bart Put*

## The government's responses to COVID-19 in Belgium and challenges for social work

Compared to other Member States, and even from a global perspective, Belgium was hit very hard (in relative terms) by the COVID-19 virus. The strategy chosen by the national government to tackle the spread of the virus was aimed at shutting down most of the public life in Belgium and was even frequently referred to as a 'lockdown light'. It entailed among other things the closure of educational institutions, bars, cafes, restaurants, museums, fun parks, 'non-essential' shops, a general ban on organised social events (i.e., sports, culture, religion), as well as firm restrictions on the number of people allowed to gather informally and on 'non-essential' movements in the public space (both inside the country, as well as cross-border), and the obligation for everyone to telework except for who works at an essential organisation[1] (Federale overheid 2020a). This strategy was also adopted in many other European countries during the first wave in March and April of 2020 (e.g., Ireland, Finland, Estonia, etc.), and fell somewhat between the very strict strategy adopted in Italy and the more liberal approach taken by the Swedish government.

Specifically, with regard to social work and its clientele, a number of government actions and decisions should be mentioned. Firstly, from the very first start of the pandemic, communication about the need for extra attention to specific groups has been pervasive. Compliance with health and safety measures, for instance, was emphasised as being even more crucial in the proximity of physically vulnerable people, such as elderly, people suffering from lung diseases, chronic illnesses, or immune disorders. These people are most likely to develop serious illness or die as a result of a COVID-19 infection (Federale overheid 2020b). Secondly, a Ministerial Decree was issued granting many organisations and sectors employing social workers the status of an 'essential service' (e.g., services providing care for elderly, minors, people with disabilities, or other vulnerable persons such as victims of domestic violence), thus exempting them from the formal obligation to telework[1]. However, the same document urges all essential services to re-organise their operations in such a way that the basic

DOI: 10.4324/9781003374374-10

health and safety guidelines are respected as much as possible, including a shift to telework if possible, adherence to social distancing rules, and so on. Thirdly, very early into the crisis, both federal and regional governments took a whole range of measures to avoid people from falling into poverty and experiencing difficulties with access to basic goods and services, such as schemes aimed at alleviating loss of income caused by temporary unemployment, mortgage repayment postponement for certain groups, a moratorium on evictions, continuity in the services for homeless (Steunpunt tot bestrijding van armoede, bestaansonzekerheid en sociale uitsluiting 2020). Fourthly, as part of the launch of the 'Federal phase' of the crisis (Federale overheid 2020a), two new government bodies were established: the Working Group Social Impact COVID-19 Crisis (WG SIC) and the Taskforce Vulnerable Groups, charged with the monitoring of the social impact of the crisis (measures) (WG SIC) and the provision of advice and input for COVID-19 related policy measures concerning vulnerable groups (Taskforce) respectively (Federale overheid s.d.; POD Maatschappelijke Integratie 2020).

It is clear that such initiatives have created significant challenges for social workers and clients. Social work values, ethics, and practice have been challenged, not only in Belgium (Blomme et al. 2020; Bocklandt 2020; Debruyne et al. 2020; Kinderrechtencommissariaat 2020; Maenhout 2021; Nijs et al. 2020; Schepens et al. 2020; University of Antwerp 2020a, 2020b) but worldwide (Amadasun 2020, 754–755; Dominelli et al. 2020; Ham 2020; Harrikari et al. 2021; Richardson et al. 2020; Walter-McCabe 2020, 69–71). In addition, social work is also expected to continue to play an important role in post-pandemic actions. Studies such as the one presented here can therefore be of great value, as the chapter focuses on the dynamics or adaptations that social workers in Flanders, Belgium, experienced during this crisis and on what they would like to preserve in the future ('good practices'), as well as the challenges or barriers ('bottlenecks') they experienced and would like to eliminate.

## A comprehensive survey in the broad landscape of social work in Flanders, Belgium

Collection of the data took tween 6 April and 4 May 2020. Data were collected using a standardised questionnaire in the form of an online survey. Invitations to participate in the survey were distributed via two channels. On the one hand, social sector stakeholders were contacted with whom the *Anonymous*[2] department as well as the *Anonymous* centre had collaborated in the past. On the other hand, organisations were selected from an existing directory of social organisations in Flanders and Brussels, called 'de sociale kaart' (the social map). This directory contains an overview of care facilities and care providers in Flanders and Brussels. We selected all organisations from this directory except for organisations specialised in physical health care, residential mental health care, health care professions (except for remedial education professionals), nursing homes, police, courts, lawyers, job placement services, and special needs education. These subsectors were excluded because they mainly employ other professional groups than social workers.

In order to reach the right persons within the organisations (contacted by email), we provided a description of the target group by way of an address to 'social workers or other professionals active in the broad field of social work'. This resulted in the participation of 2815 respondents, out of which 1703 fully completed their questionnaires. The findings discussed below result from a thematic coding analysis of the answers to the following open questions: '*What dynamics or adaptations related to your job or organisation emerged during the COVID-19 crisis and would you like to preserve after the COVID-19 crisis?*' and '*What challenges or barriers related to your job or organisation did you experience during the COVID-19 crisis and would you like to eliminate structurally?*' The first question (RQ1) was answered by 1717 respondents and the second question (RQ2) was answered by 1584 respondents. The sectoral characteristics of the realised sample for this question can be found in Table 8.1; respondents can belong to more than one (sub)sector.

*Table 8.1* Sectorial characteristics of the realised sample for the research question

| Sector | RQ1 | | RQ2 | |
|---|---|---|---|---|
| | N | Percentage | N | Percentage |
| General social welfare | 841 | 49.0 | 782 | 49.4 |
| Children and families | 284 | 16.5 | 263 | 16.6 |
| Youth care | 214 | 12.5 | 196 | 12.9 |
| Poverty and deprivation | 213 | 12.4 | 205 | 12.4 |
| Youth work | 208 | 12.1 | 186 | 11.7 |
| Disabilities | 183 | 10.7 | 163 | 10.3 |
| Mental health care | 169 | 9.8 | 155 | 9.8 |
| Governmental | 150 | 8.7 | 150 | 8.7 |
| Elderly care | 142 | 8.3 | 138 | 9.5 |
| Budget councelling | 131 | 7.6 | 124 | 7.8 |
| Home care | 118 | 6.9 | 116 | 7.3 |
| Housing/social housing | 115 | 6.7 | 111 | 7.0 |
| Work and (social) economy | 113 | 6.6 | 99 | 6.3 |
| Education and training | 96 | 5.6 | 88 | 5.6 |
| Homeless care | 88 | 5.1 | 87 | 5.5 |
| Migration and integration | 85 | 5.0 | 88 | 5.6 |
| Community development | 83 | 4.8 | 75 | 4.7 |
| Culture and leisure | 65 | 3.8 | 56 | 3.5 |
| Justice | 58 | 3.4 | 55 | 3.5 |
| Relationships and sexuality | 51 | 3.0 | 43 | 2.7 |
| Physical health care | 33 | 1.9 | 35 | 2.2 |
| Legal services | 31 | 1.8 | 24 | 1.5 |
| Living environment and international cooperation | 6 | 0.3 | 6 | 0.4 |
| Other | 49 | 2.9 | 41 | 2.6 |

The thematic coding analysis was based on a grounded theory approach (Glaser and Strauss 1967): categories were constructed on the basis of the reading and analysis of the content itself, without a fixed set of pre-established categories to guide the classification of the answers. This approach was chosen because of the exploratory nature of the research question on the one hand, the need to attune to the individual perspectives and the experiences of the respondents on the other hand. Answers were categorised into thematic groups and subgroups. In principle, the answer of each respondent could fall into multiple thematic (sub)groups, depending on the number and variety of the aspects mentioned in the answer. Answers were compared (i.e., scanned for both common and differing thematic content units) and grouped on the basis of this thematic logic.

## Good practices to strengthen and bottlenecks to eliminate

### Good practices

We would first like to address good practices that emerged during the COVID-19 crisis and that respondents would like to preserve. To do so, we zoom in on dynamics or adjustments to the job or within the organisation that respondents indicated.

Respondents mentioned several dynamics or adaptations related to the job or organisation that they would like to preserve after the crisis. The dynamic or adaptation that is mentioned most frequently is the *opportunity to work from home*. Almost half of the respondents (n=836, 48.7 %) who answered referred to this type of dynamic or adaptation. According to them, digitalisation nowadays also facilitates work(ing) from home (WFH). WFH is preferred to be preserved, however mostly partially. Three main interrelated reasons were mentioned by the respondents.

The first main reason relates to efficiency, as most respondents mentioned that WFH reduces traffic jam and associated stress, or stress related to parking the car. In addition, it cuts travel expenses, saves time, and/or reduces distraction due to chit-chat with colleagues or other distractions when working in a shared office. Furthermore, several tasks are well suited to be performed from home. Respondents are mostly referring to administrative tasks, phone or online calls with clients or colleagues, permanency, research, and preparation for client visiting.

The second main reason relates to flexibility. It is mentioned that the opportunity to work from home facilitates flexibility to properly organise the day and therefore to find a more efficient balance between work tasks and/or the combination with household tasks. For example, being able to visit clients in their home environment and work from home afterwards because it is more efficient instead of returning to the office of the organisation. The flexibility to avoid traffic during peak hours, drive children to school without the need to rush to the office of the organisation afterwards, to work from home if children are ill or the opportunity to shop groceries or perform household tasks during breaks is also mentioned. For some respondents, this flexibility provides breathing space and contributes to a better work-life balance. The third reason relates to trust in employees WFH. It is believed by some respondents that trust from supervisors in employees WFH increased during the COVID-19 crisis.

The dynamic or adaptation that is mentioned second most frequently is the *use of digital tools*. Again, almost half of the respondents (n=754, 43.9%) who answered refers to this type of dynamic or adaptation. Four main reasons were addressed why respondents would like to preserve the use of digital tools after the COVID-19 crisis:

Firstly, digitalisation nowadays offers a wide range of opportunities for online communication with colleagues, external partners, clients, or for administration. The respondents mentioned mostly synonyms for video calling or specific tools like Zoom, Microsoft Teams, Skype, WhatsApp, Facebook, or Hangouts without further specification. Secondly, because of the various possibilities of digital tools, it is believed by many respondents that the use of online communication (in combination with face-to-face contact) can be in the best interest of the client and respond to what works for him. Respondents mentioned that this can be the case for clients who experience difficulties visiting the organisation (e.g. mobility), but also for clients from target groups that could not be reached or are less reachable before the COVID-19 crisis (e.g., youth). Social media makes it possible to chat and share tips, tasks, or videos. Online communication does not necessarily increase distance, as several respondents mentioned that with some clients there is even more contact.

Thirdly, several respondents mentioned that online communication with clients enables them to work easily accessible, monitor situations, respond quickly, and create time for other tasks. Intake or follow-up interviews with clients can be organised online. Online communication (e.g., meetings) between colleagues is also deemed to be more efficient (faster, shorter, and more productive) because the number of trips declines, the communication is more goal-oriented or because participants let each other finish talking more often instead of interrupting. Some respondents, however, missed full-fledged social interaction when communicating online because it is harder to emphasise with each other and there is less involvement. One respondent stated that online communication is mostly suited for already existing partnerships. Online communication is nonetheless seen as an opportunity to communicate with far-located possible partners. A part of the respondents also mentioned that digitalisation of administration (e.g., applications and client files) improves efficiency, transparency, and collaboration. Several respondents mentioned that they had the opportunity to get documents signed digitally or consider confirmation by email a valid signature. This was intended to simplify administrative processes during the COVID-19 crisis. According to some respondents, the reduced use of paper is also a positive effect of the digitalisation of administration.

The fourth reason relates to new social interaction dynamics within organisations, as online meetings during the COVID-19 crisis contained e.g., a daily song to start the workday, online coffee, or lunch breaks, a daily online get-together at the end of the workday or on Friday to end the workweek. Although respondents are willing to preserve online communication after the COVID-19 crisis, they often consider this additional to face-to-face contact rather than replacing it.

The third most frequently mentioned dynamic or adaptation is an *increased feeling of solidarity* (n=189, 11%). Respondents point out that attention for physical and psychological well-being of employees increased (e.g., working by appointment only, strict hygiene measures for both employees and clients and attention for professional workload and mental health of employees). Some respondents address the increased trust in WFH and providing IT support for this. Further, several respondents mentioned that information gets shared more easily within and between organisations. Some respondents also mentioned that they noticed colleagues being more flexible to help each other when organisations had to adapt during the COVID-19 crisis. This resulted in new experiences for professionals and challenges to be creative. A few respondents related an increased feeling of solidarity also to the number of volunteers that wanted to help.

## Bottlenecks

Secondly, we would like to address bottlenecks that emerged during the COVID-19 crisis and that respondents would like to eliminate. More specific, we zoom in on challenges or barriers related to the job or the organisation that respondents mentioned.

Respondents who answered this question are of the opinion that the most common bottleneck to be eliminated was the *reduced or lack of face-to-face contact with clients and colleagues* (n=484, 30.6%). It was often stated that human contact is essential for practising social work, especially in a context of proximity and connection. Several interrelated reasons were mentioned by the respondents. Face-to-face contact was considered essential for building and maintaining a good relationship with clients. It was stated by many respondents that face-to-face contact is needed to really engage with clients, get in their comfort zone, build a relationship of mutual trust at a client's pace, and/or get a correct overall picture of his situation, his understanding (facial expressions) and/or needs. This is even more important with children, families, elderly or persons who do not possess the necessary language skills and/or to correctly assess the safety or health of clients. In general, the warmth and humanity of face-to-face interaction is regarded highly valuable. Face-to-face contact was also found important to maintain a good relationship with colleagues, as many respondents valued spontaneous work-related and non-work-related face-to-face conversations with colleagues (e.g., support, reassurance, advice, inspiration, appreciation). Because such spontaneous conversations with colleagues were absent during the COVID-19 crisis, it was believed that the threshold to ask a question or talk to a colleague online or by phone was higher.

In addition, reduced or lack of face-to-face contact was perceived as a threat to the accessibility of aid services. Several respondents mentioned that not all target groups can be reached online (e.g., digital gap, language barrier). Reduced or lack of face-to-face contact had implications for the content of conversations with clients as well, as respondents addressed that difficulties are expressed less quickly and that certain topics are less suitable to discuss online or over the phone or cannot be discussed at all (e.g., emotional topics when involved third parties are possibly present, situations involving intrafamily violence, conflict mediation, divorce situations). According to these respondents, expressing empathy and providing emotional support was hampered. Reduced or lack of face-to-face contact also impacted the content of conversations with colleagues, as these conversations were more often described as business-like, work-related and goal-oriented. Face-to-face contact was believed essential to facilitate the application of certain methodologies in practice. Several respondents indicated the importance of sitting down with clients to go over and complete documents together, going to certain agencies together or visiting clients in their home environment.

The second most frequently mentioned bottleneck relates to *difficulties regarding the sudden switch-over to digitalisation and WFH* (n=462, 29.2%), including the lack of experience, hardware and software, and concerns regarding digital literacy, validity of legal documents, data protection, and security. At first, many respondents did not have experience with the use of digital tools and WFH. This lack of experience became a challenge when suddenly organisations were forced to re-organise operations. Concerns were raised about the availability and usability of hardware and software. Several respondents addressed that an outdated laptop or phone and/or the absence of a printer, scanner, headset, or working webcam complicated teleworking. Also, little was known about the use of digital tools (e.g., chat assistance) and difficulties were experienced (e.g., connectivity or login problems, not being able to share the screen), whereby some respondents or colleagues of respondents avoided online communication and developed a negative attitude towards digitalisation.

Because many social workers and clients lacked means and/or knowledge, concerns were raised regarding the digital literacy of both social workers and clients. Several respondents addressed that digitalisation demands language skills, whereby also many clients experienced difficulties with digital information and online communication. Further, high expectations about online availability and accessibility were mentioned by several respondents, which caused stress and challenged guarding the work-life balance. The validity of legal documents, data protection, and security was also questioned, due to the access and use of certain digital tools, secure connections, digitalisation of administration, and information sharing (e.g., by email). Respondents indicated that they were often hampered by this. In addition, the sudden switch-over to WFH meant for many respondents primarily doing desk work alone. Having enough space and/or a separate room for this purpose and/or being able to work with focus and in compliance with ergonomic prescriptions was nevertheless not evident to some respondents (e.g., using only a laptop because a second screen is not provided, working at the kitchen table).

The third most frequently mentioned bottleneck to be eliminated was *the problematic accessibility of organisations* (n=236, 14.9%) *and clients* (n=218, 13.8%). As many organisations re-organised operations to respect the basic health and safety guidelines to the extent possible (e.g., teleworking), respondents raised the difficulties to reach organisations (e.g., unions, mutual aid societies, city services, police services, schools, first-line assistance). Respondents considered that it was more difficult and time-consuming to get hold of the right people and information to help clients. Several organisations closed or limited their services, were only reachable by telephone (waiting lists) and/or responded late. As a consequence, clients were often left with questions and concerns, especially more vulnerable clients (e.g., homeless, elderly, isolated individuals). Respondents also experienced difficulties reaching clients, as many clients lack the language and/or do not have a laptop, tablet, or phone to email or call or a printer or scanner to complete documents (digital gap). Clients with a phone did not always answer phone calls (e.g., fear, language barrier), especially when social workers use a private phone number to protect their privacy. Due to this problematic accessibility of organisations and clients, several respondents fear hidden crises.

The fourth most flagged bottleneck was the *overload of unclear communication, lack or absence of information within and between organisations and/or governmental bodies* (n=402, 25.4%). Respondents pointed out that, in their view, managers and coordinators suddenly found themselves under additional pressure when operations had to be re-organised to respect the basic health and safety guidelines as much as possible. Direct, clear, streamlined, and timely communication within the organisation was required but was not provided. Many respondents mentioned an abundance of mail traffic, newsletters and rapidly changing information, policies, or guidelines, without being involved. According to several respondents, clear guidance, or a well-thought-out approach about WFH and digitalisation was missing and uncertainty among colleagues emerged about how to respond to certain issues or needs. A few respondents also raised that little was known about other colleagues' tasks when they are absent due to illness. Further, several respondents addressed the lack of communication at policy level (Flemish and local government) and the absence of human impact of the COVID-19 crisis such as mental health. Information of colleagues from different departments or organisations could also have been transferred more smoothly, as some respondents indicate the lack of clarity about services provided by other departments or organisations (e.g., some organisations were in lockdown while other organisations still allowed home visits) and the extra work and time to collect this information. External services or partners were less or not accessible, with the result that collective projects were often put on hold.

## Discussion and conclusion

The COVID-19 crisis has challenged social workers globally. In this chapter, we addressed dynamics or adaptations that social workers in Flanders, Belgium, experienced and what they would like to preserve in the future ('good practices'), as well as challenges or barriers ('bottlenecks') they experienced and would like to eliminate. This study shows that social work organisations and social workers were not prepared for such a crisis but quickly adapted to this new situation and to the best of their abilities. In doing so, they noticed several good practices related to WFH, digitalisation, and solidarity. In addition, they also experienced bottlenecks related to reduced or lacking face-to-face contact, digitalisation, accessibility, and information flow. These good practices and bottlenecks should be thoughtfully considered when establishing systems that benefit the client, the social worker, and the organisation. In this regard, we want to derive three themes from the conclusions for further consideration.

A *digital transformation* within social work is a first theme and puts social work in a dilemma. The results showed some positive and negative aspects on different levels. At the level of the relationship between social worker and client, digitalisation can enable low-threshold, fast, and efficient work if social workers and clients have the necessary tools and knowledge. It is, however, more often necessary to assess situations from a distance and to trust what clients report, and also to question how vulnerable clients can be reached.

While systematic research on the impact of the pandemic on social work has just recently started to arise, many social workers and researchers have pointed out several corresponding challenges that this pandemic has brought to the professional field. The balance between digitalisation and proximity is an attention point. Proximity is seen as a building block on which social work is based and relates to being engaged in the lifeworld of service users (Vandekinderen et al. 2019, 882–883). Accessibility is a pivotal condition for enabling proximity and means getting rid of all kinds of thresholds and provide services that are affordable, physically accessible, available, understandable, and useful. This requires flexibility and involvement in the client's lifeworld. Although the study results shed light on the potential of digitalisation in terms of availability, usability, and flexibility, *the question remains how social work can sustainably undergo a digital transformation in the coming period without compromising its proximity.* After all, the daily lives of individuals, families, and communities were heavily affected by the COVID-19 measures. Concerns about this were voiced not only in our study but also in public debate by social workers (Blomme et al. 2020; Ham 2020; Harrikari et al. 2021; Maenhout 2021; Schepens et al. 2020). Subsequent scientific studies also indicated that health and safety measures had some (unexpected) latent effects that increased existing and instigating new vulnerabilities (Dominelli et al. 2020; Kinderrechtencommissariaat 2020; Richardson et al. 2020; University of Antwerp 2020a, 2020b). Already vulnerable groups' circumstances frequently worsened and new vulnerable groups arose. The demand for social work was more apparent than ever, but less evident to carry out given that attention for proximity had to be redefined. Additionally, social workers had to find other ways to reach out to clients (Bocklandt 2020; Nijs et al. 2020). In addition, some authors also wonder if telehealth practices are reaching all clients that need to be reached and whether everyone has equal access to it (Amadasun 2020, 754–755; Walter-McCabe 2020, 69–71). Personal contact remains very central to social work, but it has partially disappeared during the pandemic, putting pressure on the most vulnerable clients given the negative consequences of isolation and being closed off from the personal aspect of aid (Debruyne et al. 2020; Walter-McCabe 2020, 69–71). Some clients might therefore not be reached anymore.

Still, there already exists a wide range of digital tools and there are differences between clients, which means that dialogue with clients is needed to find the best way of working for them. In some cases, this can be a hybrid format that involves both face-to-face and online contacts and communication and where proximity, in other words being present in the life of clients (Debruyne et al. 2020), is still paramount and is matched with the client. In this way, it is also a question of to what extent and in what way suddenly necessary work-related skills such as IT skills in the context of the shift from face-to-face interactions to remote connections will be part of the basic competencies of a social worker in the future. Other research (Harrikari et al. 2021) in this case also highlights the importance of interaction skills for a social worker in a shift in interaction skills that enables proximity from a distance. At the level of the social worker, digitalisation offers opportunities to work place-independently and to avoid inefficient travel and meetings and to increase the flexibility to structure the day themselves, which is more beneficial for the work-life balance. A digital transformation also offers perspectives at the level of organisations. If structures are created at the organisational level that improves the flow of information within and between organisations, this would benefit clients and social workers as well. Moreover, a new client base for social work might be reached.

A second theme is *a shift to a hybrid working model*, in which social workers work place- and time-independent. An important social and economic consequence of a lockdown is a shift to WFH, including many industries that did not previously embrace WFH. Research by Timo Harrikari et al. (2021) indicates that managers' attitudes toward teleworking in social work in Finland were unfavourable and, as a result, there was limited support for it. In contrast, other research shows that employers have had predominantly positive experiences with WFH since lockdown (Forbes et al. 2020). This has subsequently influenced the likelihood that managers and organisations will support more place- and time-independent working in the future. Further, a decrease in the stigma around place- and time-independent working and less concern that WFH has a negative impact on the employee performance were noticed (Forbes et al. 2020). Organisations increased the support available for home-based employees by providing tools and professional support, and this is something they plan to continue in the future. These conclusions are largely in line with the results of our study, but *it remains a question of what the significance of new ways of working will be for social work and how they will be implemented.* Respondents suddenly started WFH and experienced certain benefits, such as a positive contribution to the work-life balance—which is also reported by Harrikari et al. (2021). It was also mentioned in our study that the confidence of managers in WFH had increased, but in order to structurally give place to place-independent work within social work, it seems advisable to ensure equipment and knowledge of its use and possibilities but also to think about monitoring systems so that work can also be followed up from a distance. We don't intend to monitor social workers, but to support them in obtaining their goals. It can in fact ensure the trust of managers in WFH, follow-up and flexibility for the social worker, so that the work of social workers does not always have to be physically visible in the office and an overview is still maintained. When flexible work arrangements are adopted structurally, it is also relevant to consider how to keep employees involved in the organisation and avoid isolation.

A third theme is the *exchange of information within and between organisations*. An impeded information flow and sharing within and between organisations was not a new concern that emerged during the study, but rather a concern that became even more visible during the crisis. Although exceptions were mentioned by several respondents and solidarity and flexibility was noticed when organisations had to adapt quickly, which was also addressed by Pascale Debruyne et al. (2020) who mentioned that several new coalitions and alliances emerged in which social workers, actors from civil society, local governments, and private actors cooperated in order to protect the persons that have become most vulnerable during the pandemic, *it can be persistently addressed that structures should be reviewed so that information is accessible and open*. A digital transformation can facilitate this, but then issues regarding validity of legal documents, data protection, and security must be clarified. Such new structures can strengthen flexible work arrangements. The use of digital tools for remote communication, which was new to many social workers in our study and the organisations where they work, aligns with the theory of digital adaptation (Castillo de Mesa 2021). However, the possibilities of the present and future digital era go even much further, including the exchange of information within and between organisations, governments, and clients. The idea of the digital social work paradigm (which implies an evolution of digital adaptation, transition, and disruption) is based on the idea that social workers fully utilise technology to give voice to the most vulnerable, humanise technology with ethical criteria and battle to preserve citizens' digital rights (Castillo de Mesa 2021). This requires the participation of social workers in the design and prototyping of digital solutions and reducing the various digital gaps. It will therefore be interesting to follow up if and how these first digital adaptations will influence the full utilisation of the potential of digitalisation and thus the evolution towards digital disruption in social work, where accessible and open information is evident.

It appears from the results that the crisis challenged social workers in Flanders when, among other things, face-to-face contact largely disappeared. Human contact proved essential in practising social work, but the crisis also taught that work can be done more flexibly, efficiently, and effectively through existing digital possibilities. When interpreting the results of this study, it should be mentioned that the survey was done shortly after the start of the first and most strict lockdown. It could be that respondents now have a different view on good practices and bottlenecks. For one thing, WFH and working with digital tools were still new at that time. The question therefore is what will remain after the crisis and whether will it soon become business as usual again. In any case, social work will continue to play an important role after the pandemic. Answers were also given from a variety of (sub)sectoral perspectives within the field of social work. Further research will be needed to generate clear results on the good practices and bottlenecks within each of these subsectors. Although the shortcomings of this study should be taken into account, it contributes to the emerging literature concerning the practice of social work during the pandemic. It seems sensible to proceed with the three themes that emerged and to take good practices further and eliminate bottlenecks that have emerged to find what works best for clients, social workers, and organisations. For this, frameworks are needed that provide social workers space to organise their services and to practice social work in an effective and efficient way.

## Notes

1 Belgium. Ministry of Home Affairs. 2020. Ministerieel besluit houdende dringende maatregelen om de verspreiding van het coronavirus COVID-19 te beperken. C – 2020/ 30331. Adopted 18 March 2020. http://www.ejustice.just.fgov.be/eli/besluit/2020/03/18/ 2020030331/justel
2 This information is redacted in order to preserve and protect the anonymity of informants.

## References

Amadasun, Solomon. 2020. "Social Work and COVID-19 Pandemic: An Action Call." *International Social Work* 63 (6): 753–756. 10.1177/0020872820959357

Blomme, Anke, Sylvia Hubar, and Karolien Morelli. 2020. "Sociaal werkers in coronatijden: 'Mensen in de ogen kijken, is levensbelangrijk'." Sociaal.net, 27 October 2020. https://sociaal.net/opinie/sociaal-werkers-in-coronatijden-mensen-in-de-ogen-kijken-is-levensbelangrijk/.

Bocklandt, Philippe. 2020. "Geluk bij een ongeluk: 'Onlinehulp zorgde voor extra veerkracht'." Sociaal.net, 17 June 2020. https://sociaal.net/opinie/onlinehulp-zorgde-voor-extra-veerkracht/

Castillo de Mesa, Joaquin. 2021. "Digital Social Work: Towards Digital Disruption in Social Work." *Journal of Sociology and Social Welfare* 48 (3): 117–133. HeinOnline.

Debruyne, Pascale, Jan Naert, and Hans Grymonprez. 2020. "Sociaal werk in tijden van corona." Samenleving & Politiek (n.d.). https://www.sampol.be/2020/04/sociaal-werk-in-tijden-van-corona

Dominelli, Lena, Timo Harrikari, Joseph Mooney, Vesna Leskošek, and Erin Kennedy Tsunoda, eds. 2020. "COVID-19 and Social Work: A Collection of Country Reports." N.p.: N.p. https://www.researchgate.net/publication/343219006_COVID-19_AND_ SOCIAL_WORK_A_COLLECTION_OF_COUNTRY_REPORTS

Federale overheid. 2020a. "Coronavirus: Fase 2 gehandhaafd, overgang naar federale fase en bijkomende maatregelen." Coronavirus COVID-19 [Federale overheid Belgie]. Last modified 12 March 2020. https://www.info-coronavirus.be/nl/news/archive/fase-2-gehandhaafd-overgang-naar-de-federale-fase-en-bijkomende-maatregelen/

Federale overheid. 2020b. "Help jezelf en anderen te beschermen." Last modified 10 March 2020. https://www.info-coronavirus.be/nl/news/archive/help-jezelf-en-anderen-te-beschermen/

Federale overheid. s.d. "Monitoring van de sociale impact van de COVID-19-crisis in België." Federale Overheidsdienst – Sociale Zekerheid. Accessed 11 October, 2021. https://socialsecurity.belgium.be/nl/sociaal-beleid-mee-vorm-geven/sociale-impact-covid-19#:~:text=De%20interdepartementale%20Werkgroep%20Sociale%20Impact, opgericht%20om%20ECOSOC%20te%20ondersteunen

Forbes, Sarah, Holly Birkett, Lori Evans, Heejung Chung, and Julie Whiteman. 2020. *Managing Employees during the COVID-19 Pandemic: Flexible Working and the Future of Work.* Birmingham: Equal Parenting Project. https://kar.kent.ac.uk/85918/1/managerial-experiences-during-covid19-2020-accessible.pdf

Glaser, Barney G. and Anselm L. Strauss. 1967. *The Discovery of Grounded Theory: Strategies for Qualitative Research.* Chicago: Aldine.

Ham, Marcel. 2020. "Coronacrisis vraagt niet enkel medisch, maar ook sociaal antwoord." Sociaal.net, 20 March 2020. https://sociaal.net/achtergrond/coronacrisis-vraagt-ook-sociaal-antwoord/

Harrikari, Timo, Marjo Romakkaniemi, Laura Tiitinen, and Sanna Ovaskainen. 2021. "Pandemic and Social Work: Exploring Finnish Social Workers' Experiences through a SWOT Analysis." *The British Journal of Social Work* 51 (5): 1644–1662. 10.1093/bjsw/bcab052

Kinderrechtencommissariaat. 2020. *Laat kinderrechten nooit meer in lockdown gaan.* Brussel: Kinderrechtencommissariaat. https://publicaties.vlaanderen.be/view-file/39703

Maenhout, Klaas. 2021. "Er moet nu hulp komen of er gebeuren ongelukken, dit weekend." *De Standaard,* 6 March 2021. https://www.standaard.be/cnt/dmf20210305_98175715

Nijs, Davy, Stijn Custers, Jan Dekelver, and David Loyen. 2020. "Een lockdown biedt unieke kansen voor digitale inclusie." *Sociaal.net,* 15 May 2020. https://sociaal.net/achtergrond/lockdown-biedt-kansen-voor-digitale-inclusie/

POD Maatschappelijke Integratie. 2020. "Synthese van de werkzaamheden van de TaskForce Kwetsbare Groepen." Accessed October 13, 2021. https://www.mi-is.be/nl/tools-ocmw/synthese-van-de-werkzaamheden-van-de-taskforce-kwetsbare-groepen

Richardson, Dominic, Alessandro Carraro, Victor Cebotari, Anna Gromada, and Gwyther Rees. 2020. *Supporting Families and Children Beyond COVID-19 – Social Protection in High-Income Countries.* Florence: UNICEF Office of Research – Innocenti. https://www.unicef-irc.org/publications/1165-supporting-families-and-children-beyond-covid-19-social-protection-in-high-income-countries.html

Schepens, Brigitte, Ringo Vandermeeren, and Lise Deschoemaker. 2020. "Begeleid wonen: 'Ondanks fysieke afstand, staan we nu heel dicht bij de jongeren'." Sociaal.net, 22 April 2020. https://sociaal.net/verhaal/begeleid-wonen-ondanks-fysieke-afstand-staan-we-nu-heel-dicht-bij-de-jongeren/

Steunpunt tot bestrijding van armoede, bestaansonzekerheid en sociale uitsluiting. 2020. *Overzicht van COVID-19-maatregelen, ter ondersteuning in situaties van armoede en bestaansonzekerheid.* Brussel: Steunpunt tot bestrijding van armoede, bestaansonzekerheid en sociale uitsluiting. https://www.armoedebestrijding.be/wp-content/uploads/2020/04/200409-overzicht-covid-19-NL.pdf

University of Antwerp. 2020a. "Resultaten twintigste enquête." Accessed 21 December 2021. https://www.uantwerpen.be/nl/projecten/coronastudie/resultaten/resultaten-twintigste-enquete/

University of Antwerp. 2020b. "Resultaten enquête 22." Accessed 21 December 2021. https://www.uantwerpen.be/nl/projecten/coronastudie/resultaten/resultaten-enquete-22/

Vandekinderen, Caroline, Rudi Roose, Peter Raeymaeckers, and Koen Hermans. 2019. "The DNA of Social Work as a Human Rights Practice from a Frontline Social Workers' Perspective in Flanders." *European Journal of Social Work* 23(5): 876–888. 10.1080/13691457.2019.1663408

Walter-McCabe, Heather. 2020. "Coronavirus Pandemic Calls for an Immediate Social Work Response." *Social Work in Public Health* 35 (3): 69–72. 10.1080/19371918.2020. 1751533

Section III

# Vulnerabilities and Adaptive Capacities at the Client Interface

# 9 Medical Social Workers' Context of Practice during COVID-19 in Iran

*Sareh Abri and Maryam Zabihi Poursaadati*

## Introduction

The 2020s began with a new coronavirus that radically changed many aspects of people's lives. Conditions have worsened for those with whom social workers usually work (i.e., those already on the margins of society, suffering poor health, poverty, and other forms of inequalities). The COVID-19 pandemic has undoubtedly challenged social workers to engage with the health pandemic and provide essential services in conditions of uncertainty and high risk (Dominelli 2021). Several studies about social work during COVID-19 show that the pandemic has exacerbated many social workers' and clients' issues. In this regard, medical social workers dealt directly with patients and their families. Their roles and tasks have been changed in the COVID-19 situation, with an expectation to protect the patients and also to improve the human relations that are damaged. The mechanisms offered to services and support have changed dramatically during COVID-19 pandemic (Brennan et al. 2020). Social work is under threat today because the value of social justice is challenged by the deleterious impact of the pandemic on powerless groups. More so, 'the value of human dignity tanks' in the face of resource and economic deprivation among many citizens who cannot access medical care (Amadasun 2020, 754).

## COVID-19, the Iranian context and social work

The outbreak of Coronavirus in Iran was officially confirmed to be in Qom on 19 February 2020. However, previously suspected cases of Coronavirus have been reported in Iran. The fast-moving global COVID-19 pandemic caught many countries such as Iran unprepared and exposed several flaws, including social inequities in public health, economic and social welfare institutions. Public trust in the authorities' capacity to deal with the virus had been undermined by the government's initial response to the outbreak. Also, a shortage of masks and disinfectant gels, even in hospitals, has been widely reported (Dominelli et al. 2020).

Social workers have played a crucial role during the COVID-19 crisis in Iran, meeting people's most urgent social needs. However, research has been focused on other health professionals, and less is known about social workers on the frontline, including those working in hospitals.

DOI: 10.4324/9781003374374-12

The Social Work Bureau and the Deputy of Health have designed guidelines for psychosocial support in care centres for COVID-19 patients and have designed a Psychosocial Intervention Protocol against the Coronavirus for hospital social workers (HSWs). Educational programs are held online through the Instagram page of the Scientific Association of Social Work of Iran. The Iranian Association of Social Workers has released the contact numbers of some experienced experts (social workers or related specialists) to provide expert and supervisory advice and technical assistance in various fields across the country if needed. These individuals work voluntarily, free of charge, to help experts in the context of the coronavirus crisis (Dominelli et al. 2020).

Previous to the pandemic health social workers were performing a variety of roles using the person in environment context. Some of the major roles included identification of patients in need of social work services, conducting psychosocial assessment with interviewing client and family, paying home visits, keeping records of all stages of assistance, participating in the development and implementation of an intervention plan to reduce social problems by using community social work method, providing individual and group counselling, preparing for case conference and working with other professionals in addressing social and psychological problems of the patients with adherence to professional ethics; arranging for financial support and facilitating referral for clients to receive medical, psychological, and psychiatric services; providing financial support, addressing concerns of patients introduced through judicial or police intervention, collaborating with Crisis intervention team, planning for discharge and post discharge follow-up and developing skills and competencies through training and professional development courses (Ministry of Health and Medical Education 2020).

Although COVID-19 pandemic has undermined and, in some instances, overturned most of these roles, in Iran, health social workers have risen to the challenges of providing services despite inadequate personal protective equipment; limited supervision and support; along with experiences of death and dying, grief and loss, isolation, and safety concerns. They needed to adapt to the situation and prioritise the most urgent and essential aspects of their roles during these unprecedented times. They continued to do their jobs at the time of COVID-19 pandemic, with a much-reduced face-to-face delivery of services. They have changed their work hours and practices to achieve social distancing protocols with their clients and colleagues. This article highlights the perception of medical social workers about new situations and challenges caused by the pandemic and the new roles and activities that have been imposed on them to replace the previous roles, by drawing on the experiences of a purposively drawn sample of social workers working in general hospitals, using a qualitative research design.

## Study framework

In this study, bio-psychosocial model, ecological framework, and systems theory were applied as the guiding theoretical frameworks for the study. The bio-psychosocial model considers health as the interactions of genetic and psychological makeup with the environment and thus explicitly relates to social work as the profession is inherently concerned with the perspective of the person (biological and psychological factors) in the environment (social). The biological (relating to genetics, diet, and physiology) and psychological (such as emotions, cognitive functioning, anxiety, depression) systems interact with contextual factors (such as the social factors such as social support, cultural practices, policies, laws, and other interrelated factors) dynamically, to shape health over the life span (Lehman et al. 2017). While COVID-19 pandemic is characterised by significant morbidity and mortality with disruption of and damage to human biological systems, it is imperative to appreciate the psychosocial and cultural context of the pandemic (Chigangaidze 2021). For researching and addressing health-related illness conjunctive to social work practice (Zittel et al. 2002), and for interdisciplinary and multifaceted focus that posits the interrelations among the biological, psychological, and socio-environmental influences on health and disease (Frazier 2020), bio-psychosocial model is the favoured choice.

The Ecological Systems theory illustrates that human behaviour, development, and socialisation are influenced by different environmental circles, including the microsystem, mesosystem, exosystem, macrosystem, and chronosystem (Chigangaidze 2021). The ecological approach provides strategies that allow the social worker to impact a client system at a micro-level of intervention, such as psychotherapy to a macro-level of social treatment such as policy and planning. Thus, direct and indirect practice strategies for intervention can be combined into a congruent practice orientation when working with a client system through the ecological approach (Pardeck 1988). The ecological approach recognises the existence of bi-directional and cyclic interrelationships with clients and other systems. In human terms, this means that as a person enters each new situation, he or she usually adapts to its demands and, by his or her presence, changes the situation at least structurally. A person is constantly creating, restructuring, and adapting to the environment even as the environment affects the person (Greif and Lynch cited in Ungar 2002, 38).

System theory approach is regarded as another relevant framework for this paper, to focus on interactions and dynamics within the environment (Kirst-Ashman 2009). Thus, within the hospital setting different professionals such as doctors, nurses, health unit coordinators, and social workers collaborate to meet the patients' needs. Bradford Sheafor and Charles Horejsi (2008) identify four key components that are interrelated in systems theory. These components are input, conversion operations, output, and feedback (Fusenig 2012). Medical social workers perform the element of input by interviewing patients and families for needed information, reading electronic medical records, and obtaining other pertinent information in order to treat patients. The component of conversion operations has the medical social worker translating this information and then interacting with other systems or disciplines within the hospital to provide continuity of care within this system which completes the output function within systems theory. Finally, the social worker can complete this task by providing feedback to the interdisciplinary team or facility management to provide optimal patient care.

## Methodology: Design, sample, and data collection and analysis

The present study used a qualitative research design due to the exploratory nature of research. It was considered a more appropriate method for understanding the meaning of what the participants say, their perspectives and unravel the story behind their actual experiences. The data was collected between June and August 2021 while emergency conditions were in force in Iran. The researchers used purposive sampling technique to select social workers working in general hospitals, who were known to them and could provide indepth and detailed information about the phenomenon under investigation. Researchers considered only those participants who were willing and agreed to participate in the study, after they were duly informed about the research purpose, anonymity, the voluntary basis of the study, and the permission to publish the data anonymously. The semi-structured interview commenced after researchers and social workers mutually agreed on convenient time.

The study participants comprised 16 individuals from different cities, including Tehran (4), Tabriz (2), and one each from the cities of Hamedan, Bandar Abbas, Khorramabad, Borujerd, Kermanshah, Bookan, Kerman, Mashhad, Sari, and Ahvaz. Data collection was continued until data saturation was achieved. The interviews were conducted using an interview guide with the following open-ended questions:

Please explain how you felt about COVID-19 during its outbreak. Explain your thoughts, feelings, and understandings.

What challenges are you facing/have faced during the pandemic?

Which of your roles and tasks have been changed during the pandemic?

If the participants mentioned a specific point about their perception and experience of COVID-19 exposure, the interviewer would ask them to provide further explanations. All interviews were conducted in Persian language, using WhatsApp, which was the most commonly available application in Iran, whereas other social media applications have some difficulty connecting. The interviews were recorded digitally with the respondents' consent and then transcribed. The researchers were familiar with qualitative studies.

Qualitative content analysis was used for data analysis (Graneheim and Lundman 2004). The researchers transcribed the text of each interview verbatim in Persian immediately after the interview and these were analysed using MAXQDA12. In this method, the analytic section of the text relevant to the research objectives was selected from the interview text. This process led to extraction of initial codes based on the meaning units derived from the participants' descriptions. Then, the initial codes were reduced to subcategories based on similarities and differences. Finally, the subcategories were classified into abstract categories and themes (Priest et al. 2002), based on continuous comparison of the data and authentic interpretation by the researchers.

Trustworthiness, seen as bedrock of qualitative research, is promoted by four criteria of (a) credibility (in preference to internal validity), (b) transferability (in preference to external validity/generalisability), (c) dependability (in preference to reliability), and (d) conformability (Lincoln and Guba 1986). For this study, credibility was established using the participants' observation and member checking. Transferability was achieved with explicit connections with the cultural and social contexts where the data was collected. For dependability, another researcher (not involved in the data collection and analysis processes) examined these processes and the research results and confirmed them.

## Results and discussion

### Individual experience and perception

At the beginning of the pandemic, the HSWs had a similar understanding of the situation as the general public. In unstable and ambiguous pandemic conditions, where the extent of the disease was unknown and routine treatments had failed, society was in shock due to the crisis, and psychological reactions such as denial, anger, panic, stress, and anxiety were evident in the society. HSWs also suddenly faced many clients, which the health system in Iran initially denied, adding to the ambiguity, concern, and anger of the hospital staff, including HSWs.

Some participants reported that seeing other patients dying made them feel how close they were to their own death and that not knowing enough about the virus added to their fears. They frequently reported concern about risk of illness of their own or family members.

> At the same time, I was concerned about my health and family. Anyway, we had a lot of contact with the sick during the day, and then we went home. We also had children and the elderly at home, and we were more concerned about endangering their health than our own (P3).

Participants also referred to their extreme reactions to the crisis. Although severe fear first caused repetitive behaviour like frequent hand washing in HSWs, over time and numbness to crisis and death, the rate of adherence to social distancing protocols also decreased. The medical staff witnessed many patients admitted to hospitals without being able to provide appropriate services. They were also unable to maintain their health and witnessed the death of their colleagues and patients every day. On the other hand, insufficient facilities were available to meet the clients' needs, which added to the depth of the tragedy, and they felt unable to meet the clients' needs.

As the days passed and the top managers of the Ministry of Health still denied this issue, fear, and despair overwhelmed me. I was very disappointed. I looked everywhere and saw nothing but death (P11).

### Professional-related perception

During the pandemic, a significant portion of the cost was spent saving lives from disease-related deaths. As a result, the efforts of the HSWs to prevent and reduce the psychosocial consequences of the disease for the patient and their family were marginalised.

> For the first six months of Coronavirus, I did around 500 rounds to be at the patient's bedside. Stress worsened the patient's symptoms and reduced confidence in treatment, so I used stress reduction techniques. Our work was complementary to the biomedical treatment, but all this was ignored, discouraging HSWs (P13).

Participants complained about the ignorance of hospital managers about the ability of HSWs to deal with the crisis. Some participants believed that a biological approach governs the Iranian health system and other aspects of health, such as the psychosocial dimension are ignored, so non-medical professions are marginalised in the health system due to the attribution of lack of knowledge and skills in crisis management among HSWs.

> The most significant challenge we faced was the unreasonable expectations of our managers (tasks that were far from our professional work). Of course, this was due to the unusual circumstances of the crisis. Still, in our case, it has always been the case that temporarily entrusted tasks usually become permanent tasks after a while (P4).

In the early months of the pandemic, HSWs did not have specific professional instructions for intervention and were engaged in non-specialist activities, which increased their burnout.

The Social Work Bureau in the Ministry of Health, responsible for setting policies and guidelines and supervising the HSWs was practically surprised by the pandemic, as in the case of other sections of the Ministry. Furthermore, due to the lack of a supervisory structure, HSWs could not use the support of their officials and felt left out in the crisis. They considered themselves as caregivers who were left unattended.

> My biggest challenge was the lack of support from the Ministry. Although we, social workers, are expected to endure hard work, at this time, the incompatibility of the workload with the available facilities and lack of support caused irreparable physical and mental damage to us (P11).

## Health system-related challenges

Participants attributed some of their challenges to macro-policies in the health system. At the beginning of the pandemic, despite the signs of the virus entering the country, high-level officials in the Ministry of Health denied the disease. They had virtually no plan to deal with the virus crisis. Many healthcare providers, including HSWs who were in direct contact with patients and observed symptoms, expressed concern about the unpreparedness of the health system. Lack of hospital beds, medicine, and medical equipment caused dissatisfaction for the clients in the treatment system and increased the burden on the medical staff.

> I thought that the virus would enter our country soon, why the health care system did not take any measures, and why the hospitals were not ready to respond in time (P1).

The lack of protective items such as masks and disinfectants, especially for medical staff, has led the Ministry of Health to downplay some precautionary measures, such as masking, to reduce public criticism. On the other hand, due to the contradictory policies of the government and comprehensive sanctions against the government and the people of Iran (Abdoli 2020), the access of the Iranian health system to countries producing drugs and vaccines was limited. Receipt of medicines, vaccines, and other medical equipment was slow despite support from international institutions and has affected a number of COVID-19 victims in Iran.

> Policies heavily depended on the community's economic conditions and material resources. For example, in the early days, due to the scarcity of masks and rising prices, the Ministry of Health announced to the people that not everyone had to wear a mask, making it very difficult for us who worked in hospitals (P1).

In pre-COVID-19 phase, Iran faced severe inflation due to sanctions and declining oil sales. With the advent of the pandemic and implementing preventive social policies such as closure and quarantine, people faced numerous economic problems. Some lost their jobs or faced declining incomes. In addition, treatment and hospitalisation costs increased due to inflation, too. Under these circumstances, the government could not support people who had lost their jobs or were experiencing declining incomes. As a result, access to people with other chronic physical and mental illnesses was severely reduced. Finding support for vulnerable groups was increasingly on the agenda of HSWS, while support resources were also weakened.

> The most major problem during the epidemic was the increase in the economic vulnerability of the people. Many families lost their income and then faced a crisis such as illness, while the cost of treatment skyrocketed (P13).

On the other hand, [...] we had cancer patients or heart patients or people with psychiatric disorders, and when they came to continue their treatment, we could not admit them because we had reduced the non-COVID-19 wards, and most of the beds were for patients with COVID–19 signs. We had to spend much time convincing these people that the priority of treatment is COVID–19 (P16).

### Ethical challenges

Social work is a profession based on ethical principles and values, and observing ethical codes is one of the duties of social workers in any situation (Farkas 2020). Participants believed that they faced numerous ethical dilemmas that made professional work difficult for them in a pandemic situation. They pointed out that one of the most important ethical principles was to have the necessary professional competence to work with clients in crises. In contrast, they had been deprived of training in this field for years, and the lack of specific instructions led to non-specialist interventions in this area.

One of the challenges I faced was what competency I had to help these people [...] I felt the need to train for psychosocial intervention in personal crises and extreme stress (P10).

One of the main goals of social work is to achieve social justice for society. Participants acknowledged that pandemic conditions created situations in which they saw injustice and could not intervene, especially when there was increase in the number of vulnerable people with COVID-19, such as the homeless, who had difficulty paying hospitalisation costs and during discharge, leading to an increase in the number of abandoned patients, particularly the elderly. Support organisations such as the Welfare Organisations were closed or teleworked due to quarantine policies. Accommodation centres did not accept new patients due to the COVID-19 outbreak, which had increased the workload of HSWs.

One of our significant challenges during this period was the increase in the number of patients. This phenomenon increased considerably, especially among the elderly. The residential centres themselves had a disease crisis and did not accept patients. We were under pressure from the hospital's managers to discharge these patients by any means, but we could not leave them without proper shelter (P9).

It was also difficult to communicate professionally due to the circumstances of patients with COVID-19. In cases where the patient needed to be interviewed, HSWs were in the isolation ward. Sometimes, it was difficult to maintain professional confidentiality and patient privacy. Participants also noted that in many Iranian sub-cultures, especially in the country's southern and western regions, mourning follows specific customs, which completely contradict the public health advisories in COVID-19. They had to ignore some cultural considerations to maintain their own safety and that of other patients as also general health, which led to the anger of the mourners.

> You see [in pre-COVID-19] we used to walk freely in the wards, and we could meet patients who needed social work services in a safe and private space. Nevertheless, during the pandemic, we have to go to the patient's bed with [protective equipment such as] guns, gloves, masks, and shields while other patients are in the room and get information that is a private matter, but we cannot take the patient out of the ward to get this information (P15).

### Work-related challenges

Routine interventions of HSWs were disrupted with the adoption of appropriate decisions like isolation during health emergency. Before the pandemic, HSWs were required to conduct a daily round, identify patients needing social work services and adhere to case management process that included psychosocial assessment, counselling, advocacy, and referral. However, participants in the study reported a change in this process:

> This pandemic impacted the HSWs and changed the description of our routine tasks. For example, daily tasks such as the daily round of all patients admitted to the wards were disrupted. To the best of my belief, a series of jobs have lost their importance, such as home visits due to COVID-19 conditions (P13).

On the other hand, during this period, HSWs faced an increase in high-risk groups of patients, such as child abuse or elder abuse and other domestic violence cases. The number of patients with psychiatric disorders with high-risk behaviours due to relapse increased as also suicides. Moreover, the challenge of finding resources to support these cases persisted, amidst the general lack of support:

> We had more child abuse and violence cases than ever before, and it was challenging to communicate with organisations such as Welfare organisations and the police (P7).

In this situation, HSWs had to adopt remote interventions instead of face-to-face communications. In many cases, they provided their services over the phone. Still, in some cases, which required longer consultations or more detailed assessment sessions, they needed to use new technologies and smartphones, while some clients were not familiar with working with a smartphone. Also, some HSWs were untrained to communicate remotely and may not be aware of the ethical implications of remote intervention.

Sometimes, to comply with social distancing protocols, we had to be in shifts in the hospital and intervene remotely. Our clients were mostly from economically vulnerable groups and unfamiliar with the technology. We could only do some things over the phone (P5).

Although the quality of these relationships was not as good as face-to-face interventions, they significantly reduced the negative psychosocial consequences of COVID-19 pandemic. For example, they used video communication to educate patients and families during the inpatient and post-discharge. They also provided some psychological interventions for patients through family-friendly video calls during hospitalisation.

### Previously existing roles accentuated by COVID-19

During the pandemic, one of the most critical challenges faced by HSWs was conflicting information and rumours that changed the health-seeking behaviours of clients. During the pre-COVID-19 phase, HSWs played an essential role in increasing patient and family awareness of disease and self-care, which became more prominent during the pandemic.

During this time, I think our role was more informative. Giving information to clients who had many questions and ambiguities about the virus, doubling their stress (P4).

Participants also noted the accentuating role of the HSWs as a mediator. When medical staff was increasingly involved in reducing physical symptoms and treating the COVID-19 patients, it became HSWs' duty to provide the necessary information about the patient's condition and prepare family members for post-discharge care as they were not allowed to see patients:

We were the link between the family and the treatment team because the hospitals were quarantined, and families were not allowed to visit their patients (P13).

Financial support was another role of HSWs that was highlighted during this period. While COVID-19 severely impacted people's living conditions, medicines also became costly. Patients who needed an ICU paid higher charges for hospitalisation, and the combination of these conditions led HSWs to strengthen their data base of financial resources.

Another task was to raise financial support from donors for clients who had lost their jobs and income due to COVID-19 pandemic and were now family members or themselves were patients (P2).

Although HSWs were members of the bad news team during pre-COVID19 time, they also played a vital role during the pandemic. Due to the limited access of specialist members for grief counselling, they had to provide initial grief counselling to families who had lost their patients and then refer them to specialists for further complex psychological services if any.

## Newly imposed roles by COVID-19

Pandemic conditions severely impacted the mental health of medical and hospital staff. Increasing workload at the peak of the disease, facing the death of patients and colleagues, lead to high physical and mental fatigue. The interviewees describe how their role was providing psychological support to staff members:

> In addition to the clients, we also provided psychosocial support to our colleagues. The difficult working conditions and lack of facilities undoubtedly put a lot of psychological pressure on the medical staff, and there was no source of support. Some had reactions such as crying and screaming, while others did not emotionally react but showed physical symptoms such as sudden fainting, which was due to fatigue (P7).

One of the roles redefined for HSWs due to pandemic conditions is post-discharge follow-up and care. Due to its significance, HSWs maintained contact and provided remote interventions to the patient and family.

> The follow-up after discharge was much longer, and I think this was one of the perfect things that happened in the HSW units (P16).

Participants mentioned using group and community approaches in interventions. Before COVID-19 pandemic, HSWs in Iran focused on interventions at the individual and family levels and used fewer other methods, especially community work. However, during the pandemic and the need for social care, they added the role of social planning to their roles.

> On the other hand, to reduce the workload of the hospital, we had to inform the public. Therefore, social awareness was put on the agenda to strengthen the psychosocial skills of the general public, and we presented a community plan (P10).

One of the significant challenges for HSWs was stigmatisation of the disease. In the early months, due to ignorance about the virus, infected people experienced high social stigma after treatment. People believed the disease occurred due to a lack of hygiene and disregard for social distancing protocols and blamed the patients. Fear of spreading the disease also kept people away from those who were ill or even recovered. This stigma affected their mental state. Sometimes families refused to accept the patient because of this stigma. Thus, HSWs presented their interventions for de-stigmatisation.

Our other role is to try to convince the families of the sufferers that this disease is not a disgrace and a cause of shame and that anyone can get it (P2).

## Conclusion

This study conducted with the Iranian HSWs has brought out significant pointers to the challenges faced by social workers in a complex and dynamic social reality. The person-in-environment context applies not only to the hospital patients in need of care and treatment but also to the social workers. Both are embedded in the specific social contexts which have a significance for micro-level and macro-level interventions.

At the micro level, HSWs had to contend with their own fears, uncertainty, and ambiguity in the provision of services due to the lack of knowledge about the disease and the due to the unknown nature of illness. There emerged major challenges to handle emotions, fatigue, and the need for self-care when working in unsafe and stressful circumstances. The study participants reported significant ethical challenges while prioritising patients' needs and demands, and maintaining empathic relationships concerning privacy and confidentiality. In particular, these issues became evident when HSWs could not address grief and loss while their patients, colleagues, family, and friends perished to COVID-19 and they felt they were unable to support people during moments of loneliness and isolation, which intensified social workers' feelings of powerlessness.

Work-related challenges concerned transformation in HSWs roles for providing awareness of disease and self-care, providing services when resources were unavailable, seeking financial support, providing initial grief counselling to families losing a loved one and referral to specialists in case of need. They also faced an increase in high-risk groups of patients, such as child abuse, elder abuse, and other domestic violence cases. Providing psychological support to staff members, remote follow-up after discharge, social planning, and interventions to de-stigmatisation were the new tasks for HSWs imposed by COVID-19.

The systems perspective is useful to understand the importance of COVID-19 patients' psychosocial interventions provided by HSWs which were unrecognised from hospital managers. Moreover, HSWs had to deal with the fears of the patients and their family members, and to address the economic distress by seeking financial resources in a macro context of economic downturn. The whole healthcare system was already constrained when COVID-19 epidemic struck, due to constrained international support systems for medicines and medical equipment, decline in international price of oil, and strained international relations. Inadequate protective facilities and lack of medical equipment increased these worries.

The study points to the need for preparedness planning of hospital-based social workers in the pandemic situations, highlighting the need for recognition of the significant service rendered by them and the need to address their own vulnerabilities as those whom they are attempting to support, with possible organisational support of their own. There is a critical need to focus on macro policy for providing health and social support services that are integrated and accessible to all. Future research could possibly investigate the differential impacts experienced by different cultural groups in the context of health inequalities.

# References

Abdoli, Amir. 2020. "Iran, Sanctions, and the COVID-19 Crisis." *Journal of Medical Economics* 23 (12): 1461–1465. 10.1080/13696998.2020.1856855

Amadasun, Solomon. 2020. "Social Work and COVID-19 Pandemic: An Action Call." *International Social Work* 63 (6): 753–756. 10.1177/0020872820959357

Brennan, John, Patrice Reilly, Kerry Cuskelly, and Sarah Donnelly. 2020. "Social Work, Mental Health, Older People and COVID-19." *International Psychogeriatrics* 32 (10): 1205–1209. 10.1017/S1041610220000873

Chigangaidze, Robert K. 2021. "Risk Factors and Effects of the Morbus: COVID-19 through the Biopsychosocial Model and Ecological Systems Approach to Social Work Practice." *Social Work in Public Health* 36 (2): 98–117. 10.1080/19371918.2020.1859035

Dominelli, Lena, Timo Harrikari, Joseph Mooney, Vesna Leskošek, and Erin Kennedy Tsunoda, eds. 2020. *COVID-19 and Social Work: A Collection of Country Reports.* N.p. https://www.iassw-aiets.org/covid-19/5369-covid-19-and-social-work-a-collection-of-country-reports/.

Dominelli, Lena. 2021. "A Green Social Work Perspective on Social Work during the Time of COVID-19." *International Journal of Social Welfare* 30 (1): 7–16. 10.1111/ijsw.12469

Farkas, Kathleen J., and J. Richard Romaniuk. 2020. "Social Work, Ethics and Vulnerable Groups in the Time of Coronavirus and COVID-19." *Society Register* 4 (2): 67–82. 10. 14746/sr.2020.4.2.05

Frazier, Leslie D. 2020. "The past, Present, and Future of the Biopsychosocial Model: A Review of 'The Biopsychosocial Model of Health and Disease': New Philosophical and Scientific Developments by Derek Bolton and Grant Gillett." *New Ideas in Psychology* 57: 100755. 10.1016/j.newideapsych.2019.100755

Fusenig, Elizabeth. 2012. "The Role of Emergency Room Social Worker: An Exploratory Study." Social Work Master's Clinical Research Papers, 26. St. Catherine University. https://sophia.stkate.edu/cgi/viewcontent.cgi?article=1026&context=msw_papers

Graneheim, Ulla H. and Berit Lundman. 2004. "Qualitative Content Analysis in Nursing Research: Concepts, Procedures and Measures to Achieve Trustworthiness." *Nurse Education Today* 24 (2): 105–112. 10.1016/j.nedt.2003.10.001

Kirst-Ashman, Karen K. 2009. *Introduction to Social Work & Social Welfare: Critical Thinking Perspectives.* 3rd ed. Belmont: Brooks.

Lehman, Barbara J., Diana M. David, and Jennifer A. Gruber. 2017. "Rethinking the Biopsychosocial Model of Health: Understanding Health as a Dynamic System." *Social and Personality Psychology Compass* 11 (8): e12328. 10.1111/spc3.12328

Lincoln, Yvonna S., and Egon G. Guba. 1986. "But Is It Rigorous? Trustworthiness and Authenticity in Naturalistic Evaluation." *New Directions for Program Evaluation* 1986 (30): 73–84. 10.1002/ev.1427

Ministry of Health and Medical Education (Iran). 2020. *Classification of Jobs in Medical Sciences and Health Services Universities.* Tehran: Ministry of Health and Medical Education.

Pardeck, John T. 1988. "An Ecological Approach for Social Work Practice." *Journal of Sociology & Social Welfare* 15 (2): 11. https://scholarworks.wmich.edu/jssw/vol15/iss2/11

Priest, Helena, Paula Roberts, and Leslie Woods. 2002. "An Overview of Three Different Approaches to the Interpretation of Qualitative Data. Part 1: Theoretical Issues." *Nurse Researcher* 10 (1): 30–42. 10.7748/nr2002.10.10.1.30.c5877

Shafor, Bradford W., and Charles R. Horejsi. 2008. *Techniques and Guidelines for Social Work Practice.* 8th ed. Boston: Pearson Education.

Ungar, Michael. 2002. "A Deeper, More Social Ecological Social Work Practice." *Social Service Review* 76 (3): 480–497. 10.1086/341185

Zittel, Kimberly M., Shawn Lawrence, and John S. Wodarski. 2002. "Biopsychosocial Model of Health and Healing: Implications for Health Social Work Practice." *Journal of Human Behavior in the Social Environment* 5 (1): 19–33. 10.1300/J137v05n01_02

# 10 Experiences of Social Service Officers Working at Safe Home during COVID-19 in Bangladesh

*Priyanka Bhattacharjee and Tulshi Kumar Das*

## Background of the study

Bangladesh, considered a developing country, did not change much of its welfare policy, in line with the neoliberal policy of the west, rather it carried on with the state responsibility to serve the poorest. Thus, the Social Welfare Ministry emerged as an independent one, separating from the Labour and Social Welfare Ministry in 1989, focusing more on different social welfare services for older persons, widows, and people with disability. The Ministry of Social Welfare primarily assists the poor and the marginalised regardless of their religion, caste, creed, and gender (Ministry of Social welfare 2021). Of all social service programs under the Ministry of Social welfare, Safe Home or safe custody home was built to prevent the social degradation of Bangladeshi society. It is a crucial shelter house introduced for women, children, and adolescents who are awaiting a judicial decision for their case lodged in the court and they can stay here for weeks, months, or even years under Section 31 of the Suppression of Violence against Women and Children Act-2000 (Department of Social Service 2021).

Generally, victims of sexual and gender-based violence are picked up by the police and sent to the Safe Home through the court instead of sending them to the jail, where the safety and basic needs of the inmates are ensured in a congenial atmosphere (Ameen 2003). In each Safe Home, there are 13 personnel working, who have different responsibilities such as providing care, maintenance, legal assistance, education, medical service, vocational training, and counselling to the inmates. One social service officer is working in charge of each Safe Home, and the rest of the staff are incumbent (Department of Social Services 2021). As there is no special provision for recruiting social work graduates in the social service department of Bangladesh, officers are recruited from different academic backgrounds such as economics, sociology, anthropology, and so on (Hossain and Mathbor 2014). So, the Department of Social Service (DSS) introduced additional training for social service officers of the Safe Homes, after their recruitment, on providing psychosocial support and therapy to the inmates, practising social casework with them, and getting familiar with referral techniques (UNICEF et al. 2021). Though social work is not a recognised profession in Bangladesh, some of its methods and techniques are used by

DOI: 10.4324/9781003374374-13

the trained social service providers of government and non-government organisations (Das 2018, 33; Hatta et al. 2021, 477; Islam 2011).

Like all other countries in the world, Bangladesh also faced three consecutive waves of COVID-19 pandemic. The first wave of COVID-19 started spreading in Bangladesh on 8 March 2020, which negatively impacted social and healthcare services because of Bangladesh's dense population and limited resources (Anwar et al. 2020). The government declared a nationwide 'general holiday' on 26 March 2020, which was later extended several times. All government and non-government institutions were closed during the two-month lockdown, with only emergency service providers (such as healthcare and law enforcement) and businesses providing vital services (such as food and grocery delivery) remained open (Das 2020). Court activities were formally closed since the shutdown began but the Safe Home remained open to provide shelter for the inmates, although no new inmates were admitted. Since 11 May 2020 virtual courts started working with a limited capacity across the country, allowing the judges to handle hearings digitally using video-conferencing technology during the pandemic (Kamal 2020). They have to stay in the Safe Home until the situation becomes normal. As a result, social service officers working at Safe Home had to work like other frontline workers of Bangladesh during the pandemic. Shammi et al. (2020) found that a significant number of emergency service providers in Bangladesh were infected and felt forced to remain in isolation and many of them died from COVID-19. The workers' families, especially their children, were also at risk of contracting the virus (UNICEF et al. 2021). Social service officers also experienced challenging situations while providing services to the inmates of Safe Home due to the COVID-19 crisis. They had to ensure their own safety alongside managing the well-being of the inmates of the Safe Home and protecting them from this infectious disease. This qualitative study was conducted to investigate the nature of the challenges social service officers and their families faced at the Safe Home, and the strategies they adopted to work directly with the inmates during the pandemic.

## Literature review

The rate of violence towards women and children increased during the pandemic which was closely related to unemployment and other financial constraints within family (Alif 2022). As Bangladesh is a patriarchal society, so gender-based violence is a common phenomenon, which can take many forms like physical assault, psychological abuse, and sexual harassment including rape. To empower women microfinance was introduced and emphasis was given to provide equal employment opportunities for women in various industries. Such initiatives were taken based on neoliberal policies imposed by the World Bank and the International Monetary Fund (IMF). But culturally children and adults are supposed to be taken care of mostly by the female family members. Neoliberalism prioritises competition and efficiency, but it does not create an environment that is hospitable to women. It hasn't abolished the system that has oppressed the women in the past and therefore women continue to suffer today. As a result, when women are faced with different kinds of oppression at different places, they get limited supports (Murshid 2016).

The government of Bangladesh tries to protect women and children from violence by taking legislative measures and providing safe shelter homes. There are six government Safe Custody Homes (Safe Home) located in six divisional cities where only three hundred (each Safe Home can accommodate 50 victims only) women and adolescent girls who are raped, rescued from the sex trade, oppressed or deserted by their husbands, or experiencing a marriage dispute can stay (Department of Social Services 2021).

The recent pandemic has impacted each organisation and all types of professional services (Martínez-López et al. 2021, 61; Rao et al. 2020). Employees' ability to manage and positively overcome unfavourable situations, which are termed resilience at work, has been highlighted as a significant asset for maintaining the performance of an organisation (Fletcher and Sarkar 2013). The crisis management and resilience framework suggests that employees who develop cognitive, behavioural, emotion-regulation, and relational capabilities are better able to anticipate crises and adapt and respond more successfully to them (Williams et al. 2017). The model also proposes a feedback loop leading from individuals' crisis experiences to preparations for future crises. Finally, according to Trenton Williams et al. (2017) model, resilience may lead to both positive (e.g. increased perseverance) and negative outcomes (e.g. resistance to change, failure to adapt).

Okafor (2021) found that during disasters, pandemics, and other public emergencies social workers deliver exceptional services such as raising awareness, providing psychosocial assistance, and fighting for social inclusion for the most disadvantaged people. Some studies across the world investigated social workers' roles (Okafor 2021), opportunities (Harrikari et al. 2021), and obstacles (Farkas and Romaniuk 2020; Harrikari et al. 2021) during this pandemic. Social workers who worked as frontline workers during pandemics encountered a variety of unpleasant conditions (Shuja et al. 2020). Some factors contributed to creating such a hostile situation i.e. lack of crisis management training for social workers (Amadasun and Omorogiuwa 2020; Harrikari et al. 2021); limited infrastructure disrupting working from home, and internal division among the colleagues and shrinking focus areas of the social workers (Harrikari et al. 2021); lack of preparation for pandemic outcomes, shortage of personal protective equipment (PPE) for social workers, changes to official guidelines and protocols (Redondo-Sama et al. 2020). Social workers innovated different techniques to handle the hectic situation at their workplace originating from this pandemic such as forming mutual support groups to provide aid to the service users (Cabiati 2021; Redondo-Sama et al. 2020); using virtual media for carrying on the therapeutic relationship with clients instead of face to face interaction (Mishna et al. 2021; Redondo-Sama et al. 2020), and cooperation from the service users (Redondo-Sama et al. 2020). Based on the crisis management and resilience framework, organisations could design and implement human resource management practices (e.g. training, performance management) that supported the employees in building resilience and successfully anticipating and responding to crisis events.

Early research on COVID-19 pandemic in Bangladesh mainly focused on the experiences of health workers and bankers (Rana and Islam 2021; UNICEF et al. 2021). Social work is directly and indirectly practised by the government and non-government social service organisations since the independence of Bangladesh (Samad and Das 2014). Social service providers worked in harsh conditions during the pandemic as frontline workers. Although field-based social services were closed during the pandemic, some organisations such as Safe Home remained open for its inmates, who were awaiting justice pending in the court. This qualitative study was carried out on the social service officers of Safe Home who continued their services for the inmates during the pandemic. Their experiences and expectations for handling a crisis could be helpful for the policymakers to deal with such a situation in the future.

## Methods

This study used a qualitative research method to explore the responses and strategies used by the social service officers working at six Safe Homes during the pandemic. The qualitative method of social research helps the researcher provide a detailed understanding of participants' experiences (Tong et al. 2012). The participants of this study were the social service officers who supervise six Safe Homes. They are neither probation workers nor volunteers; rather they practice professional social work with the inmates of Safe Home after receiving short training on social work. Six of them were purposively selected as the participants of this research. Their address and contact number were collected from the website of the Department of Social Services (2021). Social service officers working at Safe Home are the source of primary data as they have deeper knowledge about their organisation. Verbal consent was taken from the research participants before the interview (Tremblay et al. 2021). Each participant was given freedom to withdraw from the interview if required. Researchers did not force or harm any participants before, during, and after the interview.

For collecting data, a semi-structured interview guide containing 12 open-ended questions was used. One data collector was appointed to collect data from 5 June 2020 to 15 July 2020 through web channels like Skype and WhatsApp. The data collector used video calling instead of face-to-face interviews to avoid COVID-19 infection. Stephanie Tremblay et al. (2021) found that rapport-building with the participants was challenging during an online interview because of time constraints and physical distancing. For building trusting relations with the research participants, the data collector took consent from them by explaining the research objectives. Before data collection a flexible interview schedule was agreed with each participant over the phone. However, the data collector faced difficulties to confirm a schedule with two of the research participants due to their heavy workload at the workplace because of COVID-19.

So, the interview schedule with those participants had to be conducted outside of office hours, and the data collector shortened the length of the interview stretching from 30 to 40 minutes. The rest of the interviews finished within 45–55 minutes. The data collector recorded these interviews with the consent of the participants. The data were first transcribed and then translated into English.

Collected data were analysed thematically following the steps outlined by Mojtaba Vaismoradi et al. (2013). The researchers read the data thoroughly to get an initial idea. Relevant data were sorted into different columns and groups according to the research questions. Later, different codes were developed such as personal experience, organisational experience, challenges, personal safety, and inmates' well-being. Selected codes were organised to create themes. Lastly, each theme was analysed and redefined with the narratives of the participants.

### Findings

The pandemic created an unusual and challenging working situation for social service officers of Safe Homes, but they had to take immediate actions for continuing their activities during COVID-19. Their capabilities to handle the situation have been thematically analysed here under the following themes, 'Changes in service delivery system during pandemic', 'Practical issues confronted by the social service officers', and 'Support to and from others'.

### Changes in service delivery system during pandemic

The COVID-19 pandemic created some deviations in providing services to the inmates of the Safe Home. The basic needs of the inmates such as food and informal education were ensured in the same way during the pandemic. But vocational training programmes were stopped, and the nature of counselling sessions changed during the first wave of COVID-19. Typically, the social service officers treated each inmate equally and provided one-to-one counselling and psychotherapy based on their problems. However, according to the government instructions, social service officers had limited working hours at the Safe Home during the first wave of COVID-19 and so they categorised the necessities of inmates and arranged group counselling according to their needs. Three officers said that '*During the pandemic, based on the urgency of inmates we divided all of them into several groups for providing counselling. We converted one-to-one sessions into group counselling*'. In most of these sessions, they provided cognitive-behaviour therapy (CBT) for the inmates to cope with this crisis in a better way. One of the officers explained that '*During the pandemic, we increased their engagement in indoor activities so that they could keep themselves away from negative thinking*'. Instead of physically attending court during the pandemic, the inmates residing at the Safe Home were brought to the court online after the proceedings had begun. All of the participants said that '*We received short training on using ICT so that we could present the inmates in front of the judge virtually*'.

Usually, the family members, relatives, and friends of the inmates could interact face-to-face at the Safe Home within a given time. But during the first phase of the pandemic, the social service officers restricted physical communication of the inmates with the outsiders to ensure their safety. Surprisingly, the officers noticed that the inmates broke down emotionally because of this decision. Considering this, communication over the phone with friends and family for the inmates was introduced at the Safe Home. A glass was set separating both the parties so that they could see each other and talk over the phone. One of them explained that 'A *meeting room within the Safe Home was arranged where a glass was set up separating both the parties*'. Video calling with COVID-19-affected family members was also arranged for the inmates.

## Practical issues confronted by the social service officers

Social service officers faced difficulties handling the inmates of the Safe Home as there were frequent changes in COVID-19 guidelines. Increasing responsibilities, lacking PPE (Personal Protective Equipment), and worrying about the safety of inmates put pressure on the participants at their workplaces. But there was no counselling session to reduce officers' stress. Two officers described this by saying that '*This pandemic affected us not only physically but also mentally. During the first wave we felt helpless as there was no PPE for us at the office [...]. Limited working hours increased our workload*'. They used masks during the conversation with the inmates. Communication problems arose with the deaf inmates who had to be understood through lip-reading. Three social service officers shared that, '*We always wear a mask during the conversation with the inmates, but we face trouble communicating with the deaf inmates*'.

Officers had to attend the virtual meeting with the higher authorities and other stakeholders of the Safe Home through Zoom application. Communication, however, was disrupted because of the low speed of the internet and recurrent load shedding. Two officers explained: '*Virtually decision-making was not easy during the pandemic because of frequent interruption of electricity and internet speed*'. Information and Communication tools (ICT) were introduced during the pandemic for communicating with the higher authorities. A short training on ICT was virtually arranged for the officers. Some of the officers, however, could not learn it properly from virtual training. One of the aged interviewees said that, '*Learning ICT within a limited time was impossible for me, as I was not habituated to using this before the pandemic*'.

Inmates of the Safe Home had a lot of misconceptions regarding COVID-19 testing. So, when any symptoms of COVID-19 were found among the inmates, social service officers found it difficult to send them to the testing centre. Two of the officers explained that '*they developed misconceptions about testing like—testers would take huge blood from them, or they would use a big syringe, or they might get infected with different diseases after testing. As a result, they refused to go to the medical centre for a COVID-19 test*'. Getting test results was a time-consuming issue. As there was no particular place for the inmates to be tested quickly, it took more than 14 days to get the result. Thus, it became difficult for the officers to know whether they were infected with COVID-19 or not. They were in a fix to decide regarding whether to send such an inmate for quarantine and providing medicine. One of the officers narrated,

> [...] we faced a huge problem to differentiate COVID patients from the rest of the inmates. Generally, the COVID-19 test result helped us to take a decision for the infected person. But when the cases were rising in Bangladesh, it took a long time to get the test result for inmates.

All of the respondents said that their family members were worried about their safety due to highly contagious nature of COVID-19 and non-availability of vaccines and drugs for treatment. One of the participants who was affected by COVID-19 expressed her concern saying that:

> [...] My family members became heavily tensed when I tested COVID-19 positive. Because, I could not manage a bed in the hospital for treatment as the hospitals were overloaded with patients. I had to stay at home in an isolated room and continued my treatment with doctors' consultations. But if my health condition deteriorated i.e., if I needed oxygen or any other emergency medical services I and my family members did not know what to do [...] how helpless we were!! By the grace of God, I cured fully after one and half months.

## Support to and from others

Fulfilling the needs of the inmates within limited capacities was a challenging task for the social service officers during the pandemic. Almost all of the participants shared their satisfaction when they could support the inmates at their best. Sometimes the social service officers became stressed at their workplace but there was no counselling for them to reduce the stress. They had informal support from their family members, friends, and colleagues. A group was virtually formed by themselves to eliminate their workplace stress. They discussed and shared their daily challenges on this platform, finding out possible solutions. Two research participants clarified that '*We created a WhatsApp group where we could discuss the challenges we faced at our organisation. From this discussion, we found the idea to overcome the situation*'. Social service officers acknowledged the caring attitude of their family members, friends, and the organisation during the pandemic. Despite limited resources, whenever social service officers took any decisions for the inmates, they got all kinds of support from the higher authorities of the Safe Home. To keep family members safe from this infectious virus, female social service officers handed over their family responsibilities to other members. When one of the social service officers was infected by COVID-19, she isolated herself from family members to ensure the safety of others.

## Discussion

This qualitative study was undertaken to comprehend the experiences of social service officers who were in charge of the Safe Home during the pandemic. The COVID-19 virus was new to everyone and most of us had no clear idea about it. When the government declared a nationwide lockdown, the court suspended all its activities. Inmates who were waiting for justice had to stay at the Safe Home during the pandemic, and the authorities did not allow them to go to their own houses. The findings of this study revealed that each of the social service officers encountered a series of challenges while working at the Safe Home as there were no crisis management guidelines to handle the pandemic. All of the participants became stressed when the government asked them to carry on the services of the Safe Home during lockdown. Findings by Neil Greenberg (2020, 425–426) also showed that a lack of preparation to handle the pandemic was a reason frontline workers faced such challenges. They faced new challenges every day at their workplace and daily lives. Inmates residing at the Safe Home were fearful during the first phase of the pandemic, and thus the social service officer provided counselling to them following social work ethics.

Three themes were developed based on the findings: changes in the service delivery system during the pandemic, practical issues confronted by the social service officers, and support to and from others. The goal of social service officers was to maintain a balance between their professional duty and personal and family well-being. They had to bring some changes in the service delivery such as providing group counselling instead of individual sessions. Most of the inmates were traumatised due to the pandemic. Officers increased inmates' engagement in the indoor activities such as gardening, cleaning, etc. to shift their focus; introducing different meeting styles with the outsiders and video calling with their relatives to ensure safety. Timo Harrikari et al. (2021) considered these as innovations and observed service users' life from a different perspective during the pandemic, describing them as opportunities for the social workers. Sarah Banks et al. (2020) found that managing a balance between clients' complex needs and limited resources within the organisation was a struggle for the social worker. Social service officers of the Safe Home faced multifarious problems during the first wave of COVID-19 pandemic. They could not manage PPE for themselves and their staff at the office; besides, limited office hours and increasing responsibilities towards the inmates contributed to their stress. Gisela Redondo-Sama et al. (2020) also found that the stress in the workplace was common for the social worker due to some unavoidable stressors that arose from the pandemic. Social service officers of the Safe Home showed their resilience and endurance to work with the inmates with these obstacles. However, they were in a dilemma to decide about quarantining those inmates waiting a long time for COVID-19 test results. The officers had to handle the misconceptions of the inmates regarding COVID-19. Generally, a social worker plays role of a counsellor and an educator to address these misconceptions (Okafor 2021). It was also difficult for the social service officers to use virtual communication tools with different stakeholders after receiving a short training on ICT. Most of the participants expressed their inability in using ICT, causing challenges to cope with the crisis. Faye Mishna et al. (2017) found that experienced social workers lacked training in using technology to deliver services for the clients. Added to these complexities, wearing a mask also created a communication barrier for those inmates who had hard of hearing.

However, as they had no professional counselling, informal social networks helped the social service officers reduce their internal stress through sharing. Harrikari et al. (2021) accepted the fact that the spirit of teamwork was helpful for the social workers to handle the pressure of their work. The participants used a virtual group to share their experiences and find solutions as every officer was going through the same situation. Geert Hofstede (2013) described Bangladesh a collectivist society where family, colleagues, friends, relatives, and neighbours played a significant role to provide a person with mental health support. It can be concluded, as Williams et al. (2017) proposed, that social service officers developed cognitive and behavioural capacities to adapt to the crisis caused by COVID-19. Resilience helped them positively, handling every critical situation with perseverance.

## Conclusion

Generally, services being offered to the inmates of the Safe Home were not affected due to the adoption of neoliberal policy in Bangladesh. The DSS of Bangladesh continues to perform its functions and activities towards serving the most vulnerable without disruption. Welfare activities of different organisations were impacted because of COVID-19 as some of the organisations stopped their services and some others remained open as per the government's decision. This study shows how the social service officers working at the Safe Home were completely unprepared for the pandemic but adapted to this new situation quickly and innovated new ways of working. According to crisis management and resilience framework, the resilience of the social service officers became stronger during the pandemic, which pushed them to be determined to help the inmates of the Safe Home. But the bureaucrats and policymakers were literally oblivious about the essentiality of such social work services in a crisis. The social service officers involved in providing such services should be properly trained as social workers so that they could undertake innovative steps to deal with a pandemic of this sort. It may be noted that human service professionals like social workers are hardly valued in a developing country like Bangladesh. Social service officers should be well-trained as frontline social workers like doctors, nurses, and police who can defend against the deteriorating mental health of the disadvantaged caused by a sudden pandemic.

*Notes (Description of the Safe Home):

The government of Bangladesh takes initiatives to keep the girls, women, juvenile prisoner safe and detached from the criminals of jail. According to Children's Act, 1974 and the Prevention of Violence against Women and Children Act, 2000 of Bangladesh, six Safe Homes were established across the country. The Safe Custody Homes will help victims to avoid future sufferings and humiliation for their confinement in jail with hardened criminals (DSS 2021).

## References

Alif, Abdullah. 2022. "MJF: 4,249 Women Subjected to Domestic Violence during the Lockdown." *Dhaka Tribune*, 6 May 2020. https://archive.dhakatribune.com/bangladesh/2020/05/06/mjf-4-249-women-endure-domestic-violence-amid-lockdown

Amadasun, Solomon, and Tracy B.E. Omorogiuwa. 2020. "Applying Anti-Oppressive Approach to Social Work Practice in Africa: Reflections of Nigerian BSW Students." *Journal of Humanities and Applied Social Sciences* 2 (3): 197–213. 10.1108/JHASS-12-2019-0082

Ameen, Nusrat. 2003. "Children and Females in Safe Custody – A Violation of Legal Rights in Bangladesh." *The Dhaka University Studies* 14 (1), 71–100.

Anwar, Saeed, Mohammad Nasrullah, and Mohammad J. Hosen. 2020. "COVID-19 and Bangladesh: Challenges and How to Address Them." *Frontiers in Public Health* 8: 154. 10.3389/fpubh.2020.00154

Banks, Sarah, Tian Cai, Ed de Jonge, Jane Shears, Michelle Shum, Ana M. Sobočan, Kim Strom, Rory Truell, María Jesús Úriz, and Merlinda Weinberg. 2020. "Practising Ethically during COVID-19: Social Work Challenges and Responses." *International Social Work* 63 (5), 569–583. 10.1177/0020872820949614

Cabiati, Elena. 2021. "Social Workers Helping Each Other during the COVID-19 Pandemic: Online Mutual Support Groups." *International Social Work* 64 (5): 676–688. 10.1177/0020872820975447

Das, Tulshi K. 2018. "Social Work Practice with Abused Married Women." In *Social Work Case Analysis: Global Perspective*, edited by Lolita Vilka, Olafs Brūvers, Anita Ābele, Marika Lotko, and Ilvija Razgale, 33–64. Riga: Rīgas Stradiņa Universitāte.

Das, Tulshi K. 2020. "Bangladesh." In *COVID-19 and Social Work: A Collection of Country Reports*, edited by Lena Dominelli, Timo Harrikari, Joseph Mooney, Vesna Leskošek, and Erin Kennedy Tsunoda, 24–30. N.p. https://www.iassw-aiets.org/wp-content/uploads/2020/07/IASSW-COVID-19-and-Social-Work-Country-Reports-Final-1.pdf

Department of Social Services. 2021. "Safe-Home." Department of Social Services, Bangladesh. Accessed 25 August 2022. http://www.dss.gov.bd/site/page/fd7fbd4a-ee0c-4417-9200-a1984894130f/Safe-Home &-Shelter-Home

Farkas, Kathleen J., and J. Richard Romaniuk. 2020. "Social Work, Ethics and Vulnerable Groups in the Time of Coronavirus and COVID-19." *Society Register* 4 (2): 67–82. 10.14746/sr.2020.4.2.05

Fletcher, David, and Mustafa Sarkar. 2013. "Psychological Resilience: A Review and Critique of Definitions, Concepts, and Theory." *European Psychologist* 18 (1): 12–23. 10.1027/1016-9040/a000124

Greenberg, Neil. 2020. "Mental Health of Health-Care Workers in the COVID-19 Era." *Nature Reviews Nephrology* 16 (8): 425–426. 10.1038/s41581-020-0314-5

Harrikari, Timo, Marjo Romakkaniemi, Laura Tiitinen, and Sanna Ovaskainen. 2021. "Pandemic and Social Work: Exploring Finnish Social Workers' Experiences through A SWOT Analysis." *The British Journal of Social Work* 51 (5): 1644–1662. 10.1093/bjsw/bcab052

Hatta, Zulkarnain A., Zarina M. Saad, Tulshi K. Das, Isahaque Ali, Md. Anwar Hossain, and Mohd H. Yahaya. 2021. "Islamic and Local Knowledge on Social Work in Malaysia and Bangladesh." *Journal of Religion & Spirituality in Social Work: Social Thought* 40 (4): 475–493. 10.1080/15426432.2021.1949425

Hofstede, Geert. 2013. *Culture's Consequences.* 2nd edition. Thousand Oaks: Sage.

Hossain, Md. Ismail, and Golam M. Mathbor. 2014. "Social Work Practice for Social Development in Bangladesh: Issues and Challenges." *Asian Social Work and Policy Review* 8 (2): 123–137. 10.1111/aswp.12030

Islam, Fardeen. 2011. "Social Work Education and Practice in Bangladesh: Past Effort and Present Trends." In *Social Work Education in Countries of the East: Issues and Challenges,* edited by Selwyn Stanley, 27–45. New York: Nova Science Publishers Inc.

Kamal, Syed M. 2020. "How Bangladesh Is Addressing the Covid-19 Pandemic." *Observer Research Foundation.* Last modified 4 May 2020. https://www.orfonline.org/expert-speak/how-bangladesh-is-addressing-the-covid19-pandemic-65601/

Martínez-López, José Á., Cristina Lázaro-Pérez, and José Gómez-Galán. 2021. "Death Anxiety in Social Workers as a Consequence of the COVID-19 Pandemic." *Behavioral Sciences* 11 (5): 61. 10.3390/bs11050061

Ministry of Social Welfare. 2021. "Department of Social Service." Accessed 25 August 2022. https://msw.gov.bd/

Mishna, Faye, Sophia Fantus, and Lauren B. McInroy. 2017. "Informal Use of Information and Communication Technology: Adjunct to Traditional Face-To-Face Social Work Practice." *Clinical Social Work Journal* 45 (1): 49–55. 10.1007/s10615-016-0576-3

Mishna, Faye, Elizabeth Milne, Marion Bogo, and Luana F. Pereira. 2021. "Responding to COVID-19: New Trends in Social Workers' Use of Information and Communication Technology." *Clinical Social Work Journal* 49 (4): 484–494. 10.1007/s10615-020-00780-x

Murshid, Nadine S. 2016. "Violence: Neoliberalism at the Root of It." *The Daily Star – Column – #ResearchMesearch,* 28 December 2016. https://www.thedailystar.net/opinion/researchmesearch/violence-neoliberalism-the-root-it-1336330

Okafor, Afomachukwu. 2021. "Role of the Social Worker in the Outbreak of Pandemics (A Case of COVID-19)." *Cogent Psychology* 8 (1): 1939537. 10.1080/23311908.2021.1939537

Rana, Rezwanul H., and Ariful Islam. 2021. "Psychological Impact of COVID-19 among Frontline Financial Services Workers in Bangladesh." *Journal of Workplace Behavioral Health* 36 (3): 238–249. 10.1080/15555240.2021.1930021

Rao, H. Raghav, Naga Vemprala, Patricia Akello, and Rohit Valecha. 2020. "Retweets of Officials' Alarming vs Reassuring Messages During The COVID-19 Pandemic: Implications for Crisis Management." *International Journal of Information Management* 55: 102187. 10.1016/j.ijinfomgt.2020.102187

Redondo-Sama, Gisela, Virginia Matulic, Ariadna Munté-Pascual, and Irene de Vicente. 2020. "Social Work during the COVID-19 Crisis: Responding to Urgent Social Needs." *Sustainability* 12 (20): 8595. 10.3390/su12208595

Samad, Muhammad and Tulshi K. Das. 2014. "Contextualizing Social Work Practice in Bangladesh." In *Social Work Education and Practice: Scholarship and Innovations in the*

*Asia Pacific*, edited by Baju R. Nikku, and Zulkarnain A. Hatta, 72–88. Brisbane: The Primrose Hall Publishing Group.

Shammi, Mashura, Md. Bodrud-Doza, Abu R.M.T. Islam, and Md. M. Rahman. 2020. "COVID-19 Pandemic, Socioeconomic Crisis and Human Stress in Resource-Limited Settings: A Case from Bangladesh." *Heliyon* 6 (5): e04063. 10.1016/j.heliyon. 2020.e04063

Shuja, Kanwar H., Muhammad Aqeel, Abbas Jaffar, and Ammar Ahmed. 2020. "COVID-19 Pandemic and Impending Global Mental Health Implications." *Psychiatria Danubina* 32 (1): 32–35. 10.24869/psyd.2020.32

Tremblay, Stephanie, Sonia Castiglione, Li-Anne Audet, Michèle Desmarais, Minnie Horace, and Sandra Peláez. 2021. "Conducting Qualitative Research to Respond to COVID-19 Challenges: Reflections for the Present and Beyond." *International Journal of Qualitative Methods* 20. 10.1177/16094069211009679

Tong, Allison, Kate Flemming, Elizabeth McInnes, Sandy Oliver, and Jonathan Craig. 2012. "Enhancing Transparency in Reporting the Synthesis of Qualitative Research: ENTREQ." BMC *Medical Research Methodology* 12: 181. 10.1186/1471-2288-12-181

UNICEF, International Federation of Social Workers, The Alliance for Child Protection in Humanitarian Action, and Global Social Service Workforce Alliance. 2021. *Social Service Workforce Safety and Wellbeing during the COVID-19 Response: Recommended Actions*. N.c.: N.p. https://www.unicef.org/media/68501/file/Social-Service-Workforce-Safety-and-Wellbeing-during-COVID19-Response.pdf

Vaismoradi, Mojtaba, Hannele Turunen, and Terese Bondas. 2013. "Content Analysis and Thematic Analysis: Implications for Conducting a Qualitative Descriptive Study." *Nursing & Health Sciences* 15 (3): 398–405. 10.1111/nhs.12048

Williams, Trenton A., Daniel A. Gruber, Kathleen M. Sutcliffe, Dean A. Shepherd, and Eric Y. Zhao. 2017. "Organizational Response to Adversity: Fusing Crisis Management and Resilience Research Streams." *Academy of Management Annals* 11 (2): 733–769. 10.5465/annals.2015.0134

# 11 Social Vulnerability of Older Adults and COVID-19: Findings from Surveys of Professionals Providing Care in Japan

*Junko Wake and Mie Ohwa*

## Background and the framework of the study

With the increase of natural disasters due to climate change, many studies have been conducted focusing on vulnerability (Borden et al. 2007; Cannon 2008; Cutter 1996; Morsut et al. 2021). In recent years, research has also focused on social vulnerability (Burton et al. 2018; Cutter and Finch 2007; Otto et al. 2017; Singh et al. 2014). Social vulnerability is 'determined by physical, social, economic, and environmental factors or processes, which increase the susceptibility of community to the impact of hazards and is conceptually located at the interaction of nature and culture' (Singh et al. 2014, 78). According to Christopher Burton et al. (2018), vulnerability is an underlying condition, caused by stress on the system, including natural hazards. Susan Cutter, Bryan Boruff, and W. Lyn Shirley further developed the definition of social vulnerability as follows, 'social vulnerability is a multidimensional concept that helps to identify those characteristics and experiences of communities (and individuals) that enable them to respond to and recover from environmental hazards' (Cutter et al. 2003, 257).

We discuss the social vulnerability with regard to older adults with the support of evidence from our study. The first case of COVID-19 in Japan was reported on 16 January 2020, and since then, the infection rates have repeatedly increased. In order to accurately assess the situation, it is necessary to clarify when the survey was conducted, as frequent changes in the infection status affect the social vulnerability situation, hence the results of the survey. We discuss in this chapter, the findings of our survey, conducted in February 2021, when vaccination was not yet in full swing and a second state of emergency declaration was still in effect for Tokyo and three other prefectures in the Kanto region of Japan.

In 2020, Japan's ageing rate was 28.8 percent, making it the most aged country in the world. According to Japan's Ministry of Health, Labour and Welfare (MHLW), as of 1 February 2021, there were 928 clusters of residential facilities for older adults nationwide—more than the 796 clusters of medical institutions (Ueda and Koizumi 2021). In residential facilities where vulnerable older adults live together, doctors are not always available to treat them, and there was initially a lack of protective equipment for COVID-19. In this regard,

DOI: 10.4324/9781003374374-14

it is important to identify and mitigate the social vulnerability of professionals involved in the care of older adults.

The aims of the study are to describe the social vulnerability of older adults and professionals who care for them during the COVID-19 pandemic and to provide an exploratory analysis of the associated factors. We first present a review of previous studies on the social vulnerability faced by older adults in Japan during this pandemic. The situation of the elderly residing at home was ascertained, based on preliminary interviews with care managers. This was followed by a questionnaire survey to obtain and analyse the perceptions and feelings including negative effects towards the pandemic, among the three types of professionals (social workers, facility managers, and chief care workers) who work in the welfare and health care facilities for older adults. Finally, we present our discussion on ways to address the social vulnerability of older adults and the professionals who care for them.

## Social vulnerability of the older adults during COVID-19 pandemic in Japan

In Japan, during the early stages of the pandemic, there was initially a tendency to restrict persons from going out to prevent COVID-19 infection; this tendency was particularly strong among older adults. Some nursing homes also restricted visits of family members and prevented residents from going out; local governments also required facilities to close after a cluster outbreak. As a result, older adults remained confined to their homes and facilities. There have been warnings of the mental health effects of isolation since the early stages of the pandemic. The high-risk population for mental health during a pandemic is said to include the following: infected persons, quarantined persons, their families and related persons, medical personnel, helping professionals, people with a low socioeconomic status, people with physical disabilities, people with mental disabilities, racial minorities, older adults, pregnant women, and children (Shigemura et al. 2020).

The stressors and their psychological impact on pandemic isolation can be divided into two stages: stressors during isolation and post-isolation stressors. Stressors during isolation include frustration with restrictions, boredom, lack of supplies and medical care, lack of information, extensions to the restriction period, and fear of becoming infected or infecting others. Post-isolation stressors include financial loss, stigma, and the time it takes to readjust to 'normal' routines. Several studies have been conducted on the physical and psychosocial effects in older adults. In July 2020, after the first state of emergency was lifted, a study showed that only 25 percent of a sample of 1,000 men and women between the ages of 65 and 85 years had returned to their way of life before the spread of COVID-19, with many reporting that they were less active (53.8%) or felt physically unwell (34.5%) (Omron Healthcare 2020). The impact of infection prevention measures on independent older adults in the community was a decrease in the frequency of going out, where the purpose of going out was related to social health, such as cultural and community activities

(Ouchi et al. 2021; Yamauchi et al. 2021). These containment measures were intended to protect this population, but they concurrently had negative effects, such as reduced motor function (Watanabe et al. 2021), which ultimately exacerbated social vulnerability.

The Dementia Care Research Center, which plays a central role in dementia care at nursing homes and other facilities, conducted a survey of care workers and nurses across Japan. The survey found that 85 percent agreed that, refraining from going out or visiting had an impact on the progression of dementia. Compared to five months before the pandemic, the most noticeable effects were behavioural and psychological problems, such as 'wanting to see family members' (49%), 'irritability' (40%), and 'becoming restless' (29%). In addition, on the physical side, 28 percent of the respondents reported a 'decline in health conditions' (Yomiuri Newspaper 2020). When a person with dementia who is receiving care at home is hospitalised after being infected with COVID-19, the sudden change in environment is known to cause discomfort and delirium in older patients (Japan Medical Association COVID-19 Expert Committee 2020).

## The impact of the COVID-19 pandemic on care managers working with older adults in the community

Previous studies have shown that the COVID-19 pandemic has exacerbated the social vulnerability of older adults, and has a significant negative impact on professionals such as social workers, care workers, and care managers who support older adults. In August 2020, we conducted preliminary interviews with 21 care managers who participated in the regional training program. The following is a summary of how care managers responded to the problems they faced (Ohwa 2021).

Older adults, their families, and officials occasionally had different feelings and perceptions about COVID-19, and care managers found it difficult to deal with them. In some cases, both the clients and their families were highly anxious. In other cases, the client wanted to use the daycare service, but the family was too anxious about infection to make use of it. Some care managers were troubled as some clients began to refuse medical care and home services. In some cases, there were family members with disabilities, and there was a limit to the amount of support that could be provided to family members. Although insurance for long-term care was originally intended for older adults only, there may be a need for social work that includes their families. Care managers said that it took a lot of time to deal with difficult cases, such as dealing with families with complex needs; the rewards were often not commensurate with the effort spent.

As described above, with regard to the older adults' care services, the COVID-19 pandemic, which is novel, placed older adults, their families, and the care managers themselves in a state of uncertainty and anxiety. Despite the risk of infection, care managers had to visit the homes of older adults on a regular basis to provide accurate information and support to older adults and their families, since the long-term care insurance law mandates the care manager to physically meet the client in person at home to make accurate monitoring and assessment. They felt as if they were constantly being asked on how to provide support in a situation where there were no right answers.

## A questionnaire survey of health and welfare facilities for older adults

The COVID-19 pandemic has profoundly affected older adults, and those who are institutionalised in residential facilities and nursing homes were the most vulnerable. A study of 20 countries in Europe and North America found that nursing home residents accounted for 0.73 percent of the total population, while 46 percent of deaths from COVID-19 were in nursing homes (Comas-Herrera et al. 2020). In addition to the lack of adequate infection control measures and difficulty in protecting patients, many older adults in nursing homes are unable to report their symptoms, which can lead to delays in the detection of infection and outbreaks.

Unlike Western countries, deaths in residential facilities and nursing homes in Japan account for less than 20 percent of all deaths among older adults in Japan (Japanese Association of Medical Care for Chronic Illness 2021). Although the details are not clear, this could be attributed to the efforts of facilities and nursing homes, their collaboration with medical institutions, and the thorough measures taken to prevent COVID-19 infection on a daily basis. However, the prohibition of family visits and constraints on socialisation resulted in a decline in the cognitive function and quality of life (QOL) of residents (Kanamori et al. 2021). There is also concern about the enormous amount of stress placed on staff over the long term.

The research presented in this section aims to clarify the perception and negative impacts experienced by the three professional groups (social workers, facility managers, and chief care workers) working in two different types of nursing homes in Japan: welfare facilities and healthcare facilities for older adults (Wake and Lee 2022). A welfare facility is an institution where residents receive care and live until the end of their lives; only those who require moderate or severe care can be admitted. Meanwhile, healthcare facilities for older adults are medium-term institutions where users receive care and rehabilitation. Both facilities operate under the public long-term care insurance system. We analysed differences in the nature and extent of negative impacts among different types of institutions and professional groups and distilled the factors and determinants of their social vulnerability.

We used simple random sampling to select 500 welfare facilities for older adults and 500 healthcare facilities in Tokyo and six neighbouring prefectures in the Kanto region. A questionnaire survey was conducted in February 2021. As mentioned previously, it was the time when the second state of emergency declaration was still in effect for Tokyo and three other prefectures in the Kanto region of Japan. Three survey forms were enclosed with each facility, requesting that a social worker, a facility manager, and a chief care worker each respond to the survey.

## Basic characteristics of the facilities and respondents

Due to the differences in the historical development of the two types of facilities, there were differences in the year of establishment and the type of corporation. Welfare facilities have a longer history and majority of them are operated by social welfare corporations, while about three-quarters of healthcare facilities are operated by medical corporations. Differences in admission capacity and average lengths of stay were also found. The average length of stay in welfare facilities is 1115 days, while those of health care facilities are 466 days.

Within the three professional categories, there were differences in gender, age, job qualifications, and family living arrangements. In the case of facility managers, the majority of respondents were male and older. However, the largest proportion of social workers and chief care workers were in their 40s, and more than 30 percent of chief care workers were in their 20s or 30s. In terms of the number of years of service in the current facility, chief care worker worked the longest at over 13 years.

In addition to the basic attributes, another important item is the facility's availability to secure human power. In recent years, the shortage of care workers has become a serious issue in Japan. In both facilities, only about a quarter of the respondents answered that the situation was 'favourable', while more than three-quarters of the respondents answered that recruitment was 'somewhat difficult', 'fairly difficult', or 'extremely difficult'.

## Perceptions of work under COVID-19 pandemic

Respondents were asked about their perceptions of work using a five-point scale on 16 items, with scores ranging from 1 = 'totally disagree' to 5 = 'totally agree'. Because this pandemic was a first-time event, this scale was constructed from our preliminary interviews with facility staff, rather than from existing standardised measures. As shown in Table 11.1, there was a high level of 'fear of infecting' residents, staff, and family members, and a high level of 'feeling unsafe while working' in situations where 'residents cannot take sufficient infection control measures'. In addition, respondents were also concerned about the extent to which they could interact with the local community.

Although there was no major difference in perceptions between respondents from the two types of facilities, statistically significant differences were found in several items between the professions. For the four items of 'fear of spreading my infection to residents', 'spreading my infection to staff', 'spreading my infection to my family', and 'lack of sufficient support from the corporation', the concerns of social workers and chief care workers were higher than those of facility managers. Meanwhile, in the categories 'discrimination from the community' and 'anxiety about management' facility managers expressed greater anxiety than the other two professions.

For a more structural understanding of the 16 items, a factor analysis (principal component analysis, and varimax rotation) was conducted, and five

Table 11.1 Perceptions of work under the COVID-19 pandemic

| | Welfare facility | | Healthcare facility | | T-Test | Social worker | | Facility manager | | Chief care worker | | One-way ANOVA |
|---|---|---|---|---|---|---|---|---|---|---|---|---|
| | M | SD | M | SD | | M | SD | M | SD | M | SD | |
| **Factor 1:  Fear of Infecting Others (α=.94)** | | | | | | | | | | | | |
| I feel fear of passing my infection to residents without knowing it. | 4.36 | 0.80 | 4.36 | 0.88 | | 4.5 | 0.77 | 3.94 | 0.95 | 4.56 | 0.67 | *** |
| I feel fear of infection through contact with other staff members. | 3.88 | 0.90 | 3.78 | 0.99 | | 3.82 | 0.99 | 3.79 | 0.91 | 3.91 | 0.89 | *** |
| I feel fear of passing my infection to family members without knowing it. | 4.24 | 0.87 | 4.29 | 0.94 | | 4.34 | 0.92 | 3.92 | 0.94 | 4.46 | 0.71 | *** |
| **Factor 2:  Fear of Being Infected (α=.72)** | | | | | | | | | | | | |
| After the COVID-19 crisis, I feel that it is dangerous to carry out my work. | 3.96 | 0.85 | 3.84 | 0.85 | | 3.9 | 0.83 | 4.05 | 0.80 | 3.8 | 0.90 | |
| I feel fear of infection through contact with residents. | 3.45 | 1.13 | 3.42 | 1.09 | | 3.5 | 1.12 | 3.3 | 1.05 | .48 | 1.14 | |
| I feel fear of infection through contact with other staff members. | 3.88 | 0.90 | 3.78 | 0.99 | | 3.82 | 0.99 | 3.79 | 0.91 | 3.91 | 0.89 | |
| Inability of residents to take adequate infection control measures themselves. | 4.03 | 1.05 | 4.13 | 0.95 | | 4.02 | 1.05 | 3.98 | 1.04 | 4.23 | 0.91 | |

| | Mean | SD | Mean | SD | | Mean | SD | Mean | SD | Mean | SD | |
|---|---|---|---|---|---|---|---|---|---|---|---|---|
| **Factor 3: Difficulty in Communication (α=.71)** | | | | | | | | | | | | |
| Insufficient communication between residents and staff. | 3.00 | 1.02 | 2.94 | 1.07 | | 2.92 | 1.05 | 2.98 | 1.05 | 3.04 | 1.03 | |
| Staff do not communicate well with each other. | 2.98 | 1.02 | 2.77 | 1.09 | * | 2.9 | 1.08 | 2.81 | 1.03 | 2.94 | 1.05 | |
| It has become difficult to balance work and family life. | 2.48 | 0.99 | 2.49 | 0.96 | | 2.46 | 1.03 | 2.52 | 0.93 | 2.51 | 0.95 | |
| I felt discriminated against by the community because I work in a nursing home. | 1.99 | 0.97 | 2.14 | 0.98 | | 1.94 | 0.97 | 2.24 | 1.00 | 2.03 | 0.93 | * |
| **Factor 4: Concern about Survival due to Increased Burden (α=.5.8)** | | | | | | | | | | | | |
| I feel increased anxiety about management. | 3.74 | 1.02 | 3.78 | 1.03 | | 3.7 | 1.12 | 4.06 | 0.87 | 3.56 | 0.96 | *** |
| It is hard to communicate with the local community. | 4.04 | 1.14 | 3.98 | 1.11 | | 4.04 | 1.17 | 4.11 | 0.97 | 3.86 | 1.18 | |
| Workload has increased and physical and mental fatigue has increased. | 3.62 | 1.05 | 3.44 | 1.07 | | 3.48 | 1.06 | 3.51 | 1.03 | 3.65 | 1.07 | |
| **Factor 5: Lack of Support from Corporation & Government (α=.76)** | | | | | | | | | | | | |
| Lack of adequate support (information, supplies) from the corporation. | 2.44 | 0.91 | 2.64 | 1.06 | * | 2.55 | 1.02 | 2.35 | 0.86 | 2.65 | 1.00 | * |
| Lack of adequate support (information, supplies) from the government. | 2.97 | 0.97 | 3.05 | 1.06 | | 3.06 | 0.99 | 2.85 | 1.05 | 3.07 | 0.99 | |

*** p <.001, **p <0.1, * p <.05

dimensions were extracted, namely 'fear of infecting', 'fear of being infected', 'communication difficulties', 'concern about survival due to increased burden', and 'lack of support from corporation and government'. Social workers and chief care workers were more inclined than managers to cite 'fear of infecting', while chief care workers were more inclined to cite 'lack of support from the corporation and government'.

## Negative impact of the spread of COVID-19

Respondents were asked to score the negative impact of the pandemic on six categories, (1) themselves, (2) residents, (3) family members of residents, (4) family members of respondents, (5) staff, and (6) facilities/corporations on a scale from 1= 'no impact at all' to 10 = 'impacted extremely negatively'. The results (mean scores) are presented in Figure 11.1.

For the six variables, the highest negative impact was shown for 'family members of residents', followed by the impact on facilities and corporations. No significant differences were found by facility or profession.

Next, all the negative impact points by subject were used as a dependent variable, and multiple regression analysis was performed to examine the factors influencing the high and low scores (Table 11.2). The independent variables

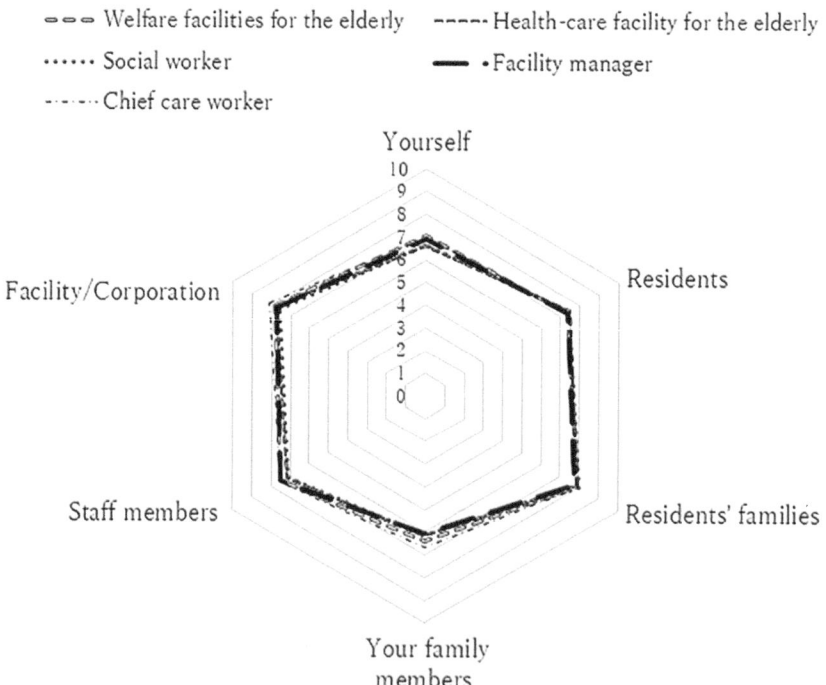

Figure 11.1 Negative impact of the spread of COVID-19.

*Table 11.2* Determinants for the negative impact of the COVID-19 (multiple regression analysis)

| | Yourself β | Resident β | Residents family β | Your family β | Staff β | Facility/ corporation β |
|---|---|---|---|---|---|---|
| **Facility Factors** | | | | | | |
| Facility type | −0.09 | 0.03 | −0.03 | −0.03 | −0.06 | 0.02 |
| Year of establishment | 0.02 | 0.10 | 0.05 | −0.03 | 0.07 | 0.07 |
| Location population size | 0.04 | 0.09 | 0.08 | 0.07 | 0.08 | 0.16** |
| Recruiting care workers | 0.10* | 0.12* | 0.08 | 0.08 | 0.15** | 0.16** |
| Infection of residents | 0.04 | 0.08 | −0.04 | −0.00 | 0.08 | −0.04 |
| Staff turnover due to pandemic | −0.10 | −0.03 | −0.04 | −0.05 | −0.07 | −0.08 |
| **Individual Factors** | | | | | | |
| Sex | 0.16** | 0.14** | 0.13* | 0.13* | 0.16** | 0.16** |
| Age | −0.17* | −0.16* | −0.17* | −.14* | −.17* | −0.20** |
| Being a facility manager | 0.15* | 0.08 | 0.04 | 0.05 | 0.15* | 0.11 |
| Total years of experience | −0.01 | 0.02 | 0.06 | −0.02 | 0.00 | 0.03 |
| Adjusted R $^2$ | 0.05** | 0.04** | 0.02* | 0.02 | 0.07** | 0.10** |

**p<0.01 *p<0.05

included were the facility type, the year of its establishment, the population size of the facility's location, the respondent's gender, age, whether the respondent was the manager of the facility, the respondent's sense of difficulty in recruiting care workers, the presence of infection among residents, the presence of staff turnover due to the spread of COVID-19 infection, and the respondent's total years of experience in health and social care services.

The results of the analysis showed that gender and age were the determining factors for all the negative effects, with a correlation between 'female' and 'younger' with a more negative evaluation. We also found that the perception of 'difficulty in recruiting care workers' had a negative impact on 'oneself', 'residents', 'staff', and 'facilities/corporations'. Furthermore, the negative impact on the institution was greater in urban areas with larger populations. In the preliminary analysis, we found different associations between the two professional categories of facility managers and others, so we included a binary variable for facility managers and others. The results indicate that being a facility manager had a strong negative impact on 'oneself' and on the 'facility/corporation', suggesting that respondents took their responsibility as a leader of an organisation more seriously.

## Discussion

As evidenced by previous studies, the COVID-19 pandemic has had many negative impacts on older adults living in the community as well as in institutions. Before the spread of COVID-19, there were many active efforts to promote social participation and preventive care for older adults such as day services and gathering places. However, due to infection prevention measures, it became difficult to provide such a place for people to gather. As a result of the lack of contact with others in the community, a decline in physical function in older adults due to confinement and the psychosocial effects of high anxiety were observed. It is paradoxical that these protective measures have resulted in the exacerbation of social vulnerability among older adults.

There is an urgent requirement for social work to support older adults in the community in order to mitigate social vulnerability. To support older adults who tend to be isolated in the community, the first step is to make social connections. It is necessary to devise IT equipment that enables non-face-to-face connections and also face-to-face meetings with a small group of people with adequate infection control measures in place. In addition, for older adults living in the community, it is difficult to receive correct information about unknown infections such as COVID-19 pandemic, which may cause anxiety and result in unnecessary self-imposed regulation of their behaviour. Therefore, it appears that the role of social workers is to provide appropriate information to older adults and their families from a professional perspective.

We did not find any major difference in perceptions around COVID-19 across facility types and across the three types of professions among the respondents. They were more concerned about infecting residents and staff than themselves, with families being the most affected. However, social workers and chief care workers were more fearful of infecting residents and staff, whereas facility managers felt more challenged by community relations and management. Furthermore, there were differences by gender and age, with women and the younger generation being more negatively affected, including by understaffing in institutions. These factors have exacerbated the social vulnerability of professionals in institutions as essential workers, and thus in affecting institutional care. The results suggest the importance of monitoring for post-traumatic stress disorder (PTSD) and critical incident stress in staff who are more affected by the pandemic, and to provide the necessary psychosocial and post-traumatic care. In addition, the shortage of staff is a structural problem that has existed in Japanese society before the pandemic began, and it is an issue that must be addressed in the post-COVID-19 era.

It is clear that the pandemic has created a more critical situation in facilities for the older adults than expected. Outbreaks of clusters have resulted in staff becoming infected or being in close contact with infected people, making it difficult to provide services; in addition, these facilities with limited infection control equipment, knowledge, and experience have had to care for residents who could not be admitted to the hospital. Since long-term care services for the older adults are essential for their QOL, 'continuity of services', 'ensuring the safety of users', and 'ensuring the safety of staff' are essential elements that must be secured in the time of crisis.

As a result, Japan's MHLW has mandated for the first time that long-term care insurance facilities and home-care service providers to have business continuity plans (BCPs) from FY2021, with a three-year transitional period. The MHLW published guidelines in December 2020 for developing two types of BCPs, one for COVID-19 and the other for natural disasters. The key points for preparing a BCP for COVID-19 are (1) information sharing and division of roles among relevant parties, including those within the facility or office, and the establishment of a system that facilitates decision-making; (2) measures to be taken in the event of a person being infected or a suspected infection; (3) securing staff; (4) organising work priorities; and (5) the dissemination of information and training on a regular basis so that the plan can be implemented. BCPs can be seen as systematic tools of minimising social vulnerability of older adults in need of care and professionals who provide care for them.

However, it is difficult for small social welfare corporations to formulate feasible BCPs by themselves. Previous studies have shown that comprehensive health and welfare corporations were able to avoid the spread of cluster infections by taking appropriate infection control measures and securing human resources. It is necessary for local governments, prefectures, and even the national government to provide support in formulating BCPs by forming networks and urging collaboration among different corporations across prefectures.

This study did not specifically identify unique role of social workers in responding to the pandemic in facilities for older adults. This may have been due to the emergent need for a facility-wide response that involved other care professionals. However, social workers have a significant role in the development and implementation of BCPs in areas such as family support, the promotion of social participation and advocacy for facility residents. Online interviews and visits by family members have recently become common and information and communications technologies (ICTs) have been used to innovate local multi-professional and multi-agency collaboration. The use of robots to provide non-contact care is also being tried. Social work plays an important role in the integration of technological innovations and human interaction in social care. Social work researchers need to further examine social workers' experiences of the pandemic and identify the unique role that social work can and/or should play in a pandemic situation.

In conclusion, COVID-19 pandemic brought to the fore, not only the physical vulnerability but also the social vulnerability of older adults. Even in Japan, where the mortality rate among older adults was relatively low, we found that the social vulnerability, both at home and in institutions, was exacerbated not only by the inherent effects of the disease, but also by the social measures taken to protect against infection.

Age, gender, and difficulty in securing care workers were also identified as factors that exacerbated the social vulnerability of professionals working in the facilities. The Japanese government has announced a policy to mandate the formulation of BCPs in order to deal with such social vulnerability. It is hoped that social workers, who comprehensively contribute to the quality of life of older adults, will play a decisive role in identifying and overcoming the factors of social vulnerability.

# References

Borden, Kevin A., Mathew C. Schmidtlein, Christopher T. Emrich, Walter W. Piegorsch, and Susan L. Cutter. 2007. "Vulnerability of U.S. Cities to Environmental Hazards." *Journal of Homeland Security and Emergency Management* 4 (2): 5. 10.2202/1547-7355.1279

Burton, Christopher, Samuel Rufat, and Eric Tate. 2018. "Social Vulnerability." In *Vulnerability and Resilience to Natural Hazards*, edited by Sven Fuchs and Thomas Thaler, 53–81. Cambridge: Cambridge University Press.

Cannon, Terry. 2008. "Reducing People's Vulnerability to Natural Hazards Communities and Resilience." WIDER Research Paper No. 2008/34. The United Nations University World Institute for Development Economics Research (UNU-WIDER), Helsinki, April 2008. http://hdl.handle.net/10419/45089

Comas-Herrera, Adelina, Joseba Zalakaín, Elizabeth Lemmon, David Henderson, Charles Litwin, Amy T. Hsu, Andrea F. Schmidt, Greg Arling, and Jose-Luis Fernández. 2020. *Mortality Associated with COVID-19 in Care Homes: International Evidence.* N.p.: International Long-term Care Policy Networks. March 24, 2021. https://ltccovid.org/wp-content/uploads/2021/02/Mortality-associated-with-COVID-among-people-living-in-care-homes-14-October-2020.pdf.

Cutter, Susan L. 1996. "Vulnerability to Environmental Hazards." *Progress in Human Geography* 20 (4): 529–539. 10.1177/030913259602000407

Cutter, Susan L. and Christina Finch. 2007. "Temporal and Spatial Changes in Social Vulnerability to Natural Hazards." *Proceedings of the National Academy of Sciences (PNAS)* 105 (7): 2301–2306. 10.1073/pnas.0710375105

Cutter, Susan L., Bryan J. Boruff, and W. Lynn Shirley. 2003. "Social Vulnerability to Environmental Hazards." *Social Science Quarterly* 84 (2): 242–261. 10.1111/1540-6237.8402002

Japan Medical Association COVID-19 Expert Committee. 2020. "在宅医療と介護における COVID-19対応の課題と　解決策、提言タスクフォース　報告書[Issues and Solutions for COVID-19 in Home Healthcare and Nursing Care]." *Recommendations Task Force Report.* https://www.covid19-jma-medical-expert-meeting.jp/topic/2942

Japanese Association of Medical Care for Chronic Illness. 2021. "日本慢性期医療協会定例記者会見[Regular press conference materials]" February 18, 2021. http://jamcf.jp/chairman/2021/chairman210218.pdf

Kanamori, Takuya, Mizue Suzuki, and Masao Kanamori. 2021. "Influence of COVID-19 Pandemic on Community-Dwelling Older Adults and Nursing Home Residents." *Journal of Geriatric Nursing* 26 (1): 17–22.

Morsut, Claudia, Christian Kuran, Bjørn I. Kruke, Kati Orru, and Sten Hansson. 2021. "Linking Resilience, Vulnerability, Social Capital and Risk Awareness for Crisis and Disaster Research." *Journal of Contingencies and Crisis Management* 30 (2): 137– 137. 10.1111/1468-5973.12375

Ohwa, Mie. 2021. "<研究ノート> 新型コロナウにルスと高齢者: グローバル・ソーシャルワークの視点から [The COVID-19 and the Elderly: From a Global Social Work Perspective]." *Human Welfare* 13 (1): 139–149. http://hdl.handle.net/10236/00029641

Omron Healthcare. 2020. "65歳以上の高齢者1000人に聞いた"withコロナ"実態調査. ['With Corona.' Survey of 1,000 elderly people aged 65 and over]." *Omron healthcare Japan.* Last modified 13 July 2020. https://www.healthcare.omron.co.jp/corp/news/2020/0713.html

Otto, Ilona M., Diana Reckien, Christopher P.O. Reyer, Rachel Marcus, Virginie Le Masson, Lindsey Jones, Andrew Norton, and Olivia Serdeczny. 2017. "Social Vulnerability to Climate Change: A Review of Concepts and Evidence." *Regional Environmental Change* 17: 1651–1662. 10.1007/s10113-017-1105-9

Ouchi, Junko, Yuko Hayashi, Michiko Matsuhara, Kumiko Miyata, Michiyo Yamamoto, Yuto Ichinohe, and Hirofumi Sanada. 2021. "新型コロナウにルス感染症の感染拡大防止策が地域在住高齢者の活動および主観的な健康に与えた影響：北海道の感染第 1 波における検討 [The Impact of Measures to Prevent the Spread of Novel Coronavirus Infections on the Activities and Subjective Health of Elderly People Living in the Community: A Study of the First Wave of Infection in Hokkaido]." *Journal of Japan Society of Nursing Research* 44 (4): 599–609. 10.15065/jjsnr.20210322114

Shigemura, Jun, Sho Takahashi, Misari Oe, and Mie Kurosawa. 2020. "Toward the Understanding of the Psychosocial Effect of COVID-19 Pandemic." *Japanese Journal of Traumatic Stress* 18 (1): 71–79. https://jglobal.jst.go.jp/en/detail?JGLOBAL_ID= 202002245518772650

Singh, Sapam R., Mohammad R. Eghdami, and Sarbjeet Singh. 2014. "The Concept of Social Vulnerability: A Review from Disasters Perspectives." *International Journal of Interdisciplinary and Multidisciplinary Studies* 1 (6): 71–82. http://www.ijims.com/uploads/2a1a7b4810a19951ea42z10.pdf

Ueda, Atsushi, and Tomoko Koizumi. 2021. "Corona Frontline at Nursing Home: Fear of Sudden Infections in Residents, No Hospitalization, Staff at Their Limit." Yomiuri Newspaper 5 February 2021.

Wake, Junko and Sunin Lee. 2022. "Attitudes of Elderly Care Facility Staff in the COVID-19 Pandemic: Differences and Determinants by Facility Types and Occupational Groups." *The Journal of Social Science and Humanities* 518 (3): 93–108.

Watanabe, Hidehiro, Akihiro Yoshida, Koki Taniguchi, Haruhi Funato, Fumihiko Goto, Hisanori Ido, Naoki Okayama, and Ryuichi Hasegawa. 2021. "Current Status of Staying Home because of COVID-19 Infection on the Physical and Mental Function in Community-Dwelling Older Adults." *Health Support* 23 (1):15–20.

Yomiuri Newspaper. 2020. "Dementia Progresses 85% under Coronas." 23 November 2020.

Yamauchi, Satsuki, Kan Shimazaki, Masae Kojima, Takashi Yonekawa, Natsuka Takeda, Hiroko Shinkai, and Hirofumi Aoki. 2021. "Changes of Behavior and Mobility in Elderly during COVID-19 Epidemic." *Proceedings of the Society of Automotive Engineers of Japan* 52 (5): 1143–1148.

# 12 Social Work and Lost Contacts with Clients during the COVID-19 Pandemic: Experiences of Shared Trauma from Three Different Civil Society Organisations

*Kristofer Hansson and Charlotte C. Petersson*

## Introduction

Early in the COVID-19 pandemic, social workers at battered women's shelters and night shelters and church deacons in Sweden warned that they were at risk of losing contact with their clients. This was reported in the media, among other things, and it was something we were told when we started conducting short telephone interviews with 25 social workers in March 2020. The telephone interviews were a way to gather empirical data with which we could follow the development of the pandemic through civil society organisations, and at the same time study what changes they made to create a more resilient form of social work. To begin with, it was mostly the social workers at battered women's shelters and deacons working in the church who highlighted and discussed these risks of not hearing from their clients. The social workers feared that the women and their children were not contacting them because they were being controlled by their assailants, who were now also spending more time in the home. But they could not be sure because there were, for the most part, no requests for support or help from clients. The situation was more obvious for the deacons, because from one day to the next the elderly were suddenly absent from church activities and were instead self-isolating in their homes. The social workers at the night shelters raised the alarm much later and told us of their worries about the cold as the winter of 2020 was approaching. Thus, even though Sweden was never subject to a lockdown in 2020 or 2021, many of the signals we were receiving from the social workers indicated that their clients were at risk of increased ill health, mental illness, and violence due to the situation produced by the pandemic.

Our goal as ethnographic researchers with no formal education in social work but with long experience researching topics concerning social work is to develop a theoretical and empirical understanding of this vulnerable position that was imposed on these client groups by the COVID-19 pandemic. But we also want to argue that these developments created fear and worry among the social

DOI: 10.4324/9781003374374-15

workers themselves, when it became clear to them that they were at risk of losing contact with their clients. Theoretically, then, we need to understand not only the vulnerable position through which the pandemic increased the risk for exclusion from society (Agamben 1998; Esposito 2008), but also the risk that the position of the social workers became more vulnerable than it had been prior to the pandemic. This is also something that many previous studies have clarified that the outbreak of an emergency or disaster increases the risk for negative psychological impacts on those working as care workers (Okafor 2021; Lee et al. 2018; Raven et al. 2018, Si et al. 2020; Tam et al. 2004). This reasoning will be further elaborated using the concept of shared trauma developed by Dr Carol Tosone, Professor of Social Work, which focuses on the way in which care workers are exposed to similar impacts of collective traumatic events as their clients (Tosone 2012, 2021).

We therefore want to argue that the concept of the vulnerable position in a shared trauma must be understood as a dialectical relationship between the social worker and the client being hard to contact as a result of rapidly changing circumstances. Our aim is then to study in what ways the COVID-19 pandemic illuminates this dialectical relationship, and how it affected the vulnerable positions of both the clients and the social workers at three different civil society organisations in Sweden. In doing so, we hope to make a contribution regarding how social care during a pandemic can be understood, with a special focus on those clients who were perceived as having been 'lost'.

## Background—The vulnerable position and shared trauma

'Vulnerable groups' can be said to constitute a central discourse in the development of social work, which has its historical origins in caring for specific groups in society (Farkas and Romaniuk 2020; OECD 2015). The discourse may involve people who are homeless, women who live in violent relationships, or children who grow up in exposed environments. This discourse also comes with a high risk of reproducing different forms of paternalistic power. At the same time, in the context of the civil society organisations that constitute the focus of this chapter, there is a clear and unspoken logic that the individuals in these 'vulnerable groups' should be given the opportunity to exercise their own power. We are here following Judith Butler's argument that vulnerability is not only passivity but needs to be understood as social relations that are embodied in different ways (Butler 2020). This perspective, Butler argues, also provides us with a theory to understand how practices of resistance can be understood as constituting part of these relations. In this chapter, this reasoning is used more conceptually and something we return to in our discussion.

Furthermore, we want to argue that it is not enough to view the pandemic as having increased the hazards faced by groups in vulnerable positions (Agamben 1998; Esposito 2008). Instead, we would like to argue, with Butler's help, that it is not individual bodies that we should focus on, but that our theoretical focus should instead be directed at dependency on other bodies (Butler 2020). It is with a focus on dependency in relation to other bodies that we can also understand the problematic development manifested in the disappearance of clients during the pandemic. Butler's argument is here more ontological, since she views the body as something that becomes a body through social relations, a phenomenological argument that can also be found in Maurice Merleau-Ponty's philosophy on intersubjectivity, for example (Merleau-Ponty 1968; see also Daly 2016). On the basis of this non-dualist ontology, individual bodies are biological entities that are at risk of becoming infected by viruses, and in this way becoming bodies dangerous to others. Further on, bodies cannot remain distinct from other bodies, at the same time as they are not fully merged (Butler 2020). This is something that becomes problematic in a pandemic, in which an important practice required to reduce the spread of a virus is maintaining distance from other bodies, and even isolating oneself and completely avoiding this intersubjectivity with other people. Our understanding of the body becomes intertwined with medical knowledge of immunity and of how new and emerging viruses—as well as bacteria—can threaten those infrastructural conditions of life that enable bodies to live an everyday life (Brown 2019).

With this said, we do not want to reduce bodies to 'bare life'—to use Giorgio Agamben's philosophical arguments (Agamben 1998)—as a means of understanding the nature of vulnerable positions, but instead to investigate what infrastructural conditions of life enable or limit dependency on other bodies in the event of a pandemic. Butler argues that when infrastructural conditions of life are imperilled—to use her word—there is a risk that 'the immanent features of life itself' are endangered (Butler 2020). The social world is in this way always in the background, structuring people's everyday lives, opening or closing the available, and sometimes affordable, lifelines (Ahmed 2006). This is even more the case when people are forced—for different reasons—to isolate themselves and their families. When it comes to the pandemic, this is a central perspective that has been emphasised in other social research, particularly research with a focus on how social work needed to adapt to the societal changes brought about by the pandemic.

The infrastructural conditions of life appear to have changed rapidly at the beginning of the pandemic. Reflecting on the pandemic in the United Kingdom, Tom Kingstone and Lisa Dikomitis have argued that: 'To continue providing care during the pandemic, social workers often had to make difficult decisions and adapt quickly to new ways of working with little or no time to prepare' (Kingstone and Dikomitis 2021). This is a central observation which can be said to illustrate the possibilities open to social work to maintain individuals' opportunities to continue with their lives. This kind of quick adaptation is something we have also seen in our research on civil society organisations and their social work (Hansson 2021a; Petersson and Hansson 2022). It was not a question of leaving people without care, but instead of trying to find new ways to reach out to people who vanished from their regular meeting places from one day to the next (Hansson 2021b). But at the same time that we can see that social workers in the civil society organisations had a strong capacity for social innovation and adapting to new situations, the social workers themselves also became a 'vulnerable group' who were at risk of being infected by the virus. In this chapter we therefore want to argue that it is a misunderstanding if we fail to see that all individuals can find themselves in a vulnerable position, where one's position can be downgraded or impeded (Butler 2004). Or, what we will argue in this chapter as well, becoming bodies dangerous to others. In relation to the virus, this is an important lesson, and is something we may have to learn to live with given that so-called emerging infectious diseases are increasing globally.

Central to this argument is also the view that the COVID-19 pandemic should be seen as a traumatic event that creates a risk for producing shared trauma for both clients and social workers (Tosone 2021). We here follow Tosone's definition of shared trauma, which she has stated as the 'affective, behavioural, cognitive, spiritual, and multimodal responses that mental health professionals experience as a result of primary and secondary exposure to the same collective trauma as their clients' (Tosone 2012, 625). Examples of this may involve secondary trauma when meeting people experiencing trauma, various stress disorders such as moral stress, for example, powerful anxiety of becoming a body dangerous to others and taking the virus home to the family, burnout, and so forth (Tosone 2021).

## Rapid ethnographies in a pandemic

Ethnographic methods can be said to be a useful means of quickly starting a research project and beginning to gather empirical data. Therefore, when the COVID-19 pandemic became more and more visible in Sweden, we quickly wrote a preliminary research plan together, which was to form the basis for the research questions we wanted to examine in relation to the social work being conducted in different civil society organisations, and how this work changed in relation to the pandemic. The project aims were to investigate the ability of social work to continue its core activities under the pressures created by COVID-19. A discovery we made early was that the social workers' experiences of lost clients made us change direction on some of our research questions.

We want to argue for the importance of developing a social science that dares to throw itself into the field without lengthy preparations, although development of these methods may be needed in the long term. In our data gathering, we have been inspired by so-called rapid ethnographies (Baines and Cunningham 2013; Isaacs 2013; Vindrola-Padros and Vindrola-Padros 2018). These can be seen as a fusion of different methods with a focus on gathering data from a field in which there is a limited amount of time available. In our fieldwork, time constituted an ethical dilemma. The social workers had their daily work with clients, and we tried to avoid disrupting this and limiting them in their work. But researchers may also be short of time when a project has to start without funding, and all one's other university tasks must be handled simultaneously. Central to rapid ethnographies is also an ability to relate to the methodological weaknesses that risk arising from the use of this method, which also constitutes an ethical dilemma in these projects. This may for example be due to reduced reflexivity, when interviews are short, and that too few interviews risk creating substandard data (see Isaacs 2013; Vindrola-Padros and Vindrola-Padros 2018). In our data gathering we have related to these challenges in different ways, for example by conducting recurrent interviews with the same social workers, and also by presenting preliminary analyses to them and getting feedback (Hansson and Petersson 2021; Petersson and Hansson 2022; see for a more extensive discussion).

From the start of the project in March 2020, we have used telephone interviews to follow social workers at battered women's shelters, night shelters, and church deacons, primarily in southern areas of Sweden. These three groups of participants have comprised 15 social workers at battered women's shelters, five social workers at night shelters, and five deacons. A total of 25 different civil society organisations have been followed, all women and of varying ages. The number of times each social worker has been interviewed has varied, from two to seven times (between March 2020 and October 2021). We have used the same semi-structured interview guide throughout the interviews but have adapted it in relation to pandemic developments. The interviews lasted anywhere from 10 to 30 minutes, with the majority taking around 15 minutes. They were conducted in Swedish and subsequently transcribed verbatim. For this chapter, they have also been translated into English, and adapted slightly for ease of reading. Our reading of the data has focused on looking for common and recurring themes (Braun and Clarke 2006). We have used theoretical models to refine this reading and have also sought a more abstract view. In this chapter, we want to highlight two themes that emerged during the interviews and that are particularly important as a means of understanding the vulnerable positions associated with the shared traumas that emerged during the pandemic. In the first theme—*Being vulnerable*—we want to empirically argue that the vulnerable position needs to be understood as a dialectical relationship, and in the second theme—*Who is lost?*—we focus on the feelings that arise when such a relationship is not possible.

There are many ethical dilemmas that arise during pandemic research. One is to avoid spreading the infection through one's research activities. In this fieldwork we have used telephone interviews to minimise the risk of spreading the virus. At the same time, however, the use of this method risks creating new ethical dilemmas. It is difficult to have the same level of sensitivity as in a regular interview face-to-face, and to know when to stop asking questions, and when to move on. Another problem is that the researcher cannot control the environment of the interview participants, with a risk that other persons may be listening. We have requested an advisory opinion from the Swedish Ethics Review Authority (Dnr 2020-01533), and all participants have been anonymised.

## Losing contact

An initial theme in the interviews that emerged as early as March 2020 was the risk of losing contact with clients, and not really knowing where they were or how they were coping with the pandemic. It was no surprise that this theme came up, because our questions were directed at social as well as immunological perspectives on risk (see Brown 2019). We therefore quickly added a question to the interview guide to focus on this further: 'Are there any visitors that you feel you have lost contact with?' This type of question resulted in short answers from everyone. But the questions also generated narratives about how social work in civil society organisations was changing due to the pandemic, and how they were in many ways experiencing a form of stress.

## Being vulnerable

In this section, we argue that to understand the concept of the vulnerable position experienced by clients, we also need to understand how the social workers became a vulnerable group during the COVID-19 pandemic. This is a perspective that we draw from research conducted in the field of shared trauma (Tosone 2021), but something that we want to theoretically develop through Butler's work, with more focus on the way that all individuals can find them-selves in a vulnerable position (Butler 2004), particularly during a pandemic. By focusing on vulnerability, and how vulnerability is understood as a dialectical relationship, we can develop a better understanding of how we all live an 'immunitary life' (Brown 2019), even if we are not made aware of this in our everyday lives.

At the beginning of the pandemic, this kind of 'immunitary life' immediately became visible in how we dialectically related to one another's bodies, when we were suddenly all required to keep our distance. For people working at the night shelters this became problematic, because the clients did not have the same level of risk awareness.

> I have not been there that much, I have [...] I feel a little myself that I 'mm' [...] some are a little [...] some of the people who go there, huh, they are very cuddly and that, and I think it feels a little hard. And then it also feels hard to, how can I put it, say to them, I think, that 'oh no, I do not want to hug now' and like, huh, and it feels like 'mm'. That's a thing, I think (Lill).

Before the pandemic a hug was unproblematic and it was something important to creating a trusting relationship in social work. '*Cuddly*' could here be seen as a form of intersubjectivity, a social relation that acknowledges the other body and also its dependency on other bodies (Butler 2020; Merleau-Ponty 1968). But this social worker felt vulnerable in the early stages of the pandemic, and the thought of having to hug others seemed daunting, as did the thought of saying no to a hug. There was a fear of ruining the relationship with the client. In this way, the social worker also ended up in a vulnerable position.

Even the simplest cold now became problematic because it not only signalled the risk of being the initial symptoms of COVID-19, but also that the individual had a body that was dangerous to others. New practices were quickly introduced to handle the risk that might be linked to a simple cold or other symptoms associated with this kind of infection. In one battered women's shelter, most of the staff had been tested for COVID-19, even though it was initially perceived as strange:

> Almost everyone in the staff has taken the test, there is only one who has not done it, but all results have been negative; there have always been colds and other things, but as soon as this happens there is a different concern than there is otherwise when you get a cold (laughter) (Teresia).

Maybe the laughter highlights the absurdity many felt in relation to the pandemic at the beginning of spring 2020, at how easily one's body was transformed from being a strong body that took care of other people in vulnerable situations, to become a body that could be dangerous both to others and oneself. This mix of emotions is important if we want to understand how the shared trauma seemed to put the individual in a new position. The roles of the clinician and the client were starting to become blurred, and it was no longer obvious how the professional should relate to the client (Tosone 2021).

In our analysis we want to argue that this new form of position also occurred when the professionals lost their usual ways of relating to and building trusting relationships with their clients. In a different battered women's shelter, this form of vulnerable situation became a reality:

> We got sick here last autumn, 90 percent of the staff had Corona, so unfortunately, there were one or two who worked, but then we closed the office and then you could only call. We have not had any cafes since Corona started. You miss a lot of young people, this social aspect, you feel isolated, you are outside, you don't know what to do, so the social aspect is terrible (Sanella).

In the above quote, it is unclear who the person '*outside*' is, but we find this telling. It was not only the clients who experienced the pandemic as terrible, the staff also found it difficult to combine their work with having closed the office. The only way to be in contact with other persons was by telephone and via the internet.

We must also remember that the vulnerability also manifested itself in relation to the fact that many of the volunteers who work at battered women's shelters, night shelters, and churches were retired, elderly people. The elderly were particularly vulnerable to the pandemic, and were quick to disappear from these organisations, thus creating a void in the workforce. One social worker from a night shelter said:

> There are many who want to help, who are volunteers, who don't dare to come, who are like in the risk zone themselves, and them, they get like a

bit of a bad conscience and that, you know, and then they come further and further from the work. And there are some who sit on our board who then also feel that, 'No, we are not doing any work here now' (Hannalena).

Being vulnerable should be viewed as a complex phenomenon, where it is not obvious how the vulnerability arises or develops. What is clear is that the shared trauma goes back to a form of risk where the professional—or the volunteer— finds themself in a similar position to the client, with a powerful anxiety about the risk associated with the virus, but also the moral stress of not being able to help more (Tosone 2021). The battered women's shelters, night shelters, and churches became 'risk zones' for some people, at the same time as all the organisations argued that they could not shut down. Because where else would people go?

## Who is lost?

It was not enough to stay open, however. Many of the clients disappeared anyway, and in our interviews, the social workers talked about which groups they felt they had lost contact with. This was in the spring of 2020, when the COVID-19 virus was not so widespread in the southern parts of Sweden, but when there were clear guidelines from the Swedish Public Health Agency on how civil society organisations, as well as individuals, should act to prevent the virus from spreading. One of the deacons clarified that this was a recurring theme among her colleagues:

> It comes up almost every week, that it is these people that we meet in certain groups, or that we meet at the church office, that we do not have contact information for. We can't reach those. We wonder how they feel. We can't reach them, but we have to wait (Anna).

In the spring of 2020, the deacons lost contact with many of the elderly who, due to the risk of becoming very ill from the COVID-19 virus, decided to self-isolate in their homes. They had been regular visitors to the various activities of the church, where they had developed a fellowship with other elderly persons. Because they came voluntarily, however, the deacons had no contact information for them and were therefore unable to reach them all. At the same time, the church in Sweden worked to remain open and, in this way, to continue giving help to people that needed them:

> You must be able to go somewhere with the anxiety we have and carry on, and the church works to be an open place, where you can meet in the crisis, and then it doesn't work if you completely shut down. At the same time, you also have to cover safety, both those of us who are working, and

those who come here. So, it has not been logical to just shut down completely. [...] It is also good to be able to be open to those who usually come and ring the doorbell at this time, because they know it is open (Hilleborg).

While people were at risk of contracting the COVID-19 virus, the deacons also argued that they could not close the church, because people in vulnerable situations needed them. In this way, their argument can be seen as a form of non-dualist ontology, in which bodies are not seen only as biological entities that should be protected against viruses, but also as bodies that need other bodies (Butler 2020). This dependency on other bodies is of course central to social work, but it is clear from the first quote that it was not obvious how this work would progress.

At the same time, it is central to see that the vulnerable situation is not the same for different groups or even different individuals. In the interviews with the deacons, the focus was first and foremost on the elderly, while the interviews with the women's shelters showed that their experiences were different. Their experiences of lost clients were focused on women and children. The following quote highlights these groups as having gone missing during the pandemic:

What we have seen above all this year in the sheltered housing is that mothers with children seeking support have kind of disappeared. So, we have had such a low number of children in our sheltered housing. We have always asked ourselves the question, 'Where have the children gone?' A new target group that has become clear to us is young women without children. That is, women who are living in what is perhaps their first love relationship or first marriage, who do not have children in those relationships, so. We've seen them (Gjertrud).

The women and their children were already in a vulnerable situation at home, and the self-isolation due to the pandemic risked increasing this separation from society. When the perpetrator was also at home to a greater extent, there were fewer opportunities to contact the shelters and other authorities. One possible analysis is that the women also felt a need to protect their families due to the increased risk associated with the COVID-19 virus. That they were simply making an effort to keep the family together, even though this increased the risk for abuse. In other articles we have argued that the pandemic increased the risk for these women and children of being deprived of the possibility of developing relationships with the communities that the women shelters offer (Hansson and Petersson 2021; Petersson and Hansson 2022).

If we turn instead to the night shelters, these have previous experience of their clients losing contact with the shelters from time to time. For this reason, their experience of the pandemic seemed to be slightly different:

These groups always include those who are [...] have a double diagnosis, i.e. mental illness and substance abuse; they always fall between the cracks a lot of the time; so because they have a hard time going to meetings, and you report anxiety and stuff, of course, about them, if they get sick, of course, but it's still the same, of course, that we have to be observant. I have called a girl now too; she's been feeling very bad. But as I said, we have very good contacts with social workers here, and our guests know about it, and they have given their approval that we can make contact, if you are going to book meetings and so on. But it is those who have a double diagnosis who are the ones who fall between the cracks sometimes (Siri).

The persons seeking this form of shelter were in a way already in danger with regard to the 'immanent features of life itself' (Butler 2020). Their vulnerable situation did not immediately create a perception among the professionals that they had lost the contact with them. The shared trauma seemed to come later, when it became clear that the pandemic would continue through the winter. This immediately created a concern and raised questions about where these people would self-isolate if they became infected by the virus. There was a fear among the interviewees that the cold would worsen the situation.

## Discussion—Shared trauma as practices of resistance

Trauma is a strong word, and some of the research which has focused on the vulnerability of care workers in similar situations has instead used terms such as negative psychological impact (Okafor 2021; Lee et al. 2018; Raven et al. 2018; Si et al. 2020; Tam et al. 2004). Taking the perspective of losing contact with clients seriously, we want to argue that the concept of shared trauma has the potential to provide an understanding of the function of the social worker during the pandemic. At the same time, losing contact with the clients means that it is empirically not a shared trauma anymore, because the social workers are then not sharing the experience together with their clients. But this non-sharing can also create feelings among social workers that can be defined as part of the shared trauma concept. Social workers, and especially those working in civil society organisations, have extensive experience and special knowledge about the specific vulnerable groups whom they care for. Not knowing where they are and how they are coping with the pandemic can be very worrying.

Using Butler's (2004, 2020) theoretical perspective on the vulnerable position we would argue that shared trauma can be developed as something that is related to the human experience of being dependent on other bodies. Although the discourse of the pandemic was initially focused on the individual responsibility to self-isolate, this does not provide any deeper understanding of the vulnerability people are at risk of finding themselves in. Instead, based on a non-dualist ontology of humans always being in a dialectical relationship (Merleau-Ponty 1968), we would argue that both clients and social workers need support as part of the community (Hansson and Petersson 2021). It may be important not to differentiate between the social worker and the client, but rather to see that this dialectical relationship can provide us with an understanding of the negative psychological impact of the pandemic. It can also help us to understand that the infrastructural conditions of life are imperilled 'when the immanent features of life itself' cannot function in the usual way (Butler 2020).

Understanding shared trauma from this perspective of vulnerability should therefore not only be seen as something passive, but instead in terms of embodied social relations, as well as a form of practices of resistance. We are here following Butler's argument that vulnerability can evoke political agency and different forms of infrastructural mobilisations (Butler 2020; Butler et al. 2016). In relation to the civil society organisations and their social work, we argue that this work should be seen as a struggle to counteract the forces that in various ways increased the risk among the clients they support during the pandemic. On the basis of our interviews, this practice can be seen as a form of practices of resistance. This was something that emerged in our interviews, which focused on how to work with equality, diversity, and inclusion during and after the pandemic. This exposure to the collective trauma so importantly identified by Tosone (2012) also creates practices of resistance. Providing social work under the impact of the pandemic has had significant implications for the organisations participating in our research. The social workers in our study have worked actively and creatively throughout the pandemic to provide support to their clients in various ways. Focusing on resistance can be an important input for future research and development, not least to discuss the opportunities of social work during societal crises.

# References

Agamben, Giorgio. 1998. *Homo Sacer: Sovereign Power and Bare Life*. Stanford: Stanford University Press.

Ahmed, Sara. 2006. *Queer Phenomenology: Orientations, Objects, Others*. Durham: Duke University Press.

Baines, Donna, and Ian Cunningham. 2013. "Using Comparative Perspective Rapid Ethnography in International Case Studies: Strengths and Challenges." *Qualitative Social Work* 12 (1): 73–88. 10.1177/1473325011419053

Braun, Virginia, and Victoria Clarke. 2006. "Using Thematic Analysis in Psychology." *Qualitive Research in Psychology* 3 (2): 77–101. 10.1191/1478088706qp063oa.

Brown, Nik. 2019. *Immunitary Life: A Biopolitics of Immunity*. London: Palgrave Macmillan.

Butler, Judith. 2004. *Precarious Life: The Powers of Mourning and Violence*. London: Verso.

Butler, Judith. 2020. *The Force of Nonviolence: An Ethico-Political Bind*. London: Verso.

Butler, Judith, Zeynep Gambetti, and Leticia Sabsay, eds. 2016. *Vulnerability in Resistance*. Durham: Duke University Press.

Daly, Anya. 2016. *Merleau-Ponty and the Ethics of Intersubjectivity*. London: Palgrave Macmillan.

Esposito, Roberto. 2008. *Bíos: Biopolitics and Philosophy*. Minneapolis: University of Minnesota Press.

Farkas, Kathleen J., and Richard Romaniuk. 2020. "Social Work, Ethics and Vulnerable Groups in the Time of Coronavirus and COVID-19." *Society Register* 4 (2): 67–82. 10.14746/sr.2020.4.2.05

Hansson, Kristofer. 2021a. "'Inställt tillsvidare': Diakonernas arbete att hitta nya vägar ut under covid-19-pandemin." ["Suspended Indefinitely": The Deacons' Work to Find New Ways Out During the COVID-19 pandemic] *Socialmedicinsk Tidskrift*, 24 February 2021 (98 [1]). https://socialmedicinsktidskrift.se/index.php/smt/article/view/2399/2283

Hansson, Kristofer. 2021b. "Att hålla ihop det sociala arbetet: Hur covid-19-pandemin påverkade tre olika sivilsamhällesorganisationer." [Keeping Social Work Together: How the Covid-19 Pandemic Affected Three Different Civil Society Organisations] *Socialvetenskaplig tidskrift* 28 (4): 499–516. 10.3384/SVT.2021.28.4.4371

Hansson, Kristofer, and Charlotte C. Petersson. 2021. "Den sårbara gemenskapen: Kvinnojourer under covid-19-pandemin." [The Vulnerable Community: Women's Shelters During the COVID-19-Pandemic] *Sociologisk forskning* 58 (1–2), 33–51. 10. 37062/sf.58.22106

Isaacs, Ellen. 2013. "The Value of Rapid Ethnography." In *Advancing Ethnography in Corporate Environments. Challenges and Emerging Opportunities*, edited by Brigitte Jordan, 92–107. Walnut Creek: Left Coast Press.

Kingstone, Tom, and Lisa Dikomitis. 2021. "The Pandemic Transformed How Social Work was Delivered—And These Changes Could be Here to Stay." *The Conversation*, 19 August 2021. https://theconversation.com/the-pandemic-transformed-how-social-work-was-delivered-and-these-changes-could-be-here-to-stay-165993

Lee, Sang M., Won S. Kang, Ah-Rang Cho, Tae Kim, and Jin K. Park. 2018. "Psychological Impact of the 2015 MERS Outbreak on Hospital Workers and Quarantined Hemodialysis Patients." *Comprehensive Psychiatry* 87: 123–127. 10.1016/j.comppsych.2018.10.003

Merleau-Ponty, Maurice. 1968. *The Visible and the Invisible: Followed by Working Notes.* Evanston: Northwestern University Press.

OECD. 2015. *Integrating Social Services for Vulnerable Groups: Bridging Sectors for Better Service Delivery.* Paris: OECD Publishing. 10.1787/9789264233775-en

Okafor, Afomachukwu. 2021. "Role of the Social Worker in the Outbreak of Pandemics (A Case of COVID-19)." *Cogent Psychology* 8 (1): 1939537. 10.1080/23311908.2021. 1939537

Petersson, Charlotte C., and Kristofer Hansson. 2022. "Social Work Responses to Domestic Violence During the COVID-19 Pandemic: Experiences and Perspectives of Professionals at Women's Shelters in Sweden." *Clinical Social Work Journal* 50 (2): 135–146. 10.1007/s10615-022-00833-3

Raven, Joanna, Haja Wurie, and Sophie Witter. 2018. "Health Workers' Experiences of Coping with the Ebola Epidemic in Sierra Leone's Health System: A Qualitative Study." *BMC Health Services Research* 18: 251. 10.1186/s12913-018-3072-3

Si, Ming-Yu, Xiao-You Su, Yu Jiang, Wen-Jun Wang, Xiao-Fen Gu, Li Ma, Jing Li, Shao-Kai Zhang, Ze-Fang Ren, Ran Ren, Yuan-Li Liu, and You-Lin Qiao. 2020. "Psychological Impact of COVID-19 on Medical Care Workers in China." *Infectious Disease of Poverty*, 9: 113. 10.1186/s40249-020-00724-0

Tam, Cindy W.C., Edwin P.F. Pang, Linda C.W. Lam, and Helen F.K. Chiu. 2004. "Severe Acute Respiratory Syndrome (SARS) in Hong Kong in 2003: Stress and Psychological Impact Among Frontline Healthcare Workers." *Psychological Medicine* 34 (7): 1197–1204. 10.1017/S0033291704002247

Tosone, Carol. 2012. "Shared Trauma." In *Encyclopedia of Trauma: An Interdisciplinary Guide*, edited by Charles R. Figley, 625–627. Thousand Oaks: SAGE Publications.

Tosone, Carol, ed. 2021. *Shared Trauma, Shared Resilience During a Pandemic: Social Work in the Time of COVID-19*. Cham: Springer.

Vindrola-Padros, Cecilia, and Bruno Vindrola-Padros. 2018. "Quick and Dirty? A Systematic Review of the Use of Rapid Ethnographies in Healthcare Organisation and Delivery." *BMJ Quality & Safety* 27 (4): 321–330. 10.1136/bmjqs-2017-007226

# Section IV

# Restarting the Dynamics, Relationships, and Connectivity in Social Work

# 13 'And I Say, "Yes" Because I Want to Help'—Social Workers' Reflections on Practice in Ireland During COVID-19

*Joseph Mooney, Declan Coogan, Caroline McGregor, and Olive Lyons*

## Introduction

The centrality and importance of social workers as frontline responders during the SARS-CoV-2 global pandemic has been starkly elucidated (Dominelli et al. 2020). Showing a dynamic and varied response to social work within a COVID-19 context, numerous studies, personal stories, practice guidance, and peer-reviewed papers have focused on multifaceted themes of ethics, values, and addressing basic material and human needs while operating to challenge injustice. Studies have illuminated the distorting and disproportionately negative impact of the pandemic on those most marginalised and least resourced to respond or thrive within such changed conditions, affecting education and service support (e.g. the digital divide), health services (unequal access to preventative health measures and protective health measures), welfare (increase in poverty and disadvantage), family violence (reduced access to outside help alongside shut downs locking families away from sources of help and support), and a wider range of social problems. Addressing the needs of persons across the life course who were disconnected through isolation and lack of access to routine services as well as support has been central to social work during the pandemic (Alston and Chow 2021).

The COVID-19 pandemic brought our shared global challenges into sharp focus. Supporting connections and managing disconnections for those whom they work with has been central to social work practice responses to the COVID-19 pandemic (Miller and Lee 2020). So too has been the challenge of social workers managing their own connections and disconnection in this ever-changing context. Connection takes many forms in the recent literature which has tended to focus on:

1 emotional connectedness for frontline health care workers (Bender et al. 2021);
2 digital connectivity and the impact on the practice of social work (Gibson et al. 2020; Pink et al. 2022);

DOI: 10.4324/9781003374374-17

3   how social workers, through mutual support, interconnected to offer 'practical and organisational, methodological and ethical, and personal and emotional' assistance (Cabiati 2021, 676);
4   the connection between the personal and professional lives of social workers (e.g. Schiff et al. 2021); and
5   the direct experiences of practice (Ashcroft et al. 2022; Harrikari et al. 2021).

In this chapter, we contribute to this growing body of knowledge and insight about social work experiences by focusing on learning from an Irish context. The chapter initially provides a brief synopsis of the Irish context and our rationale for this study. Our methodological and analytical approaches are then described, followed by a presentation and discussion of our identified core categories of connection, disconnection, and reconnection.

## The first responses to COVID-19 in Ireland

On 29 February, 2020, the first case of COVID-19 was confirmed in the Republic of Ireland. Following this, the Irish Government closed schools, childcare facilities, universities and other public buildings, and hospitality services. People's movements were restricted to within two kilometres except for the use of essential services, with the physical distancing of two metres put in place. The children, families, and adults usually served by social workers were impacted by the closing of day services, social clubs, and residential respite services, where vulnerable persons and their families received significant support in dealing with their already substantial life challenges (Coogan and Mooney 2020). The Child and Family Agency, Ireland's dedicated state agency responsible for improving outcomes and well-being for children, together with practitioners in voluntary and other statutory agencies, continued to provide key services during the pandemic across core areas, including child protection and welfare services, services for children in care, and domestic, sexual, and gender-based violence services (Coogan and Mooney 2020). Like some other health and social care practitioners, social workers continued to work throughout the pandemic and as data from this study show, the impacts were varied and nuanced.

### Rationale for the study

We conceived our study as part of a wider backdrop of social work and social science research being conducted globally in the context of the pandemic. We were part of a wider global network of social work academics led by Professor Timo Harrikari, University of Lapland, who discussed the pandemic as a 'black swan', an unprecedented and unexpected event of significant magnitude (Mooney et al. 2020). Due to the societal impact of this global phenomenon, we wondered whether the role of social work was potentially of increased importance during this period, as children were not accessing the other traditional forms of in-person support in their lives, such as biological parents, grand-parents, teachers, sports coaches, and community supports. As the early phases of the pandemic resulted in child protection and welfare social workers completing only essential home visits and social work practice taking place both in-person and remotely, we wondered whether and how practice might be affected. Our study examined social workers' reflections on their work practices through the pandemic and related lockdown; what were social workers' experiences, thoughts, and feelings, and their views about the future? Our findings provide learning for social work practice, policy, and education in these areas and beyond.

## A constructivist grounded theory methodology—Discovering the concepts of connection, disconnection, and reconnection

Our study received ethical approval from the University of Galway, University College Dublin, and the Research Ethics Board of the Child and Family Agency. We asked social workers to reflect on their own practice and did not invite commentary on individual casework or case management. Our study gathered data from ten participants across Ireland via two separate data collection methods: A reflective diary stream (n=5) and a semi-structured qualitative interview stream (n=5). The study was conducted during the latter part of 2020. We recruited five child and family social workers via a regional service area in the west of Ireland for the diary stream. We recruited five social workers for the semi-structured interviews nationally via the Irish Association of Social Workers, a representative body for the profession. Levels of professional experience varied across the sample, from senior management to a student social worker who was on placement during periods of lockdown associated with COVID-19. Participants developed their reflective diaries over a six-week period, and those who participated in the semi-structured interviews did so on a once-off basis via Zoom. We use pseudonyms throughout this chapter and the brackets (D) or (I) indicate reflective diary or semi-structured interview data, respectively. In the following section, we briefly outline the development of grounded theory methods and present our analytical approach and research design.

We chose a constructivist grounded theory (CGT) methodology, as this approach seeks to privilege the perceptions of research participants, particularly in common social settings that are not well understood and have not been exhaustively researched (Farragher and Coogan, 2020; Hunter et al. 2011). CGT places a strong emphasis on the exploration of the meanings that participants attribute to their experiences (Kenny and Fourie 2015). Understanding the variants of grounded theory methodologies enabled us, as the researchers in this project, to make informed choices about methodology.

Barney Glaser and Anselm Strauss, working together with Jeanne Quint, first developed the grounded theory approach as a response to the extreme positivism that permeated contemporary social research at the time. The grounded theory approach proposes that scientific truth results from both the act of observation and the emerging consensus within a community of observers as they make sense of what they have observed (Hunter et al. 2011). In their seminal book, *the Discovery of Grounded Theory*, Glaser and Strauss (1967) described an approach in which research was conceptualised as an organic process of theory emergence based on:

1   the 'fit' between the data and the conceptual categories identified by an observer/researcher;
2   how well the categories accounted for ongoing interpretations; and
3   on whether the categories are relevant to the core issues that the researcher is exploring.

Researchers using grounded theory methods do not set out to develop a set of definitive findings or an exhaustive description in relation to a problem. The goal is to develop a conceptual theory that will be recognisable to people familiar with the social settings in which the research problem was explored and which will be adaptable to similar social settings (Farragher and Coogan 2020; Hunter et al. 2011). This original grounded theory approach is often termed *classical grounded theory* (Edwards 2012).

CGT (Charmaz 2000a), on the other hand, recognises that the data and the analysis of the data emerge through interaction between the 'viewer' (researcher) and the 'viewed' (subject of the research), with the researcher aiming to present an interpretive representation of the understandings of the research subjects. Researchers adopting CGT methods are conscious that both the process of carrying out research, and any description of it, is a particular research narrative about the problem that the researchers focused upon (Charmaz 2000a, 2000b; Farragher and Coogan 2020).

For our study, data were analysed through *line-by-line* coding which facilitated our immersion in and detailed exploration of the data. Juliet Corbin and Anselm Strauss (2008) describe the work of analysing data and theorising in grounded theory studies as involving the two main analytic strategies—asking questions of the data and making constant comparisons between incidents, codes, and categories. They explain the constant comparison process in this way:

> As the researcher moves along with analysis, each incident in the data is compared with other incidents for similarities and differences. Incidents found to be conceptually similar are grouped together under a higher level descriptive concept such as 'flight'. This type of comparison is essential to all analysis because it allows the researcher to differentiate one category/ theme from another and to identify properties and dimensions specific to that theme (Corbin and Strauss 2008, 73).

This process of constant comparative analysis, which continues until a grounded theory is fully developed, is common to the literature on the three main variants of grounded theory methods (e.g. Bryant and Charmaz 2007; Corbin and Strauss 2008; Glaser 1992). Cathy Urquhart (2002) argues that the constant comparison method ensures rigour in the research as it facilitates researchers in 'grounding' the theory in the data as they develop a deeper understanding of the data. We followed an analysis process adapted from Corbin and Strauss (2008, 163), Melanie Birks and Jane Mills (2011), and Jacqueline Low (2019), engaging in a process of constant comparison of incidences of concepts in the data and writing detailed memos to capture ideas and reflect on theories identified within the data. This process of analysis created an extensive pool of memos upon which we further reflected and reworked in preparation for theory development and discussion between members of the research team.

During the analysis of the interviews, it initially appeared to the second author that social workers' experience of practice during the pandemic could be conceptualised primarily as one of 'connection' or 'dis-connection'. This perspective appealed to the previous experiences and theoretical biases (solution-focused, strengths-based, and relationship-based theories) of the second author as a social work educator/practitioner and psychotherapist. Independent of this process, the first and third authors also engaged in this process in respect of data collected via the semi-structured interview stream. They identified initial codes such as 'fear', 'hidden harm', and 'engagement', and following a discussion of the overall body of data, they identified the core categorisation of 'connection'. The four members of the research team were guided by the question 'Would the participants recognise this as a core theme in terms of their experiences?' As an example of our analysis, we take the following quote from Rachel, where she remarks that technology helped break down barriers:

> [...] people got to connect, foster carers and children got to connect more, and they got to see the child more which allowed for better relationships ... the rush wasn't there, the in and out of the car, the upset before and after access, the hard sessions that they might have done in play therapy, it was just paused and I think children, ... like they just had the time (Rachel (I)).

In this example, we reflected upon the *in vivo* concept of 'connect' during our analysis and this was also reflected upon in our research memos. We then compared this example of connection with other examples across data from other participants to explore differences and similarities in meanings and properties to develop further our understanding of participants' perceptions. As a theoretical concept, we identified its relationship to other developing categories. We then met to discuss the analysis process and the 'candidate' core concept of 'connection' and ultimately adopted this core concept, including its variations of disconnection and reconnection.

We used the core category of 'connection' to develop a grounded theory as follows: We developed codes as properties of categories (e.g. what, where, when, how do participants describe and experience connection?). These categories (conceptual elements of a theory) in turn became properties of the core category and supported theoretical codes or narratives that explain the relationships between categories, their properties, and the substantive theory

(Hunter et al. 2011). The subcategories of 'disconnection' and 'reconnection' then contributed to the development of the theoretical model grounded in the data. For example, there are many instances in the data, as discussed below, where participants reflect these concepts of connection, disconnection, and reconnection as they practice social work during the early stages of the pandemic.

## Social workers' experiences: connection, disconnection, and reconnection

The choice of 'connection' as a core category was justified by instances of related concepts across the data. Connection appears in many forms throughout the data and the following findings section presents the variants of connection, disconnection, and re-connection.

### Connection

COVID-19 in Ireland, as in many other countries, brought with it a series of lockdowns, and periods of time where the public was confined to geographic spaces, with limits on social contact. Despite this, our data showed that social workers saw opportunity in this. Many spoke about the use of technology breaking down previous barriers and facilitating and enriching communication between services, between workers, and between families. *Rachel(I)* spoke about her experience of working with foster carers and children in foster care and the impact of using existing technologies in new ways, *'people got to connect, foster carers and children got to connect more, and they got to see the child more which allowed for better relationships'*. Rachel went on to describe why she felt these technologies made a difference, '[...] *the rush wasn't there, the in and out of the car, the upset before and after* [family contact], *the hard sessions that they might have done in play therapy, it was just paused and I think children, [...] like, they just had the time' (Rachel(I))*.

All participants spoke about connections being easier to foster in terms of online meetings, but this was often coupled with technology difficulties. *Margaret(I)*, a line manager, told us that due to new IT systems put in place in recent years, the social work teams were able to connect quickly to each other and to their administrative tasks; *'you know, within two weeks everybody was connected'*. Another social worker, *Paul(I)*, highlighting a new efficiency in communication, summed this up by saying that the *'death of the in-person meeting has been a god send'*. This level of technological connection, using video calls and video conferencing, also led to efficient communication and connection with partner agencies in the community. With home visiting restricted and public lockdowns in place, these agencies were more heavily relied upon to be the 'eyes and ears' for child protection in the community: *'—we had strong working relationships with them and they were our eyes and ears in the Community, and they knew that, when we didn't have [information] from schools' (Margaret(I))*.

Notwithstanding that some clients did not have access to online technology, for the most part, participants conveyed an overall sense of optimism about greater communication with clients. Communication between social workers, foster carers, and families can be challenging in child protection work, however, online platforms provided greater access for families to connect with their social worker. In addition, greater connection was observed between foster carers, biological families, and foster children, as evidenced through sharing of videos, texts, and video calling. Participants commented on biological parents now being a more connected part of their child's care in foster care, with families forging different, potentially more individualised connections.

Rachel(I) related a story where she was responsible for supervising contact between a young boy in care and his biological sister. The young boy had chronic asthma and part of the COVID-19 restrictions in place required the siblings not to have any physical contact during these visits. Rachel found this difficult to police and during her interview she shared this account of a visit where the siblings hugged:

> [...] it was two weeks later on, where they did, you now, embrace, and it was a hug, but it was like, it was really emotional [...] and it just happened! You know what I mean, there was no way you could step in, but a social worker needed to be there at those two occasions when it was never the case [before COVID-19].

Connection also related to worlds being connected via COVID-19 that previously were separate. The reality of the lockdown was that many social workers were operating, in part or wholly, from their homes. The separation of the two environments often being a critical component of self-care, identity, and respite. Rachel(I) spoke about the pace at which the COVID-19 context developed and its initial impact on her, '[...] I think myself, I needed to get my own head straight for a day just to work it out and how I was going to make this work with family, and [...] my husband and all of that you know'.

## Dis-connection

The core concept of connection encompasses variants of disconnection and re-connection. On the one hand, we see data highlighting the value of relationships and also the benefits observed, for example, when foster families were just 'allowed to get on with it'. Social workers spoke about more natural, human, relationships forming at their own pace, without 'the rush' as one participant noted. On the other hand, however, disconnection was also present. Social workers expressed genuine worry and fear over what they were failing to see in their communities. Being disconnected from families they worked with, and those families, in turn, being disconnected from their communities. Social workers also expressed concern for children attending special services and the disconnection from these services, supports, and their peers, potentially leading to a fallout that we have yet to see. Louise(I) highlighted the importance of such informal support for young people saying, '... you know if a young person is experiencing ... mental health issues, *their friends turning around saying 'oh that's fine, I feel like that too', sometimes is worth 100 professionals turning around saying that, you know'.*

Participants also referred to missing connections with clients and colleagues and the abilities to meet with people face-to-face. *Rachel(I)* spoke about this in the context of 'Irish hospitality': *'There would be some families that you have a toasted sandwich [...] and a cup of tea and it's just [...] that Irish hospitality thing is gone [...] all of that is taken away'.* Ava(D) illustrated this dilemma as she describes the difference in practice before and during COVID-19:

> Normally [...] I would telephone a parent, inform them of the referral and then try to make an opportunity to meet. Whilst this does take longer [...] I find I reach more positive outcomes quicker, because you have a bigger opportunity to make a connection with a person. I am finding it hard to connect with every client I am speaking to by phone I am now missing the relationship side of my practice. I no longer get to empathise with a family by body language or non-verbal communication. It relies solely on the tone of my voice.

In her diary entry three to four weeks later, Ava(D) returned to the concept of connection or lack thereof with her colleagues, highlighting the importance of collegial support previously available and now replaced by solitude or disconnection. Amelia(D) described similar experience by saying that her connections had become much more problem based: 'My work certainly feels more problem orientated, it's now at home and I'm alone when these calls come in'.

Participants spoke of acutely feeling this loss of support particularly in completing visits alone and particularly when social workers had to deal with a high level of risk, such as domestic violence. *Margaret(I)* stated that workers *'were going out on their own in their own cars, they didn't have the benefit of joint work, two staff going out, they didn't have that benefit of the debriefing, debriefing was taking place over the phone. That was a huge challenge'* (Margaret(I)). Because many workers were working remotely during this period, it meant that they were receiving complex referrals while working in their homes, travelling to the scene, and returning to their homes, all on their own in many instances. In her reflective diary, Ava(D) emphasised the toll this disconnection had on her professional and personal life:

> I know it's not necessary to reflect on [annual] leave, however I feel this was directly impacted by covid and so I want to. For the first time ever in my years as a child protection social worker, I felt a sense of "burn out" which led to me taking this leave. As I have [a health condition] which puts me in the 'vulnerable' category, I am not allowed do face-to-face meetings with families.

### Re-connection

Many of the participants spoke about disconnection from their colleagues in a physical sense but also that the context of the pandemic had also brought them closer together as a team. At the beginning of the pandemic, the Child and Family Agency in Ireland prioritised their responses to three key areas: Child protection, children in care, and domestic violence. Social workers moved to remote working from their homes, and contact with children and families was reduced to essential visits only. Despite these unprecedented restrictions on connection, for social workers who participated in this study, it seems that the pandemic also inadvertently strengthened relationships.

Many of the participants spoke about the value of or a revaluing of 'team'. *Paul(I)* stated that '[COVID-19] *brought us closer as a team* [...] *the support is fantastic because I suppose we have been through the most historically significant event of our lives together* [...] *and we have done it locked up in a room together* [...] *and we haven't killed each other'. Rachel(I)* spoke about a new level of understanding by management of the juggle between personal and professional life and that it's '*important* [...] *that is recognised – – that people really stood up to the mark, they showed their resilience, they worked through, were creative, you know'* with *Margaret (I)* supporting this by saying that '*the adaptability and the commitment of staff was huge you know that certainly came to the fore'*.

Given that the context of our study was child and family social work through the pandemic, it was heartening that participants spoke about witnessing strengthened relationships, particularly between foster carers and parents. *Margaret(I)* spoke about the impact on child-in-care placements also whereby children were more stable with less distraction and had more time to engage with their foster carers. Via the use of technology, participants also shared a view that this area of connection became more natural and served to reconnect foster and biological families around the child:

> I've noticed that we'll say if a foster carer takes photographs of the family that she can send it on to the birth family and also [...] I suppose you see foster carers and parents interacting and that respect. The importance of that for the children [...] foster carers showing that respect to the mother and father I think has strengthened an awful lot (Rachel(I)).

The use of technology to connect with young people and their families also highlighted the participant's person-centred practice. It was clear from our data that participants were thinking about what was working best for their clients. *Jennifer(I)*, speaking about the authorised use of WhatsApp, stated that '[...] *because it's on the Wi-Fi, like, my clients can send me a text and say, listen I don't have any credit I can't ring you'.* Participants also spoke of working more efficiently with less travel time due to COVID-19 restrictions. *Louise(I)*, referring specifically to this aspect, suggested: '[...] *you know that time could be pumped into a young person or a family or someone else in need so, yeah I think, I mean it just made us more kind of aware of communicating and how important even, like, emails and text messages and checking in and all the things that we say that we're going to do all the time, do you know'.*

## Discussion and Conclusion

Through our analysis, we developed theorisations and candidate categories concerning many different issues. The notion of struggle arose strongly considering the 'new normal' placing significant pressures on frontline social work staff, their managers, and the children and families they worked with. These struggles brought a sense of guilt for some social workers as they sought to balance their working lives with their personal lives; two spheres previously separated and now thrust together. We heard from social workers who needed time to adjust to their own personal lives before feeling they were able to help others in a professional capacity.

While other theorisations and categories developed, the core concept of connection remained and the findings endorsed what social workers have always known—that as humans, we are hardwired to connect. Building and maintaining relationships is the linchpin of the social work profession (Ruch et al. 2018). Our findings attest to the centrality of relationships and highlight all that is best about social work practice: Workers trying against the odds to maintain and in some instances create new connections with the people we are privileged to serve, children, their parents, and foster parents. This study illustrated that social workers remain one of the most skilled professions in navigating human relationships.

However, COVID-19 resulted in these relationships often crossing the threshold into the workers' home life, and what was once a binary of work and home became a fusion. This blurring of the lines made some workers feel disconnected from informal support from colleagues, case discussions, and advice. Social work was never conceptualised or practiced as a solitary profession, and without careful attention from organisations and individual workers, this is a potentially unwelcome trajectory for the profession. Further research is required to assess the impact of remote work practices on new and recently qualified social workers who rely on more experienced colleagues for advice and guidance. A balance will need to be found to ensure that all staff are supported.

Adopting a new way of connecting with clients through technology existed in more nascent forms before COVID-19 (Mishna et al. 2012). However, out of necessity, these practices overshadowed the in-person format during the pandemic. In the main, participants were energised by the flexibility that technology brought to their role during COVID, seeing many benefits to using multiple methods of communication. Our findings echo similar research highlighting that the merit of digital communication depends, among other factors, on the child's age, quality of the pre-existing relationship with family, and access to technology (Alston and Chow 2021; Baginsky and Manthorpe 2021; Copson et al. 2022). Child protection social work, particularly visits to children and families, remain a sensory role—at times influenced by our emotions, experiences, and intuitive responses, which is best undertaken in person (Ferguson 2016; Munro 2020). Caution is warranted to ensure that technology is used as a complementary tool and not at the expense of in-person relationship building (Pink et al. 2022).

In this context, we were heartened to find that the concept of re-connection demonstrated a (re)establishment of links between practitioners and core social work ethics and values. Our findings demonstrate the practice of person-centredness in establishing communication with families and children. Elements of compassion and empowerment were particularly evident in the context of foster care where families, in some sense forced to get on with things themselves, thrived and established their own new connections with biological parents. The sense of team was evident throughout and something which all participants seemed to value, particularly during the pandemic, whether through realising its absence or through its provision of resilience. However, these positives were starkly contrasted with the darker side of the pandemic where social workers expressed anxiety in dealing with risk in isolation, uncertainty about the 'hidden harm' within the community, and the fear of what impacts and effects are yet to emerge.

Looking forward, this study resonates with social worker's experiences elsewhere (e.g. Ashcroft et al. 2022; Harrikari et al. 2021; Pink et al. 2022) and highlights the ethical challenges involved and the centrality of value-based practice during the pandemic (Banks et al. 2020). COVID-19 ushered in a recalibration of the profession in terms of embracing a more technological focus while at the same time a return to our core function as a helping and social justice profession. This is best illustrated through the ability of social workers to build, promote, and maintain relationships—our greatest asset. To conclude, there is cause for optimism going forward as connection and reconnection with core social work values and ethics place the profession in good stead to face the next black swan.

## References

Alston, Margaret and Amy Y.M. Chow. 2021. "Introduction – When Social Work Meets Disaster: Challenges and Opportunities." *The British Journal of Social Work* 51 (5): 1525–1530. 10.1093/bjsw/bcab154

Ashcroft, Rachelle, Deepy Sur, Andrea Greenblatt, and Peter Donahue. 2022. "The Impact of the COVID-19 Pandemic on Social Workers at the Frontline: A Survey of Canadian Social Workers." *The British Journal of Social Work* 52 (3): 1724–1746. 10.1093/bjsw/bcab158

Baginsky, Mary and Jill Manthorpe. 2021. "The Impact of COVID-19 on Children's Social Care in England." *Child Abuse & Neglect* 116 (2). 10.1016/j.chiabu.2020.104739

Banks, Sarah, Tian Cai, Ed de Jonge, Jane Shears, Michelle Shum, Ana M. Sobočan, Kim Strom, Rory Truell, María Jesús Úriz, and Merlinda Weinberg. 2020. "Practising Ethically During COVID-19: Social Work Challenges and Responses." *International Social Work* 63 (5): 569–583. 10.1177/0020872820949614

Bender, Anna E., Kristen A. Berg, Emily K. Miller, Kylie E. Evans, and Megan R. Holmes. 2021. "'Making Sure We Are All Okay': Healthcare Workers' Strategies for Emotional Connectedness During the COVID-19 Pandemic." *Clinical Social Work Journal* 49 (4): 445–455. 10.1007/s10615-020-00781-w

Birks, Melanie and Jane Mills. 2011. *Grounded Theory: A Practical Guide*. Thousand Oaks: Sage Publications.

Bryant, Anthony and Kathy Charmaz, eds. 2007. *The Sage Handbook of Grounded Theory.* London: Sage Publications.

Cabiati, Elena. 2021. "Social Workers Helping Each Other During the COVID-19 Pandemic: Online Mutual Support Groups." *International Social Work* 64 (5): 676–688. 10.1177/0020872820975447

Charmaz, Kathy. 2000a. "Looking Back, Moving Forward: Expanding Sociological Perspectives in the Twenty-First Century – 2000 Presidential Address to the Pacific Sociological Association." *Sociological Perspectives* 43 (4): 529–547.

Charmaz, Kathy. 2000b. "The Teachings of Anselm Strauss: Remembrances and Reflections." *Sociological Perspectives – Supplement: A Tribute to Anselm Strauss* S163–S174. 10.2307/41888823

Coogan, Declan and Joseph Mooney. 2020. "Report of Ireland." In *Covid-19 and Social Work: A Collection of Country Reports*, edited by Lena Dominelli, Timo Harrikari, Joseph Mooney, Vesna Leskošek, and Erin Kennedy Tsunoda, 68–77. N.p. https://www.iassw-aiets.org/covid-19/5369-covid-19-and-social-work-a-collection-of-country-reports/.

Copson, Ruth, Anne M. Murphy, Laura Cook, Elsbeth Neil, and Pernille Sorensen. 2022. "Relationship-Based Practice and Digital Technology in Child and Family Social Work: Learning From Practice During the COVID-19 Pandemic." *Developmental Child Welfare* 4 (1): 3–19. 10.1177/25161032221079325

Corbin, Juliet M. and Anselm L. Strauss. 2008. *Basics of Qualitative Research: Techniques and Procedures for Developing Grounded Theory.* 3rd ed. Los Angeles: Sage Publications.

Dominelli, Lena, Timo Harrikari, Joseph Mooney, Vesna Leskošek, and Erin Kennedy Tsunoda, eds. 2020. *Covid-19 and Social Work: A Collection of Country Reports.* N.p. https://www.iassw-aiets.org/covid-19/5369-covid-19-and-social-work-a-collection-of-country-reports/.

Edwards, Jane. 2012. "We Need to Talk About Epistemology: Orientations, Meaning and Interpretation Within Music Therapy Research." *Journal of Music Therapy* 49 (4): 372–394. 10.1093/jmt/49.4.372

Farragher, Róisín and Declan Coogan. 2020. "Constructivist Grounded Theory: Recognising and Raising the Voice of Young People With Experience of Care Systems." *Child Care in Practice* 26 (1): 38–49. 10.1080/13575279.2018.1521377

Ferguson, Harry. 2016. "Researching Social Work Practice Close Up: Using Ethnographic and Mobile Methods to Understand Encounters Between Social Workers, Children and Families." *British Journal of Social Work* 46 (1): 153–168. 10.1093/bjsw/bcu120

Gibson, Allison, Shoshana H. Bardach, and Natalie D. Pope. 2020. "COVID-19 and the Digital Divide: Will Social Workers Help Bridge the Gap?" *Journal of Gerontological Social Work* 63 (6–7): 671–673. 10.1080/01634372.2020.1772438

Glaser, Barney G. and Anselm Strauss. 1967. *The Discovery of Grounded Theory – Strategies for Qualitative Research.* Chicago: Adeline Publishing Co.

Glaser, Barney G. 1992. *Basics of Grounded Theory Analysis: Emergence Vs Forcing.* Mill Valley: Sociology Press.

Harrikari, Timo, Marjo Romakkaniemi, Laura Tiitinen, and Sanna Ovaskainen. 2021. "Pandemic and Social Work: Exploring Finnish Social Workers' Experiences Through a SWOT Analysis." *The British Journal of Social Work* 51 (5): 1644–1662. 10.1093/bjsw/bcab052

Hunter, Andrew, Kathy Murphy, Annmarie Grealish, Dympna Casey, and John Keady. 2011. "Navigating the Grounded Theory Terrain. Part 1." *Nurse Researcher* 18 (4): 6–10. 10.7748/nr2011.07.18.4.6.c8636

Kenny, Méabh and Robert Fourie. 2015. "Contrasting Classic, Straussian, and Constructivist Grounded Theory: Methodological and Philosophical Conflicts." *Qualitative Report* 20 (9): 1270–1289. 10.46743/2160-3715/2015.2251

Low, Jacqueline. 2019. "A Pragmatic Definition of the Concept of Theoretical Saturation." *Sociological Focus* 52 (2): 131– 19. 10.1080/00380237.2018.1544514

Miller, Vivian J. and HeeSoon Lee. 2020. "Social Work Values in Action During COVID-19." *Journal of Gerontological Social Work* 63 (6–7): 565–569. 10.1080/01634372.2020. 1769792

Mishna, Faye, Marion Bogo, Jannifer Root, Jami-Leigh Sawyer, and Mona Khoury-Kassabri. 2012. ""It Just Crept in": The Digital Age and Implications for Social Work Practice." *Clinical Social Work Journal* 40 (3): 277–286. 10.1007/s10615-012-0383-4

Mooney, Joseph, Timo Harrikari, and Lena Dominelli. 2020. "Covid-19: A New Challenge for Social Work." In *COVID-19 and Social Work: A Collection of Country Reports*, edited by Lena Dominelli, Timo Harrikari, Joseph Mooney, Vesna Leskošek, and Erin Kennedy Tsunoda, 1–6. N.p. https://www.iassw-aiets.org/covid-19/5369-covid-19-and-social-work-a-collection-of-country-reports/.

Munro, Eileen. 2020. *Effective Child Protection*. 3rd ed. Los Angeles: Sage Publications.

Pink, Sarah, Harry Ferguson, and Laura Kelly. 2022. "Digital Social Work: Conceptualising a Hybrid Anticipatory Practice." *Qualitative Social Work* 21 (2): 413–430. 10.1177/14733250211003647

Ruch, Gillian, Danielle Turney, and Adrian Ward, eds. 2018. *Relationship-Based Social Work: Getting to the Heart of Practice*. 2nd ed. London: Jessica Kingsley Publishers.

Schiff, Miriam, Shiri Shinan-Altman, and Hadas Rosenne. 2021. "Israeli Health Care Social Workers' Personal and Professional Concerns During the COVID-19 Pandemic Crisis: The Work-Family Role Conflict." *The British Journal of Social Work* 51 (5): 1858–1878. 10.1093/bjsw/bcab114

Urquhart, Cathy. 2002. "Regrounding Grounded Theory–Or Reinforcing Old Prejudices? A Brief Reply to Bryant." *The Journal of Information and Technology Theory and Application (JITTA)* 4 (3): 43–54.

# 14 Transformative Disruption?— Reflections on Care in Social Work Under a COVID-19 Pandemic Lockdown

*Andreas Møller Jørgensen, Mie Engen, and Maria Appel Nissen*

## Introduction

This chapter focuses on social workers' experiences and reflections on the possibilities for sustaining care during a pandemic lockdown and discusses if disruption of normal practices can be a source for learning and transformation. In part one, we outline a concept of care and reflect on how a pandemic lockdown can disrupt and challenge professional care, but may also reveal structural weaknesses and offer paths for critical reflective transformation. In the second part, we exemplify this by presenting an empirical case from a research project on the possibilities for care in social work (2018–2022). We introduce the current structural challenges in the context of Danish social work with vulnerable children and families related to expectations of cost-effectiveness, efficiency, scarce resources, and time. Next, we present an analysis of an online interview with a group of social workers conducted during the Danish pandemic lockdown in 2020. The analysis shows that the capacity to prioritise scarce resources and time and work in new and creative ways to enable caring practices is paramount when normal practice is disrupted. Moreover, disruption becomes an impetus for critical reflection on normal practice and conditions for care. The social workers share positive experiences of (re)discovering the 'essence of social work'. They experience an intensified sense of solidarity, community, and reciprocity with children and families. At the same time, they feel 'worn out' and worry if the conditions under the COVID-19 lockdown will constitute a 'new normal'. For example, will management acknowledge and prioritise the need for resources and time for care or will they translate the experiences from the lockdown into potentials for increasing efficiency and cost-effectiveness? In the third part, we discuss how the pandemic disruption can contribute to recognition of the caring purpose and the societal value of social work. We will relate this discussion to the broader findings from our research project based on in-depth empirical investigations of care in social work with vulnerable children and families.

DOI: 10.4324/9781003374374-18

## The concept of care—Pandemic disruption and critical reflective transformation

Seeing, understanding, and responding to human problems and needs for help—developing relationships that enable this, are considered core values of the social work profession (Phillips 2007). In this way, social work is oriented towards ideals and practices of care (Engen et al. 2019). Theories of care are diverse but build on a relational ontology that sees relations of interdependence and dependence as basic features of existence (Robinson 2011). *Care* as a concept and practice calls attention to the importance of others and their needs. Human beings depend upon each other for fulfilment of basic material, social, and psychological needs, and individuals, communities, and societies cannot exist without care (Sevenhuijsen 1998; Tronto 1993). The ideal is to develop caring practices and societies where human well-being and flourishing are at the centre (Tronto 2013). However, realising this ideal is challenging.

Care is relational, and relationships are embedded in asymmetrical power structures and 'conditions of vulnerability and inequality' (Tronto 1993, 21). Therefore, conditions and practices of care are continuously negotiated among individuals, groups, and institutions in specific socio-cultural contexts (Nissen and Engen 2021). Needs for care are typically ascribed to vulnerable and dependent people, while 'control for meeting these needs is placed in the hands of those who are deemed competent and independent' (Tronto 2013, 108). According to Tronto (1993, 2013), caring practices rely on the five moral qualities: attentiveness, responsibility, competence, responsiveness, and trust. Attentiveness involves perceiving and recognising needs. Responsibility means recognising that action is necessary and possible and making decisions to respond to needs. Competence is necessary to fulfil needs, and responsiveness involves the willingness to consider the response of the other person in order to evaluate if needs are met. A precondition to these qualities is trust linked with solidarity and a broader collective responsibility for care in society based on respect for difference and plurality (Tronto 2013). In late modern capitalist societies, the underlying process for realising these five qualities can be put to the test.

Hartmut Rosa argues that *resonance* is the process through which our encounters and experiences of relationships are constituted, and 'we seek and need resonance, connections, and experiences of resonance to have a good life' (Schiermer 2020, 4). Like care, resonance is relational and characterised by four crucial qualities. First, affection: 'We feel truly touched or moved by someone or something we encounter [...] [a]ffection has an emotional, but also a cognitive and certainly a bodily element' (Schiermer 2020, 3). Second, emotion: 'We feel that we answer this "call", we react to it with body and mind, we reach out and touch the other side as well—in a word, we experience self-efficacy in this encounter'. Third, in this process of being moved and of responding, we transform ourselves and the other is transformed as well. Fourth, elusiveness: 'We cannot predict or control resonance because it arises relationally and interactively' (Schiermer 2020, 4). According to Rosa, people are resonant beings—we strive for being in relationships of resonance—but importantly, resonance does not imply consonance. Rather, it involves a relationship of care transcending difference:

> […] only something that is and remains utterly different can actually speak to us in its own voice. Resonance is not consonance, it requires the active presence of something that is beyond my grasp, elusive, and in this sense remains alien (Schiermer 2020, 4).

It can be argued that late modern, capitalist societies, characterised by an incessant and accelerated focus on reproducing their social and institutional structures through economic growth, innovation, and public managerial imaginaries about future potentialities (Andersen and Pors 2016; Beckert 2016), have changed our relationships to each other in a direction that can hinder resonance. Rosa (2021) terms this a condition of 'dynamic stabilisation', which creates poor conditions for resonance. Resonance requires mutual trust and low levels of fear, which in turn require 'time and stability as background conditions' (Rosa 2021). Modes of competition, optimisation, and speed significant for capitalist societies create time-pressure and stress and enforce 'a non-resonant, instrumental, reified mode of approaching the world' (Schiermer 2020, 4). This leads to alienation in relation to both subjects and objects; "a particular mode of relating to the world of things, to people, and to one's self in which there is no responsivity, i.e., no meaningful inner connection. It is a relationship without genuine relation" (Rosa 2021, 41).

The COVID-19 pandemic has caused the world to stop and pause—non-voluntarily. It has led to a 'deceleration', a significant reduction of speed, activities, and movement, which 'is not a solution or a liberation, it rather resembles an accident' (Rosa 2021). Many communities or societies are experiencing a serious disruption of life causing economic hardship, anxiety, and uncertainty (Corrêa et al. 2021), and the impact of the pandemic crisis will vary depending on the available resources and capacities of communities or societies to 'cope' with both short- and long-term effects (UNDRR 2019). In that sense, COVID-19 is a bio-medical and social phenomenon that reveals inequality in access to economic, political, social, technological, educational, material, and human resources. Disruptive disasters can both reveal and exacerbate weak economic and social infrastructures and a lack of organisational capacities, staff, and resources that can place vulnerable parts of the population at risk of both immediate and long-term suffering (Cronin and Jones 2015). According to Rosa, COVID-19 fosters `a serious distortion in our relationship to the world', since it installs a fundamental distrust and feeling of not being at home in the world anymore (Corrêa et al. 2021, 120). As a global pandemic, it shows the uncontrollability of the world, and this should make us think deeply about how we relate to it and to each other:

[…] as we seek to understand, control and dominate the world scientifically, technologically, politically and so on, the virus is totally beyond our control on all these levels. Perhaps this situation, in the end, might help us to collectively re-think our mode of being in the world and lead us to less alienating forms of life in the future (Corrêa et al. 2021, 120).

Thus, the pandemic may also open a window of resonance, where we are moved by, respond to, and change our relations with each other and the world. Despite the devastating consequences, the pandemic disruption can be *transformative* and lead to processes of learning, reflection, and social change (Caron et al. 2020; Truell 2020).

According to International Federation of Social Workers (IFSW), social workers globally have struggled for making governments recognise the importance of a social response to the crisis. They have advocated for access to social services during lockdown and faced similar 'ethical challenges in the face of inadequate resources and collapsing health and welfare systems' (Truell 2020, 545–46). Consequently, they have struggled to adapt and transform social work practices. Even though the effects of the pandemic will show in the years to come, 'it is already clear that social work is becoming fundamental to not only rebuilding but transforming our world' (Truell 2020, 548). Thus, it is assumed that if societies, communities, organisations, and professionals are attentive to needs and experiences arising from being in the midst of disruption and encourage responsiveness to these experiences, the disruption can be a valuable source for learning, critical reflection, and social change. However, this will depend on the capacity, time, and resources for approaching the experience of disruption as an unusual event that reflects existing weaknesses in normal social practices in the context of structural and social inequalities in access to resources. We will now illustrate this challenge as it appears in the context of Denmark.

## Practices and reflections on care in times of a lockdown—A case of social work with children and families in Denmark

Our case is concerned with social work with children and families in Denmark, embedded in a particular economic, political, and institutional infrastructure of social services. Within this context and over the last ten years, there has been an intensified focus on cost-effectiveness. The former Social Democratic Social Minister encouraged municipalities to 'invest in methods that work' and to 'do away with ineffective services' (Ministry of Social and Internal Affairs 2012). Following this, Local Government Denmark (2015) actively encouraged municipalities to organise social services as cost-effective 'temporary pit-stops' and to search for alternatives to expensive long-term placements in institutional care. Internationally, such governmental and bureaucratic attempts 'to control processes and outcomes in order to ensure their efficiency and transparency' are pervasive (Rosa 2021), and research shows how social workers struggle to translate ideas about cost-effectiveness into discourses that resonate with social work (Fallov and Blad 2018; Nissen et al. 2018).

From research, we know that caring for and keeping children safe depends on establishing a relationship with the family based on trust. This requires time, resources, and thus governmental, organisational, and professional backup of practices that enable face-to-face contact and in-depth understanding of the needs and lives of the families (Engen et al. 2019). If such backup does not exist, there is a risk of individualising the responsibilities, uncertainties, and worries embedded in this work, which can lead to burnout and losing sight of the well-being of children (Ferguson et al. 2020). In our research project, from where this case derives, we have identified two significant ways of shaping social work with vulnerable children and families that connect to governmental discourses of cost-effectiveness. One is a targeted and instrumental collaboration with parents strictly focused on protecting vulnerable children's needs, while at the same time promoting parental responsibility and self-sufficiency as fast as possible. Services are regularly evaluated in terms of how children and parents are progressing in order to stop ineffective services. The other constitutes an enduring and often long-term collaboration with families, with a focus on both children and parents' needs and the relationship between them, in order to keep the child at home and avoid expensive and potentially ineffective long-term placements (cf. Nissen 2021). One way or the other, expectations of cost-effectiveness are an integrated aspect of the organisational and professional climate, as one manager conveys it: 'I think you will find many variations, but maybe such a pressure is dependent on how well a particular agency of social services is performing. If expenses are going up, a local manager might come under some pressure'.

This was the governmental context of social work with families, when the Danish COVID-19 lockdown was announced on 11 March, 2020 involving a widespread lockdown of the public and private sectors. Social services for vulnerable children and families were defined as a critical societal function and municipalities continued core functions such as responding to reports on suspicion of child neglect and offering special support for vulnerable children (Ministry of Social and Internal Affairs 2020). Some social workers were included in emergency responses at the workplace, but the majority worked from home equipped with computers and telephones. Knowing that even before COVID-19, the Danish child protection system was vulnerable to financial pressure and struggles for time (Nissen 2021), we wondered how social workers would experience and respond to the disruption of social work practices. How did the lockdown affect their ability to care for and sustain a relationship with vulnerable children and their families, and what can we learn from this disruption?

These questions were investigated in an online focus group interview with social workers in the child welfare and protection services. The interview was set up as a part of the research project *Does social work care? Exploring the relational, emotional, and embodied practices in social services for vulnerable children and their families* (2018–2022). The purpose of the project is to generate knowledge about forms of and possibilities for care in social work with children and families in vulnerable positions. The project is based on ethnographic field studies closely following and observing the practices of social workers and their encounters with children and families in multiple settings of statutory social case work, home-based counselling, and family treatment in two Danish munici-palities. Due to the lockdown, the field study was paused in March 2020. However, in April 2020, we arranged the online group interview with social workers from one of the municipalities. Three social workers participated: Jane, a statutory social worker; Stephanie, who works with home-based family support for families with small children; and Rebecca, a contact person for young people. The interview lasted for approximately 1.5 hours, and it was conducted in an open and dialogic fashion but with a focus on experiences of the possibility of care during the lockdown. Since the interviewer had already met and estab-lished relationships with the social workers during the fieldwork, it was possible to establish a relaxed and trusting atmosphere and dialogue online. The inter-view was transcribed verbatim and the social workers were given pseudonyms. The interview provides a rich account of experiences of caring for children and families in a disrupted context. We have identified three core experiences that point to essential but often unnoticed practices as well as structural and social resources, capacities, and challenges in making care possible. The following part of our case is structured according to these experiences, practices, capacities, and challenges in order to illustrate potential sources for learning and for making disruptions transformative.

## Working creatively to enable caring practices

As noted, the impact of a disaster is dependent on the available resources and capacities (UNDRR 2019). In relation to this, Jane reflects: 'When there is a crisis, the challenges our families face are amplified'. Because of this, the social workers find it essential to keep a close connection and relationship with the families. However, staying close to the families, gaining knowledge about their evolving needs, and offering support are difficult during the lockdown. Thus, the social workers intensively prioritise the families, who are in most need of care. The social workers start using alternative means of communication including digital devices creatively to keep in contact with and seeing the children in the family (Truell 2020, 547). Prevented from visiting the families, Jane calls all the families, *'just to hear, how they are'*. While this means that she is talking with some families more than normally, she also experiences a greater need to prioritise, who should receive home-based support from the emergency response team. *'I have 36 children* [in her caseload], *so it is about choosing, who should be seen more than others'*, she explains, prioritising calling families, who do not get visits at home. In relation to this, Stephanie describes how home visits offer unique insights:

> [...] when you enter into a home, if there is a high level of conflict for example, then there is this atmosphere [...] you can just feel the whole house reeks of something, and you see, what it is. You cannot uncover this in a phone conversation.

When a lockdown disrupts the possibility of making home visits, the social workers become more aware of the home as an important place to do social work. Home visiting is a deeply embodied practice in which all senses and emotions come into play (Ferguson 2018). It is pivotal for gaining a socio-material experience of the atmosphere of the home and in extending caring relations into the private domain (Fallov and Nissen 2018). Thus, creating resonance with the material setting of the home is an important way of generating knowledge and understanding. Entering the home affects the social workers both cognitively, emotionally, and bodily and enables them to be attentive to and respond to the situation and needs in the family (Rosa 2021; Tronto 1993).

Reflecting on the shortcomings of phone calls, Jane says that she will never conduct initial meetings with families over the phone, since '*you have only one attempt*'. Building relationships of resonance and care with families is a fragile affair that depends on attentiveness to and understanding of even the smallest clues in the interaction. Related to this, Rebecca tells about a young boy, who has just lost his father, and says, '*in such situations, I just want to go and hold, hug and be close, and just talk about how it is to experience a loss*'. Phone and online conversations can make it hard to show empathy—especially in situations involving deep human emotions (Mørk 2020). Resonance and care are embodied experiences that digital communication distorts. When time and resources have already been invested in creating mutual relations of trust, it is easier to maintain contact and relationships through phone and online conversations. In these cases, the families also initiate contact themselves and call to tell the social workers about problems. Thus, the importance of establishing and sustaining relationships of mutual trust becomes even more evident than under normal conditions (Tronto 2013).

## (Re)discovering 'the essence' of social work

The social workers also report positive experiences of (re)discovering 'the essence' and value of social work practices that are attentive to, take responsibility for, and respond to the needs of children and families (Tronto 1993):

> We have had to lower our ambitions a bit, and focus on and do what is helpful. It offers an opportunity to reflect on, what usually takes time in our everyday work. What is the essence, what turns us on in terms of making a difference? It has been interesting to slow down a bit, this slowness in my relationship to the young people. I have walked a lot with them. It is about being together and being present. I have had a chance to see, what is most important in my work (Rebecca).

I agree [...] This feeling of crisis makes you move a little closer and 'get to the bone', and this is wonderful. Time to prepare properly for home visits, not hasting from one meeting to another (Stephanie).

The experience of slowness and maintaining only essential social work activities opens a 'window of resonance', a sense of responsivity and connection, a sense of opening up towards each other and of being together, a sense of being affected by and responding to each other (Rosa 2021). To the social workers, this creates a sense of 'getting to the bone' of what makes a difference in people's lives. Sometimes parents have expressed concern for the social worker as well, which has affected and touched the social workers *because usually it is only the other way around*, Stephanie tells. In this way, a '*strange*' sense of community, solidarity, and reciprocity has appeared:

> We need to be aware that we are a huge part of their network, and if they do not hear from us for a month, then maybe they do not hear from anyone at all. I want to be in contact and I miss them like crazy. I am okay with them knowing that I miss them [...] Sometimes, I also get sad, and in some way, I'm a part of their life too. We have different functions. They are the family, I am the social worker, but we all want the same thing, and we are able to face difficult things together and be together, when things turn out well (Jane).

The disruption has brought about a sense of shared human vulnerability that heightens awareness of and ethical reflection on human interdependence. In the midst of crisis, the social workers become intensely aware that human beings—including themselves—can only exist within networks of care and social resonance and therefore depend on each other (Robinson 2011; Rosa 2021). Due to different '*functions*', as Janes puts it, the sense of reciprocal caring relations is somewhat unfamiliar. The lockdown fosters a sense of community that stems from being in a common situation of human anxiety and opens for reciprocal attentiveness, responsiveness, and reflection about shared human needs and conditions. However, this capacity is also dependent on the resources for making care possible.

Practicing creatively, prioritising, and initiating new forms of contact in a situation marked by uncertainty and anxiety is also emotionally demanding. This is expressed by Stephanie: '*I have also felt a huge need for self-care. I'm the one to give hope. I can do it, and I'm doing it, but I feel a bit more worn out*'. According to the social workers, the management has told them to '*keep their nerves steady*' and accept that it is not possible to uphold normal ambitions. However, the social workers do not find this easy. As Jane says: '*I'm the one who has to look this little girl in the eyes, and see how she is withdrawing*'. The emotional burden of perceiving and recognising other persons' need for care without having the possibility to act can go unnoticed. The social workers experience a gap between their responsibility for being attentive to and responding to basic human needs for care and support (Tronto 2013) and their possibilities for doing so that are not addressed by the management. This gap causes worries about what will happen after the lockdown.

## After the lockdown: What will be the new normal?

The social workers reflect upon the experience of being in a state of emergency and worrying for what will come after. Jane, Stephanie, and Rebecca have experienced that most of the families manage the lockdown '*surprisingly well*'. Their explanation is that everyday demands and pressures, such as getting the children to school and participating in social and unemployment services, are suspended (Ministry of Employment 2020). However, Stephanie suggests, '*There will be a huge work now, getting them back on track with structure in daily life*'. This concern for the long-term consequences of the lockdown is not unique for a Danish context (The British Academy 2021). Furthermore, the social workers worry that the management will not recognise this problem and will conclude that '*everything has gone perfectly well*'; the families have been well; social workers' sick leaves have decreased; costs have not increased. The social workers do not recognise this as unambiguous sign of neither decreasing social problems nor enhancing the quality and effectiveness of social work. What counts as good and effective social work, depends on the criterion for success, as Jane notes:

> There is a difference between keeping the children alive and creating improvement. Many children remain, perhaps, at status quo, or they have developed for the worse. It may well be that the parents have kept the children alive. If that is the success criterion, then it has gone really well.

The social workers understand the aim of social work as promoting human well-being and social inclusion through actual processes of change sensitive to people's past and present life world (Lorenz 2006; Parton and Kirk 2009) but worry if management is of the same understanding.

## Possibilities for transformative disruption and social change—Recognising the caring purposes and social value of social work

As we are writing this in winter 2021, Danish social workers have returned to their workplaces. The lockdown disrupted normal practices of social work creating tensions and difficult emotions but also a 'free space', where social workers have experienced key moments of the 'essence' of social work. They have prioritised and (re)discovered a practice based on in-depth knowledge, caring, and providing safety for vulnerable children and their families obtained through informal conversations, home visits, and actions that foster social resonance, energy, and hope. This grows from a basic solidarity and orientation towards the value of being together to enable humane relations and new possibilities for trust and social change (Tronto 2013). Our case seems to reflect a more general experience under the lockdown of having more time to do essential social work and being present, listening, and responding to needs (Paulsen 2020). These key moments and discoveries are valuable knowledge for making disruptions transformative and a source for organisational and practice learning. Social workers have been part of an intense and unforeseeable process of learning. After a process of intense learning, organisations can reflect on how to use a period of uncertainty to develop resilience instead of amplifying exhaustion, destabilisation, and vulnerabilities (Andersen and Pors 2016). We are yet to see how social problems, social work organisations, and social work will develop, and if the disruptions will become a source for critical reflection, learning, and social change. The worry, as one social worker expressed it, is that 'unfortunately, it will most likely just become a parenthesis in me and my colleagues' work life' (Paulsen 2020). This worry is shared by Rosa (2021), who points to the fact that the pandemic has not changed the modes of competition, optimisation, and speed characteristic of late capitalist societies. Thus, the fundamental structures that foster instrumental, non-resonant relationships have not been altered.

However, while governmental expectations of cost-effectiveness shape the conditions for care in social work practice in Denmark and internationally, the pandemic may have opened 'a window' for care practices and responses to emerge. In Denmark, we see that a governmental focus on cost-effectiveness can lead to a strict focus on the child's needs, responsibilisation of parents, and expectations of quick individual change despite vulnerability and inequality. Social workers must generate quick returns on investments, and, consequently, attention to needs requiring long-lasting interventions and involvement are easily considered an overinvestment (Jørgensen 2022; Nissen 2021). However, we also see that social work struggles for more sustainable and caring alternatives; social work practices that exercise solidary authority by integrating child-focused practices with family-oriented practices and a balanced focus on risk and support (Engen 2022). Enduring long-term relationships with families are based on feelings and values concerning what is fair for disfavoured children and parents and a deep qualitative knowledge of their life circumstances (Nissen forthcoming). Caring social work requires time and resources invested in establishing enduring relationships. Thus, a starting point for social change and transformation in the aftermath of the pandemic is recognising the caring purpose and the societal value of social work practices that sustain relational and socio-material welfare (Engen et al. 2019). This involves a critical reflection and questioning regarding the sustainability of our modes of relating to each other and the world that pervade practices and relations of care.

## References

Andersen, Niels Å. and Justine G. Pors. 2016. *Public Management in Transition: The Orchestration of Potentiality*. Bristol: Policy Press.

Beckert, Jens. 2016. *Imagined Futures. Fictional Expectations and Capitalist Dynamics*. Cambridge: Harvard University Press.

Caron, Roxane, Edward O.J. Lee, and Annie Pullen Sansfaçon. 2020. "Transformative Disruptions and Collective Knowledge Building: Social Work Professors Building Anti-Oppressive Ethical Frameworks for Research, Teaching, Practice and Activism." *Ethics and Social Welfare* 14(3): 298–314. 10.1080/17496535.2020.1749690

Corrêa, Diogo S., Gabriel Peters, and João L. Tziminadis. 2021. "'Human Beings Are First and Foremost Resonant Beings'. Interview With Professor Hartmut Rosa of Universität Jena and Director of Max-Weber-Kollegs." *Civitas - Revista de Ciências Sociais* 21 (1): 120–129. 10.15448/1984-7289.2021.1.39974

Cronin, Michael and David N. Jones. 2015. "Social Work and Disasters". In *International Encyclopedia of the Social & Behavioral Sciences*. 2nd ed., edited by James D. Wright, 753–760. Elsevier.

Engen, Mie. 2022. "Solidary Authority – Conceptualising Relations of Care in Statutory Social Work With Vulnerable Children and Families." *European Journal of Social Work*. Published ahead of print, 20 June, 2022. 10.1080/13691457.2022.2094344

Engen, Mie, Stina K. Petersen, Line S. Bjerre, and Maria A. Nissen. 2019. "Does Social Work Care? Practising Care in Social Work With Vulnerable Children and Their Families." *European Journal of Social Work* 24 (1): 34–46. 10.1080/13691457.2019.1615869

Fallov, Mia A. and Cory Blad, eds. 2018. *Social Welfare Responses in a Neoliberal Era: Policies, Practices and Social Problems*. Leiden: Brill.

Fallov, Mia A. and Maria A. Nissen. 2018. "Social Work in and Around the Home: Using Home as a Site to Promote Inclusion." In *Social Welfare Responses in a Neoliberal Era*, edited by Mia A. Fallov and Cory Blad, 160–181. Leiden: Brill.

Ferguson, Harry. 2018. "Making Home Visits: Creativity and the Embodied Practices of Home Visiting in Social Work and Child Protection." *Qualitative Social Work* 17 (1): 65–80. 10.1177/1473325016656751

Ferguson, Harry, Lisa Warwick, Tarsem S. Cooner, Jadwiga Leigh, Liz Beddoe, Tom Disney, and Gillian Plumridge. 2020. "The Nature and Culture of Social Work With Children and Families in Long-Term Casework: Findings From a Qualitative Longitudinal Study." *Child & Family Social Work* 25 (3): 694–703. 10.1111/cfs.12746

Jørgensen, Andreas M. 2022. "Time for and Timing in Social Work With Vulnerable Families: Responding to Needs in Neoliberal Times." *European Journal of Social Work*. Published ahead of print, February 17, 2022. 10.1080/13691457.2022.2040435

Local Government Denmark. 2015. *De udsatte børn – Fremtiden er deres*. https://www.kl.dk/media/15890/udspil-_de_udsatte_b-rn_-_fremtiden_er_deres_-2015.pdf. Copenhagen: KL

Lorenz, Walter. 2006. *Perspectives on European Social Work: From the Birth of the Nation to the Impact of Globalization*. Opladen: Barbara Budrich Publishers.

Ministry of Employment. 2020. *Jobcentre lukker ned: Går ikke ud over udbetalingen af ydelser*. Press Release, 12 March, 2020. Accessed 30 September, 2021. https://bm.dk/nyheder-presse/pressemeddelelser/2020/03/jobcentre-lukker-ned-gaar-ikke-ud-over-udbetalingen-af-ydelser/

Ministry of Social and Internal Affairs. 2012. *Milliarder at spare med bedre indsats for udsatte børn og unge*. News letter, 15 March 2012.

Ministry of Social and Internal Affairs. 2020. *Udsatte børn og unge skal fortsat have den nødvendige hjælp og det gælder også nødpasning*. Press release, 20 March 2020. Accessed 30 September, 2021. https://sim.dk/nyheder/nyhedsarkiv/2020/mar/udsatte-boern-og-unge-skal-fortsat-have-den-noedvendige-hjaelp-og-det-gaelder-ogsaa-noedpasning/

Mørk, Mette. 2020. "Det er svært at snakke håb og drømme over telefonen." *Socialrådgiveren*, no. 6, 28 May 2020. https://socialraadgiverne.dk/faglig-artikel/mette-bechsgaard-hoegh-det-er-svaert-at-snakke-haab-og-droemme-over-telefonen/

Nissen, Maria A. 2021. "Time Matters: Changes in the Time Horizon in Social Services for Vulnerable Children and Their Families in Denmark in an Era of Productivity and Competition." *European Journal of Social Work* 24 (3): 430–441. 10.1080/13691457. 2019.1651253

Nissen, Maria A. Forthcoming. "Emotional Practices and Ideas About Professional Care in Social Work With Children and Families in Denmark: Responses to Expectations of Cost-Effectiveness?"

Nissen, Maria A. and Mie Engen. 2021. "Power and Care in Statutory Social Work With Vulnerable Families." *Ethics and Social Welfare* 15 (3): 279–293. 10.1080/17496535. 2021.1924814

Nissen, Maria A., Mia A. Fallov, and Pia Ringø, eds. 2018. *Menneskesyn i Socialt Aarbejde: Om Udviklingen af det Produktive Menneske.* Copenhagen: Akademisk Forlag.

Parton, Nigel and Stuart Kirk. 2009. "The Nature and Purposes of Social Work." In *The SAGE Handbook of Social Work Research*, edited by Ian Shaw, Katherine Briar-Lawson, Joan Orme, and Roy Ruckdeschel, 23–36. London: Sage Publications.

Paulsen, Susan. 2020. "REFLEKSION:' Jeg kan arbejde på en måde, som vi ofte kun drømmer om.'" *Socialrådgiveren*, no. 6, 28 May 2020. https://socialraadgiverne.dk/faglig-artikel/refleksion-jeg-kan-arbejde-paa-en-maade-som-vi-ofte-kun-droemmer-om/

Phillips, Judith. 2007. *Care.* Cambridge: Polity Press.

Robinson, Fiona. 2011. *The Ethics of Care: A Feminist Approach to Human Security.* Philadelphia: Temple University Press.

Rosa, Hartmut. 2021. "The Idea of Resonance as a Sociological Concept." *Global Dialogue*, 8 July, 2018. https://globaldialogue.isa-sociology.org/the-idea-of-resonance-as-a-sociological-concept/

Schiermer, Bjørn. 2020. "Acceleration and Resonance: An Interview With Hartmut Rosa." *Acta Sociologica—E-Special: Four Generations of Critical Theory in Acta Sociologica.* Accessed 15 August, 2022. https://journals.sagepub.com/pb-assets/cmscontent/ASJ/Acceleration_and_Resonance.pdf

Sevenhuijsen, Selma. 1998. *Citizenship and the Ethics of Care: Feminist Considerations on Justice, Morality and Politics.* London: Routledge.

The British Academy. 2021. *The COVID Decade: Understanding the Long-Term Societal Impacts of COVID-19.* London: The British Academy. 10.5871/bac19stf/9780856726583.001

Tronto, Joan C. 1993. *Moral Boundaries – A Political Argument for an Ethic of Care.* New York: Routledge.

Tronto, Joan C. 2013. *Caring Democracy: Markets, Equality, and Justice.* New York: New York University Press.

Truell, Rory. 2020. "News From Our Societies – IFSW: COVID-19: The Struggle, Success and Expansion of Social Work – Reflections on the Profession's Global Response, 5 Months on". *International Social Work* 63 (4): 545–548. 10.1177%2F0020872820936448

UNDRR (United Nations Office for Disaster Risk Reduction). 2019. *2019 Annual Report.* Geneva: United Nations. https://digitallibrary.un.org/record/3895941?ln=en

# 15 A Shift in Social Interaction in Social Work during the COVID-19 Pandemic

*Līga Rasnača, Mareks Niklass, and Endija Rezgale-Straidoma*

## Introduction

Work-related practices during the COVID-19 pandemic and the associated restrictions of direct contact forced social workers to adapt to new processes and practice. This applies to how 1) to work with service users, and 2) how to participate in social interaction with colleagues and administration. Everyday social interactions have to be re-evaluated. Social interaction is a process that involves a reciprocal stimulation or a response between two or more individuals. Persistent social interaction between specific individuals leads to the formation of social relationships (Tronick 2008). The authors are interested in social interaction in the social work environment during the COVID-19 pandemic. Communication is a mutual exchange of information implying participants' orientation to the reciprocal openness of the partner (Prokopenko and Omelyanenko 2018). Changes in social interaction mean not only a much wider use of digital technologies but also much less frequent conversations and a lack of non-verbal communication.

Changes in social interaction are related to how and what decisions are made when performing social work tasks. Heuristics is a term describing the adaptation process in contrast to rationality. It implies the simplification of decision making (Gigerenzer and Gaissmaier 2021). How did social workers make decisions in rapidly changing circumstances during the pandemic? The authors are interested in whether the decision-making process can be interpreted using the heuristic theory. In everyday interaction, conversations with colleagues and service users, non-verbal communication is used that is difficult to include in written and also virtual social interaction. The informal interaction in the social work process is a part of social workers' sense-making encouraging a more careful reflection on the work with service users. Informal and formal interaction social processes and relationships in the social work environment have changed with the digital transformation (Helm 2017). During COVID-19 pandemic, these transformations were more rapid and unprecedented. The use of digital technologies and work from home became a usual form of work even for those jobs where the form of teleworking was not used before (Bela et al. 2021; Drašler et al. 2021). When they interact, people become more aware of others and begin

DOI: 10.4324/9781003374374-19

to build relationships and mutual understanding necessary in the social work and decision-making processes.

## Research and methodology

The empirical data have been drawn from a large-scale project called 'Life with COVID-19: Evaluation of overcoming the coronavirus crisis in Latvia and recommendations for societal resilience in the future', which was carried out by a team of researchers.[1] One of the objectives of the project was to assess the effectiveness and coverage of social protections provided by state institutions and municipalities and to measure their impact on the support of various socio-demographic groups during the pandemic (Riga Stradins University 2021). This article is aimed to find out:

1) how social interactions among social workers, service users, and administration have changed;
2) whether and how communication channels have changed;
3) how decisions were made in rapidly changing circumstances during the COVID-19 pandemic.

In total, 84 semi-structured interviews with social workers and other representatives of social services organisations were carried during the fall of 2020. For this analysis presented here, 47 full interview transcripts have been used. These interviews were recorded, transcribed, and verified. The empirical data were coded and analysed using a qualitative data analysis software NVivo. In addition to the interviews from 2020, a follow-up study from November 2021 until January 2022 was carried out involving ten social workers working with different groups of service users. The acquired empirical data were analysed using the constant comparative method.

## Literature review and theoretical background

A North American social work professor and the author of 'strengths perspective' Dennis Saleebey (2002) pointed out that dialogue and collaboration are necessary for successful communication and cooperation. An individual can only develop and grow in interaction with others. Changes in social interactions are especially important at difficult times. Experience in overcoming difficulties allows individuals to solve problems in the future (Saleebey 2002).

A Web of Science search was performed to review previous research publications in the database. By entering the keywords 'social communication', 'social work', and 'COVID-19' in September 2021, 345 publications were identified. Those publications that met the purpose of the study were selected. Several publications were devoted to the development of theoretical knowledge of social work, especially in the acquisition of practice and conducting research (Azman et al. 2020; Lee and Johnstone, 2021). Some publications analyse how the COVID-19 and related restrictions influence groups and communities (for example, people with mental health problems, older adults) focusing on vulnerability (Campbell 2020; Cox 2020). A significant part of publications focused on the use of digital technologies in social work during COVID-19 (Felder 2021; Trenerry et al. 2021). The social worker-client relationships are described as essential to social work but are a broad and multi-layered concept. These relationships are strengthened and challenged by digitalisation (Mitchuk et al. 2021).

Adaptation to the environmental change can be explained by the theory of ecological rationality that emphasises environmental constraints. The notion of ecological rationality allows us to analyse the decision making in its complexity with the adaptation to the environment. Ecological rationality emphasises the interaction between the strategy of actions and the structure of the environment in producing good decisions. *Heuristics* mean that some parts of new information could and have to be ignored in the adaptation process when it is difficult to adapt to all conditions. A part of the information is ignored during the adaptation process. These are understood as *heuristic decisions*. Individuals and organisations often rely on simple heuristics in an adaptive way. It can lead to a simpler and easier decision but could prevent more accurate judgements (Barkoczi 2016; Gigerenzer and Gaissmaier 2011; Mata et al. 2012). This can be very important at a time of a significant change when social workers are forced to change their usual behaviour under the conditions of increased stress. For example, making judgements from the experience in the similar environment. This may be justified when working with specific service user groups. It can also be used to describe positive practices, such as talking to service users or explaining the epidemiological situation. It can be difficult to consider all available information. In addition, the information may not always be precisely targeted. A heuristic approach can, if successful, help to select only the information that seems useful to a particular situation or a group of customers. A heuristic is a strategy that ignores a part of the information, with the goal of making decisions more quickly, frugally, and/or accurately than more complex methods (Gigerenzer and Gaissmaier 2011, 454).

There is growing evidence that the pandemic has had a negative impact on the wellbeing of social workers and organisational arrangements in their institutions. Kate Holmes et al. (2021) surveyed 181 social workers in the United States and found out that 64 percent of the surveyed social workers reported average burnout (Holmes et al. 2021, 495). Furthermore, organisational support and opportunities for co-workers to help each other have significantly decreased during the pandemic (Holmes et al. 2021, 498–502).

José Martínez-López et al. (2021) conducted a survey of 273 social workers in Spain in September 2020 and identified high levels of emotional exhaustion and depersonalisation and a low level of personal accomplishment. Spanish scholars conclude that teleworking and poor psychological treatment have a negative effect on emotional exhaustion.

Claudia Bacter et al. (2021) surveyed 94 social workers in May 2020 in Romania. Their aim was to explore the 'vulnerabilities and challenges imposed by these rapid and unprecedented changes in daily routine activity' caused by the pandemic (Bacter et al. 2021, 8). A significant part of daily activities was held online or by phone. Procedures were introduced, which limited direct contact with partners and clients. Losing direct contact has a negative impact on their work. The pandemic also created uncertainty and stressful situations at work. Sometimes it led to increased workload and bureaucracy. (Bacter et al. 2021, 1–15)

Mareks Niklass (2021) analyses the results of an online survey of 443 social services sector employees carried out in October and November 2020 in Latvia. The study was aimed to find out how social services were delivered, whether restrictions imposed have any effect on services, as well as how employees coped with the pandemic. The pandemic limited direct contact, thus facilitating remote work and communication by ICT or phone. About one-third of the surveyed employees were exposed to a high risk of burnout (Niklass 2021, 580).

To sum up, the pandemic has a significant impact on social service organisations both at organisational and individual levels. Several studies indicate that remote work and indirect contacts by ICT or phone have become more widespread in the social work. Some scholars point out that it leads to more workload and stress, resulting in increased burnout. Organisations slowly adapt to the pandemic and try to provide the necessary support for their employees. However, it is a rather difficult task because of a loss of direct contact and fewer opportunities for face-to-face interactions between management and staff and among employees themselves.

## Results and discussion

This section discusses the results of an empirical study carried out from October 2020 to January 2022 in Latvia. Firstly, the study briefly describes the main characteristics of interviewed social workers and service providers. Secondly, it identifies the main themes discussed during interviews. Thirdly, the section elaborates how social interactions and communicational channels changed and how decisions were made during the pandemic.

To briefly describe the characteristics of the interviewees, we must note that there were 29 principals of social services organisations and 20 social workers of which 36 worked for various local municipalities, ten interviewees represented NGOs operating in the social services sector, and finally, three interviewees were from other organisations. Most of them had long tenures in their respective organisations (5–10 years). We have to emphasise that principals elaborated more than social workers and were generally more open about challenges facing their organisations. Social workers were somewhat reluctant or concise in providing information about their work and problems.

Table 15.1 provides an overview of thematic coding applied. It shows what themes were covered during the interviews. Codes are not mutually exclusive

*Table 15.1* The most used thematic codes in the interviews with stakeholders

| Thematic codes | Number of interviews | Number of references |
|---|---|---|
| Service users | 45 | 751 |
| Means of communication | 47 | 540 |
| Social workers | 46 | 510 |
| Information sources | 46 | 375 |
| Social services | 43 | 358 |
| Families of clients | 39 | 304 |
| Municipalities | 40 | 273 |
| Disinfection | 46 | 248 |
| Health concerns/problems/services | 41 | 191 |
| Consultations | 33 | 146 |
| Ministry of Welfare | 33 | 138 |
| Collaboration/cooperation | 40 | 131 |
| Food/provision of food items | 32 | 129 |

and themes can overlap. Respondents could have discussed clients and their health problems in the same passage.

Service users, their families, and their concerns were the focal points of all interviews. The pandemic caused the disruption and sometimes discontinuation of various social and health care services. Social workers had to communicate that with service users using different means of communication. In the context of severe health risks and uncertainty, everyday communication and decision making had to be adjusted accordingly. Ever more information about the pandemic as well as numerous guidelines and instructions flowed from various institutions such as municipalities and ministries. As a few interviews suggest, it did not make decision making easier.

To understand the interplay and overlap of various thematic codes more clearly, Table 15.2 presents the results of matrix coding queries where codes 'means of communication' and 'information sources' were included in a context with other thematic codes.

Various means of communication and information sources most often appeared when discussing the concerns of service users and social workers. Means of communication also appeared frequently in a context of consultations. At last, it should be noted that the Ministry of Welfare was more often cited as a source of information than the colleagues of social workers.

All face-to-face contacts with clients were cut to the minimum during the first wave of the pandemic. Most service users understood the gravity of the situation and adapted to a 'distance regime'. However, the seniors and those with mental health problems felt disorientated. Those individuals do not have necessary skills, communication devices, and Internet access to contact their social workers by phone or other means (WhatsApp, Skype, etc.). The social workers had to make

*Table 15.2* Means of communication and information sources in various contexts

| Thematic codes | Means of communication in a context with other thematic codes (number of references) | Information sources in a context with other thematic codes (number of references) |
|---|---|---|
| Means of communication | - | 70 |
| Service users | 162 | 85 |
| Social workers | 96 | 44 |
| Information sources | 70 | - |
| Consultations | 57 | 17 |
| Families of clients | 37 | 26 |
| Health concerns/problems/services | 29 | 35 |
| Municipalities | 19 | 25 |
| Social services | 18 | 24 |
| Ministry of Welfare | 17 | 55 |
| Collaboration/cooperation | 15 | 13 |
| Disinfection | 10 | 16 |
| Food/provision of food items | 8 | 17 |

decisions as soon as possible to reach the service users. It was a positive example of a heuristic decision.

Physical contacts were limited and sometimes even cut off at older people's nursing homes because the evidence from other countries showed that the spread of the COVID-19 had dire consequences for these institutions. Social workers had to negotiate with their clients and relatives and solve conflicts arising from these restrictions. Service users and relatives often did not perceive the risk of infection. Social workers were struggling to isolate one group of people from another within institutions. Buildings are largely ill suited and not built with the pandemic restrictions in mind. In other words, social workers had to change established interactions with clients and their relatives and adjust these to the circumstance of the pandemic.

Most respondents acknowledge that consultations were provided by phone during the first wave of the pandemic. Clients do not usually have smartphones with Internet access and necessary communication apps (WhatsApp, Skype, Zoom, etc.). If they had smartphones, there was no stable Internet connection or no money to pay for the service. Finally, many clients did not have necessary skills to communicate with social workers by other means. As a result, most respondents regarded a phone as the most reliable means of communication:

We used a different option like communicating by phone (A representative of an NGO in a small town).

[...] we had already mastered Zoom technology but there were clients who couldn't use it or they didn't have technical devices (A representative from an NGO in the capital city).

Internet coverage is very weak in the countryside (A social worker from a rural municipality).

Other means of communication were used less frequently. As the excerpts below show, these communication channels were less trusted and required necessary devices and certain user skills. WhatsApp was sometimes mentioned among tools used by social workers to contact their clients:

A WhatsApp group was also created for clients, but it was not so successful with this target group. They're pretty suspicious. If some use but the others do not, then it's not as operational and successful. In my opinion, the group did not live up to our expectations (A representative from an NGO).

I know that many social workers working with families used WhatsApp, with younger clients. WhatsApp messages were sent, photographed and, of course, all Zoom calls (A social worker from a small town).

Except telephones, other communication channels are less frequently used and considered as an alternative option for communication. Older adult clients are less likely to trust and use them in everyday life. They do not have necessary devices and skills. Social workers are aware of that and adapted to the situation accordingly:

The social service provider advised to provide the service to this target group on the Zoom platform but none of the clients had learned the program (A social worker from a city).

Digital applications, such as Zoom or Skype, were seldom mentioned in the interviews of social workers. It is safe to argue that the uptake of ICT technologies is slow among service users despite a widespread use of smartphones and increased Internet access in general public. For example, a survey carried out by the Latvian Central Statistical Bureau indicates that the share of households with Internet access in 2020 has reached 90 percent in comparison with 60 percent in 2010 (Central Statistical Bureau 2020).

Among social workers, ICT was used more widely and frequently. Social service organisations have more resources to support their staff in various ways (providing devices, IT support, etc.). Social workers are also more aware of a need to learn new skills. At last, organisations needed to adapt to a 'distance work regime' to stop the spread of the virus among their staff members. Here are some examples from interviews to support the argument:

[…] we learned to use electronic means, too, to send documents to WhatsApp, print them out of WhatsApp, a lot of things we have not used until then. Meetings, workshops […] let us say this happened electronically on the Zoom platform (The head of municipal social service organisation in a small town in Latvia).

Yes, we felt that computer skills needed to be increased for those employees. Now those skills with Zoom and all of them. Well, we felt it (The head of municipal social service organisation in a rural municipality in Latvia).

Some interviewees learned to use these tools quite efficiently. For example, they found out that remote supervisions can be more productive than those in physical presence.

Supervisions took place once a month before the pandemic. We introduced a weekly supervision but a remote one using the Zoom platform. Then, when the first wave ended, we found out that these remote supervisions were more productive than physical meetings once a month. At the moment, we are continuing with our remote supervisions (A social worker, NGO).

However, it is too early to suggest there is a radical shift in social interaction patterns. Such examples are rare. Most respondents viewed these changes as a response to the pandemic. ICT only substitutes physical contacts for a while. Here is another example of how some workers viewed the change:

Well, we will see how this epidemiological situation will develop if we have to move to a service where physical presence will be restricted, then we will act in the same way as we did in this time of the pandemic (Head of social services centre in a small town).

Many interviewed social workers believed that the introduction of ICT and different communication channels was needed to cope with the pandemic. These alternatives are no substitute for real-life contacts with clients and colleagues. The measures introduced to curb the spread of the virus were often seen as temporary. Social workers suggested, however, that the pandemic will have positive effects on the social work in the future. More and more clients will learn how to use WhatsApp or Zoom. It will enable them to contact people outside their immediate surroundings and solve their problems. Moreover, the pandemic forced social service organisations to invest more in physical and human capital. They obtained necessary devices for remote communication, taught their staff how to use new apps, and found out how these devices and apps could be used more productively. At the same time, some vulnerable groups (especially, the seniors and persons with mental health problems) will remain at a risk of isolation and neglect because new ICT and communication channels will be beyond their reach. Delivering devices to them and teaching them necessary IT skills would not be any viable options either.

From November 2020 to January 2021, we conducted a follow-up study involving ten social workers working with families, those with substance abuse issues, young people, and older adults, both at municipal and non-governmental organisations. Empirical data gathered from semi-structured interviews were analysed by using the constant comparative method. In the follow-up study, social workers in the mentioned fields described how their relationship with clients had become superficial:

> Some clients tend to be very manipulative, aggressive, they affect other clients at the same time. When working with clients who do not understand the information provided, there may be a feeling that all the work is useless (A social worker working with young people with disabilities).

Difficulties in relationships with service users affected social workers' psychological mood and their relations with co-workers. The good teamwork skills benefited social work during COVID-19.

Social workers were aware of their professional duty and the necessity to adapt to the new situation:

> Our task as social work specialists is to adapt to the current situation, whatever it may be, and to find effective solutions and support for clients (A social worker working with seniors in long-term care institution).

Moreover, the adaptation to new conditions (social distance, remote work, use of technologies) impacts the psychological mood of social workers and relationships with different service users. Overall, interviewed social workers felt tired and were dissatisfied with their work during the pandemic. Some responses indicated hopelessness, especially for social workers working in remote areas with fewer resources.

> A remote work in social work is not a work. You must see a human, to talk to him or her. To assess the need for a particular service, one must assess a human (A social worker in a rural municipality).

The heuristic decision-making process has been most apparently exemplified in instances when social workers receive instructions and recommendations from various ministries, state organisations, and municipalities. Social workers pointed out that the management of their respective organisations sorted out and selected information passed to social workers because of the enormous and ever-changing information flow from the institutions 'above'. In some instances, social workers did not receive original instructions and recommendations. The information was disseminated in online meetings, emails, or in-person encounters.

> Of course, the heads of departments first read all the information. Then they assessed, which information to be passed to social workers (A social worker with families with children in a municipal social service).

In the first wave of the COVID-19 pandemic in 2020, securing disinfectants and protective gear and the closure of organisation for in-person contacts were the main concerns for many social workers. Regarding the later waves, social workers pointed out a frequent change of preventive measures and the feasibility of social work, including the need for face-to-face interactions.

Heuristic decisions were made considering the kind of service and the needs of target groups. Although the government introduced a stricter lockdown in October and November 2021, social workers working with adolescents with behavioural challenges and young people with intellectual disabilities still provided services outside institutions. Social workers admitted that they faced a dilemma whether follow the law or provide the necessary support to the target groups. Documents providing guidelines during the pandemic are often formulated in general terms, ignoring the specificity of a service or the needs of certain target groups.

> A lot of information was also annoying. Sometimes it was difficult to identify what exactly referred to our institution because our target group was not often addressed (A social worker working in day care centre for disabled persons).

Social workers took their own decision in such circumstances according to their own understanding of what restrictions are to be followed or not be followed. Heuristic decision making first refers to the social work management, which decides what information is relevant in their field. Secondly, social workers themselves took decisions which of the preventive measures are to be considered in the context of the needs of a particular target group. Thirdly, the style of instructions, guidelines, and recommendations were not user friendly:

> The language of instructions is long and extensive [...] There are many questions that remained unanswered (A social worker in a long-term care institution for seniors).

Social workers did not have time to find relevant information, therefore, they often took decisions based on social work values. Fourth, a mobile phone was very frequently chosen as a more accessible means of communication among others.

In the follow-up study, social workers revealed those kinds of interactions that became commonplace as a result of the pandemic during the second half of 2021. Face-to-face contacts became increasingly rare and more restricted. The use of mobile phones was mentioned in all interviews. Social workers operated in a hybrid mode to adapt to the current epidemiological situation:

> A lot of work with clients, lots of phone calls, I am not able to answer all the phone calls. We are currently working in a quasi-remote, a quasi-in-person mode (A social worker with families with children in a municipal social service).

When operating in a remote mode, a few problems arise concerning the recipients of social services and a number of target groups. The lack of physical contacts is one of them. Some groups, such as families with children, young people, and persons with mental disorders, are hard to reach and work with if physical contacts are restricted:

> Clients disappear, they don't come to consultations, are hard or impossible to reach by phone (A social worker with families with children in a municipal social service).

To sum up the results of the follow-up study, it should be emphasised that the COVID-19 pandemic had a negative effect on social work, that is, it reduced the number of face-to-face interactions and visits by clients. Social workers knew less about clients, their circumstances, and problems. Some groups, such as young people with behavioural problems and persons with mental disabilities, become ever harder to reach and to put social work into practice with them. The use of ICTs may alleviate the problem only to a degree. Only those with necessary skills, devices, and internet access were able to contact social workers. Finally, social workers were overwhelmed by the flow of information (instructions, guidelines) from various institutions. The instructions and guidelines were often very long, and in general, rarely addressing the concerns of social workers. Consequently, they interpreted various measures according to their circumstances and applied heuristics in their decision making when there are no clear rules to follow.

## Discussion

The COVID-19 pandemic changes the conditions of environment where social work takes place. In 2020, the main attention was paid to the new precautionary measures how to limit the spread of the disease, how to fulfil all regulations, and how to obtain and pass on information. The most severe concerns were for the provision of a secure environment for social workers and service users. The frequency of code use identifies the main actors and social interactions among them during the COVID-19 pandemic. The heuristic features of the communication process are characterised by a hierarchical approach to the transfer of information, management, and administration decisions about the information to be transferred. Dramatic changes took place as well in the relationship between social worker and service users, social workers, and their co-workers and between social workers and the representatives of the administration and policy makers. Frequent changes in decisions at the political and administrative levels encouraged social workers to make heuristic decisions. Policy makers and administrators did not always pay attention to the diversity and specific needs of social work target groups. To compensate this, social workers had to simplify their own decision making, making it understandable to recipients and their relatives.

The results of the empirical study presented here support the conclusions of other studies measuring the psychological wellbeing of social workers during the pandemic. Social workers feel more stressful and constrained by various preventive measures. It is exacerbated by the lack of face-to-face interactions between social workers and service users as well as among social workers themselves. Many problems can be more easily solved, and information can be more quickly exchanged and explained through contacts in person. Long instructions and guidelines were very detailed. However, they are often too general and hardly address the immediate concerns of social workers. Overwhelmed by these constraints, some social workers may have felt depressed and exhausted.

## Conclusions

Finally, we would like to present some main conclusions based on our analyses. First of all, during the COVID-19 pandemic, the social interaction patterns changed among social workers, services users, and administration. Direct face-to-face contacts were limited or sometimes cut off. The exchange of information and the provision of services were difficult, especially for some groups such as seniors and those with mental disabilities. Regarding communication channels, the mobile phone was the most frequently used communication channel. Zoom and WhatsApp were other digital communication channels often mentioned in interviews. Many service users though did not have necessary skills, devices, and internet access to use the digital communication channels. In this regard, social workers were more equipped and skilful.

During the pandemic, various institutions have produced dozens of instructions and guidelines on how to cope with the pandemic and how to implement preventive measures. Social workers have been overwhelmed by the flow of those documents, which are often formulated in general terms and do not address the concerns of social workers working with specific groups such as persons with mental health problems. In the absence of clear guidelines and relevant information, social workers use heuristics in their decision making. Heuristic decision making was also manifested in the choice of communication channels. Some specific groups, such as the older adults and persons with mental disabilities, were easier to reach by phone or in person. Sometimes social workers were meeting service users outdoors.

To conclude, during the pandemic, social workers had to change their usual way of interacting with service users and in some cases take on the role of health care workers. However, the introduction of ICTs for interactions with clients and colleagues was often regarded as a temporary measure. Social workers did not see it as a viable option that may substitute face-to-face interactions with clients. However, some interviewed social workers acknowledge that online supervision and meetings among colleagues can be effective and reduce the time necessary for such activities.

## Note

1 Researchers from the University of Latvia, Riga Stradins University, Rezekne Academy of Technologies, Vidzeme University of Applied Sciences, as well as the Institute of Electronics and Computer Science.

## References

Azman, Azlinda, Paramjit S.J. Singh, Jonathan Parker, and Sara Ashencaen Crabtree. 2020. "Addressing Competency Requirements of Social Work Students During the COVID-19 Pandemic in Malaysia." *Social Work Education* 39 (8): 1058–1065. 10.1080/02615479.2020.1815692

Bacter, Claudia, Sorana Săveanu, and Cristiana Marc. 2021. "Social Work During the COVID-19 Pandemic. Administrative and Personal Response to New Challenges." *Social Change Review*. Published ahead of print, 11 October, 2021. 10.2478/scr-2021-0004

Barkoczi, Daniel. 2016. "Ecological Rationality of Social Learning." Dr. rer. nat. dissertation, Humboldt University of Berlin. https://edoc.hu-berlin.de/bitstream/handle/18452/18120/barkoczi.pdf?sequence=1.

Bela, Baiba, Anna Broka, Feliciana Rajevska, and Liga Rasnača. 2021. "Transformative Change in Social Service Delivery and Social Work Practice in Latvia During the COVID-19 Pandemic" *European Journal of Social Work*. Published ahead of print, 17 September, 2021. 10.1080/13691457.2021.1977255

Campbell, Anthony D. 2020. "Practical Implications of Physical Distancing, Social Isolation, and Reduced Physicality for Older Adults in Response to COVID-19." *Journal of Gerontological Social Work* 63 (6–7): 668–670. 10.1080/01634372.2020.1772933

Central Statistical Bureau. 2020. Over the Ten Years Availability of Internet at Households Has Risen by 30 %. *Official Statistics Portal – Official Statistics of Latvia – Press Release*. Published 2 November, 2020. https://stat.gov.lv/en/statistics-themes/information-technologies/computers-and-internet/press-releases/2182-internet.

Cox, Carole. 2020. "Older Adults and Covid 19: Social Justice, Disparities, and Social Work Practice." *Journal of Gerontological Social Work* 63 (6–7): 611–624. 10.1080/01634372.2020.1808141

Drašler, Varineja, Jasna Bertoncelj, Mojca Korošec, Tanja Pajk Žontar, Nataša Poklar Ulrih, and Blaž Cigić. 2021. "Difference in the Attitude of Students and Employees of the University of Ljubljana Towards Work From Home and Online Education: Lessons From COVID-19 Pandemic." *Sustainability* 13 (9): 5118. 10.3390/su13095118

Felder, Stephanie S. 2021. "Reflections on a Pandemic: Disruptions, Distractions, and Challenges of a Clinical Social Worker on the Frontline in New York City." *Qualitative Social Work* 20 (1–2): 404–409. 10.1177/1473325020981076

Gigerenzer, Gerd and Wolfgang Gaissmaier. 2011. "Heuristic Decision Making." *Annual Review of Psychology* 62 (1): 451–482. 10.1146/annurev-psych-120709-145346

Helm, Duncan. 2017. "Can I Have a Word? Social Worker Interaction and Sense-Making." *Child Abuse Review* 26 (5): 388–398. 10.1002/car.2463

Holmes, Megan R., C. Robin Rentrope, Amy Korsch-Williams, and Jennifer A. King. 2021. "Impact of COVID-19 Pandemic on Posttraumatic Stress, Grief, Burnout, and Secondary Trauma of Social Workers in the United States." *Clinical Social Work Journal* 49 (4): 495–504. 10.1007/s10615-021-00795-y

Lee, Eunjung and Marjorie Johnstone. 2021. "Resisting Politics of Authoritarian Populism During COVID-19, Reclaiming Democracy and Narrative Justice: Centering Critical Thinking in Social Work." *International Social Work* 64 (5): 716–730. 10.1177/00208728211011627

Martínez-López, José A., Cristina Lázaro-Pérez, and José Gómez-Galán. 2021. "Predictors of Burnout in Social Workers: The COVID-19 Pandemic as a Scenario for Analysis." *International Journal of Environmental Research and Public Health* 18 (10): 5416. 10.3390/ijerph18105416

Mata, Rui, Thorsten Pachur, Bettina von Helversen, Ralph Hertwig, Jörg Rieskamp, and Lael Schooler. 2012. "Ecological Rationality: A Framework for Understanding and Aiding the Aging Decision Maker." *Frontiers in Neuroscience* 6: 19. 10.3389/fnins.2012.00019

Mitchuk, Olha, Inna Penchuk, Nataliia Podluzhna, Olena Malovichenko, Olga Shirokobokova, and Angelina Tregub. 2021. "Changes in Social Communication as a Tool of Social Work Under the Influence of Digitalization." *Studies of Applied Economics (Estudios de Economía Aplicada)* 39 (3). 10.25115/eea.v39i3.4717

Niklass, Mareks. 2021. "Burnout During the COVID Pandemic: A Case of the Social Services Sector in Latvia." In *Nr. 55 Economic Science for Rural Development: Proceedings of the International Scientific Conference*, edited by Anita Auzina, 576–589. Jelgava: Faculty of Economics and Social Development, Latvia University of Life Sciences and Technologies. 10.22616/ESRD.2021.55.059

Prokopenko, Olha and Vitaliy Omelyanenko. 2018. "Marketing Aspect of the Innovation Communications Development." *Innovative Marketing* 14 (2): 41–49. 10.21511/im.14(2).2018.05

Riga Stradins University. 2021. "Life With COVID-19: Evaluation of Overcoming the Coronavirus Crisis in Latvia and Recommendations for Societal Resilience in the Future." Accessed 16 August, 2022. https://www.rsu.lv/en/project/life-with-covid-19.

Saleebey, Dennis. 2002. *The Strengths Perspective in Social Work Practice*. 3rd ed. Boston: Allyn and Bacon.

Trenerry, Brigid, Samuel Chng, Yang Wang, Zainal S. Suhaila, Sun S. Lim, Han Y. Lu, and Peng H. Oh. 2021. "Preparing Workplaces for Digital Transformation: An Integrative Review and Framework of Multi-Level Factors." *Frontiers in Psychology* 12. 10.3389/fpsyg.2021.620766

Tronick, ed. 2008. "Social Interaction." In *Encyclopedia of Infant and Early Childhood Development*, edited by Marshall M. Haith and Janette B.B. Benson, 207–215. Amsterdam: Elsevier. 10.1016/B978-012370877-9.00150-X

# 16 COVID-19 as a Game Changer for the Digitalisation of Social Work

*Anna-Karin Bergman, Lupita Svensson, and Sanna Melling*

Digitalisation as a system for societal change has in recent years permeated deeper and more areas of society, not least due to cost-saving effects, but also due to it being an important tool for increased democratisation and accessibility in society. Since May 2017, Sweden has had a national digitalisation strategy that sets out the direction for Swedish politics. The overall goal is for 'Sweden to become the best in the world in utilising the opportunities of digitalisation' (Regeringskansliet 2017, 10). In practice, however, the digital transition occurs at different rates of speed and meets different levels of resistance. Social work in the social service, which in Sweden is mainly carried out in the public sector, is a field that has been slow in its digital transition. Previous research has defined the social services as a 'digitally insecure organisation', and as a consequence, they lag behind in the digital transition in comparison with other public service areas such as services in Library and Educational settings (Svensson and Larsson 2017; 2018).

According to Lupita Svensson and Stefan Larsson (2017), the development of digitalisation in public services can be seen in three waves. The first wave of digitalisation occurred during the 1980s and 1990s with the introduction of digital technology and digital services in the workplace. During this wave, the technology was primarily used as a way for the management to steer and control the work, and the consequences for the practice were an increased number of reporting duties and more, often experienced as complicated processes on top of existing ones (Svensson and Larsson 2017). The first wave of digitalisation further shows that the use of digital tools was defined by the needs set out by management, which matched poorly with those of the end users (Bowker et al. 1997; Ehn 1988; Greenbaum and Kyng 1991; Kensing 2003; Svensson and Larsson 2017). The second wave of digitalisation is characterised by a bottom-up use of digital channels and tools and therefore includes a form of democratisation and end-user perspective, a lot owing to social media and smartphones (Derks et al. 2015). Placing end users at the centre might also mean that power is shifted from management regulations towards a more user-generated content and perspective as well as towards users' norms, which changes the prerequisites for how an organisation can be governed and is governed (Svensson and Larsson 2017). The third wave of digitalisation is largely about digitised automation and the self-learning aspects of technology, including in the form of artificial

DOI: 10.4324/9781003374374-20

intelligence (AI) and machine learning. A development that has meant that technologies have both been democratised in their use and have become more widespread.

In 2017/2018, when we began our general study on digitalisation and social work, we were able to ascertain that to large extent social work within the public sector social services was in the first wave of digitalisation. However, at this time, many Swedish municipalities had begun to work on transferring social work into the second wave of digitalisation. Our study municipality—a medium-sized municipality in Sweden (approximately 170.000 inhabitants)—was no exception. Our study organisation—a social service organisation—had the previous year committed to the goal that by 2022 they would be able to offer everyone who needs social service support, support when they want it, and how they want it, thereby clearly indicating an expectation of social work entering the second wave of digitalisation. However, the social work practice had a long journey ahead to reach that goal. Hence, at the time of the COVID-19 pandemic, the social services in our municipality had begun the journey towards the second wave of digitalisation—at least from a top-down perspective—but had yet to implement it at a greater scale in practice.

On 11 March, 2020, COVID-19 was categorised as a pandemic (Adhanom Ghebreyesus 2020). Sweden responded with a number of restrictions, such as social (physical) distancing and a ban on meeting in larger groups (Act 2020:114, 1§). Early on, our municipal social service reached out to their employees with the information that as far as possible the organisation should follow the advice of the Public Health authorities whilst the teams should continue to deliver services in line with their core assignments. In order to continue to provide services, both professionals and service users had to act in a crisis mode and were consequently 'pushed' towards the digital transformation from a bottom-up perspective.

In this article, we examine how we can understand this shift from the first wave of digitalisation to the second wave of digitalisation and how COVID-19—as a global crisis with local consequences—has contributed to this 'push', subsequently changing the game of digitalisation of social work. In this article, we use a narrative approach to describe the results in order to highlight the process.

## Theoretical framework

We base our understanding on the framework of the *theory of reciprocal change management* and *the three perspectives on work* (Loid and Malmström 2020)[1] in combination with an analysis from a systems approach, referring to the systems theorists, such as Jürgen Habermas (1979; 1995) and Niklas Luhmann (1986; 2003). The theory of *reciprocal change management* and *the three perspectives on work* in combination with a systems approach contribute specifically to understanding how social services have been organised during the first wave of digitalisation, and why it has been challenging from the beginning to bring about a change as well as a transformation towards the second wave of digitalisation.

Even though these digitalisation efforts in both waves of digitalisation are from a top-down approach, there has been a swift transformation towards the second wave of digitalisation that needs to be understood.

### Reciprocal change management and the three perspectives on work

The theory of *reciprocal change management* (Loid and Malmström 2020) is based on a new approach in management research aiming to understand how management and employees can work with so-called *reciprocal change management*. The theory relates to a Scandinavian view of leadership and work culture and therefore differs from many other management theories that are mainly based on the Anglo-Saxon approach. In Scandinavia, we have a so-called collectivist and decentralised view of responsibility. Further, in a Scandinavian work culture— generally speaking—employees expect to have a great deal of influence over what happens in their workplace. They are expected to take responsibility for their teams functioning well and also expect from themselves to be in a position to make decisions that are beneficial for the organisation as a whole. On an operational level, they are expected to be able to spontaneously coordinate and self-organise groups on the same hierarchical level as themselves and at the same time they are expected to 'lead upwards', i.e., make higher levels in the hierarchy aware of any problems at the operational level. David Loid and Clas Malmström (2020) translate this into categories that correspond to *three perspectives on work*: Machine perspective, Contract perspective, and Community of Practice perspective. These perspectives represent different generic views on organisation, leadership, and development. It is worth mentioning that these three perspectives are found both within the Anglo-Saxon and the Scandinavian work culture. However, with regard to the Scandinavian work culture (collectivist and decentralised), a further strengthening of the Community of Practice perspective occurs which makes it a more problematic work culture to steer with a 'top-down' management approach. In this study, we will mainly focus on the Machine and the Community of Practice perspectives. Because on the one hand, they can be translated into larger management systems that are important for the readiness for change, and on the other hand, they are the perspectives that are most clearly seen in our social service organisation's pursuit of transformation into the second wave of digitalisation.

### The Machine perspective

A person with a Machine perspective views the organisation as a factory where input and output need to happen as efficiently as possible. From a management system and in our context, social services in the public sector, this can be translated into New Public Management (standardisation, synergies, measurability, etc.) where evaluation takes place based on sustained quantitative measurement in the long term. For a 'machine', the organisation as a whole is translated into numbers and the driving force is 'how can we do this more efficiently?'. The goal of the pure 'machinist' is to rationalise and do away with anything unnecessary—and goes as far as to include oneself. The 'machinist' view themselves as an advocate for good control, quality assurance, progress, and efficiency, and therefore the Machine perspective is most often found distinctly in functions such as controllers, economists, logistics, strategists, and 'change leaders' (Loid and Malmström 2020). In our study, the representation of this perspective is clearly seen in our organisation's management positions, i.e., those who advocate and drive the transformation towards the second wave of digitalisation, by producing clear (from 'the Machinist's' perspective) goals for this transformation.

## Community of Practice perspective

A person with this perspective strives to become an accepted member of a *work community* and is driven by good relationships with colleagues and identification with the profession. The stronger the person's community perspective, the more the person identifies with one's choice of profession. This can be seen in professions such as doctors, lawyers, researchers, teachers, and social workers. From a Community of Practice perspective, the work is evaluated mainly on the basis of *qualitative aspects*[2] and the work itself is designed according to a 'community standard; a design, which is based on the motto 'this is how we perform our work in this workplace' (Loid and Malmström 2020, 48). The more complex the activity, the more important it is for the community to agree on an appropriate formatting for their work (Loid and Malmström 2020, 48). The formatting is also what drives a team of Community of Practice forward and makes the work efficient—everyone knows (largely) what is expected of them and how to conduct the work in order for the operation to run smoothly. Where there is a clear Community of Practice perspective, informal leaders steer the operation as well as the development. These informal leaders can get to supervise junior colleagues because of their skills. In this way, 'community work' becomes a self-reinforcing process where the leading figures of the organisation directly influence the formatting of the work. The disadvantage of these communities is that they can become too introverted and rigid in their formatting, and hence, they need help in balancing more strategic or economic realities, something that 'the Machinists' are very good at. (Loid and Malmström 2020). Changes in the formatting of the work must be done in a way that 'fits in well' and is understood by the Community of Practice perspective, because a person or phenomenon that is considered to 'threaten' the logic of the community perspective can initiate strong reactions expressed as an internal loyalty and strong cohesion comparable to a 'we against them' attitude. In our study, a clear representation of this perspective is seen in the operational work, i.e., within the group of frontline social workers that interact with clients daily and work hands-on with the practice. This is verified by Loid and Malmström's (2020) definition in which the social work profession qualifies as a group with a strong Community of Practice perspective (David Loid, personal communication, Teams conversation with authors, 6 June, 2021).

## A systems approach

Although the theory of *the three perspectives on work* takes us quite far in our understanding in regard to the organisational transformation and the aims in terms of digitalisation and social work, COVID-19 (as a global crisis with local consequences) pushes us a bit further in realising that we need to broaden our horizon. We have chosen to do so by complementing our research with a system approach analysis. We see the connection between the Community of Practice and the systems approach from two perspectives:

1) as a way of understanding an individual's overall logic of work from a systems perspective;
2) that the perspectives' logic is driven by as well as drive their own system (depending on which community we deal with) and where the premiss/ survival of the system is in fact the basis of the establishment of and maintenance of the community.

In other words, the community will always work on the basis that the system is maintained and from that, the community decides what the *good* work entails. Our systems approach is inspired by Jürgen Habermas and Niklas Luhmann (see Habermas 1979, 1995; Jönhill 1995, 1997; Luhmann 1986, 2003) and their theories on systems communication and 'system survival' as the ability of systems to change oneself in order to strengthen one's ability to survive (self-referential systems and Luhmann's *Autopoiesis*; Luhmann 1986, 2003). In order for systems to be transformed, they must do so in order to survive. In our case, we can view *social work* as a system that is governed by its own logic upheld by its community and its practice.[3] At an operational level, our systems consist of people that maintain the logic of the system. By combining a systems approach with the *three perspectives on work* theory, we are partly able to draw the analysis to an empirical level represented by social workers and management and partly able to make the connection between 'the system' and the 'perspectives of work' (Community of Practice perspective and the Machine perspective), which are maintained by our empirical functions.

## Method

The principal methodology of the study is a repeat survey with closed- and open-ended questions. The Survey was distributed twice, once in May 2020 and then again in March 2021, to professionals working within social services.[4] Each time the survey was distributed to 724 persons, the total number of personnel in the studied organisation. The Survey was distributed by a digital link to the survey-software SUnet Survey encompassing a filter that ensures anonymity for the respondents. The Survey was designed with a focus on closed-ended questions relating to the usage of digital tools in a number of settings (internal and external collaboration) and in relation to different target groups (colleagues, external partners, and clients) before and during the pandemic (i.e., during ongoing societal restrictions). The Survey also included open-ended questions focusing on in what way the eventual usage had been implemented. The data generated from the closed-ended questions was subsequently analysed by frequencies and cross-tabulation in the statistical tool SPSS. The data from the open-ended questions was analysed in relation to the question posed, hence providing qualitative data on the *how*. The aim of Survey 1 was to produce a baseline, while the aim of Survey 2 was to capture any change in the usage of digital tools that had occurred during the months when work was carried out in accordance with the restrictions. Survey 2, therefore, included a number of questions about perceived shift in the areas of concern since the respondents last answered the survey. Survey 1 was answered by 137 people and Survey 2 by 198 people. Of these 198 people, 90 people answered Survey 1. The respondent population is small and strategically selected. Hence, the results cannot claim generalisability but, on the other hand, they can make a valuable contribution for further studies.

## Results and analysis

In the first survey in May 2020, only 15 percent of the respondents state that the COVID-19 situation with imposed restrictions has not affected their use of digital tools at all, which means that 85 percent of the respondents have changed their digital use in some way or the other. The largest change was found in how digital tools are used in internal collaboration and 73 percent indicate the adoption of new digital tools. 60 percent indicate a change in relation to collaboration *outside* its own operations. However, only 37 percent state that the use of digital tools has changed in relation to client or service user. Survey 1 indicated that the professionals' use of digital tools had shifted a bit during the two months that had elapsed between when societal restrictions were imposed and the time of Survey 1. However, the fact that 85 percent of the respondents state that they have changed their digital use in some way or the other does not necessarily entail a major change in relation to the practice given the status of digital usage before COVID-19.

Survey 1 indicates a divided and insecure organisation where previous experiences of using digital tools vary greatly between different respondents, from those who have never used digital tools (more than telephone and computer) to those who have a little experience and to those who have a lot of experience. In addition to a variation in the individuals' digital maturity and competence, several respondents also experienced that the support and prerequisites for being able to use digital tools vary within the organisation. In relation to client work, most of the respondents had at the time of Survey 1 not changed their use of digital tools, although some had tried in ways of, e.g., digital documentation:

> [We] let service users access part of the documentation digitally, in the form of e-services. [...]. We use digital channels to transfer when it is possible (Respondent F 14).

Benefit applications, from new clients, are partly accepted via digital tools (Respondent F 24).

Some respondents expressed that they did not have the option to use digital tools with their clients because some clients were digitally excluded—making them a vulnerable group in the strive towards the digital transformation of social work. As noted, there was a common and general concern from the respondents in Survey 1 that they could not meet their clients' needs. It ranged from not being able to make good pre-assessments, not being able to meet clients who have a relapse, or that they were not able to achieve continuity in the treatment work, especially if the clients were new (Respondent ÅK 5). Some respondents expressed that it was not as easy to interpret body language via digital channels, a method that is considered to be central to social work (Respondent F 179). Overall, there was a general experience in Survey 1 that the quality of service had decreased and that the clients, therefore, stay in the system longer than necessary:

> I am not able to deliver quality interventions due to the decrease in physical meetings. In many cases it is a matter of just keeping up a certain level in order for it not to be chaotic for the client. This will mean that the clients are registered with social services much longer than necessary (Respondent F, 72).

The image of a divided and insecure organisation, emerging from Survey 1, was altered somewhat by Survey 2. In Survey 2, the majority of the respondents— regardless of whether they were accustomed to or unaccustomed to digital tools at the time of Survey 1—had made a move forward in all areas, in other words, internal and external collaboration and client work. A total of 83 percent responded that their digital usage in relation to *internal collaboration* had changed since they responded Survey 1 and 69 percent responded that their digital usage in relation to *external collaborations* had changed since they responded Survey 1. Some respondents also point out that the external collaborating partners also have become better and more comfortable with digital meetings:

> [...] the different collaboration partners are different in terms of how good they are and willing they are in using technology. For example, school has been very good to have on board as a partner in video calls, whilst the health service is significantly less so which makes it harder when you can join the client in their meetings with the health service (Respondent ÅK, 21).

When it came to the use of digital tools in case work, there was also a slight shift from Survey 1 to Survey 2. A total of 56 percent of the respondents had made a move forward in regard to using digital tools in their case work since Survey 1.

During the time elapsed between Surveys 1 and 2, a part of the organisation seems to have had time to assimilate to the digital transformation by trying more and various digital tools in their work (Respondents ÅK 15; ÅK 21; ÅK 49).

Therefore, it also to a certain degree reached a level of competency in assessing which meetings ought to be face-to-face and which can be carried out digitally – without jeopardising the rights of the individuals.

> I am and others are more used to meeting digitally. It is also easier to decide which meetings still need to be physical and which (most of them) can be digital (Respondent ÅK, 18).

> I have had to learn a lot digitally in a short period of time (Respondent ÅK, 35).

Overall, Survey 2 indicates that individuals belonging to the social work profession, and therefore also—one can argue—social work, seem to have made quite a leap towards digital transformation in the ten months that elapsed between Survey 1 (May 2020) and Survey 2 (March 2021). This is foremost seen in relation to internal and external collaboration but also in relation to case work, hence contributing to the overall digital transformation of the social service organisation at large into the second wave of digitalisation. What happened during these ten months that enabled this leap to be realised? How can we understand this sudden swift in digital transformation given earlier baseline results? And why now?

## Discussion

### *Phase one—Clash of the Titans*

Our social service organisation had already begun working towards a digital transformation before COVID-19, among other things by setting up top-down objectives for the transformation. The organisations top-down steering model had (through their 'Machine' perspective), however, difficulties in implementing their proposals in practice which can be explained, at least partly, by the encounter between the two perspectives, Machine and Community of Practice. The time before COVID-19 can be viewed as a common example of what occurs when the Machine perspective encounters the Community of Practice perspective and vice versa.

Social work, as a social system, is an area where the physical meeting between client and social worker is an important tool and this way of conducting social work has thus become part of what Loid and Malmström (2020) described as *the formatting of community standards*. As mentioned above, the formatting of the Community of Practice itself is maintained—mainly by informal leaders—and in this way, 'community work' becomes a self-reinforcing process where the community themselves directly affects the formatting of the work. This means that in order to achieve a sustainable transformation of the system (social work), it must be implemented in a way that makes sense for the Community of Practice perspective and through communication that the system understands.

Seen from a systems approach, transformation ought to be carried out in such a way that the system's core logic, 'the notion of the *good* social work', is preserved—even if it is in a new format. The *good* social work represents those values that drive the system of social work and subsequently become the format that is followed by the Community of Practice. Examples of these values are the creation and the maintaining of relations to clients, empowerment, and the ability to change and care/humanity (to 'see' another human being), and so on. According to the Community of Practice perspective, these values are seen as harder to maintain through digital channels, and digitalisation is therefore seen as challenging the 'traditional' social work.

> Harder to establish relations with clients, harder to read the interaction between family members, harder to lead conversations that get out of hand or get stuck (Respondent ÅK 47).

> Nuances in the language used, spontaneity and creative solutions that are a necessity when working with soft values are lost (Respondent ÅK 63).

As mentioned above, the digital transformation in our social service organisation was initiated with a top-down perspective and mainly through 'overarching transformation objectives' with the purpose to steer the transformation for the organisation in its entirety. In Loid and Malmström's (2020) terminology, this work was initiated from a Machine perspective. Hence, the Machine perspective suggests to the community how the forthcoming work around digitalisation should proceed. If this suggestion is not viewed from a Community of Practice perspective as positively contributing to the formatting of the community standards that have already been carried out, then 'the Machinist's' proposal will be declined/ignored.

In Survey 1 there is an indication of this, especially in relation to case work, where many respondents state that—which we would interpret as the system's core logic—'the *good* social work' is in danger due to the digital transformation being imposed with a Machine perspective. 'The Machinist' on the other hand cannot understand how the Community of Practice fail to see that both the social workers and the clients will benefit from the digitalisation in the long run (e.g., by increased democratisation, greater accessibility, and better match between intervention and user needs). 'The Machinist' therefore misinterprets the reluctance of the Community of Practice as resistance and/or as an unwillingness to change. We say 'misinterpret' because the root of the problem in this encounter between the perspectives—the reason for the clash of the Titans—is not that the Community of Practice is opposed to change as such, but that the two perspectives emanate in *different* problem formulations, namely whether social work needs digitalisation or not in order to meet the notion of the *good* social work. The Community of Practice, who want to maintain what *they* consider to be the *good* social work, therefore dismisses the Machine perspectives proposal for change due to considering it as not meeting the standards (too low quality in regard to relationship building) and/or as being too uncertain. Hence, the time before COVID-19, but even at the time of Survey 1, is defined by *different problem formulations* and consequently with a slow digital transformation.

### Phase two—The uniting of the Titans and COVID-19 as a game changer

During the ten months that now pass between Survey 1 and 2, something happens—a reformation of the social work takes off, not from an external (Machine) perspective but from within the community (or within the system). What happens is that the Community of Practice are now beginning to see a possible collapse of its system, in other words, they were not able to conduct their work in the best way possible way according to the previous practice (e.g., meeting clients face-to-face) due to the fact that the COVID-19 restrictions seem to be prolonged at this point. The system must now change if it is to survive and continue to deliver social services/values it is created to deliver; it is no longer possible to postpone the use or testing of digital tools such as Skype, Teams, digital records and files, local collaboration tools, digital network maps, and so on.

> A lot of meetings with clients have been carried out over the phone or digitally (Teams, Zoom) (Respondent F 109).

> An increased usage of digital collaboration tools (Respondent F 97).

> The Covid situation has also speed up our development of digital meetings and how we with the help of digital aids can carry out some interventions, for example, drawing digital network maps (Respondent F 100).

Hence, COVID-19 has now forced social work as a system to adapt to the changing social situation communicated. Subsequently, the Community of Practice will also now be forced—due to the threat of possible system collapse—to reformat their work in practice to support this adaptation, which is made visible by the fact that they begin to test digital tools to a greater extent together with colleagues, external partners, and clients (Respondents ÅK 10; ÅK 21; ÅK 49). Expressed in relation to the reasoning above around *different* problem formulations, the Community of Practice's problem formulation now all of a sudden coincides with that of 'the Machinists', that is, in order for the social work practice to 'survive', the integration of digitalisation is a must. Hence, the digitalisation will now from a Community of Practice perspective be viewed as positively contributing to the formatting of the community standards carried out by the Community. When the Community of Practice begin to reformat their standards, they also, in parallel, begin to define which parts of social work are *not* appropriate to be digitalised. Subsequently, the community starts to develop a new 'digital best practice' by integrating digital tools and at the same time maintain the '*good* social work'. This strengthens Loid and Malmströms (2020) theory that when a transformation is consolidated by the Community of Practice perspective, the process happens fast, to the point that 'the Machinist' cannot keep up. This might cause the Machine perspective to lose control over their aims and objectives. An interesting, though currently theoretical, argument that can be put forward here is that in our case it is not digitalisation as an *efficiency tool* (a logic used by the Machine perspective) that has driven the development of social work into the second wave of digitalisation. On the contrary, it is a strong Community of Practice perspective, in combination with the pandemic (a crisis) and its feared consequences on social work, that have realised the benefits of digitalisation in order to maintain the *good* social work practice and hence opened up for its (fast) introduction.

## Summary

This article attempts to explain how we can understand the rapid digital transformation that has taken place within a public social service organisation in a medium-sized municipality in Sweden, despite the fact that it was preceded by a slow-moving progress. Our analysis mainly points to three parts:

1) the significance of COVID-19 as an enabler for change;
2) the connection between systems and its Community of Practice perspective; and
3) the importance of involving a Community of Practice perspective in the reformatting of their own standards if a transformation is to be sustainable, especially when the transformation is regarding an area that potentially threatens the survival of the community system, in this case, social work.

Our study strengthens the theory of the *three perspectives on work* in many ways, but we also attempt to add another theoretical frame on top in the form of a system approach in which the interaction between a system and its community is made visible, and we can understand Community of Practice driving forces on a broader and more complex level. Our study also points out the significance of COVID-19 as a global crisis with local consequences. Without this crisis, it is highly unlikely that our social services organisation would have made the rapid transformation into the second wave of digitalisation as they did, much owing to the crisis communicating and directly threatening the 'survival' of the Community of Practice system (social work). The importance of Community of Practice to be involved in its own reformatting for more sustainable transformation also becomes clear in our study—Loid and Malmström (2020) state that functional Community of

Practice are reliable organisations which drive and develop the community standards themselves. In our study, this becomes visible by the fact that the community has not only shifted in their digital use, but they have also gone a step further and started to reflect on their system's core logic (the *good* social work) in relation to what is to be integrated (digitalisation). In other words: The Community of Practice perspective has begun to develop a digital best practice (albeit on a test basis) that can guide the community to which parts of social work can/should be digitalised and which parts can/should not be digitalised. With the digital transformation carried out during COVID-19, our social service organisation has taken the step into the second wave of digitalisation, but whether this standard and the forthcoming best practice will be implemented in a sustainable way and on a broad scale in the organisation remains to be seen. At least, we can ascertain that with the Community of Practice both involved in and driving the transformation, there are better chances of a successful integration on an operational level, and perhaps COVID-19 will prove to have been the game changer for digital transformation of social work in the long run.

## Further research

This article has opened up a new way of looking at the intersection between social work and digitalisation. It offers a theory and an analysis why rapid changes were possible due to the circumstances of the COVID-19 crisis. There is still plenty more to research in this area in general and in regard to the proposed theory in particular. What role does the public sector (contra the corporate system) play in the understanding of the three perspectives of work theory? How do we understand the relationship between the perspectives and their self-referential systems (which characteristics/parts do they contain and how do they cooperate with their system on the whole)? How do we understand the ethical challenges faced by the Community during digitalisation? Furthermore, will this development actually lead to a transformation of the *value orientation* of social work practice, in other words, producing a new (digitisation oriented) social work Community of Practice? These are just some of the questions that need more research in order to help push this area of research into its next wave and we look forward to take part in its future formation.

## Notes

1 Original title: '*Promotivt förändringsarbete – när medarbetare och ledning drar åt samma håll*'. Translation of the title provided by original authors Loid and Malmström, whom might publish a version of this work in English in the future (Personal communication with authors 29 August, 2022).
2 Examples of qualitative aspects are that the work should contribute to good customer/client/colleague relations and high work satisfaction.

3 It is not clear whether social workers are aware of their own community of practice, but one may argue that they are aware of the *values* that are fundamental to uphold by the professionals and the social service system they are a part of.
4 Social workers working with treatment and/or the exercise of public authority and personnel working with support systems, e.g., organisational development.

# References

Act 2020:114. Om förbud mot att hålla allmänna sammankomster och offentliga tillställningar. Given in Stockholm on 11 March, 2020, Ministry of Justice. https://www.riksdagen.se/sv/dokument-lagar/dokument/svensk-forfattningssamling/forordning-2020114-om-forbud-mot-att-halla_sfs-2020-114

Adhanom Ghebreyesus, Tedros. 2020. "WHO Director-General's Opening Remarks at the Media Briefing on COVID-19" (Speech). March 11, 2020, media briefing on COVID-19, transcript, https://www.who.int/dg/speeches/detail/who-director-general-s-opening-remarks-at-the-media-briefing-on-covid-19---11-march-2020

Bowker, Geoffrey C., Susan L. Star, Willian Turner, and Les Gasser, eds. 1997. *Social Science, Technical Systems, and Cooperative Work: Beyond the Great Divide.* Mahwah: Lawrence Erlbaum Associates.

Derks, Daantje, Desiree van Duin, Maria Tims, and Arnold B. Bakker. 2015. "Smartphone Use and Work–Home Interface: The Moderating Role of Social Norms and Employee Work Engagement. *Journal of Occupational and Organizational Psychology* 88 (1): 155–177. 10.1111/joop.12083.

Ehn, Pehr. 1988. *Work-Oriented Design of Computer Artifacts.* Stockholm: Arbetslivscentrum.

Greenbaum, Joan and Morten Kyng, eds. 1991. *Design at Work: Cooperative Design of Computer Systems.* Hillsdale: Lawrence Erlbaum Associates.

Habermas, Jürgen. 1979. *Communication and the Evolution of Society.* London: Heinemann Educational Books.

Habermas, Jürgen. 1995. *Diskurs, rätt och demokrati. Politisk filosofiska texter i urval av ErikOddvar Eriksson och Anders Molander.* Göteborg: Bokförlaget Daidalos.

Jönhill, Jan-Inge. 1995. "Människan som individ i sociala systems omvärld. Om individ och person i Niklas Luhmanns systemteori." *Sociologisk Forskning* 23 (3): 66–88. 10.37062/sf.32.18594.

Jönhill, Jan-Inge. 1997. Society as System and Its Ecological Environment: A Study in the Sociological Systems Theory of Niklas Luhmann. PhD Dissertation, University of Lund.

Kensing, Finn. 2003. Methods and Practices in Participatory Design. PhD dissertation, IT University of Copenhagen.

Loid, David and Clas Malmström. 2020. *Promotivt förändringsarbete – När medarbetare och ledning drar åt samma håll.* Stockholm: Liber.

Luhmann, Niklas. 1986. "The Autopoiesis of Social Systems." In *Sociocybernetic Paradoxes: Observation, Control, and Evolution of Self-Steering Systems,* edited by Felix Geyer and Johannes van der Zouwen, 172–192. London: Sage Publications.

Luhmann, Niklas. 2003. "Organisation." In *Autopoietic Organization Theory: Drawing on Niklas Luhmann's Social Systems Perspective,* edited by Tore Bakken and Tor Hernes, 31–52. Copenhagen: Copenhagen Business School Press.

Regeringskansliet. 2017. *För ett hållbart digitaliserat Sverige – en digitaliseringsstrategi.* Stockholm: Regeringskansliet. https://www.regeringen.se/49adea/contentassets/5429e024be6847fc907b786ab954228f/digitaliseringsstrategin_slutlig_170518-2.pdf

Svensson, Lupita and Stefan Larsson. 2017. *Digitalisering och socialt arbete – en kunskapsöversikt.* Lund: Lunds universitets internetinstitut (LUii). https://lup.lub.lu.se/ search/files/22297951/Svensson_Larsson_2017_Digitalisering_och_socialt_arbete_en_ kunskaps_versikt.pdf

Svensson, Lupita and Stefan Larsson. 2018. *The digitalization of Municipal Social Services – An Empirical Study of an Organization and Profession in Transformation.* Helsingborg: Forsknings- och utvecklingsenheten för social hållbarhet. https://fou.helsingborg.se/ wp-content/uploads/sites/40/2021/12/the-digitalisation-of-municipal-social-services- research-report-rd-helsingborg-sweden.pdf

# Section V

# Conclusion

# 17 Social Work through Pandemic: Conclusions, Lessons Learned, and Future Orientations

*Timo Harrikari*

In this book, we have explored social work and how it was performed and conceived during the global pandemic. The 15 empirical chapters of the book have addressed social work actors and organising work practices in various parts of the world during the COVID-19 pandemic, specifically from 2020 to 2022. The chapters have described how social work has been prepared for the outbreak of the pandemic and how it has been able to respond to the challenges that the outbreak has created. Methodologically speaking, the empirical analyses have been implemented in many dimensions; they include surveys, interview studies, observations, and document analyses, together offering a fairly parallel, but naturally fragmentary, view of the shared research object.

In this final chapter, we bring together the empirical chapters of the book and aim to create an updated overall picture of what we know about social work during the pandemic through both theoretical frameworks and recent research. We return to the conceptualisations that we presented in the introductory chapter, deepening our view of them. Thus, we start from the social-ecological conditions under which social workers, social work communities, and organisations have had to work during the COVID-19 pandemic. These conditions include various factors that may increase or decrease the epidemiological exposure and social vulnerability of individuals, communities, and societies in the context of the pandemic and its countermeasures. After this, we will compile the chapters of the book and summarise the results of the empirical analyses. We complement this view by utilising the latest international social work research, reflecting on this in relation to general social theoretical frameworks, resilience studies, and the conceptual frames of crisis and disaster social work. At the end of the chapter, we aim to summarise what we have learned from the pandemic, to make visible the limitations of our work, and to create an overview of future challenges.

## New normal and social-ecological fabric

At the time of writing this closing chapter, it is August 2022. The COVID-19 virus and its effects are still visible to the public, but already, by the spring of 2022, the state of war in Europe and tangible signs of deepening climate change

DOI: 10.4324/9781003374374-22

have sidelined the pandemic in the news headlines. Despite the increasingly frequent cycles of the public debate these days and the fact that only one main headline seems to be newsworthy at a time, the global traces of the coronavirus are still evident.

In the early stages of the pandemic, speculations about the forthcoming effects of the pandemic were presented. These speculations culminated in a debate about the 'new normal' (e.g. Bergman et al. 2022; Blumler and Coleman 2021; Hoyt et al. 2020; Powers et al. 2021). This discussion, however, was rather vague regarding what the 'new normal' would actually mean (Sardar 2021). The effects were believed to be multicaused and multilevel, direct and indirect, and intentional and unintentional. While talking about the prevailing ecological conditions, multicaused and multilevel generative mechanisms, social structures and relationships, or social events and measures of governance, we easily ended up with thematic listings that are as wide as they are long, so to speak.

To capture the force behind these described elements, we will utilise the concept of the *social-ecological fabric*. Metaphorically, the concept refers to a fringed and network-like living organism (see Castells 2010; Durkheim 1964), which is rarely that clearly defined that we could talk about it, for example, as an 'ecosystem' in a strict system-theoretical sense (cf. Folke et al. 2005). The fabric is a fragmentary and complex collective structure (Boyd and Folke 2012; Shaw and McKay 1942) that is structured, reproduced, and transformed in time and place (Giddens 1984); it consists of factors such as, among others, *ecological conditions* (e.g. geographical location, population size and density, gender and age structure, etc.), *social structure and social networks* (e.g. in the ways and conditions of earning a living, forming culture, etc.), and *the apparatuses of governance* (e.g. social institutions, administration, politics). The collective structure is a contingent historical product (Warf 2008) and, as such, the soil on which all transformative elements settle themselves, here including both linear and nonlinear mechanisms (Chandler 2014; Klijn 2008). The fastest changes in the fabric are often caused by phenomena that threaten the existence of the whole community or its members such as natural disasters, epidemics, or wars.

This rather abstract definition of the social-ecological fabric needs to be concretised. To illustrate the concept of social-ecological fabric, as an example, we take the events during the pandemic in the border region between Finland and Sweden, which is located in the Arctic Circle and separated by a natural ecological landmark: The Tornio River. For centuries, the population of the area has lived in an inseparable connection with each other in a way where earning a living or building family relationships have not followed the riverbed but have been built organically over it. Those who live on the west side of the river are Swedish, and those who live on the east side are Finnish. However, it has not been customary to divide the people and their status based on citizenship. For example, the Sámi, who are the indigenous people of the region (see Järvensivu et al. 2016; Ness et al. 2020), live in the Arctic regions of Norway, Sweden, Finland, and Russia. In general, the Arctic region is sparsely populated (in the Finnish province of Lapland, the population density is two inhabitants/square kilometre), and its densely populated areas, such as a few sparse population centres, form their own ecological entities.

As the COVID-19 virus began to spread globally, nation-states and their regional governing bodies took countermeasures. However, the urgency of the measures and severity of the regulation were different in Sweden and Finland (Engler et al. 2021; Nielsen and Lindvall 2021; Plümper and Neumayer 2022). In Sweden, efforts were made to avoid shutting down society, and because of this national policy, the virus was able to spread much more freely than in Finland. In Finland, the level of virus infections and deaths was quite low when looked at from an international perspective, but in the densely populated capital region and Tornio River Valley on the border with Sweden, the infection rates were clearly higher than in the rest of the country. The border between the two countries was closed, and crossing the natural border line, the Tornio River, was prohibited. As a result, these countermeasures stopped cross-border trade, along with working and maintenance of family relationships. The situation in the Tornio River Valley received plenty of national and international attention in the news, which it would hardly have received without the recent move towards planetary-wide digital information transmission, which is currently moving even into the Arctic regions. Moreover, digital devices made it possible to communicate across the border in a new way, even when restrictions prevailed. Since then, crossing the border has been made possible, first for those working and later for everyone who wanted to.

The long-term effects of events and arrangements during the pandemic in the Tornio River Valley are difficult to assess in the current time frame, but the case makes visible how the natural ecology, social structure, and governance or administrative arrangements of human communities, not to mention the countermeasures against viral outbreaks, are important to analytically separate from each other, even though they are practically intertwined. Making a distinction among ecology, social structure, and governance is reminiscent of Jurgen Habermas' distinction between 'life world' and 'system' (Habermas 1987) or Edwin Lemert's distinction in social reaction theory between the degrees of and the dynamics between 'deviance' and 'tolerance', here showing how collective reactions prevail in a community (Lemert 1951). From a broader perspective, it is important to understand how the described local and regional fabrics are connected, form joint network-like fabrics, and are nowadays parts of the global ecology because of a drastically increased and intensified interdependence between different regions of the globe (e.g. Gomez et al. 2013). Various administrative entities and their activities, such as nation-states, regional governments, or local governments, are parts of the fabric, but forcing the whole phenomenon to be 'national', 'provincial', or 'municipal' fundamentally reduces the overall view (Beck 2005). Even the most 'microlevel' local events and systems of relations are nowadays interwoven through the 'glocalising' effect (Harrikari and Rauhala 2019; Livholts and Bryant 2017) and the virtual dimension into a part of the global and planetary fabric.

## Observations of the change in social-ecological fabric

As for the claims about a 'new normal' and fundamental change in the social-ecological fabric, we prefer to avoid far-reaching claims in the current endemic phase, leaving them for later analyses; continuum or changes and their scale could be better seen from a distance. Currently, we know that the COVID-19 virus started in 2019 from Wuhan, China, and spread almost all over the world in the spring of 2020, bringing with it well-known consequences (He and Zhang 2022; LingHu and Shanjing 2022; Yu et al. 2022). Over the course of more than two and a half years, we have shifted first to the epidemic phase, then to the pandemic phase, and, in recent weeks, to the endemic phase regarding the definitions of an infectious disease caused by a virus (Biancolella et al. 2022).

During the pandemic, we have become used to talking about the 'coronavirus' and its movement, spread, and intensity of infections as 'waves' (Plümper and Neumayer 2022). The adjectives 'first', 'second', and 'third' wave have become established in their use, all of which have been caused by different variants of the coronavirus (the British 'Alpha', Indian 'Delta', South African 'Omicron' variants, etc.). We have seen how these 'waves' have their own epidemiological rhythms, and correspondingly, the countermeasures aimed at curbing the spread of the virus have their own rhythms. In people's minds, the movements of the virus and countermeasures often become mixed up, but as said, it is important to separate them analytically. The virus has made some people ill and killed others, but many social issues that have become tense and under debate, such as the realisation of human rights (Anand et al. 2021), earning a living, or accessing services (Harrikari et al. 2021), are the results of countermeasures. The countermeasures have mainly been implemented at the nation-state level, extending to various regional and local regulations and countermeasures.

The waves of COVID-19 have varied over time in different countries, but basically, the process has followed different crisis response patterns everywhere; it has progressed from the shock phase to adaptation and further reorientation and recovering. The chain of countermeasures follows this continuum, first starting with risk reduction, mitigation, preparedness, and prevention before then responding to an ongoing crisis and finally paying attention to the measures by which communities and individuals can recover from the burden brought by the crisis. Views that the world has been poorly prepared for the rise of a phenomenon like a pandemic have been common, but the degrees of preparedness seem to have varied (e.g. Laage-Thomsen and Frandsen 2022; MacGregor et al. 2022; Plümper and Neumayer 2022). Whether the pandemic can be called a 'black swan' event is up for debate (Taleb 2010; see also Mueller and Stewart 2016; Runde 2009; cf. Mooncy et al. 2020; Sundararaman et al. 2021), but in practice, people were unprepared for the spread of the virus and quite powerless to face it, at least before the development of vaccines. Almost everywhere in the world, societies implemented restrictive measures in spring 2020 to prevent the spread of the virus, which no one dared question at that time.

The COVID-19 virus, its spread, and its consequences have had many common features around the world. The virus caused severe symptoms before vaccinations became available, which, in some places, led to mass deaths in the population. It is, however, worth specifying that, at the same time, societies, communities, and individuals have been exposed and vulnerable to varying extents and in different ways regarding both the actual effects of the virus and countermeasures (Bollyky et al. 2022). Factors at the aggregate level of the social-ecological fabric have been influencing the degree of exposure and vulnerability, for example, population density, demographic profile, standard of living, national and regional culture, and the ability of administration to initiate countermeasures. We are currently aware that national statistics on infections and deaths vary, and their reliability can be problematised (e.g. Fenton et al. 2020). However, here interpreting this case with caution, the spread of the virus has been the fastest in the populous and densely populated areas where the new variants have emerged. These types of countries have been, for example, the USA, the UK, India, Brazil, and South Africa. A different matter is how citizens have been able to protect themselves from the virus; it is known that protection against the virus tends to be most difficult among the poorest populations (Beck 1992; Therborn 2013) in the Global South (Henley et al. 2021; Kgadima and Leburu 2022), like the African continent, but at the same time, statistics from these areas may not be the most reliable. Moreover, the question remains whether the age structure of these societies may have reduced mortality at the population level because the population is younger compared with other regions (see Bollyky et al. 2022). In terms of age structure, prosperous and ageing societies, such as Japan and Italy, were particularly vulnerable in the early stages of the pandemic, when vaccines were not yet available. However, the social-ecological fabric and its susceptibility to the virus do not follow national borders, and regional variations in susceptibility occur within national borders. The population of the northern part of Italy has been particularly aged, which may have increased the vulnerability of the regional fabric, eventually leading to the mass deaths of elderly people (see Guastafierro et al. 2021).

In addition to regional, demographic, cultural, and social group-specific factors, the effects of the pandemic and its countermeasures have followed lines according to gender, age, and family structure. The epidemiological significance of the life phase that people are living has been brought out above, but in pandemic conditions, it has social effects in light of the provision of age-specific society services, too. For example, Junko Wake's and Mi Ohwa's analysis in Chapter 11 concretely demonstrates that, because of the closing of services, the elderly people became isolated, felt themselves to be isolated, and had their well-being deteriorate (see also Callow et al. 2020; Gorenko et al. 2021). It also remains to be seen whether—and if so, to what extent—the pandemic will become a shared generational experience for young people (Lundström 2022; Mannheim 1952). Moreover, studies on gender and family structure have been connected to the impact that restrictions have had on everyday life. For example, in families with heterosexual parents, where both parents had been in paid work before the pandemic, it was the mother who stayed home more often than the father to take care of the children in a situation where restrictive measures required so (Reichelt et al. 2020). Here, the children moved to distance education and both spouses worked remotely, but in addition to this, the woman had to take care of her children's education and organising family meals, a fact that has become evident in a social work research, too (Czymara et al. 2020; Fodor et al. 2020). The everyday life of those who were not in paid work before the pandemic was less changed by the restrictions, but the transitions of other family members to work at home changed their everyday lives as well. In terms of these arrangements, the different families have undoubtedly been in unequal positions because the degrees of freedom of the wealthy families regarding the spatial arrangements have been wider than those of the poor families. Moreover, homeless people may have been in the weakest position because the opportunities to protect themselves from the virus and comply with lockdowns and other restrictions were nonexistent (e.g. Fenley 2020; Fujii 2022; McCosker et al. 2022).

In addition to ecological and social factors, extensive national, regional, and local variations in the governance of exposures, risks, and vulnerabilities emerged, a factor that constitutes the third element of the mutual dynamics of the social-ecological fabric (Hasselman 2017; He and Zhang 2022). National agents, governments, and ministries, as well as other central and local authorities, have played a key role in the initiation, development, guidance, and supervision of countermeasures (Laage-Thomsen and Frandsen 2022; MacGregor et al. 2022; Plümper and Neumayer 2022). Theoretically speaking, together, they form a multilevel and multidimensional apparatus of governance that aims to guide the behaviour of the population in the geographical area it controls (Dean 1999; Foucault 2000). Before developing vaccinations, the most common technologies of governance were restricting citizen's mobility and closing facilities. National and regional variations in the levels of tolerance, the severity of the restrictions, and their compliance, as well as in the sanctioning of noncompliance, have emerged (Plümper and Neumayer 2022; Toshkov et al. 2022). Likewise, compliance with receiving vaccinations has differed by region and social group. Within political populism, we have seen the world's political leaders' varying understanding and attitudes towards the spread of the deadly virus, which, in places, have influenced the thresholds, reactions, and measures of public administrative bodies (e.g. Kritzingera et al. 2021). During the pandemic, some state leaders have aimed to appear strong, even immortal, in the eyes of their citizens (Christensen 2022; Li et al. 2022). This has resulted in downplaying the danger of the virus and delaying measures, with the result being the virus spreading and citizens dying.

Summing up all the above, we may say that much is known about the pandemic era around the globe, but the overall view will be complemented and can only be estimated over a longer period of time. The COVID-19 pandemic has had its epidemiological and social effects on humankind, but these effects seem to be polarised in a way where the most vulnerable societies, communities, and their members have faced the worst of this situation (Kusumaningrum et al. 2021). In prosperous democracies, not to understate the number of deaths and all the suffering, the question has been more about a lifestyle crisis and fear of social decline. The public debate seems to maintain the notion that the pandemic period has only produced negative effects and losers, but the pandemic period has also produced its niches and has had its winners. In September 2022, it seems that, for example, digital capitalism has not fundamentally weakened from the power of the pandemic; the global accumulation of wealth in the hands of the few has only shown an accelerating trend during the pandemic (Oxfam 2022). After a short hesitation, the wealthy masses of people have continued to feed the international entertainment industry (events, sports, movies, music, etc.), which generates billions for the owners and actors. Taking into account the recent radicalising signs of deepening climate change and the total threat it produces to the existence of humankind, the question of social scientists—supporting a humane, rational, and research-based social policy—is where we as humankind are going and whether we have learned anything from the pandemic. Quite often, we are left with the dystopian impression that we are living in a 'carnival of the end of the world' between the tail end of the pandemic and looming climate change. The key question is how to maintain hope, solidarity, and the principles of fairness (Slavich et al. 2021) under circumstances where living conditions and resources are becoming irreversibly scarce, the atmosphere of fear and the reactivity of societies increase, irrational activity takes over the field, and human dignity is repeatedly put to the test (Harrikari and Rauhala 2019).

## Social work through pandemic: Empirical perceptions, conceptual reflections

Social workers around the world have been an integral part of everything described above. They have been forced to experience the pandemic and its effects both as residents of the global village and citizens of the state, and from their various social positions, one of which is the professional role of a social worker. Social workers have lived, worked, and been parts of varying social-ecological fabrics, all of which define their professional operating environment. The pandemic and its effects on the lives of social workers have been pervasive and comprehensive in such a way that the boundaries between social workers' private and working lives have faded away (Ben-Ezra and Hamama-Raz 2021; Schiff et al. 2021). Social workers represent different gender, age, and race groups, have diverse family statuses, and belong to different income groups in terms of their income; the factors that have certainly conditioned their options to act as social workers during the pandemic at the interface between private and work life.

In a global comparison, the epidemiological susceptibility of the social-ecological fabric to the COVID-19 virus, its spread and wounding effects, and surrounding social workers' professional activities have varied. It is challenging to present exact comparable numbers simply because the fabrics rarely have a clear boundary and because many factors, such as the mobility of people or digitisation, remind us that the whole phenomenon is a cross-border one. However, if we briefly compare the ecological factors of the empirical analyses framing this book, we may notice that, in terms of population density, social workers in Delhi, India (9,294 inhabitants/square kilometre), and Lapland, Finland (two inhabitants/square kilometre), as well as in terms of the age structure of the population, social workers in Japan (Median age 48.6) and Bangladesh (Median age 27.9), operate in quite different environments. Likewise, the question of social workers' and their clients' options to protect themselves from the virus may appear different in Iranian health care than in Irish child protection services.

The first part of the book introduced three empirical analyses that have examined social workers' actions during the pandemic but that have also shed light on the circumstances and boundary conditions in which they have been forced to act. Both Tadeja Kodele et al.'s multilevel analysis from Slovenia (Chapter 2) and Melinda Madew (Germany), Marcin Boryczko (Poland), and Daniela Gaba's (Romania) comparison among Poland, Romania, and Germany (Chapter 3) suggest that many developments that undermine social workers' working conditions arose long before the pandemic, but during the pandemic, their effects have become particularly visible, with their developments escalating. Both analyses refer to the austerity policies and efficiency measures of public administration implemented in the name of neoliberal governance, which may have succeeded in weakening social work organisations and their resources. These observations are not new: Several social work studies have suggested that all kinds of standardisation, management, and governance from outside social work, strange regarding its own ethos, have increased (e.g. Brown 2021; Wallace and Pease 2011). However, politicians demanding efficiency, as well as administrative bureaucracies around the world, were powerless to respond to the challenges that arose when facing the reality in the spring of 2020. Moreover, the opportunities and obstacles offered by the technological and administrative structures that support the work of social workers vary by region and organisation. Fiorentino et al.'s analysis (Chapter 4) sheds light on how the IT infrastructure available to social workers and its functionality conditioned their opportunities to switch to remote working and online meetings with their clients. This was influenced, among other things, by the availability and functionality of data networks, computers, mobile devices, software, and applications. The social workers' own attitudes and instructions given by employers also affected these work opportunities.

As noted, social workers have had to experience the pandemic and its effects both as residents of the global village and citizens of the state, among other positions. The analyses included in the second part of this book demonstrate how the pandemic and its effects on a social worker's life have been pervasive and comprehensive in a way where the boundaries between private and working life have faded. As citizens, social workers have been under the same restrictions to curb viral outbreaks as any other people, but their professional status has brought some additional burdens to their lives. Reeli Sirotkina, Airi Mitendorf, and Kersti Kriisk's analysis (see Chapter 6) in the Estonian context shows how, in local communities, not only social work clients but also employees, were subjected to fearful stigmatisation because of their professional status during lockdown (see also Onyeaka et al. 2021). Indeed, Paula McFadden, Ruth Neill, and Jill Manthorpe's analysis (Chapter 5) illustrates how the pandemic era has caused social workers a serious workload and symptoms of burnout, which only seem to have increased from the crisis phase at the beginning of the pandemic to the present (see also Ben-Ezra and Hamama-Raz 2021; Cadell et al. 2022; Currin-McCulloch et al. 2022; Gur et al. 2022; McFadden et al. 2021; Ravalier et al. 2022). The social work literature is used to describe how the effects of phenomena like the pandemic fall most severely on the most vulnerable client groups. This is, no doubt, true, but it must be kept in mind that during the pandemic, both clients and social workers have been in 'the same boat', so to speak. Kristofer Hansson and Charlotte C. Petersson's analysis (see Chapter 12) aptly describes the emergence of shared trauma and its effects (Holmes et al. 2021; Levi-Belz and Zerach 2022; Wampole and Kohli 2022).

During the pandemic, social workers around the world have worked in exceptionally challenging circumstances. These circumstances and their everyday contexts have been filled with concern and justified the fear towards COVID-19 (Chow et al. 2022; Saraniemi et al. 2022). In general, ageing societies such as Japan have been more vulnerable to the effects of the virus. In services for older adults, the fear of the virus spreading to collective residential units has had a variety of intended and unintended consequences (see Wake and Ohwa, Chapter 11; see also Chan et al. 2022; Yildirim et al. 2021). Hygiene has been enhanced and specific attention paid to preventing the virus from spreading, but, at the same time, because all collective activities were ceased, the residents felt isolated and lonely. Media reports about the cases where the virus had succeeded in entering a residential unit, spread there, and caused the deaths of residents did not decrease the state of panic in society and supported organising proper measures. Likewise, viral deaths seen from a close distance when a social worker works in health care or at its interface, helplessness felt in front of them, and the fear of infecting loved ones or clients with the deadly virus have all been present (see Abri and Poursaadati, Chapter 9; see also Chow et al. 2022). While social workers have been challenged to respond to new dynamics and new clients, they have also been forced to take care of their old clients and challenges, as well as administrative requirements. During the restrictions, intimate partner violence and the need for child protection, among other things, remained hidden, and the availability of services weakened or was interrupted, which is why many statistics turned downward (see Bhattacharjee and Das, Chapter 10; see also Cortis et al. 2021; Wake and Kandula 2022).

The first phase of the pandemic tore social work communities apart, and several studies have shown that, with physical limitations and remote working, social workers felt they were left alone with their decisions (see Cook and

Carder, Chapter 7; see also Cabiati 2021; Cadell et al. 2022). The quick and reflective 'door-to-door conversations' that were a part of the everyday offering of collegial support were suddenly unattainable, and colleagues started to appear more as potential virus carriers and sources of fear (Saraniemi et al. 2022). In the middle of the crisis, where no information about the virus and no ready-made guidelines for action existed, a huge self-organisation of social work communities (of course also in almost all other areas of social practice) was initiated and launched. Self-organisation in social work—in other words, innovating and creatively launching activities amid the fear of viruses and various restrictions—was started a few weeks after the viral outbreak and in the so-called edge-of-chaos context to secure the existence of systems (Ferguson et al. 2022; Harrikari et al. 2021; Phillippo et al. 2022; Ren et al. 2022).

As for the basis of this type of self-organisation, the role of social work teams, professional capital, and adaptive capacity to mobilise resources have been decisive in a situation where organisational guidelines have been missing and management is in crisis (Hawkins and Maurer 2010; Mathbor 2007; Romakkaniemi et al. 2021; Yeong-Tsyr Wang et al. 2020). In terms of mobilising adaptive capacity during crises, the allocation of resources can be used to conceptualise it as a matter of promoting various forms of *human and social capital* (Hawkins and Maurer 2010; Rapeli 2018). One of the subforms of social capital, in other words, *the professional capital of social work*, is a crucial collective archive to allocate individual, group, and community resources for responding to crisis situations and recovering from a crisis (Aghabakhshi and Gregor 2007; Hawkins and Maurer 2010; Nahapiet and Ghoshal 1998; Wu 2021). This can be defined as a form of symbolic capital, here referring to a sense of collective identity and offering adaptive capacities such as congruent values, a knowledge base and knowledge production, reciprocal relationships with other professions, and distinctive contributions to social well-being (Beddoe 2010). In crisis situations, social workers provide their specific professional competencies and mobilise collaborative relationships in a way that makes it difficult to distinguish between individual skills and the resources provided by the professional community such as ethical principles or know-how. Resource allocation can be understood and conceptualised as the mobilisation of social capital in terms of protecting individuals, groups, and communities from their hazard-specific vulnerabilities, but on the other hand, it can be seen as increasing their resilience to anticipate, respond to, and recover from crises (Yeong-Tsyr Wang et al. 2020). In sum, from the perspective of social work, mobilising professional capital in crisis situations requires two types of arrangements and measures:

1) mobilising the social worker's competencies, skills, and know-how, and
2) mobilising community resources to allocate bonding, bridging, and linking capital (Romakkaniemi et al. 2021; see also Rapeli 2018, 1055).

The mobilisation of adaptive capacity has not only been limited to social work communities and organisations during the pandemic, but social work has had a specific and more extensive role in the initiatives and actions that have been developed to respond to the direct and indirect consequences of the pandemic (see Massart et al., Chapter 8; see also Craig et al. 2022). Here, the special competence of social work and the strength of the profession have been condensed into a holistic approach and its organisation across organisational and institutional boundaries (Wang and Liu 2022). With a holistic approach, social workers have held on to their clients (bonding capital) in contexts where other service providers have closed their doors or restricted access to their services. In a very concrete manner, Mooney et al.'s analysis (Chapter 13) demonstrates how relations, not only with colleagues but also with clients, became disconnected in the early stages of the pandemic and how the re-establishment of connections was intentionally pursued according to the ethos of social work and its ethical principles. Likewise, social workers have bridged (bridging capital) cross-sectoral service channels for their clients (cross sectoral) and linked (linking capital) institutional actors together and initiated professional collaboration (Romakkaniemi et al. 2021; Yu et al. 2022). Moreover, Jorgensen et al.'s analysis (Chapter 14) shows how opening the 'windows of resonance' (see also Ferguson et al. 2022), in other words, creating meaningful and constructive activities both in the social work community, among professionals, especially between the social worker and client, requires mobilising a flexible, creative, interactive, and relation-based approach; doing this requires an understanding of systemic effects in a complex, multidimensional, and nonlinear environment.

## A fundamental and irreversible change in the operating environment of social work?

In general, the pandemic period has raised the question of how the social worker's operating environment may be changing. Social workers' operating environment is one of the classic themes of the social casework tradition (Richmond 1917; person in environment, circumstantial evidence, etc.), not to mention the agendas of community social work (Addams 1912) or critical, structural, and radical social work (Germain and Gitterman 1980). Several empirical analyses included in this book have relied on and applied ecological and systemic frameworks in social work. In the introduction and conclusion, we have illustrated the dynamics of these multidimensional agendas through the concept of social-ecological fabric, gathering various elements under it.

It seems that the pandemic period has made it visible how the spatial, temporal, and interactive dimensions of the structuring of the world—consequently also the operational environment of the social work environment—have changed rapidly and in a fundamental way over the past few decades. As early as the 1990s, the 'condensation of time and place' (Giddens 1990) and the 'death of distances' (Janelle 1991) were discussed in sociological contemporary analyses in a way that became realised in everyday social work during the pandemic. Looking back, this seems a bit disheartening because the world has changed much since then; for example, digitalisation had not even started when the concept of the 'condensation of time and place' was first discussed. During the pandemic, the effects of the forced digital leap and working online were evident. The advantages and disadvantages of the digital leap are debated, but it seems clear that Waldo Tobler's (1970) first law of geography—'everything is related to everything else, but near things are more related than distant things'—requires a fundamental re-evaluation.

In parallel, ecological and systemic theorising in social work, in which the systemic circles or 'levels' of physical operating environments and social relations gradually expand (micro, exo, mezzo, macro, chrono; see, e.g. Bronfenbrenner 1977; Garbarino 1977), would require updating (Harrikari and Rauhala 2019). The domain of virtual and hybrid reality, where flexible and quick interaction, even in the farthest corners of the globe, is made possible, increases, for example, the probability that even the most meaningful human relationships do not have to be defined through the physical dimension of the real world like in modern times. The current world is much more liquid and complicated (Bauman 2000). Thus, space, social relations, and temporal rhythms are becoming increasingly separated from each other, which has to be considered in renewing social work theory and research. Instead of living in the institutional boxes that are characteristic of the modern world, the social-ecological fabric of the current world is becoming increasingly constituted and organised outside these boxes, within the scope of a global network-like weave of civil society, digital platforms, and virtual reality.

The spatial changes are inextricably linked to changes in interaction and temporal rhythms in social work; as the spatial dimension is compressed, the temporal rhythms will also condense. During the pandemic, with restrictions and remote working, social workers' transitions to client and team meetings, among other things, decreased and were left out. In the early stages of the pandemic, the rhythms of organisations, teams, and client work slowed down or even stopped because of restrictions. However, the forced digital leap and transition to working on digital platforms (see Bergman, Svensson, and Melling, Chapter 16; see also Copson et al. 2022; Mishna et al. 2021) accelerated the rhythms, soon leading to breathless chains of several online meetings and meetings without breaks from which to recover. To solve this problem, social work organisations began to offer their employees telework instructions to protect their well-being and switch to a hybrid work model that alternates office and remote work as soon as possible, depending on the limitations. The changes in interaction patterns with clients are probably what social workers have been the most concerned about. Fiorentino et al.'s analysis (Chapter 4; see also Copson et al. 2022) has shown how the transition from face-to-face to virtual interaction as the fundamental social work elements caused resistance among social workers. Social workers have also been concerned that not all dimensions of perception and methods of information acquisition are possible in online interactions. On the other hand, client reachability and clients' access to services through digital platforms and online applications have improved since the first phase of the pandemic.

The described tendencies have been conceptualised in social theory, for example, within the theory of social acceleration (Rosa 2013; Wajcman 2015). The idea of acceleration is anything but new, already found in Karl Marx's and Friedrich Engels' writings, where they address the relations between the effects of producing added value in capitalist systems and accelerating the rhythms of industry and, thus, also of society as a whole (Marx and Engels 1998). However, the reminder of the pandemic era for social work may be that there is not just one concept of time; the rhythms and timespans of face-to-face and virtual interaction differ from each other in a way that causes asynchrony in both team activities and employee–client relationships, a case especially true in the early stages of the pandemic. In addition, the social workers and teams had to adapt their activities to the changing organisational rhythms, the rhythms of countermeasures against the virus and movements of the virus itself. Interestingly, the system of disciplinary power, as characterised by Michel Foucault (1977), and maintaining the social order of social work became visible at these breaking points. It seems that the diverse and complex conceptualisations Foucault developed in his work may have many other fruitful connections to the pandemic, considering, for example, his writings on biopower or total institutions as experimental laboratories for the technologies of power. As we know, the roots of 'lockdown' lie in the prison world and in the contexts where the prison riot is threatening or starting.

The questioning of the social orders and disciplinary system of social work has often brought experiences in which we live in disorder or even chaos. The ontological question of whether our lives are basically living in 'order in the midst of chaos' or vice versa is important while locating what kind of fundamental assumptions social work contains and in examining the reality in which social work acts. In the midst of crises, in times of rapid change and when there is a feeling of things being out of control, a tendency to overestimate the effects of a crisis and its causes can emerge (cf. Walter-McCabe 2020). Many societies are very well organised and structured, and even fairly minor disturbances in their operating systems may seem large. Based on the classic social reaction theory (Lemert 1951), which highlights societal problems, tolerance, and reactions as independent variables, one can hypothetically ask whether the feeling or perception of the world turning complex or chaotic during a pandemic is more a characteristic of well-organised and stable societies than others. Moreover, global digital and real-time communication has required us all to carry out frequent reflection, be more alert, and form a personal position on the acute issues related to the pandemic. Thus, the pandemic period may have increased the charm of regarding social work and a reality especially complex in nature. Considering these starting points, the belief that the surrounding world is perhaps fundamentally chaotic may have been strengthened. Understanding the pandemic as a 'black swan', the emergence of which we could not have expected, easily leads to such an interpretation.

Of course, the complexity and chaos theories (see Horn 2008; Klijn 2008) can make the elements of the prevailing reality understandable, contribute to the structuring of events in social work during the pandemic, and open their dynamics. In general, any conceptual frameworks of interpretation should not be taken as a given or granted because they easily formulate fundamental assumptions and expand and become established in contemporary reality. Critical reflection and practice (Adams et al. 2002) by both social work researchers and practitioners require extensive social theoretical reading. The more conceptual networks and theoretical frameworks to structure various social work phenomena during the pandemic are available, the more diverse reality appears and the more finely detailed we can describe its many nuances. In other words, the more lenses, the more nuanced the world, and the more potential options for action there will be. Calls for research and development funding often fuel 'new and innovative openings', but from a social scientist's point of view, for example, going back to the classics and rereading them often seems the most useful. We may ask what the pandemic era looks like, for example, in the light of Emile Durkheim's (1984) forms of solidarity, Max Weber's (1978, 956–1003) bureaucracy theory, Hannah Arendt's (1986) writings on totalitarianism, or Ulrich Beck's risk society thesis (1992). More specifically applied to social work, what kind of data do the pandemic era offer for preparing a social diagnosis (Richmond 1917), how can the principles of community social work implemented at Hull House be applied in digital services (Addams 1912), or how can we promote social questions in pandemic conditions (Jebb 1906)?

## Towards a recovering and post-COVID period? Lessons learned and future perspectives

One question remains as follows: What have we learned about social work during the pandemic? It is often the case that offering easy answers only raises new questions and that it may be good to just wait for time to pass so that we can see better from afar. The dynamic of the pandemic has shown that we almost always do not know what will happen in terms of virus infections in the coming months. It is justified to remain cautious.

Some answers, however, seem almost self-evident. The first is that, in the future, we should be better prepared for societal crises like the pandemic, avoid risks, and try to reduce the probability of their occurrence, in other words, the adaptive governance of social-ecological fabric (Ansell 2019; Boyd and Folke 2012; Hasselman 2017; Walch 2019). The current view of the future of the globe and humankind is rather dystopian, but the key tasks of social work are to maintain hope and an atmosphere of trust, especially during the darkest moments of humankind (Slavich et al. 2021). Different natural and human disasters require qualitatively slightly different preparation, so one should be able to distinguish both their common and special features. This preparation certainly has its limits, and while facing phenomena that are not directly dependent on human activity, such as earthquakes, volcanic eruptions, floods caused by drought and heavy rains, or aggressively spreading deadly viruses, we must be humble and recognise the limits of our influence when the phenomenon comes up (see Berkes 2007). However, everything like this to happen can be foreseen. Settlements can be avoided from being built in fire-prone areas, buildings can be made more durable than usual, and dams can be built in areas suffering from severe rainy seasons. Regardless of the location, the functionality and development of technical and communication infra-structures are key issues (Asprone and Manfredi 2014). We have learned from the pandemic era that social work is not an island, and it should be even more closely involved in a form of contingency planning that anticipates crises and promotes preparedness in the future (Rapeli 2018; Yeong-Tsyr Wang et al. 2020; Zakour 1996).

The better social work anticipates and gets prepared for crisis situations, the faster and more convincingly it will be capable of responding to external shocks (McConnell 2011). This statement may be a cliché, but it is rather difficult to question it. The first phase of the pandemic showed the importance of capable management in social work. In crisis situations, management must be accessible to employees, and communication should occur openly. In contingency and preparedness planning that envisions possible worlds, scenarios can be produced for varying situations and challenges through which basic formats and models for instructions for different contexts can be prepared. Based on these, social workers can be trained, and exercises for preparation can be organised in the social work organisations. Different professions and other agents have their basic work, strengths, and areas of expertise in contingency planning and responding to acute crises. In respect to preparedness planning, the specific competence of social work is related to its holistic approach, as well as explaining to other actors how the problems of people in a particularly vulnerable position should be considered in various disaster situations and what kind of actions should be initiated. The status of social work as a mandatory emergency profession has varied in countries during the pandemic (Cadell et al. 2022; Cheung 2022; Dominelli et al. 2020; Mešl et al. 2022), and it would be important to emphasise the importance of social work among other social practices and actors.

As mentioned above, the key issue in facing disasters is the adaptive capacity of social workers and social work communities. The pandemic period has shown that the global ethical principles of social work are the core of social work practice that has been put to test in pandemic conditions (Banks and Rutter 2021; Banks et al. 2020; Farkas and Romaniuk 2020). A social worker can rely on them in chaotic disaster situations where legislation, government regulations, or organisational instructions are not available. In addition to shared professional codes and other professional capital, the functionality of the communication structure, the per-manence of employees, and the cohesion between team members can increase the adaptive capacity to prepare for and act in disaster situations. In light of the current ecological and social tendencies around the globe, one can rightly em-phasise teaching the principles of structural and ecological social work in the basic education of social workers (Matthies and Närhi 2017).

Finally, in a broad sense, the whole pandemic era may raise the question of whether—and, if so, to what extent—the pandemic and its consequences could be viewed as indicators of a new world age or even of modernisation. Combined with many other current escalating and tangible ecological hazards, natural disasters, wars, and other humanitarian catastrophes, it is becoming more obvious that we may be living in a particularly erratic and unstable historic era. We have seen how these unexpected events can kill masses of people and threaten living conditions and the survival of humankind. Because of global interdependence, any corner of the world will not be outside of these developments (Asprone and Manfredi 2014; Harrikari and Rauhala 2019; Rifkin 2008). In this context, we would like to highlight how the presence and voice of social workers, among many other actors, are extremely important. In humanitarian disasters, the task of social work is to mobilise its functional capacity and maintain hope through a holistic approach.

## Limitations of the epistemological gaze and methodologies

We conclude this book with epistemological and methodological reflections. We briefly consider the specific perspectives this book opens for social work and under what limitations the reader should understand these. Our first notion relates to the geographical limitations of the empirical analyses. Our purpose has been to offer examples of social work during the pandemic and promote forming views while not presenting an overall picture of it. In certain spots in this book, we speak about the planetary dimension, but in light of the geographical coverage of the empirical analyses, there is no justification for talking about such a thing. The coverage is quite good, from the European perspective and in the direction of the East–West latitudes (Ireland–Japan), but there are no, for example, African, Oceanian, or American analyses included.

Second, we would like to remind the reader that, considering the entire pandemic period, the time span of the book and its empirical analyses is rather front oriented. The main part of the empirical analyses addresses the relationship between social work and problem of the pandemic no later than 2021—in other words, emphasising the shock and adaptation phases in terms of overall crisis models. Academic book editing and publishing processes are always delayed in relation to the need for information. The same applies to articles in high-standard scientific social work journals, even during the pandemic. We may see a certain development arc in the publications. In the summer and fall of 2020, social work journals published some concerns from practitioners, as well as editorials, many of which have become quite cited only because nothing else was available (e.g. Amadasun 2020; Walter-McCabe 2020). In the fall of 2020, the first texts, three to six pages long, which had received 'article' status but did not contain any empirical data, were published (e.g. de Jonge et al. 2020; Yuan et al. 2020). In November 2020, BJSW and QSW published calls for their thematic special issues that addressed the pandemic. The issues were published in late spring 2021. Social work research on the pandemic started slowly, but as it stands now, there is already plenty of empirical research (Cheung 2022). An early exception was the report of our COVID-19 SWRF research network in July 2020, which presented social work perspectives on the pandemic in 16 countries.

The third notion is related to the previous one in the sense that, in terms of the pandemic period, the front-oriented empirical analyses have most obviously been affected by the boundary conditions of the gathering of the research data. In some places, strict restrictions on movement and closures in institutions made it difficult for the researchers to reach clients or observe social work practices from a close distance. Many of the analyses included in the book have been conducted as online surveys for social work professionals, a methodology best suited to the circumstances. In addition, social workers were reached through diary requests and online interviews. It is still difficult to find any ethnographies on social work, not to mention the lives of social work clients, made during the pandemic that would include, for example, participatory observation methods. We believe, however, that various memory data studies from the pandemic will be published in abundance.

# References

Adams, Robert, Lena Dominelli, and Malcom Payne, eds. 2002. *Critical Practice in Social Work*. Basingstoke: Palgrave.

Addams, Jane. 1912. *Twenty Years at Hull House With Autobiographical Notes*. New York: The MacMillan Company.

Aghabakhshi, Habib and Claire Gregor. 2007. "Learning the Lessons of Bam: The Role of Social Capital." *International Social Work* 50 (3): 347–356. 10.1177/0020872807076048

Amadasun, Solomon. 2020. "Social Work and COVID-19 Pandemic: An Action Call." *International Social Work* 63 (6): 753–756. 10.1177/0020872820959357

Anand, Janet C., Sarah Donnelly, Alisoun Milne, Holly Nelson-Becker, Emme-Li Vingare, Blanca Deusdad, Giovanni Cellini, Riitta-Liisa Kinni, and Cristiana Pregno. 2021. "The Covid-19 Pandemic and Care Homes for Older People in Europe – Deaths, Damage and Violations of Human Rights." *European Journal of Social Work*. Published ahead of print, 12 August, 2021. 10.1080/13691457.2021.1954886

Ansell, Christopher K. 2019. *The Protective State*. Cambridge: Cambridge University Press.

Arendt, Hannah. 1986. *The Origins of Totalitarianism*. London: André Deutsch.

Asprone, Domenico and Gaetano Manfredi. 2014. "Linking Disaster Resilience and Urban Sustainability: A Global Approach for Future City." *Disasters* 39 (S1): S96–S111. 10.1111/disa.12106

Banks, Sarah and Nikki Rutter. 2021. "Pandemic Ethics: Rethinking Rights, Responsibilities and Roles in Social Work." *The British Journal of Social Work*. 10.1093/bjsw/bcab253

Banks, Sarah, Tian Cai, Ed de Jonge, Jane Shears, Michelle Shum, Ana M. Sobočan, Kim Strom, Rory Truell, María J. Úriz, and Merlinda Weinberg. 2020. "Practising Ethically During COVID-19: Social Work Challenges and Responses." *International Social Work* 63 (5): 569–583. 10.1177/0020872820949614

Bauman, Zygmunt. 2000. *Liquid Modernity*. Cambridge: Polity Press.

Beck, Ulrich. 1992. *Risk Society: Towards a New Modernity*. London: Sage Publications.

Beck, Ulrich. 2005. *Power in the Global Age*. Cambridge: Polity Press.

Beddoe, Liz. 2010. "Building Professional Capital. New Zealand Social Workers and Continuing Education". PhD diss., Deakin University, 2010. http://dro.deakin.edu.au/eserv/DU:30032402/beddoe-buildingprofessional-2010A.pdf

Ben-Ezra, Menachem and Yaira Hamama-Raz. 2021. "Social Workers During COVID-19: Do Coping Strategies Differentially Mediate the Relationship Between Job Demand and Psychological Distress?" *The British Journal of Social Work* 51 (5): 1551–1567. 10.1093/bjsw/bcaa210

Bergman, Solveig, Margunn Bjørnholt, and Hannah Helseth. 2022. "Norwegian Shelters for Victims of Domestic Violence in the COVID-19 Pandemic – Navigating the New Normal." *Journal of Family Violence* 37 (6): 927–937. 10.1007/s10896-021-00273-6

Berkes, Firket. 2007. "Understanding Uncertainty and Reducing Vulnerability: Lessons From Resilience Thinking." *Natural Hazards* 41 (2): 283–295. 10.1007/s11069-006-9036-7

Biancolella, Michela, Vito L. Colona, Ruty Mehrian-Shai, Jessica L. Watt, Lucio Luzzatto, Giuseppe Novelli, and Juergen K.V. Reichardt. 2022. "COVID-19 2022 Update: Transition of the Pandemic to the Endemic Phase." *Human Genomics* 16: 19. 10.1186/s40246-022-00392-1

Blumler, Jay and Stephen Coleman. 2021. "After the Crisis, A 'New Normal' for Democratic Citizenship?" *Javnost – The Public* 28 (1): 3–19. 10.1080/13183222.2021.1883884

Bollyky, Thomas J., Erin N. Hulland, Ryan M. Barber, James K. Collins, Samantha Kiernan, Mark Moses, David M. Pigott, et al. 2022. "Pandemic Preparedness and COVID-19: An Exploratory Analysis of Infection and Fatality Rates, and Contextual Factors Associated With Preparedness in 177 Countries, from Jan 1, 2020, to Sept 30, 2021." *Lancet* 399 (10334): 1489–1512. 10.1016/S0140-6736(22)00172-6

Boyd, Emily and Carl Folke, eds. 2012. *Adapting Institutions: Governance, Complexity and Social- Ecological Resilience.* Cambridge: Cambridge University Press.

Bronfenbrenner, Urie. 1977. "Towards an Experimental Ecology of Human Development." *American Psychologist* 32 (7): 513–531. 10.1037/0003-066X.32.7.513

Brown, Catrina. 2021. "Critical Clinical Social Work and the Neoliberal Constraints on Social Justice in Mental Health." *Research on Social Work Practice* 31 (6): 644–652. 10.1177/1049731520984531

Cabiati, Elena. 2021. "Social Workers Helping Each Other During the COVID-19 Pandemic: Online Mutual Support Groups." *International Social Work* 64 (5): 676–688. 10.1177/002087282097544

Cadell, Susan, Rachelle Ashcroft, Jessica Furtado, Keith Adamson, Sheri M. McConnell, and Samantha Teichman. 2022. "COVID-19 and Social Work in Health Care in Canada: What Are the Impacts?" *Social Work in Health Care* 61 (4): 218–242. 10.1080/00981389.2022.2104985

Callow, Michael A., Daniel D. Callow, and Charles Smith. 2020. "Older Adults' Intention to Socially Isolate Once COVID-19 Stay-at-Home Orders Are Replaced With "Safer-at-Home" Public Health Advisories: A Survey of Respondents in Maryland." *Journal of Applied Gerontology* 39 (11): 1175–1183. 10.1177/0733464820944704

Castells, Manuel. 2010. *The Rise of the Network Society.* 2nd ed. Chichester: Wiley-Blackwell Publishing.

Chan, Chak K., M.Y. Tang, and M.L. Lee. 2022. "Delivering Social Services During the COVID-19 Pandemic: The Case of Older People Centers in Hong Kong." *Journal of Social Service Research* 48 (1): 1–11. 10.1080/01488376.2021.1956670

Chandler, David. 2014. "Beyond Neoliberalism: Resilience, the New Art of Governing Complexity." *Resilience* 2 (1): 47–63. 10.1080/21693293.2013.878544

Cheung, Johnson C.-S. 2022. "Responses to COVID-19 in Major Social Work Journals: A Systematic Review of Empirical Studies, Comments, and Editorials." *Research on Social Work Practice* 32 (2): 168–185. 10.1177/10497315211046846

Chow, Amy Y.M., Margaret H.P. Suen, Keyuan Jiao, Yong H. Ng, Juan Wang, and Cecilia L.W. Chan. 2022. "Fear of Contamination, Perceived Social Support and Physical Health of Health Social Workers in Hong Kong: A Cross-Sectional Survey." *Social Work in Health Care* 61 (4): 280–297. 10.1080/00981389.2022.2076766

Christensen, Kyle. 2022. "Unmasking the Ageism of Whiteness During COVID-19." *Communication and Critical/Cultural Studies* 19 (1): 15–21. 10.1080/14791420.2021.2020863

Copson, Ruth, Anne M. Murphy, Laura Cook, Elsbeth Neil, and Pernille Sorensen. 2022. "Relationship-Based Practice and Digital Technology in Child and Family Social Work: Learning From Practice During the COVID-19 Pandemic." *Developmental Child Welfare* 4 (1): 3–19. 10.1177/25161032221079325

Cortis, Natasha, Ciara Smyth, Kylie Valentine, Jan Breckenridge, and Patricia Cullen. 2021. "Adapting Service Delivery During COVID-19: Experiences of Domestic Violence Practitioners." *British Journal of Social Work* 51 (5): 1779–1798. 10.1093/bjsw/bcab105

Craig, Shelley L., Toula Kourgiantakis, Alexa Kirkland, Barbara Muskat, and Deepy Sur. 2022. "Riding the Wave: Pandemic Social Work in Hospitals." *Social Work in Health Care* 61 (5): 323–337. 10.1080/00981389.2022.2085232

Currin-McCulloch, Jennifer, Qi Chen, Shivani Kaushik, Dede Sparks, and Barbara Jones. 2022. "The Courage to Continue: Healthcare Social Worker's Resilience During COVID-19." *Journal of Social Work in End-Of-Life & Palliative Care* 18 (2): 177–192. 10.1080/15524256.2022.2070330

Czymara, Christian S., Alexander Langenkamp, and Tomás Cano. 2020. "Cause for Concerns: Gender Inequality in Experiencing the COVID-19 Lockdown in Germany." *European Societies* 23 (sup1): S68–S81. 10.1080/14616696.2020.1808692

Dean, Mitchell. 1999. *Governmentality. Power and Rule in Modern Society.* London: Sage Publishing.

de Jonge, Ed, Raymond Kloppenburg, and Peter Hendriks. 2020. "The Impact of the COVID-19 Pandemic on Social Work Education and Practice in the Netherlands." *Social Work Education* 39 (8): 1027–1036. 10.1080/02615479.2020.1823363

Dominelli, Lena, Timo Harrikari, Joseph Mooney, Vesna Leskošek, and Erin Kennedy Tsunoda, eds. 2020. *COVID-19 and Social Work: A Collection of Country Reports.* N.p. https://www.iassw-aiets.org/wp-content/uploads/2020/07/IASSW-COVID-19-and-Social-Work-Country-Reports-Final-1.pdf.

Durkheim, Émile. 1964. *The Rules of Sociological Method.* 8th ed. New York: The Free Press.

Durkheim, Émile. 1984. *The Division of Labor in Society.* Basingstoke: MacMillan.

Engler, Sarah, Palmo Brunner, Romane Loviat, Tarik Abou-Chadi, Lucas Leemann, Andreas Glaser, and Daniel Kübler. 2021. "Democracy in Times of the Pandemic: Explaining the Variation of COVID-19 Policies Across European Democracies." *West European Politics* 44 (5–6): 1077–1102. 10.1080/01402382.2021.1900669

Farkas, Kathleen J. and J. Richard Romaniuk. 2020. "Social Work, Ethics, and Vulnerable Groups in the Time of Coronavirus and COVID-19." *Society Register* 4 (2): 67–82. 10.14746/sr.2020.4.2.05

Fenley, Vanessa M. 2020. "Everyday Citizenship and COVID-19: "Staying at home" While Homeless." *Administrative Theory & Praxis* 43 (2): 245–257. 10.1080/10841806.2020.1825600

Fenton, Norman E., Martin Neil, Magda Osman, and Scott McLachlan. 2020. "COVID-19 Infection and Death Rates: The Need to Incorporate Causal Explanations for the Data and Avoid Bias in Testing." *Journal of Risk Research* 23 (7–8): 862–865. 10.1080/13669877.2020.1756381

Ferguson, Harry, Laura Kelly, and Sarah Pink. 2022. "Social Work and Child Protection for a Post-Pandemic World: The Re-Making of Practice During COVID-19 and Its Renewal Beyond It." *Journal of Social Work Practice* 36 (1): 5–24. 10.1080/02650533.2021.1922368

Fodor, Evá, Anikó Gregor, Júlia Koltai, and Eszter Kováts. 2020. "The Impact of COVID-19 on the Gender Division of Childcare Work in Hungary." *European Societies* 23 (sup1): S95–S110. 10.1080/14616696.2020.1817522

Folke, Carl, Thomas Hahn, Per Olsson, and Jon Norberg. 2005. "Adaptive Governance of Social-Ecological Systems." *Annual Review of Environmental Resources* 30: 441–473. 10.1146/annurev.energy.30.050504.144511

Foucault, Michel. 1977. *Discipline and Punish: The Birth of the Prison.* New York: Random House.

Foucault, Michel. 2000. "Governmentality." In *Power: The Essential Works of Foucault 1954–1984.* Vol. 3, edited by James D. Faubion, 201–222. New York: New Press.

Fujii, Kashiko. 2022. "COVID-19 Prevention Measures Targeting Homeless People in Japan: A Cross-Sectional Study." *Social Work in Public Health* 37 (5): 468–483. 10.1080/19371918.2022.2026268

Garbarino, James. 1977. "The Human Ecology of Child Maltreatment. A Conceptual Model for Research." *Journal of Marriage and the Family* 39 (4): 721–735. https://www.jstor.org/stable/350477.

Germain, Carel B. and Alex Gitterman. 1980. *The Life Model of Social Work Practice.* New York: Columbia University Press.

Giddens, Anthony. 1984. *The Constitution of Society: Outline of the Theory of Structuration.* Cambridge: Polity Press.

Giddens, Anthony. 1990. *The Consequences of Modernity.* Stanford: Stanford University Press.

Gomez, David M., Benno Torgler, and Guillermo J. Ortega. 2013. "Measuring Global Economic Interdependence: A Hierarchical Network Approach." *The World Economy* 36 (12): 1632–1648. 10.1111/twec.12080

Gorenko, Julia A., Chelsea Moran, Michelle Flynn, Keith Dobson, and Candace Konnert. 2021. "Social Isolation and Psychological Distress Among Older Adults Related to COVID-19: A Narrative Review of Remotely-Delivered Interventions and Recommendations." *Journal of Applied Gerontology* 40 (1): 3–13. 10.1177/07334 64820958550

Guastafierro, Erica, Claudia Toppo, Francesca G. Magnani, Rosa Romano, Carla Facchini, Rino Campioni, Ersilia Brambilla, and Matilde Leonardi. 2021. "Older Adults' Risk Perception During the COVID-19 Pandemic in Lombardy Region of Italy: A Cross-Sectional Survey." *Journal of Gerontological Social Work* 64 (6): 585–598. 10.1080/01634372.2020.1870606

Gur, Ayelet, Vered Shenaar-Golan, and Ayala Cohen. 2022. "Stress, Sense of Meaningful Work, and Well-Being Among Social Workers During Covid-19." *European Journal of Social Work* 25 (5): 840–854. 10.1080/13691457.2022.2067136

Habermas, Jürgen. 1987. *The Theory of Communicative Action: Life World and System, a Critique of Functionalist Reason.* Vol. 2. Cambridge: Polity Press.

Harrikari, Timo and Pirkko-Liisa Rauhala. 2019. *Towards Glocal Social Work in the Era of Compressed Modernity*. London: Routledge.

Harrikari, Timo, Marjo Romakkaniemi, Laura Tiitinen, and Sanna Saraniemi. 2021. "Pandemic and Social Work. Exploring Social Workers' Experiences Through SWOT-Analysis." *British Journal of Social Work* 51 (5): 1644–1662. 10.1093/bjsw/bcab052

Hasselman, Lyndal. 2017. "Adaptive Management; Adaptive Co-Management; Adaptive Governance: What's the Difference?" *Australasian Journal of Environmental Management* 24 (1): 31–46. 10.1080/14486563.2016.1251857

Hawkins, Robert L. and Katherine Maurer. 2010. "Bonding, Bridging and Linking: How Social Capital Operated in New Orleans Following Hurricane Katrina." *The British Journal of Social Work* 40 (6): 1777–1793. 10.1093/bjsw/bcp087

He, Jinliao and Yuan Zhang. 2022. "Urban Epidemic Governance: An Event System Analysis of the Outbreak and Control of COVID-19 in Wuhan, China." *Urban Studies*. Published ahead of print, 8 February, 2022. 10.1177/00420980211064136

Henley, Lee J., Zoey A. Henley, Kathryn Hay, Yary Chhay, and Sonthea Pheun. 2021. "Social Work in the Time of COVID-19: A Case Study From the Global South." *The British Journal of Social Work* 51 (5): 1605–1622. 10.1093/bjsw/bcab100

Holmes, Megan R., C. Robin Rentrope, Amy Korsch-Williams, and Jennifer A. King. 2021. "Impact of COVID-19 Pandemic on Posttraumatic Stress, Grief, Burnout, and Secondary Trauma of Social Workers in the United States." *Clinical Social Work Journal* 49 (4): 495–504. 10.1007/s10615-021-00795-y

Horn, James. 2008. "Human Research and Complexity Theory." *Educational Philosophy and Theory* 40 (1): 130–143. 10.1111/j.1469-5812.2007.00395.x

Hoyt, Lindsay T., Alison K. Cohen, Brandon Dull, Elena Maker Castro, and Neshat Yazdani. 2020. "'Constant Stress Has Become the New Normal': Stress and Anxiety Inequalities Among U.S. College Students in the Time of COVID-19." *Journal of Adolescent Health* 68 (2): 270–276. 10.1016/j.jadohealth.2020.10.030

Janelle, Donald. 1991. "Global Interdependence and Its Consequences." In *Collapsing Space and Time*, edited by Stanley Brunn and Thomas Leinbach, 49–81. New York: Routledge.

Järvensivu, Linda, Anneli Pohjola, and Marjo Romakkaniemi. 2016. "Locating Sámi Social Work in Finland: Meanings Produced by Social Workers in Working With Sámi People." *International Social Work* 59 (5): 600–613. 10.1177/0020872816646817

Jebb, Eglantyne. 1906. *A Brief Study in Social Questions*. Cambridge: Macmillan & Bowes.

Kgadima, Puhti N. and Goitseone E. Leburu. 2022. "COVID-19 Ruptures and Disruptions on Grieving and Mourning Within an African Context: Lessons for Social Work Practice." *OMEGA – Journal of Death and Dying*. Published ahead of print, 1 February, 2022. 10.1177/00302228211070149

Klijn, Erik-Hans. 2008. "Complexity Theory and Public Administration: What's New?" *Public Management Review* 10 (3): 299–317. 10.1080/14719030802002675

Kritzingera, Sylvia, Martial Foucault, Romain Lachat, Julia Partheymüller, Carolina Plescia, and Sylvain Brouard. 2021. "'Rally Round the flag': The COVID-19 Crisis and Trust in the National Government." *West European Politics* 44 (5–6): 1205–1231, 10.1080/01402382.2021.1925017

Kusumaningrum, Santi, Clara Siagian, and Harriot Beazley. 2021. "Children During the COVID-19 Pandemic: Children and Young People's Vulnerability and Wellbeing in Indonesia." *Children's Geographies* 20 (4): 437–447. 10.1080/14733285.2021.1900544

Laage-Thomsen, Jakob and Søren L. Frandsen. 2022. "Pandemic Preparedness Systems and Diverging COVID-19 Responses Within Similar Public Health Regimes: A Comparative Study of Expert Perceptions of Pandemic Response in Denmark, Norway, and Sweden." *Globalization and Health* 18: 3. 10.1186/s12992-022-00799-4

Lemert, Edwin M. 1951. *Social Pathology: A Systematic Approach to the Theory of Sociopathic Behavior.* New York: McGraw-Hill.

Levi-Belz, Yossi and Gadi Zerach. 2022. "The Wounded Helper: Moral Injury Contributes to Depression and Anxiety Among Israeli Health and Social Care Workers During the COVID-19 Pandemic." *Anxiety, Stress, & Coping* 35 (5): 518–532. 10.1080/10615806. 2022.2035371

Li, Hongmei, Baojiang Chen, Zhuo Chen, Lu Shi, and Dejun Su. 2022. "Americans' Trust in COVID-19 Information From Governmental Sources in the Trump Era: Individuals' Adoption of Preventive Measures, and Health Implications." *Health Communication.* 10.1080/10410236.2022.2074776

LingHu, Yuwei and Ren Shanjing. 2022. "Analysis of the Impact of Interprovincial Migration on the First Wave of COVID-19 Transmission in China." *SAGE Open* 12 (1). 10.1177/21582440221085572

Livholts, Mona and Lia Bryant, eds. 2017. *Social Work in a Glocalised World.* London: Routledge.

Lundström, Markus. 2022. "Young in Pandemic Times: A Scoping Review of COVID-19 Social Impacts on Youth." *International Journal of Adolescence and Youth* 27 (1): 432–443. 10.1080/02673843.2022.2117637

MacGregor, Hayley, Melissa Leach, Grace Akello, Lawrence Sao Babawo, Moses Baluku, Alice Desclaux, Catherine Grant, Foday Kamara, Fred Martineau, Esther Yei Mokuwa, Melissa Parker, Paul Richards, Kelley Sams, Khoudia Sow, and Annie Wilkinson. 2022. "Negotiating Intersecting Precarities: COVID-19, Pandemic Preparedness and Response in Africa." *Medical Anthropology* 41 (1): 19–33. 10.1080/01459740.2021.2015591

Mannheim, Karl. 1952. "The Problem of Generations." In *Karl Mannheim: Essays,* edited by Paul Kecskemeti, 276–322. London: Routledge and Kegan Paul.

Marx, Karl and Friedrich Engels. 1998. *The Communist Manifesto.* London: Electric Book Co.

Mathbor, Golam M. 2007. "Enhancement of Community Preparedness for Natural Disasters: The Role of Social Work in Building Social Capital for Sustainable Disaster Relief and Management." *International Social Work* 50 (3): 357–369. 10.1177/0020872 807076049

Matthies, Aila-Leena and Kati Närhi, eds. 2017. *The Ecosocial Transition of Societies: The Contribution of Social Work and Social Policy.* London: Routledge.

McConnell, Allan. 2011. "Success? Failure? Something in-Between? A Framework for Evaluating Crisis Management." *Policy and Society,* 30 (2): 63–76. 10.1016/j.polsoc. 2011.03.002

McCosker, Laura K., Robert S. Ware, Annick Maujean, Stephen J. Simpson, and Martin J. Downes. 2022. "Homeless Services in Australia: Perceptions of Homelessness Services Workers During the COVID-19 Pandemic." *Australian Social Work.* Published ahead of print, 10 August, 2022. 10.1080/0312407X.2022.2105162

McFadden, Paula, Ruth D. Neill, John Mallett, Jill Manthorpe, Patricia Gillen, John Moriarty, Denise Currie, Heike Schroder, Jermaine Ravalier, Patricia Nicholl, and Jana Ross. 2021. "Mental Well-Being and Quality of Working Life in UK Social Workers Before and During the COVID-19 Pandemic: A Propensity Score Matching Study." *The British Journal of Social Work* 52 (5): 2814–2833. 10.1093/bjsw/bcab198

Mešl, Nina, Vesna Leskošek, Tamara Rape Žiberna, and Tadeja Kodele. 2022. "Social Work During COVID-19 in Slovenia: Absent, Invisible or Ignored?" *The British Journal of Social Work*. Published ahead of print, 11 August, 2022. 10.1093/bjsw/bcac149

Mishna, Faye, Elizabeth Milne, Marion Bogo, and Luana F. Pereira. 2021. "Responding to COVID-19: New Trends in Social Workers' Use of Information and Communication Technology." *Clinical Social Work Journal* 49 (4): 484–494. 10.1007/s10615-020-00780-x

Mooney, Joseph, Timo Harrikari, and Lena Dominelli. 2020. "Introduction. COVID-19: A New Challenge for Social Work". In *COVID-19 and Social Work. A Collection of Country Reports*, edited by Lena Dominelli, Timo Harrikari, Joseph Mooney, Vesna Leskošek, and Erin Kennedy Tsunoda, 2–6. N.p. https://www.iassw-aiets.org/wp-content/uploads/2020/07/IASSW-COVID-19-and-Social-Work-Country-Reports-Final-1.pdf.

Mueller, John and Mark G. Stewart. 2016. "The Curse of the Black Swan." *Journal of Risk Research* 19 (10): 1319–1330. 10.1080/13669877.2016.1216007

Nahapiet, Janine and Sumantra Ghoshal. 1998. "Social Capital, Intellectual Capital, and the Organizational Advantage." *The Academy of Management Review* 23 (2): 242–266. 10.5465/amr.1998.533225

Ness, Tove M., Siv Söderberg, and Ove Hellzèn. 2020. "'Contradictions in Having Care Providers With a South Sami Background Who Speak South Sami': Older South Sami People in Sweden's Expectations of Home Nursing Care." *Scandinavian Journal of Caring Sciences* 34 (2): 436–445. 10.1111/scs.12747

Nielsen, Julie H. and Johannes Lindvall. 2021. "Trust in Government in Sweden and Denmark During the COVID-19 Epidemic." *West European Politics* 44 (5–6): 1180–1204. 10.1080/01402382.2021.1909964

Onyeaka, Helen, Christian K. Anumudu, Zainab T. Al-Sharify, Esther Egele-Godswill, and Paul Mbaegbu. 2021. "COVID-19 Pandemic: A Review of the Global Lockdown and Its Far-Reaching Effects." *Science Progress* 104 (2). 10.1177/00368504211019854

Oxfam. 2022. "Profiting From Pain. The Urgency of Taxing the Rich Amid a Surge in Billionaire Wealth and a Global Cost-of-Living Crisis." Oxfam Media briefing, 23 May, 2022. https://www.oxfam.org/en/research/profiting-pain.

Philippo, Kate, Robert Lucio, Emily Shayman, and Michael Kelly. 2022. ""Why Wasn't I Doing This Before?": Changed School Social Work Practice in Response to the COVID-19 Pandemic." *Qualitative Social Work*. Published ahead of print, 11 March, 2022. 10.1177/14733250221076061

Plümper, Thomas and Eric Neumayer. 2022. "Lockdown Policies and the Dynamics of the First Wave of the Sars-CoV-2 Pandemic in Europe." *Journal of European Public Policy* 29 (3): 321–341. 10.1080/13501763.2020.1847170

Powers, Meredith, Michaela Rinkel, and Praveen Kumar. 2021. "Co-Creating a "Sustainable New Normal" for Social Work and Beyond: Embracing an Ecosocial Worldview." *Sustainability* 13 (19): 10941. 10.3390/su131910941

Rapeli, Merja. 2018. "Social Capital in Social Work Disaster Preparedness Plans: The Case of Finland." *International Social Work* 61 (6): 1054–1066. 10.1177/0020872817695643

Ravalier, Jermaine, Paula McFadden, Patricia Gillen, John Mallett, Patricia Nicholl, Ruth Neill, Jill Manthorpe, John Moriarty, Heike Schroder, and Denise Curry. 2022. "Working Conditions and Well-Being in UK Social Care and Social Work During COVID-19." *Journal of Social Work*. Published ahead of print 6 July, 2022. 10.1177/14680173221109483

Reichelt, Malte, Kinga Makovi, and Anahit Sargsyan. 2020. "The Impact of COVID-19 on Gender Inequality in the Labor Market and Gender-Role Attitudes." *European Societies* 23 (sup1): S228–S245. 10.1080/14616696.2020.1823010

Ren, Min, Binbin Wang, and Michael Rasell. 2022. "Flexibility and Professionalisation: Reflections on Adaptions by Social Work Services in China During COVID-19." *Social Work in Action* 34 (2): 87–101. 10.1080/09503153.2021.1998413

Richmond, Mary E. 1917. *Social Diagnosis.* New York: Russel Sage House.

Rifkin, Jeremy. 2008. *The Third Industrial Revolution. How Lateral Power Is Transforming Energy, the Economy, and the World.* London: Palgrave Macmillan.

Romakkaniemi, Marjo, Timo Harrikari, Sanna Saraniemi, Vera Fiorentino, and Laura Tiitinen. 2021. "'Bonding, Bridging and Linking the Last Resort Tailboard': Shifts in Social Workers' Professional Positions and Mobilising Adaptive Capital During the Coronavirus Pandemic." *Nordic Social Work Research.* Published ahead of print, 25 October, 2021. 10.1080/2156857X.2021.1992489

Rosa, Hartmut. 2013. *Social Acceleration: A New Theory of Modernity.* New York: Columbia University Press.

Runde, Jochen. 2009. "Dissecting the Black Swan." *Critical Review* 21 (4): 491–505. 10.1080/08913810903441427

Saraniemi, Sanna, Timo Harrikari, Vera Fiorentino, Marjo Romakkaniemi, and Laura Tiitinen. 2022. "'Silenced Coffee Rooms': Social Workers' Work Communities and Social Support in the Spring of 2020." *Challenges* 13 (1): 8. 10.3390/challe13010008

Sardar, Ziauddin. 2021. "Afterthoughts: Transnormal, the "New Normal" and Other Varieties of "Normal" in Postnormal Times." *World Futures Review* 13 (2) 54–70. 10.1177/19467567211025755

Schiff, Miriam, Shiri Shinan-Altman, and Hadas Rosenne. 2021. "Israeli Health Care Social Workers' Personal and Professional Concerns During the COVID-19 Pandemic Crisis: The Work–Family Role Conflict." *The British Journal of Social Work* 51 (5): 1858–1878. 10.1093/bjsw/bcab114

Shaw, Clifford and Henry McKay. 1942. *Juvenile Delinquency and Urban Areas: A Study of Rates of Delinquents in Relation to Differential Characteristics of Local Communities in American Cities.* Chicago: University of Chicago Press.

Slavich, George M., Lydia G. Roos, and Jamil Zaki. 2021. "Social Belonging, Compassion, and Kindness: Key Ingredients for Fostering Resilience, Recovery, and Growth From the COVID-19 Pandemic." *Anxiety, Stress, & Coping* 35 (1): 1–8. 10.1080/10615806.2021.1950695

Sundararaman, Thiagarajan, Vr Muraleedharan, and Alok Ranjan. 2021. "Pandemic Resilience and Health Systems Preparedness: Lessons From COVID-19 for the Twenty-First Century." *Journal of Social and Economic Development* 23 (Suppl. 2): S290–S300. 10.1007/s40847-020-00133-x

Taleb, Nassim Nicholas. 2010. *The Black Swan: The Impact of Highly Improbable.* 2nd printing. London: Penguin.

Therborn, Göran. 2013. *The Killing Fields of Inequality.* Cambridge: Polity Press.

Tobler, Waldo R. 1970. "A Computer Movie Simulating Urban Growth in the Detroit Region." *Economic Geography* 46 (Sup1): 234–240. 10.2307/143141

Toshkov, Dimiter, Brendan Carroll, and Kutsal Yesilkagit. 2022. "Government Capacity, Societal Trust or Party Preferences: What Accounts for the Variety of National Policy Responses to the COVID-19 Pandemic in Europe?" *Journal of European Public Policy* 29 (7): 1009–1028. 10.1080/13501763.2021.1928270

Wajcman, Judy. 2015. *Pressed for Time: The Acceleration of Life in Digital Capitalism.* Chicago: The University of Chicago Press.

Wake, Addisu D. and Usha R. Kandula. 2022. "The Global Prevalence and Its Associated Factors Toward Domestic Violence Against Women and Children During COVID-19 Pandemic—"The Shadow Pandemic": A Review of Cross-Sectional Studies." *Women's Health* 18. 10.1177/17455057221095536

Walch, Colin. 2019. "Adaptive Governance in the Developing World: Disaster Risk Reduction in the State of Odisha, India." *Climate and Development* 11 (3): 238–252. 10.1080/17565529.2018.1442794

Wallace, John and Bob Pease. 2011. "Neoliberalism and Australian Social Work: Accommodation or Resistance?" *Journal of Social Work* 11 (2): 132–142. 10.1177/1468017310387318

Walter-McCabe, Heather A. 2020. "Coronavirus Pandemic Calls for an Immediate Social Work Response. *Social Work in Public Health* 35 (3): 69–72. 10.1080/19371918.2020.1751533

Wampole, Donna M. and Hermeet Kohli. 2022. "Self-Compassion in Social Work Education at Times of COVID19." *Social Work in Mental Health* 20 (4): 400–417. 10.1080/15332985.2022.2028218

Wang, Leiheng and Chunyan Liu. 2022. "What Did Chinese Social Workers Do at the Worst Moment? — A Research Based on Social Workers' Participation in the Fight Against COVID-19 at Guangzhou." *Social Work in Public Health* 37 (6): 548–559. 10.1080/19371918.2022.2053633

Warf, Barney. 2008. *Time-Space Compression: Historical Geographies.* London: Routledge.

Weber, Max. 1978. *Economy and Society. An Outline of Interpretive Sociology.* Vol. 2. Berkeley and Los Angeles: University of California Press.

Wu, Cary. 2021. "Social Capital and COVID-19: A Multidimensional and Multilevel Approach." *Chinese Sociological Review* 53 (1): 27–54. 10.1080/21620555.2020.1814139

Yeong-Tsyr Wang, Kate, Tsai Wen-Hui, Tze-Yin Chuang, and His-Jing Lee. 2020. "Rethinking Four Social Issues of the COVID-19 Pandemic From Social Work Perspectives." *Asia Pacific Journal of Social Work Development* 31 (1–2): 45–51. 10.1080/02185385.2020.1819396

Yildirim, Hilal, Kevser Işik, and Rukuye Aylaz. 2021. "The Effect of Anxiety Levels of Elderly People in Quarantine on Depression During Covid-19 Pandemic." *Social Work in Public Health* 36 (2): 194–204. 10.1080/19371918.2020.1868372

Yu, Zhihong, Jinjun Liang, Liping Guo, Lirui Jiang, Jian-ying Wang, Moli Ke, Liao Shen, Ningning Zhou, and Xinxian Liu. 2022. "Psychosocial Intervention on the Dual-Process Model for a Group of COVID-19 Bereaved Individuals in Wuhan: A Pilot Study." OMEGA — *Journal of Death and Dying.* Published ahead of print, 26 March, 2022. 10.1177/00302228221083067

Yuan, Yiqing, Xuesong He, and Wenjie Duan. 2020. "A Reflection on the Current China Social Work Education in the Combat With COVID-19." *Social Work Education* 39 (8): 1019–1026. 10.1080/02615479.2020.1821637

Zakour, Michael J. 1996. "Disaster Research in Social Work." *Journal of Social Service Research* 22 (1–2): 7–25. 10.1300/J079v22n01_02

# Index